The Catholic Left
in Latin America:
A Comprehensive Bibliography

A
Reference
Publication
in
Latin American
Studies

William V. Jackson
Editor

The Catholic Left
in Latin America:
A Comprehensive Bibliography

THERRIN C. DAHLIN
GARY P. GILLUM
MARK L. GROVER

Introduction
DR. BERKLEY A. SPENCER

G.K.HALL &CO.

70 LINCOLN STREET, BOSTON, MASS.

LIBRARY
The University of Texas
At San Antonio

Copyright © 1981 by Therrin C. Dahlin, Gary P. Gillum, and
Mark L. Grover

Library of Congress Cataloging in Publication Data

Dahlin, Therrin C.
　The Catholic Left in Latin America.

　(A Reference publication in Latin American studies)
　Bibliography: p.
　Includes indexes.
　1.　Church and social problems—Latin America—
Catholic Church—Bibliography.　I.　Gillum, Gary P.
II.　Grover, Mark L.　III.　Title.　IV.　Series: Reference
publication in Latin American studies.
Z7165.L3D33　　　[HN39.L3]　　016.2618′3′098　81-778
ISBN 0-8161-8396-1　　　　　　　　　　　AACR2

This publication is printed on permanent/durable acid-free paper
MANUFACTURED IN THE UNITED STATES OF AMERICA

Contents

Contents

Contents

ABOUT THE AUTHORS: Therrin C. Dahlin earned a Master of Library
Science degree from Brigham Young University, and is currently
pursuing a doctorate at that institution. He has served as a bibliographer and cataloger in Latin American and Mexican-American
topics for six years, and is now Circulation Librarian at Brigham
Young University. His publications include articles on library
history, library sciences to Spanish-speaking people, and "Caribbean
Religion: A Survey and Bibliography," a paper read at the International Conference of the Seminar on the Acquisitions of Latin
American Library Materials, and soon to be published in Windward,
Leeward and Main: Caribbean Studies and Library Resources.

Mark L. Grover received his MLS in Library and Information
Sciences from Brigham Young University and an MA in History from
Indiana University. He is presently finishing his requirements for
a PhD in Latin American and African History at Indiana University.
He is the Latin American Studies Bibliographer at BYU and also serves
as consultant for Spanish-speaking library services in public libraries. His publications include bibliographies and articles on
religion in Latin America and the acquisition of Latin American
materials.

Gary Gillum graduated from Concordia Senior College at Fort Wayne,
Indiana, in Classical Studies, and received an MLS in Library and
Information Sciences from Brigham Young University. He is Ancient
Studies and Foreign Languages Librarian at BYU. He is also a free-
lance writer, editor, and indexer, including the regular indexing of
three scholarly journals. His publications include: The Soviet
Union: A Bibliography; How to Drive and Survive in the 80's with
Your Own Alcohol Fuel; a science fiction story; six scholarly book
reviews; essays and bibliographies; and many smaller in-house bibliographies, including the monthly Latin American Books.

Preface

The Catholic Left movement in Latin America is an intriguing phenom-
enon, involving as it does the Catholic layman, priest, and bishop
in attempts to promote social change. Fascination with this movement
prompted the compilers to investigate it in depth. As we explored
the Catholic Left topic and the related library resources, we real-
ized that bibliographic coverage was sadly lacking and that the Latin
Americanist researcher operating in the continental United States
faced special problems. So we determined to fill the bibliographic
gap by compiling a comprehensive bibliography on the Catholic Left in
Latin America. We had met together often as members of the Latin
American Studies Library Committee of Brigham Young University, and
we possessed a keen interest in collaborating on a bibliographic
project. Mark Grover, a specialist in Brazilian history, provided
the initial impetus to undertake this work.

    The aim of this bibliography is to assist the serious student,
researcher, or professor residing in the United States to locate
adequate instructional and research materials on the Catholic Left
movement in Latin America. Since the topic addresses complex social,
political, and economic issues, this compilation may serve scholars
from other disciplines as well. Sociologists will find valuable
discussions on social structure and social change. Political
scientists may encounter analyses of political conditions. Economists
will discover ample material on agricultural and economic development.
The emphasis on education in the movement will attract educational
scholars. And, of course, the Catholic clergy and theologians
should find this bibliography a rich resource for study.

SCOPE

We attempted to provide relatively comprehensive coverage for all
materials relating directly to the Catholic Left movement in Latin
America. Protestant-oriented materials appear if the subject matter
was related to the leftist movement. Of particular interest is
Iglesia y Sociedad en América Latina (ISAL), which involves representatives from a number of Protestant churches. ISAL has played a
part in the movement and has issued numerous publications.

    Necessity dictated certain delimitations in preparing this bibliography. Because of the voluminous literature on Christian democracy, education, and liberation theology, we included only a representative sample of such materials. Similarly, under such broad headings as "Agrarian Reform," "Economic Development," "Nationalism," and "Revolution," we have provided citations only to publications which show a relationship with the Catholic Left. To do otherwise would have caused the bibliography to swell beyond usable size.

Since we designed the bibliography to represent material available in research libraries within the continental United States, we have excluded publications, generally of minor or local importance, which could not be located here, as well as unpublished material which might be found in ecclesiastical archives. Nor does this bibliography contain references to news items published in newspapers or news magazines like <u>Time</u>, except for a few that seemed to be of particular value. Similarly omitted are general reference sources.

The scope of the bibliography is comprehensive for the years 1960-1978. Since our initial research indicated that the vast majority of relevant works appeared after 1960, we included only a few items of pivotal importance published before that date. To allow time for editing, typing, preparing indexes, and readying the manuscript for publication, 1978 became the cut-off date.

Geographic coverage extends to all of Latin America, including Caribbean countries and dependencies, regardless of national language. We selected materials published in any nation and in any language, as long as the theme related to the Catholic Left in Latin America. The majority of the materials, however, appeared in English, Spanish, and Portuguese. Russian titles were transliterated for the sake of the bibliography.

METHODOLOGY

The compilers searched every potentially valuable bibliographic source available to locate relevant books and articles. We examined over fifty bibliographic serial titles and periodical indexes, including <u>Anuario Bibliográfico Colombiano</u>, <u>Boletín Bibliográfico Mexicano</u>, <u>Handbook of Latin American Studies</u>, and the <u>Catholic Book and Periodical Index</u>. Hundreds of individual periodical titles and monographic bibliographies were utilized as well.

For two years, the compilers attempted to review physically each item through examining local library collections, liberal use of interlibrary loans, and research at the Benson Latin American Collection at the University of Texas at Austin. The richest stores of materials are the Library of Congress and the great university libraries that emphasize Latin American research, such as those at the University of Texas at Austin and the University of Florida at Gainesville.

When the materials could not be obtained for "in-hand" review, we made efforts to locate two separate entries in bibliographies, review sources, and indexes to verify bibliographic data, as well as to consult the <u>National Union Catalog</u> and other union lists.

Preface

Many items listed in the bibliography may not be available at libraries, both public and academic, which do not collect Latin American material extensively.

FORM OF ENTRY

Each entry contains the usual bibliographical information. For books this includes author, title, place of publication, publisher, date, and number of pages. In addition, we have added "bibl." to the pagination whenever the work contains a bibliography. In cases where it is not possible to ascertain some facts, we have used the standard indications--e.g., [n.d.] for no date of publication of articles and [n.p.] for no publisher or place of publication. Some entries lack page numbers, not for lack of effort or precision on the part of the compilers. A large percentage of these works are published by church agencies or small religious or research institutes without sophisticated equipment or editing expertise, and page numbers are often missing, incomplete, or of varying styles within one work.

References to journals consist of author, title of article, name of journal, volume number, date, and pagination. References to newspaper articles do not include pagination due to the differences in paging among various editions of the same newspapers. In a few other cases, it was not possible for us to complete a citation with the actual pagination.

In addition to personal author, there are a number of corporate entries, under names of organizations, congresses, etc. In some cases the same body may have its name in both Spanish or Portuguese and English. Given the differences in position of adjective, this may lead to separation of entries (e.g., 0445, Conferencia General del Episcopado Latinoamericano, 2d, and 0537, General Conference of Latin American Bishops, 2d). The index contains some cross references to aid the reader.

Some references appear in more than one place in the text. If a book or article treated more than one topic or geographic area, full references were entered under each of the respective headings.

In an attempt to follow an accepted style in preparing the bibliography, we adopted A Manual of Style, 12th edition, revised (1969), published by the University of Chicago Press, as our standard. Form of bibliographic entry conforms to the rules of style contained therein.

Since a large proportion of the books and articles cited (approximately 70 percent) were physically examined and annotations were not added, no attempt was made in the text to identify those references that were not seen.

The liberal use of acronyms and abbreviations by authors and publishers required the inclusion of a list of key abbreviations, which appears following the introduction.

ARRANGEMENT

The arrangement of the chapters of the bibliography is first by
country or region. We felt that many readers would be interested in
a particular area within Latin America. However, the first chapter,
"Latin America," includes those general works that treat all or a
large segment of Latin America. The term Latin America is broadly
interpreted to include all of Central America as well as all Caribbean areas of whatever language.

Proceeding from general to specific, the remaining chapters
consist of individual countries or regions listed alphabetically. We
listed countries in two areas, the Caribbean and Central America,
together as regions rather than individually because of the small
number of relevant references. Cuba is of such political importance
that we decided to treat it separately. Guyana is included in the
chapter on the Caribbean.

As the bibliography grew, it became apparent that annotating
every item would be impossible due to the constraints of limited
time and money and the comprehensive nature of the project. However,
as we examined the books and articles, we assigned one to three
subject headings to each item dependent on the number of relevant
topics treated. This approach allows subject access to the reference and insures that works providing extensive treatment to several
relevant topics will have a listing under each appropriate subject
heading.

When a book containing essays or chapters by various authors was
of sufficient importance, we cited the whole book and also individual
articles or essays in the book. Thus, a user of our tome can find
bibliographic data required under either entry. Each entry in the
bibliography provides full bibliographic information; consequently
there are no cross references.

To provide subject access to the references, we divided the
chapters alphabetically under topical headings that recur in each
chapter. The full complement of headings appears under "Latin
America," and in the other chapters as warranted by the books and
articles listed.

The subject headings that we selected were based on seemingly
logical groupings of materials encountered in research, rather than
on Library of Congress headings or another standard list. Items
listed under "General" are those that treat the Catholic Left broadly
without focusing on a specific aspect of the movement. "Documents"
encompasses materials produced as official publications of an
organization or results of congresses or meetings.

The compilers unearthed numerous works on the political aspects
of the movement, which required us to generate several closely allied
headings. "Politics" refers to the more general treatises on the
subject. "Catholic Church and State" focuses on the relationship of
the church to established governmental institutions. "Christian
Democracy," "Communism," and "Socialism" refer to those specific
movements and the political parties associated with each. "Marxism"
places emphasis on the philosophy and theory of Karl Marx.

Preface

Two persons, Hélder Câmara and Camilo Torres, figure so prominently in the movement that we established separate sections for them in the chapters devoted to Brazil and Colombia, respectively. In both cases, references in these divisions are to material <u>about</u> the man. For material that each man wrote, the reader should consult the author index. A substantial number of items written by Hélder Câmara appear in the chapter on Latin America, but a full listing of his writings is found only in the author index.

To facilitate further use of this material, we compiled author and title indexes which appear at the back of the volume. They allow a person to review all the works of a particular author or obtain full bibliographic data for a specific title.

The following example illustrates how to use the bibliography. Consider a researcher who seeks information on a subject such as the importance of agrarian reform in the Catholic Left movement. To obtain the more general works, he should consult the chapter on Latin America under the heading "Agrarian Reform." After examining the references listed, if he desires information on the topic in relation to a particular part of Latin America, he can go to "Agrarian Reform" under any other chapter, such as Argentina or Central America, and get more specific references. On the other hand, if he is seeking a work on this topic by a particular author, he should go directly to the author index. If he wants to find materials similar to a specific book title with which he is acquainted, he can find the title in the title index, go to the reference number indicated, and examine nearby references for relevance.

ACKNOWLEDGMENTS

All three compilers worked assiduously on the project. In the earlier stages, Mark Grover provided the primary efforts in preparing the bibliography. In the latter stages, Therrin Dahlin took over the responsibility, with the assistance of Gary Gillum, when Mr. Grover left to pursue doctoral studies at Indiana University. Mr. Dahlin also spent the summer of 1978 at the Benson Latin American Collection of the University of Texas at Austin doing bibliographic research on the Catholic Left.

Several other people collaborated in the presentation of the bibliography and deserve mention. Carla Kupitz, Syndee Painter, Ann Johnson, and Kathryn Christiansen worked diligently on typing and other technical tasks in coordination with a number of student workers. Larry D. Benson provided valuable service in locating sources.

We gratefully acknowledge the financial support afforded by the Harold B. Lee Library of Brigham Young University. Dr. Thomas E. Lyon, Jr., former director of the Latin American Center at Brigham Young University, gave us constant support and encouragement. We appreciate also the patience and critical suggestions of Dr. William V. Jackson and Janice Meagher.

T.C.D.
G.P.G.

Prefacio

El movimiento izquierdista católico en Latinoamérica es un fenómeno
fascinante en que colaboran el lego, el clérigo y el obispo católico
en esfuerzos de fomentar cambios sociales. Por eso los compiladores
de esta bibliografía resolvieron investigarlo intensivamente.
Explorando el tema de la izquierda católica y los recursos de estudio
relacionados con él, nos dimos cuenta de que hacían gran falta
materias bibliográficas adecuadas y que al investigador que estudia
Latinoamérica en los Estados Unidos le enfrentan problemas especiales.
Así determinamos remediar esta falta compilando una bibliografía
comprensiva sobre la izquierda católica en la América Latina. Ya nos
habíamos reunido frecuentemente como participantes en el Latin American Studies Library Committee de Brigham Young University y nos
interesaba una colaboración en un proyecto bibliográfico. El ímpetu
inicial para este trabajo nos llegó por parte de Mark Grover,
especialista en historia brasileña.

El propósito de esta bibliografía es ayudar al estudiante, al
investigador y al profesor en los Estados Unidos a encontrar materias
de instrucción e investigación sobre el movimiento izquierdista
católico en Latinoamérica. Ya que el tema comprende complejas
cuestiones sociales, políticas y económicas, esta compilación podría
servir también a los académicos de otras disciplinas. Los sociólogos
encontrarían discusiones útiles sobre la estructura y el cambio
social. Los estudiantes de la política podrían hallar análisis de la
situación política. Los economistas descubrirían materias abundantes
sobre el desarrollo agrícolo y económico. A los estudiantes de la
pedagogía les va a interesar el énfasis pedagógico del movimiento.
Por supuesto, para el clero católico y los teólogos esta bibliografía
sería un recurso fecundo de estudios.

EXTENSIÓN

Hemos tratado de recoger comprensivamente las referencias relacionadas
directamente al movimiento izquierdista católico en Latinoamérica.
Las citas tocantes al protestantismo se incluyen con tal que se
refieran al movimiento izquierdista. De alto interés es la Iglesia
y Sociedad en América Latina (ISAL), en la cual participan representantes de varias sectas protestantes. La ISAL ha tomado parte en el
movimiento y ha diseminado numerosas publicaciones.

Hemos impuesto ciertas limitaciones necesarias a esta bibliografía. Ya que existen copiosas materias sobre la democracia, la
educación y la teología de la liberación cristiana, hemos incluído
sólo una selección representativa de citas a ellas. De este modo,
bajo las clasificaciones amplias como "Agrarian Reform," "Economic
Development," "Nationalism" y "Revolution" hemos incluído sólo las
citas a publicaciones relacionadas al movimiento izquierdista. De
otro modo hubiéramos producido una bibliografía de extensión
excesiva.

Ya que proponemos una bibliografía que se refiera a las materias
disponibles en bibliotecas de investigación dentro de los Estados
Unidos continentales, hemos excluído las publicaciones, por lo
general de importancia escasa o regional, que no encuentran aquí, así
como materias inéditas que puedan hallarse en los archivos eclesiás-
ticos. Tampoco incluímos citas a noticias de periódicos o revistas
como Time, con excepción de los pocos de valor extraordinario. Ex-
cluídas también son las obras de referencia generales.

Esta bibliografía comprende los años 1960 a 1978. Ya que nuestras
investigaciones nos indicaron que la gran mayoría de trabajos sobre
el tema aparecieron después de 1960, citamos solamente las obras
indispensables publicadas antes de esta fecha. Para dar tiempo a la
redacción, imprenta, compilación de índices y corrección de pruebas,
determinamos la fecha terminante de 1978.

La extensión geográfica de la bibliografía comprende toda la
América Latina, incluso los países y dependencias caribes. Escogemos
materias publicadas en todos los países y en todas lenguas, con tal
que el tema sea relacionado a la izquierda católica en la América
Latina. La mayoría de las obras, sin embargo, se escribieron en
inglés, español o portugués. Hemos traducido los títulos rusos en
esta bibliografía.

METODOLOGÍA

Los compiladores investigaron todas las fuentes bibliográficas
disponibles para encontrar libros y artículos pertinentes. Examinamos
más de cincuenta bibliografías en serie e índices de periódicos,
incluso el Anuario Bibliográfico Colombiano, el Boletín Bibliográfico
Mexicano, el Handbook of Latin American Studies y el Catholic Book
and Periodical Index. Utilizamos también centenares de periódicos
y bibliografías monográficas.

Por dos años los compiladores mismos trataban de examinar todas
las materias citadas en las colecciones de bibliotecas cercanas, por
medio del "interlibrary loan" y por investigaciones en la Benson
Latin American Collection de la University of Texas de Austin. Las
fuentes más fecundas de materias son la Library of Congress y las
grandes bibliotecas universitarias que dan énfasis en investigaciones
latinoamericanas, como la de la University of Texas de Austin y de la
University of Florida de Gainesville.

Cuando no pudimos examinar personalmente las materias, tratamos
de encontrar dos citas distintas en bibliografías, reseña e índices,

tan bien como el National Union Catalog y otras "union lists," para
verificar los datos bibliográficos.

Muchas citas registradas en esta bibliografía no se encontrarán
en bibliotecas públicas o académicas que no recojan extensivamente
materias latinoamericanas.

ORDEN DE LAS CITAS

Cada cita contiene la información bibliográfica usual. Para libros
ésta incluye el nombre del autor, el título, el lugar de publicación,
el editorial, la fecha y el número de páginas. Colocamos la
abreviatura "bibl." al lado del último dato cuando la obra contiene
una bibliografía. En el caso de que no pudimos determinar un dato,
empleamos las indicaciones convencionales--v. gr., "(n.d.)" para
indicar la falta de la fecha de publicación de artículos y "(n.p.)"
para indicar la falta del nombre del editorial o del lugar de
publicación.

Algunas citas faltan el número de páginas, no por escasez de
esfuerzo o precisión por la parte de los compiladores. Un gran
porcentage de estas obras son publicadas por agencias de la iglesia,
pequeños grupos religiosos, o institutos de investigación sin equipo
sofisticado o experiencia en redacción, y los números de páginas son,
varias veces, ausente, incompleto, o de estilos variados.

Las citas a revistas incluyen el nombre del autor, el título del
artículo, el nombre de la revista, el número del tomo, la fecha y
las páginas en que aparece el artículo. Las citas a artículos de
periódicos no incluyen las páginas, ya que hay diferencias de
paginación entre las varias ediciones del mismo periódico. En unos
casos no fue posible determinar la paginación para la cita.

Además de citas a obras escritas por individuos, hay algunas
citas a obras que aparecen bajo el nombre de una organización, de un
congreso, etcétera. En algunos casos damos el nombre de la organización en español o portugués y también en inglés. A causa de
diferencias en la colocación de adjetivos un nombre puede ser
registrado en dos lugares (v. gr., 0445, Conferencia General del
Episcopado Latinoamericano, 2d, y 0537, General Conference of Latin
American Bishops, 2d). Para facilitar la consulta en tal caso, el
índice contiene algunas interreferencias.

Algunas citas aparecen más de una vez en el texto. Si un libro
o artículo trata más de un tema o de una región geográfica, hay una
cita completa para cada clasificación.

Adoptamos como guía de estilo bibliográfico A Manual of Style,
12th edition, revised (1969), publicado por la University of Chicago
Press. Las citas conforman a las reglas de estilo establecidas en
dicha guía.

Ya que una gran proporción de los libros y artículos citados
(aproximadamente 70%) fueron examinados personalmente pero no
anotados, no intentamos identificar en el texto las citas que no
fueron examinados.

Las muchas siglas y abreviaturas empleados por autores y

editoriales han necesitado una lista de abreviaturas, la cual sigue
la introducción.

ORGANIZACIÓN

La organización de los capítulos de esta bibliografía corresponde
a países o regiones, ya que, en nuestra opinión, muchos lectores van
a buscar información sobre una determinada región de Latinoamérica.
El primer capítulo, "Latin America," incluye citas a las obras
generales que tratan de toda o gran parte de la América Latina. Por
"Latin America" queremos decir toda la América del Sur, la América
Central y los países caribes.

Los capítulos restantes corresponden a los países individuos,
ordenados alfabéticamente. A causa del número escaso de citas, los
países de la América Central y del Caribe se registran juntos, como
dos regiones, en vez de individualmente. La importancia política de
Cuba requiere un capítulo distinto. Guyana se incluye en el capítulo
sobre los países caribes.

Tanto la comprensividad del proyecto como las limitaciones de
tiempo y fondos han imposibilitado la anotación de todas las citas.
Para cada cita, sin embargo, hemos escogido hasta tres clasificaciones
de acuerdo con los temas tratados en el libro o artículo. Así se
puede encontrar una cita por medio de su tema. Las obras que tratan
extensivamente de varios temas se registran bajo cualquiera de las
clasificaciones correspondientes.

Si un libro importante contiene ensayos o capítulos escritos por
varios autores, citamos el libro entero y cada uno de sus artículos
o ensayos. Así el lector puede encontrar los datos bibliográficos
en cualquiera de las varias citas. Cada cita de la bibliografía
contiene todos los datos bibliográficos; por eso no incluímos interreferencias.

Cada capítulo se divide en temas ordenados alfabéticamente.
Todas las clasificaciones aparecen en el capítulo "Latin America" y
en otros capítulos según los temas tratados.

Escogemos los temas según clasificaciones lógicas de investigaciones, en vez de las categorías del Library of Congress u otras
listas establecidas. Las citas clasificadas bajo el título "General"
se refieren a la izquierda católica sin énfasis en un aspecto específico del movimiento. La sección "Documents" comprende las publicaciones oficiales de organizaciones y los informes de congresos o
reuniones.

Las muchas obras que hemos encontrado sobre los aspectos políticos del movimiento han necesitado varias clasificaciones relacionadas. "Politics" se refiere a los trabajos generales sobre el tema.
"Catholic Church and State" enfoca la relación entre la Iglesia y
las instituciones establecidas del gobierno. "Christian Democracy,"
"Communism" y "Socialism" se refieren a estos movimientos específicos
y los partidos políticos asociados con ellos. "Marxism" da énfasis
a la filosofía y teoría de Karl Marx.

Dos individuos, Hélder Câmara y Camilo Torres, son tan importantes

en el movimiento que hemos establecido secciones distintas para ellos
en los capítulos sobre el Brasil y Colombia respectivamente. En
ambos casos las citas se refieren a materias sobre los hombres mismos.
Para encontrar las obras escritas por ellos hay que consultar el
índice de autores. Muchas obras escritas por Hélder Câmara se
encuentran en el capítulo "Latin America" pero una lista completa
solamente aparece en dicho índice.

Para facilitar el uso de la bibliografía hay índices de autores
y títulos al final del libro. Así se puede encontrar una lista de
todas las obras de un autor o conseguir los datos completos bibliográficos para una obra específica.

El ejemplo siguiente ilustra el uso de la bibliografía. Un
investigador que busque materias sobre la importancia de la reforma
agraria en el movimiento izquierdista católico consultaría la sección
"Agrarian Reform" en el primer capítulo, "Latin America," para
encontrar citas generales. Después de examinar las citas allí,
podría consultar la sección "Agrarian Reform" en cualquier otro
capítulo, como "Argentina" o "Central America" para obtener citas
más específicas. En cambio, si busca una obra sobre el tema escrita
por un autor específico, debe consultar el índice de autores. Si
quiere hallar materias relacionadas a un libro específico, puede
buscar la obra en el índice de títulos, consultar la cita corrospon-
diente y examinar otras citas cercanas.

RECONOCIMIENTOS

Los tres compiladores trabajaron diligentemente en este proyecto.
Inicialmente fue Mark Grover quien hizo los esfuerzos principales en
la preparación de esta bibliografía. Después, cuando el Sr. Grover
partió para seguir sus estudios doctorales en Indiana University,
Therrin Dahlin asumió la responsibilidad con la ayuda de Gary Gillum.
El Sr. Dahlin también hizo investigaciones bibliográficas sobre la
izquierda católica durante el verano de 1978 en la Benson Latin
American Collection de la University of Texas de Austin.

Varios individuos que también han colaborado en esta bibliografía
merecen reconocimiento. Carla Kupitz, Syndee Painter, Ann Johnson y
Kathryn Christiansen trabajaron dedicadamente en la mecanografía y
otras tareas técnicas en colaboración con varios ayudantes estudian-
tiles. Larry D. Benson rindió un servicio indispensable en buscar
las fuentes.

Reconocemos con gratitud el apoyo financiero de la Harold B. Lee
Library de Brigham Young University. El Dr. Thomas E. Lyon, Jr.,
ex-director del Latin American Center de Brigham Young University, nos
ayudó y animó constantemente. Agradecemos también la paciencia y los
consejos del Dr. William V. Jackson y Janice Meagher.

T.C.D.
G.P.G.

Introduction

In the eyes of many Latin Americans, "the Roman Catholic Church has been considered an enemy of the people. . . . Today even communists confess that this image is gradually changing and that the Church is engaging in a dialogue, proclaiming its own rights to such values as justice, compassion, respect for human beings, equality and progress."[1]

Not all Catholics would agree with the implications of the above statement, that the changes occurring within the Catholic Church in Latin America--indeed throughout the world--are positive. Nevertheless, all would agree that significant change has occurred in the last twenty-five years. The purpose of this introductory statement is not to evaluate all the changes which have occurred and are occurring, but simply to describe and briefly trace one of the major currents, the Catholic Left.

CHIMBOTE

In 1953, lay representatives of Catholic Action groups throughout Latin America met in Chimbote, Peru. Their purpose was introspection and self-analysis regarding the condition of Latin American Catholics. Their conclusions were that the state of Latin American Catholicism was cause for considerable concern. They found that only 14 percent of the people in what was supposedly a basically Catholic continent seriously professed and practiced the doctrine and discipline of the Church. The rest of those who called themselves Catholic could be divided among what were called "nominal" Catholics who profess belief but do not practice, and "cultural" or "folk" Catholics who follow the cultural practices and folk traditions but neither profess sincere belief nor practice the discipline of the Church.

What was felt by the participants of the Chimbote conference to be an alarming condition was attributed to various factors. First, it was felt that Latin America was experiencing rapid change from an essentially rural-agrarian society controlled by an elite oligarchy with which the Church had traditionally been allied and within which social relationships were relatively well defined, to a predominantly urban, quasi-industrial society in which masses were beginning to participate with increasingly greater frequency and stress. The urban proletariat thus created by this explosive urban migration has resulted in a condition of anomie, dehumanization, and depersonali-

zation with serious consequences indeed for the catholicity of the
masses.

In the midst of this rapidly changing socioeconomic milieu, the
Chimbote conference identified various other factors as undermining
the faith of Catholics in Latin America. These were felt to be
primarily (a) Protestantism, (b) Masonry, and (c) Marxism, with
secondary factors being (d) Liberalism, (e) Naturalism, (f) Nationalism, and (g) Spiritualism.

Primary emphasis for remedial action was placed on approaches
to evangelize more successfully and renew the spiritually weak.
Much attention was given to methods for increasing the ratio of
clergy to lay members, and how best to combat the influence of com-
peting ideologies, philosophies, and religions. However, the real
significance of the Chimbote conference lies in the redefinition of
the Latin American lay apostolate; not so much in its attempt to
discover the problems of the then current apostolate, but to define
the nature of the apostolate for the future.

The previously established pattern of the lay apostolate for
Latin America was set by Pope Pius XII at the World Congress of the
Secular Apostolate. In his second speech he mentioned four mortal
dangers for the Catholic Church in Latin America: Protestantism,
Laicism, Marxism, and Spiritualism. His primary solution for these
problems was to increase the ratio of clergy to laymen. Given the
declining number of priests being trained in Latin America, he saw
the lay apostolate as a major vehicle in overcoming this deficiency.

However, this concept of the lay apostolate was based upon a
traditional model of Latin American society which by 1953 was rapidly
becoming obsolete. Traditional Latin America was viewed as having a
stable, "tranquil" social structure, with clearly distinguished class
lines, and within which each individual had a defined and accepted
position. Relationships were largely paternalistic, familial, and
legitimated by Catholic norms and values. Conditions of poverty,
misery, and injustice were largely ignored. The power elite were
educated and formed in traditional Catholic concepts which then
became the ideological basis for controlling the masses with little
or no protest. All thinking and acting were done in strict accord
with the notion that Church and State were unified in the governance
of the masses.

The conditions of rapid urbanization and semiindustrialization
described previously required an entirely different model and role
for Catholic action. This the Chimbote conference produced. Perhaps
the most significant conclusion reached by the Chimbote conference
was that Catholics should become actively engaged in changing Latin
American society--especially in the following basic areas:

1. In the area of popular education: the "ignorant"
   masses must be educated in both secular truths
   and religious concepts.
2. In the area of economic life: "Catholics should
   strive to eliminate the purely selfish ends of
   monopolistic profiteering. . . . Moral considerations

of personal honesty, social justice and frater-
nalism should be emphasized in economic activites."[2]

3. Regarding the social structure: Catholics should
   strive for a higher unity of brotherhood, striving
   to overcome class differences, and being open to
   the possible transformation of the economic
   structure that would substitute salary payments
   for economic enterprise.
4. In political life: Catholics should strive to
   make the public and personal good the center of
   political life. This assumes the defense of the
   Christian bases of political structures.
5. In international policy: Catholics should work
   to promote a more vital contact and cooperation
   among Catholic forces internationally.

CELAM

During the International Eucharistic Congress held in Rio de Janeiro
in 1955, the Latin American bishops met from June 25 to August 4
and formed the Latin American Council of Bishops (CELAM). CELAM
was officially recognized by Pope Pius XII on September 24, 1955.
The initial objectives of CELAM were to provide a coordinating agency
for all of the bishops of Latin America and to carry out the programs
of pastoral aid proposed by the International Eucharistic Congress.
While CELAM was not called by the Holy See, it met each year to deal
with matters of vital concern to Latin American Catholics, and its
subject matter and conclusions were approved by the Holy See.

The first meeting of CELAM in 1955 dealt largely with organiza-
tional matters. However, a major substantive concern of CELAM at
its inception was the de-Christianization of the Latin American
continent. In this regard, special attention was given to the
impact of (a) industrialization, urbanization, and rapid social
change, (b) Protestant encroachment, (c) the insufficient number of
priests, and (d) the spread of Marxism-atheism.

During the first five years of CELAM's existence, the major focus
continued to be concerned with incorporating Christian principles
into new institutions in a world of ferment and change, one waning
in Catholic commitment. As a corollary of this concern, CELAM continued to focus on the renewal of Christian faith among professing
Catholics.

While the initial concerns of CELAM during these years were only
moderately progressive and were largely concerned with renewal of
faith, Christianization of institutions, and combating corrupting
external influences such as Protestantism, secularism, and Marxism,
there were a few bishops who were increasingly concerned about what
they were seeing as social injustice, exploitation, and imperialism.
Notable among these bishops were Manuel Larraín, Bishop of Talca,
Chile, and Dom Hélder Câmara, Auxiliary Bishop of Rio de Janeiro and
later Archbishop of Olinda and Recife. Bishop Larrain in Chile was

a key figure in the development of social awareness within the Chilean hierarchy, so that by 1962 it was one of the most progressive in Latin America. Dom Hélder Câmara had been the leader of the left-wing of the Brazilian Church since the early 1950s.

Under the presidency of Archbishop Miguel Dario Miranda of Mexico City, with Manuel Larraín and Dom Hélder Câmara as vice presidents, new and innovative currents began to be felt within CELAM. In the meeting in Mexico City in 1961, Dom Hélder spoke on the theme of the Catholic family, a favorite topic of conservative bishops. But he gave it a new social slant. He showed how family instability is a consequence of demographic changes and poverty. He went on to suggest that certain social changes--e.g., better housing, reduction of unemployment, better health and education, and agrarian reform--are prerequisites for counteracting the deterioration of the family in Latin America.

In spite of the prominent influence of these innovative bishops, CELAM as an organization continued to reflect largely the moderate and conservative views of the vast majority of bishops. It was not until after the encyclicals of Pope John XXIII, Pacem in Terris[3] and Mater et Magistra,[4] and the second Vatican Council,[5] which ended in 1963, that the majority of the moderately conservative bishops became convinced of the validity of the more liberal position of the innovative bishops. It was then that a significant change began to show itself in the pronouncements of CELAM.

This change led to a redefinition and reorganization of CELAM in 1963. New departments were organized in keeping with the new consensus, and all departments were headed by bishops noted for their competence in the substantive area of the department. Furthermore, department headquarters were moved from Bogota to various countries throughout Latin America. Two of the more significant departments added to CELAM which reflect the increasing concern with problems of development were Social Action and Education.

By 1966 CELAM had developed a social developmental orientation which predated the significant papal encyclical of Paul VI, Populorum Progressio, which is entirely devoted to the problems of development. This orientation is seen in the document produced by the CELAM Mar del Plata conference in 1966. The document argues that Latin American integration is necessary for regional development and lasting peace; that the existence of certain social, political, and economic structures inhibits the participation and integration of the Latin American people; that the right of private property is not absolute; that there is a real problem of expanding population; and that education of the masses is essential.

Because of its official status, developments within CELAM have had great impact on Latin American Catholicism. However, it is significant that many innovators of the Catholic Left have not been directly connected with CELAM.

THE CENTRO BELLARMINO IN CHILE

The development of an innovative Catholic Left in Chile must be understood in context of the development of a relatively unified and progressive clergy throughout Chile. Chile is one of the few countries in Latin America in which the clergy, including the episcopate, has been relatively unified in the development of a progressive social perspective.

The Centro Bellarmino is the outgrowth of the progressive thinking of a group Jesuits who taught at the Colegio San Ignacio in Santiago. The Centro Bellarmino was conceived by Fr. Alberto Hurtado in conjunction with Fr. Jean-Baptiste Janssens in the early 1950s. Father Hurtado had been active in advocating greater independence of thought and participation of the masses in political activities. He founded a confederation of labor unions called ASICH (Acción Sindical Chilena). All of these activities flew in the face of the traditional conservative party, and consequently Fr. Hurtado allied himself with the more liberal Falange-Nacional, the precursor of Christian Democracy in Chile.

Fathers Hurtado and Janssens were both concerned about the renovation of the Church in Latin America. They felt that the Jesuits could contribute most to this renovation by specializing in the analysis of social issues affecting the Church. A center with technical expertise in social analysis and commentary could make a significant contribution to strengthening the voice of the Church.

As a first step a journal was established: Mensaje. Mensaje became one of the important organs of progressive Catholic commentary in Latin America.

With time a group of highly trained Jesuit sociologists and economists gathered together in the Centro Bellarmino. These included Fr. Jaime Larraín; Fr. Ramón Angel Cifuentes; Fr. Roger Vekemans, a Belgian sociologist; Fr. Ignacio Grez; Fr. Renato Poblete, a sociologist trained at Fordham University; Fr. Neil Hurley, an American political scientist; Fr. Gonzalo Arroyo, an economist; Fr. Pauol Meneses, another political scientist; and Fr. Mario Zañartu, an economist from Columbia University. Their studies of social issues and the formulation of policy suggestions became very influential in the development of Christian Democracy in Chile. Indeed, some have said that the Centro Bellarmino was the "brain trust" of Frei's Christian Democratic party.

It is important to note that while the Centro Bellarmino was basically an institute of social research and commentary, its faculty was wholly committed to practical matters of social action. Thus, in 1962 a special edition of Mensaje was published devoted to the analysis and advocacy of nonviolent revolution as a practical strategy for social change in Latin America.

CIDOC

The Intercultural Center of Documentation (CIDOC) was founded by Ivan Illich in Cuernavaca, Mexico. Ivan Illich was trained for Vatican diplomatic service, but while working temporarily in New York City with Puerto Rican parishioners, he was struck by the fact that the priests and those working with Puerto Ricans didn't even speak Spanish, much less understand Puerto Rican cultural idiosyncracies. From New York he went to Puerto Rico, but was eventually asked to leave because he opposed the formation of a Catholic political party favored by his bishop.

From Puerto Rico he went to Cuernavaca, Mexico, where he founded CIDOC. The educational, analytical, and social-action objectives of CIDOC reflect Illich's primary concern--the relationship between Catholicism and culture.

Illich has been severely criticized by more conservative U.S. Catholics, including his Eminence, Richard Cardinal Cushing, for his radical stand on social change in Latin America. His conflict with Cardinal Cushing grew out of an article entitled "The Seamy Side of Charity" published in the Jesuit magazine America (Jan. 21, 1967). In this article Illich raised serious questions about American missionary activity in two basic ways: (1) that the culture-bound Church being bolstered by U.S. money and personnel is not applicable to Latin American reality, and (2) that American clergy act as agents of colonialism by advocating an Alliance for Progress mentality and a fanatical anti-Communist view which makes them unable to understand progressive leftist movements in Latin America which want to alter the present social structure.

Illich further advocates the need for genuine indigenous movements and solutions to Latin America's social problems. He insists that only the Latin American masses have the right to build a new society. Outside interests can only create a situation of imperialism and cultural conflict. He advocates political action; social equality; radical indigenous experimentation; the acceptance of the values of a pluralistic society; and liberation from cultural, political and economic imperialism among other things.

One of the principal activities of CIDOC is in the area of education of the masses in a process termed "conscientização," developed in Brazil as the brainchild of Paulo Freire. The assumption is made that as the masses are made aware of alternatives and the reality of their condition, they will then take steps to make the changes which are consistent with their needs and their reality. Literally translated, "conscientização" means the awakening of consciousness. This approach to education as advocated by Illich theoretically does not try to give people paternalistic answers to their problems, but rather tries to allow them to arrive at their own solutions after being awakened to the reality of their condition and the alternatives available.[6]

CIDOC also serves as a training and research center for many Catholic and non-Catholic missionaries and lay people who are preparing to work in Latin America. Language training is a primary focus, but also a great deal of emphasis is placed on making people aware of social structure and culture in Latin America.

THE REGIONAL SEMINARY OF NORTHEASTERN BRAZIL

A major experiment in the radicalization of the Church in Brazil is

the development of the Regional Seminary in northeastern Brazil.
Traditionally, seminary training in Brazil has followed a scholastic
model based on 16th- and 17th-century commentators on Aristotle
and the medieval theologians and philosophers. Study was almost
exclusively conducted in Latin. The development of the regional
seminary in Brazil's Northeast responds to two objectives. First,
that of increasing the number of priests in Brazil, and second, that
of training priests to become aware of and relevant to the social
conditions of the northeast.

In 1964 Dom Hélder Câmara became the Archbishop of Recife and
Olinda. As a part of his intense concern for the social and physical
condition of the people of the Northeast, Dom Hélder took upon himself
to become a prime mover in the development of the Regional Seminary
of the Northeast, in order to promote pastoral changes and social
relevance among the new priests.

Under his leadership radical innovations have been introduced
into the seminary training. The curriculum basically centers on
humanistic anthropology. The focus is upon putting the seminarian
in touch with the people and helping him to respond to their social
reality.

Various innovations have been introduced in order to bring the
seminary students into direct contact with the masses. Students
leave the seminary; they live under the same roofs and eat the same
food as the people. They learn experientially what it's like to be
poor in the Brazilian Northeast. In addition, they work as teams in
different social-action programs for a period of time. The result
has been a radical change in the orientation of the young priests.
They graduate with a sense of identification with the masses which
never before has been felt. At the same time they experience great
frustration at having to work within a traditional social structure
which is relatively unresponsive to their newly acquired radical
perspective on social change. What are and what will be the consequences? While few are openly Marxist in their ideology, most are
not opposed to violence as a means of effecting the revolutionary
changes which they feel are needed.

Dom Hélder Câmara is one of the most progressive and innovative
bishops in all of Latin America, and while he advocates a kind of
Christian socialist solution to the problems of the Latin American,
he is clearly against the use of violence in bringing about radical
social change.[7] It is, thus, noteworthy and ironical that the
Regional Seminary of the Northeast which he has championed is pro-
ducing young priests of an even more radical hue than Dom Hélder,
priests who are not adverse to violence as a means of change.

CAMILO TORRES, THE GUERRILLA PRIEST

The training of radical young priests in Brazil brings to mind Camilo
Torres of Colombia. Camilo Torres is a symbol of radical Catholic
action in Latin America. Father Torres was trained as a sociologist
at the University of Louvaine in France. Having despaired of the

possibility of equitable social change through peaceful means, he allied himself with Marxist guerrillas working from the Colombian jungles. His odyssey came to a tragic end when he was killed by counterinsurgent Colombian troops in 1966.

Camilo Torres is the prototype of a growing number of young priests in Latin America who have allied themselves with Marxist revolutionaries who seek a socialist society and liberation from what they perceive to be "Yankee imperialism." These young idealists see social justice and social action as primary Christian virtues. Love of Christ is manifest in service to one's fellow man, not in mere profession of truth. This service is translated into a struggle for human dignity, equality, and social justice by joining with Marxist revolutionaries in an ideological and sometimes violent struggle with oligarchy. While they are non-Communist, they are not anti-Communist. Their perception is that Communists and "true" Christians are struggling for a common social goal. Their only demand is that the socialist state allow Christians to worship God as they choose.

POPULORUM PROGRESSIO

When Pope John XXIII died many liberal Catholics—especially the innovators—feared that a conservative retrenchment might occur under Paul VI. They were greatly encouraged, even elated, by the encyclical Populorum Progressio, published in March of 1967. In this encyclical Paul VI called for all "men of good will" to use all means, political, social, economic, and diplomatic, in a world-wide effort to eliminate deprivation. He asserted that in the pursuit of justice and human dignity "property rights are secondary to the needs of those who lack the necessities."

He affirmed that the role of the Church is to make the poor and oppressed aware of their situation and to seek solidarity among Christians in combating conditions which produce inequality and deprivation. He specified that capitalism is a "despicable" economic system when it causes suffering and injustice, and supported agrarian reform where necessary for the common good.

Whether rightly or wrongly interpreted, the pronouncements in Populorum Progressio were looked upon by the Catholic Left as doctrinal justification for their position and as a great boost for their cause.

However, knowing full well the power of the traditional Church and oligarchy, many radical priests were apprehensive that the words of Paul VI had fallen on deaf ears among those who wield economic and political power. Typical of this apprehension is a statement of participants in the first seminar of priests sponsored by the Social Department of CELAM in Chile during October and November, 1967.

> The Church must be involved in human activity as the leaven in the dough. But she must be free from compromising entanglements that would prevent her from being a beacon of hope for the people of the world.

Thus, she must avoid entanglements with those who
wield economic, political, and social power, and
she cannot be the accomplice of those who try to
block necessary structural changes and the restora-
tion of rights to the dispossessed.

Granting this, we are deeply concerned over the
faint impact of the encyclical Populorum Progressio
on certain Christian sectors of the business world
that wield economic, social, and political power,
and on certain ecclesiastical circles of Latin
America. . . .

We deplore the fact that every attempt to regain
just rights, sometimes violent in cast because
there seems to be no other recourse, is labeled
communism when, in fact, it is simply mass rebel-
lion against a situation of injustice that is no
longer tolerable. It pains us that the truth about
these protests is distorted to favor the groups in
control, who own most of the communications media.[8]

HUMANAE VITAE: WILL THE REAL PAUL VI PLEASE STAND?

On July 3, Paul VI issued the long-awaited pronouncement on birth
control, Humanae Vitae. For the innovative clergy of the Left this
seemed to be not only a step backwards, but even a contradiction of
some of the most cherished statements in Populorum Progressio.
     One of the most critical problems of development in Latin America
is that the rate of growth of the population is far outdistancing
the ability of the Latin American nations to provide even the most
basic food and shelter.
     Without arguing the validity of this concern, most of those who
profess to be specialists in development assert that economic growth
can only catch population growth if massive efforts are made to
educate the masses to the need and techniques of effective birth
control. Humanae Vitae in a doctrinal sense effectively limited
that possibility among Latin American Catholics.
     Just as important, Humanae Vitae was published just twenty days
before Paul VI's departure for Colombia on what was heralded as the
Pope's pilgrimage to the poor of Latin America. He himself had said
that he would celebrate the next religious affirmation "in that Latin
America where we are so loved by the multitudes of the poor and the
humble who await a new and provident social justice." At last the
Pope was going to arm his words with action by seeing in person and
by personally attending the needs of the poor--or would he?
     Most of the radical priests were fearful that Paul VI would not
be allowed to see the reality of the masses during his visit to
Colombia. After Humanae Vitae many were of the opinion that he
didn't really want to. As a consequence, throughout Latin America

clergymen of the Left responded in fearful anticipation of the worst. In Santiago, a few priests and 200 lay Catholics assembled in the cathedral to protest against the traditional Church and express their concerns at the way Paul VI's trip was developing. The young clergy of Uruguay sent a concerned message directly to the Pope: "Brother Paul, if you do not come to commit yourself to the cause of those who struggle; if you come to consecrate the existing order, then, Brother Paul, it is better for you not to come." Letters of a similar nature were sent from almost all parts of Latin America: from Argentina, from Chile, from Peru, and from Colombia, among others.

Paul VI's visit to Colombia was without doubt disappointing to the young Church of the Left. His arrival at Bogota's El Dorado airport was greeted with delirious enthusiasm by the millions of spotless, shiny-faced peasants who had been scrubbing and saving for weeks for this singular occasion. He was thus insulated from the sordid reality of the poverty of the masses, not only by the official Church and governmental representatives who met him, but also by the very face of Bogota, which had put on a new and spotless, if false, mask to receive the pontiff. At best his visit was interpreted by the young Church as an attempt to affirm the eclectic nature of Catholicism.

THE MEDELLIN CONFERENCE OF THE LATIN AMERICAN EPISCOPATE

Immediately following the visit of Paul VI to Colombia, the Second General Conference of the Latin American Episcopate convened in Medellin. While the young radicals were clearly disappointed by Paul VI's lack of total commitment to the revolutionary cause of the downtrodden, the Medellin Conference turned out to be a seminal event which produced documents of transcendant importance to the young Church. The Medellin conference, following on doctrinal legitimation by Populorum Progressio, became for the Latin American Catholics what Vatican II had been for the entire Church.

A brief analysis of the conclusions of the Medellin conference in comparison with the pronouncements of CELAM during the late 1950s makes one aware of the degree to which the more innovative bishops, Vatican II, the social encyclical of John XXIII, and Populorum Progressio had influenced the thinking of the Latin American prelates. No longer was the major concern merely with the re-Christianization of Latin American Catholics. The focus had changed to the basic structural conditions of Latin American society which were impeding the achievement of basic human dignity by the masses. The following points made by the conference seem to illustrate this fact very clearly.

> 1. The Latin America prelates were no longer out-
>   spokenly anti-Communist in their pronouncements.
>   In fact, many had adopted Marxist terminology

and concepts as a sociological model for the analysis of Latin American reality. Grave concern was expressed for the blatant and excessive inequality between rich and poor, powerful and weak, and for exploitation, in its many forms, of the latter by the former.

2. The pluralistic secular nature of Latin American society was clearly recognized and the Church was acknowledged to be one of several forces participating in social-change problems.

3. Major concern was given to the problem of dependence of Latin American nations on multinational corporations and the developed nations. Particular mention was made of United States imperialism as a major exploitive factor. It was also acknowledged that rabid anticommunism had heretofore obscured the fact that Latin America was being exploited by foreign centers of economical and political power.

4. Great concern was expressed by the section on education for the need for the "awakening of awareness" among the masses, "conscientização," as a strategy for making people politically aware and active.

5. Both capitalism and communism were condemned as systems which violate human dignity: capitalism because it dehumanizes and materializes man by giving primacy to capital and its acquisition; communism because it advocates totalitarianism by concentrating power in the hands of the state. A kind of democratic socialism, frequently referred to as "communitarianism," was advocated as a system in which economic enterprise should be ". . . fundamentally a community of persons and unity of work, which needs capital for the production of goods."

6. Violence as a means for bringing about change was very clearly rejected by the conference, but it was also recognized that peace presupposes justice. It was felt that in the face of the inadequacy of dialogue and compromise, political pressure should be brought to bear the masses, enlightened and made aware through "conscientizaçao."

7. While the conference officially rejected family planning by artificial means, it was tacitly agreed by many that no concerted effort would be made to prevent its use.

8. It was agreed that agrarian reform was a much-needed measure to promote social and economic welfare, especially among rural people.

In general, the need was expressed and the call was issued for the formation of structures which would facilitate active, creative and decisive participation in the formation of a new society.[9]

THE CHILEAN "CHRISTIANS FOR SOCIALISM"

At about this same time social, political, and economic conditions in Chile were ripening for the ill-fated Marxist experiment of Salvador Allende. In July of 1970 Salvador Allende, representing the United Popular Front, was elected president of Chile and declared his intentions to create a new Chilean socialist state.

The leftist-oriented bishops and priests of Chile embraced Allende with great enthusiasm. Cardinal Silva Henriquez, the non-Marxist but innovative leader of the Catholic Church in Chile, indicated that he felt that ". . . socialism has great Christian values and in many ways is superior to capitalism." He also indicated that ". . . if on the road to the reforms which the new government of Salvador Allende intends to undertake, there are errors made, we nevertheless need to understand their good and honest intentions, and these we should support."[10]

In April of 1971 a group of eighty priests, who later became known as Christians for Socialism, met to express their support for Allende and solidarity with socialism as a socioeconomic system. Their position was that as Christians they were identified with the masses in their struggle against domination and exploitation by the wealthy capitalists. They saw socialism as basically a struggle to overcome capitalism. Ideologically, their position as priests was to identify with socialism as Christians in order to counter attempts by the ruling moneyed class to use Christian thought as a tool against socialism. They felt that their ideological struggle ". . . had to be an ongoing activity designed to create a new consciousness among Christians and to overthrow the ideological barriers to their participation in the process of liberation, barriers which had been erected by the oppressors in the name of Christianity."[11]

THE PERUVIAN BISHOPS

Another manifestation of the deepening of social conscience and legitimation of the Catholic Left following Populorum Progressio and the Medellin episcopal conference occurred in Peru. The pervasiveness of this point of view among the Peruvian clergy is reflected in the final document of the Thirty-sixth Peruvian Episcopal Conference held in January of 1969.

> . . . We bishops of Peru have chosen to make the people of Peru the center and guiding concern of our reflections. Their joys and hopes, their anxieties and sufferings, are ours too. We echo their effort to obtain liberation.

Introduction

We do not propose to present a complete picture of the present-day situation in our country. We propose to focus on those situations and factors where unjust social, political, economic, and cultural inequities exist. The Church denounces this situation as one of sin.

This situation of injustice is not an isolate reality in space and time. It is the result of a process that has worldwide dimensions. It is characterized by the concentration of political and economic power in the hands of a few and by the international imperialism of money, which operates in league with Peruvian oligarchy. . . .

This view of our present situation from a Christian perspective compels us to do our part in the creation of a new humanity. All our proposed social reforms are aimed ultimately at transforming our way of being human beings. This process of humanization requires the People of God to proclaim "the liberation of the oppressed. . . ."

. . . We recognize that we Christians, for want of fidelity to the gospel have contributed to the present unjust situation through our words and attitudes, our silence and inaction.

As citizens of this country, we share responsibility for the exploitation of the vast majority of our countrymen. . . .[12]

The prelates went on to specify some of the action steps which they proposed to take in order to do their part ". . . in the creation of a new humanity."

These included the following:

1. Work toward the formation of men's conscience.
2. Denounce injustice and defend the rights of the poor and oppressed.
3. Encourage and support efforts to create grass-roots organizations for social and political action.
4. Advocate appropriate legislation to protect household help.
5. Denounce excessive inequalities between rich and poor.

The prelates also declared their intention to evaluate all real-estate and other assets of the religious communities, dioceses, and church organizations in terms of their usefulness in giving service and dealing with poverty. They also expressed the desire to make the finances of Church institutions public. In keeping with these statements, several bishops then moved to less ostentatious living quarters as an expression of good faith.

GUSTAVO GUTIÉRREZ AND LIBERATION THEOLOGY

Perhaps the most important figure for the Catholic Left among the Peruvian clergy is the brilliant theologian and priest, Fr. Gustavo Gutiérrez. Gutiérrez represents for the Catholic Left of Peru, indeed for all of Latin America, the pinnacle of leftist Christian thought. With Gutiérrez's Teología de La Liberación, published in 1971, the wedding between Christian theology and Marxist social analysis is complete.

Gutiérrez bases liberation theology on the assumption that theology ". . . asks the question about the meaning of the Word of God for us in the today of history."[12] In other words, to be meaningful, theology must interpret the Word of God in terms of today's reality.

Gutiérrez then interprets the reality of Latin America as one in which the masses of poor are held in subjection and dependence by foreign entrepreneurs working in collaboration with a powerful few in Latin America who do so to maintain their position of power and wealth. He maintains that this condition of dependence can only be adequately analyzed and understood from a study of the class dialectic.

The challenge, then, for Gutiérrez as a theologian is to interpret God to the poor, exploited, dehumanized, "nonperson" masses. "Our question, therefore, is not how to announce God in an adult world; but rather, how to announce him as Father in a nonhuman world. What are the implications when we tell a nonperson that he or she is a child of God?"[14]

Gutiérrez insists that it is impossible for an appropriate theology of liberation to be formulated or even understood without entering into the world of the poor and joining with them in the struggle for liberation. Thus, he says that the Christian task is to create a grass-roots Church, to ". . . rip the Gospel from the hands of the powerful of this world." God will only be reintegrated in history when the poor ". . . expropriate the gospel from those who consider themselves its privileged owners."[15]

RETRENCHMENT OF CELAM

In 1972 the annual meeting of CELAM was held in Sucre, Bolivia. At that meeting a conservative leadership of CELAM was elected, and many of the more radical departments were dismantled. This reaction of the conservative clergy coincided with conservative reaction in other circles of Latin America.

In September of 1973 the Marxist government of Salvador Allende was overthrown by the military forces of Chile. General Augusto Pinochet of the army was installed as president by the ruling military junta. After the initial violent takeover by the junta, in which Salvador Allende was killed, known and suspected Communists, Marxist, socialists, and sympathaziers were rounded up pending investigation. Some were summarily executed, others were deported, and yet others put into prison.

Many of the active Christians for Socialism fled the country, while a few stayed. In October the Chilean bishops published a pastoral letter expressing their official condemnation of Christians for Socialism. Following a period of silence in which it appeared as though the remaining Leftist priests would capitulate to the bishops and the Pinochet government, criticism of the military government began to appear in Mensaje.

Later, the military government came under attack by a number of the less radical bishops and priests who nevertheless had supported Allende's socialist government. Cardinal Silva Henríquez asked that captured extremists be treated with mercy and strongly criticized the military government for brutality and the violation of human rights. Several priests and nuns were expelled from the country for aiding and protecting Mirista guerrillas wounded in a skirmish with the military police. In the meantime, confusion and frustration among prominent Catholic laymen spread as editorials appeared in El Mercurio and on radio decrying the tendency of the Church to become involved in political activism.

RIOBAMBA

On August 9, 1976, a group of seventeen bishops representing various countries of Latin America and the United States met in Riobamba, Ecuador, at the invitation of Monseñor Leonides Proaño, Bishop of Riobamba. The basic purpose of the meeting was pastoral: to compare notes, to discuss the situation in Latin America, and to make plans for pastoral work based on the ensuing interchange and discussions.

On August 12 at 5:15 p.m., the group was interrupted by several dozen Ecuadorian police. They were taken into custody and transported to Quito, where the foreign prelates were declared personae non grata and were deported from the country. The charge was that the meeting was subversive in nature and those involved had entered into the country surreptitiously.

Whether or not the meeting was subversive in nature depends on one's point of view. However, it is interesting to note that a wide spectrum of political and social thought was represented by the prelates. Two were rather notable innovators, Monseñor Proaño from Ecuador and Monseñor Sergio Mendez Arceo, bishop of Cuernavaca, Mexico. Others were much more conservative. The significance of the Riobamba conference, however, does not lie so much in what was discussed as in the trend reflected by the reaction of the conservative military government of Ecuador.

In seven of the countries of South America, there are presently conservative military governments in power. All of these governments have come to power through violence, five since 1973. In all seven there are serious conflicts between the Church and the ruling government. In several cases these conflicts have become violent. What was once considered to be a solid alliance between Church and State has in many cases turned into at best an uneasy coexistence.

THE IMPACT IN OTHER PARTS OF LATIN AMERICA

While the Sucre conference of CELAM in 1972, the military coup in Chile in 1973, and the events of Riobamba in 1976 seem to constitute a series of setbacks for the Catholic Left in Latin America, nevertheless the work of Vatican II, Populorum Progressio, the Medellin conference, and the development of a liberation theology have sent deep roots into the Latin American clergy. Even conservative gains by the traditionalists in the CELAM conference in Sucre in 1972 did not stifle the activities of the Left. The radical core simply shifted its activities from CELAM to the Latin American Confederation of Religious (CLAR). Between 1972 and 1976, over 170,000 priests and nuns representing 457 member orders[16] were exposed to seminars designed to awaken the clergy to the reality of the plight of the poor and the need for a liberation theology.

What is becoming increasingly apparent in Latin America is that priests and nuns are no longer blind followers of their bishops. Vatican II has breathed a new spirit of independence over the Catholic hierarchy. Furthermore, laymen and clergy alike are increasingly of the opinion that Marxist analytical symbols need not require Marxist ideological allegiance or solutions. Liberation theology has shown that one need not forsake his Christian faith to espouse the dialectic of classes, albeit with a nonviolent praxis.

The recent wave of conservatism and military authoritarianism, however, seems to have convinced most radical Catholics that the masses are not adequately prepared for grass-roots action. What too often has resulted heretofore is that the oppressed have become the oppressors when given a position of power.

Today's model of radical Catholic action strongly emphasizes liberation theology using nonviolent confrontation through the application of Paulo Freire's "conscientização." The most critical need as expressed by the leading spokesman, Dom Hélder Câmara, is to make the masses aware and capable of taking the responsibilities implied by liberation.

POPE JOHN PAUL II AND THE EPISCOPAL CONFERENCE IN PUEBLA

In his message to the Episcopal Conference held in Mexico in January of 1979, Pope John Paul II charted a moderate progressive line. While he affirmed the spirit of the Medellin Conference of 1968, he noted that some have interpreted the results of that conference in inappropriate ways.

He indicated that the Church must oppose injustice and infringement upon human dignity, but only in line with her true mission, which is to preach, educate, and help form public opinion in line with Christian truth. In this way the Church will be working for a more

equitable distribution of goods and resources, and for social justice
throughout all nations of the world, helping to ensure that the
stronger nations do not exploit the weaker.

In a clear rebuke of the more radical elements of the Catholic
Left, the Pope said that the idea that Christ was a political subversive, a revolutionary who died as the result of a political conflict, does not agree with the fact that Christ <u>freely</u> gave his life
for mankind.

The conference itself called for an end to repression and injustice on the American continent, and the final document which was
approved by John Paul II urged priests and Catholic laymen to press
for profound changes which would benefit the poor and oppressed.[17]
However, the document stopped short of advocating political activism.
The overall effect of the conference and the visit of the Pope was,
then, to maintain a progressive stance while tempering the position
of the more radical elements of the young church.

The development of the Catholic Left in Latin America is reflec-
tive and symptomatic of the dialectic drama being played throughout
all of Latin American culture and society. Which face of this dialectic within the Catholic Church will emerge victorious? As one
reads and observes from the outside it sometimes appears that the
young Church has clearly gained control. However, events of the
past two or three years make one wonder if the old Church is merely
flexing her muscles and arching her back in preparation for retrenchment. Certainly this is occurring at some levels and in some spheres.
It is safe to say, however, that after Vatican II and the social
encyclicals, the Catholic Church will never be the same. The modern
Church is certainly much more attuned and responsive in her own way
to the contemporary problems of the modern world. It is also safe to
say that within the Catholic Church in Latin America there are struggles of monumental proportions. How these will be resolved or what
the outcome will be is not clear at this time. Whatever the outcome,
however, the Catholic Left will have had an impact of lasting significance.

Berkley A. Spencer

Associate Professor of Sociology
and Latin American Studies,
Brigham Young University

NOTES

1. Hellmut Gnadt Vitalis, The Significance of Changes in Latin American Catholicism Since Chimbote, 1953 (Cuernavaca, Mexico: Centro Intercultural de Documentación, 1969), pp. 111–112.

2. Ibid., p. 319.

3. Pacem in Terris called for world peace, asserted the rights of the masses to human dignity and justice, and then opened the way for the clergy to take an active part in public life in these changes, even with non-Catholics.

4. Mater et Magistra asserted that the rich nations have an obligation to come to the aid of the poor nations and warned against economic and political colonialism.

5. Vatican II examined the role of the Church in the modern secularized world, found it lacking, and tried to make it socially significant by reaching outward, by trying to address the significant issues of living in a pluralistic, secular society, and by opening Catholics to a dialogue with the non-Catholic world.

6. It should be noted that Paulo Freire's "conscientização" was originally developed as a Marxist strategy for precipitating class conflicts as a part of the revolutionary class struggle. "Conscientização" was not designed simply to point out alternatives, but to label elements of the "class struggle" and foment class consciousness and resentment which would eventually lead to the forceful assertion of the exploited classes.

7. Hélder Câmara, "Violence in the Modern World," in Between Honesty and Hope, eds. Peruvian Bishops' Commission for Social Action (New York: Maryknoll Publications, 1970).

8. Peruvian Bishops' Commission for Social Action, Between Honesty and Hope (New York: Maryknoll Publications, 1970), pp. 72–73.

9. Thomas G. Sanders, "The Church in Latin America," Foreign Affairs 48 (1970): 285–287.

10. Teresa Donoso Loero, Los Cristianos por el Socialismo en Chile (Santiago, Chile: Editorial Vaitea, 1976), p. 119.

11. Fernando Castillo, "Christians for Socialism in Chile," in Christianity and Socialism, eds. Johann-Baptist Metz and Jean-Pierre Jossua (New York: Seabury Press, 1977), p. 109.

12. Peruvian Bishops' Commission for Social Action, 228–230.

13. Gustavo Gutiérrez, "Freedom and Salvation: A Political Problem," in <u>Liberation and Change</u>, ed. Ronald H. Stone (Atlanta: John Knox Press, 1977), p. 78.

14. Ibid., p. 79.

15. Ibid., p. 93.

16. Penny Lernoux, "Latin America's Insurgent Church," <u>Nation</u> 222 (May 22, 1976): 620-621.

17. "Latin America: Bishops Urge Reforms, Social Justice," <u>Facts on File</u> 39 (1979): 108.

Abbreviations

CEBRAP   Editora Brasileira de Ciencias and Centro Brasileiro de Análise e Planejamento

CEDIAL   Centro de Estudios para el Desarrollo e Integración de América Latina

CELAM   Consejo Episcopal Latinoamericano

CEP   Centro de Estudios y Publicaciones

CIAS   Centro de Investigación y Acción Social

CIDOC   Centro Intercultural de Documentación

CIEP   Centro de Investigación y Educación Popular

CISOR   Centro de Investigaciones Sociales y Socio-Religiosas

CLAR   Confederación Latinoamericana de Religiosos

CLASC   Confederación Latinoamericana de Sindicatos Cristianos

DESAL   Centro para el Desarrollo Económico y Social de América Latina

HUCITEC   Editorial Humanismo Ciencia de Tecnología

ICHEH   Instituto Chileno de Estudios Humanísticos

IDES   Instituto de Doctrina y Estudios Sociales

INES   Instituto Nacional de Estudios Syndicales

ISAL   Iglesia y Sociedad en América Latina

JOC   Juventude Operária Católica de São Paulo

NACLA   North American Conference on Latin America

ONIS   Organización Nacional de Iglesia Solidaria

PDC   Partido Democrata Cristão

SPEC   Secretariado Permanente Episcopal Colombiano

I Latin America

GENERAL

0001 AGUIAR, CÉSAR. "Currents and Tendencies in Contemporary
      Latin American Catholicism." IDOC-International 13
      (November 14, 1970): 50-73.

0002 ALLIENDE L., JOAQUÍN. "Hacia una pastoral de la religiosidad
      popular." In Religiosidad y Fé en América Latina, edited
      by Encuentro Latinoamericana de Religiosidad Popular,
      pp. 101-108. Santiago, Chile: Mundo, 1975.

0003 ALONSO, ISIDORO, and GARRIDO, GINES. La Iglesia en América
      Latina: estructuras eclesiásticas. Friburg, Switzerland:
      Oficina Internacional de Investigaciones Sociales de FERES,
      1964. 223 pp., bibl.

0004 ALVAREZ CALDERÓN, CARLOS. Pastoral y liberación humana.
      Lima: [n.p.], 1970. 84 pp.

0005 ALVES, RUBEM. "Dal paradiso al deserto." In La nuova fron-
      teira della teologia in America Latina, edited by Rosino
      Gibellini, pp. 411-440. Brescia, Italy: Queriniana,
      1975.

0006 _____, et al. La Iglesia y sociedad. Montevideo: Tierra
      Nueva, 1971. 284 pp.

0007 "L'America Latina e il viaggio di Paolo VI." Note de Culture
      39/40 (1968): 383-410.

0008 "Amerique Latine et conscience chretienne." Esprit 33
      (July/August, 1965): 1-222.

0009 ANTONCICH, RICARDO. "Cómo hablar hoy de Dios en América
      Latina." Medellín 9 (March, 1977): 19-43.

0010 APOLLONIA, L. "Pour le meilleur et pour le pire en Amérique
      Latine." Relations 276 (December, 1963): 363.

1

General

0011   AREVALO, CATALINO. "Thoughts on the Latin American Church
        Today." Impact 2 (February, 1973): 60–65.

0012   ARROYO, GONZALO. "Justice for Latin America." Impact 5
        (May, 1972): 172–174.

0013   _____. "La Iglesia en la década del yo." In América 70,
        edited by Carlos Nandon, pp. 243–244. Santiago, Chile:
        Nueva Universidad, 1970.

0014   ASSMANN, HUGO. "Medellín: a desilção que nos amadureceu."
        Brotería 38 (July/August, 1975): 51–57.

0015   _____, ed. Pueblo oprimido, Señor de la historia. Montevideo:
        Tierra Nueva, 1972. 276 pp.

0016   "Associate Justice W. Douglas Attacks Catholicism of Latin
        America and Vietnam." Catholic Layman 77 (December, 1963):
        42–43.

0017   Association for Latin American Studies. The Community in
        Revolutionary Latin America. Lawrence, Kansas: University
        of Kansas, Center of Latin American Studies, 1964. 36 pp.,
        bibl.

0018   _____. Midwest Council. Religious and Cultural Factors in
        Latin America. Lawrence, Kansas: University of Kansas,
        Center of Latin American Studies, 1970. 159 pp.

0019   BAGÚ, SERGIO. Estructura social de la colonia; ensayo de
        historia comparada con América Latina. Buenos Aires: El
        Ateneo, 1952.

0020   BAHMANN, MANFRED K. "Der römische Katholizismus in Latein-
        amerika." Materialdienst die Konfessions Kundlichen
        Instituts 19 (1968): 37–41.

0021   BATES, MARGARET, ed. The Lay Apostolate in Latin America
        Today: Proceedings of the 1959 Symposium Held Under the
        Auspices of the Institute of Ibero-American Studies of the
        Catholic University of America, April 10-11, 1959.
        Washington: Catholic University Press, 1960. 66 pp.

0022   BAUM, G. "The Christian Left at Detroit: Theology in the
        Americas, Detroit, August, 1975." Ecumenist 13 (September/
        October, 1975): 81–91+.

0023   BAUMGARTNER, SIEGFRIED. "Lateinamerikas Kirche." Rheinische
       Merkur 17 (1962): 3.

0024   BECKMAN, JOSEPH F. "The Church in Mexico." St. Anthony
       Messenger 81 (February, 1974): 22-31.

0025   BERMEJO, J. "Latin American Episcopal Conference, CELAM
       Meets." L'Osservatore Romano, January 15, 1970, p. 7.

0026   BIGO, PIERRE. "El congreso extraordinario del CELAM."
       Mensaje 15 (December, 1966): 690-691.

0027   BILHEIMER, ROBERT, AND SALES, E. "Latin America: Our Joint
       Christian Concern." Listening 2 (Fall, 1967): 227-236.

0028   BLISS, SHEPHERD. "Church Struggle in Latin America."
       Christianity and Crisis 36 (October 18, 1976): 236-238.

0029   BOENINGER, EDGARDO. "La reforma administrativa." Mensaje 23
       (October, 1963): 523-532.

0030   BOFF, LEONARDO. "Qué es hacer teología desde América Latina."
       Servicio de Documentación. MIEJ-JECI 20 (March, 1977):
       1-34.

0031   BOLO HIDALGO, SALOMÓN. Cristianismo y liberación nacional.
       Lima: Ediciones Liberación, 1962. 108 pp.

0032   BONINO-MIGUEZ, JOSÉ. "Prassi storica e identita cristiana."
       In La nuova fronteira della teologia in America Latina,
       edited by Rosino Gibellini, pp. 377-410. Brescia, Italy:
       Queriniana, 1975.

0033   BONO, AGOSTINO. "Church Involvement in Latin Rights Struggles
       to Continue in '76." National Catholic Reporter 12
       (January 9, 1976): 13.

0034   _____. "Right Turn in Latin America." Commonweal 96
       (September 22, 1972): 492-493.

0035   BORELLO, G. M. "Medellín y la evangelii nuntiandi." Catequesis
       Latinoamericana 8 (1976): 9-12.

0036   NO ENTRY

0037   BORISOV, S. "Ognem i mechom." Nauka i Religiia 4 (May, 1962):
       48.

General

0038   BORRAT, HÉCTOR. "El gran impulso." Víspera 2 (October, 1968): 3-5.

0039   _____. "En asamblea permanente con monseñor Parteli y Lucio Gera." Víspera 3 (November 12, 1969): 3-12.

0040   _____. "Freedom of Opinion in Latin America." In Human Rights and the Liberation of Man in the Americas, edited by Louis M. Colonnese, pp. 189-205. Notre Dame, Indiana: University of Notre Dame Press, 1970.

0041   _____. "Una opinión latinoamericana sobre el concilio; ida y vuelta." Marcha, September 17, 1965.

0042   BOZA MASVIDAL, EDUARDO. Revolución cristiana en Latinoamérica. Santiago, Chile: Editorial del Pacífico, 1963. 90 pp.

0043   BRUGAROLA, M. "Solemne ratificación de la 'Humanae Vitae.'" Roca Viva 8 (1975): 243-249.

0044   BURNS, E. B. Latin America: A Concise Interpretive History. Los Angeles: University of California, 1977. 307 pp.

0045   "By Bread as Well." Economist 221 (October 8, 1966): 144.

0046   CABRAL DUARTE, L. "CELAM's Social Action for Latin America." L'Osservatore Romano, March 9, 1972, pp. 6-7.

0047   CAMADER, RAUL ZAMBRANO. "The Latin American Church in the Decade of the Seventies." Worldmission 23 (Spring, 1972): 26-31.

0048   CÂMARA, HÉLDER. "Human Rights and the Liberation of Man in the Americas." In Human Rights and the Liberation of Man in the Americas, edited by Louis M. Cononnese, pp. 259-268. Notre Dame, Indiana: University of Notre Dame Press, 1970.

0049   _____. "Mensaje fraterno a los religiosos y a las religiosas de América Latina." Christus 41 (February, 1976): 58-60.

0050   _____. "The Bread of Life and World Hunger." Dimension 8 (Winter, 1976): 131-133.

0051   "Canada and Latin America." IDOC-International 13 (November 14, 1970): 74-95.

0052   CASTILLO, ALFONSO. "A propósito de los 15 años del CELAM." Christus 36 (March, 1971): 9-10.

0053 ____. "Después de su XV asamblea ordinaria realidad y futuro del CELAM." Christus 40 (January, 1975): 12-13.

0054 CASTRO, EMILIO. Hacia una pastoral latinoamericana. San José, Costa Rica: INDEF, 1974. 160 pp.

0055 ____. "Latin America's Revolutionary Churches." Christian Century 87 (September 16, 1970): 1081-1082.

0056 ____, comp. Pastores del pueblo de Dios en América Latina. Buenos Aires: La Aurora, 1974. 191 pp.

0057 "Catholics and Latin America." Commonweal 79 (February 21, 1964): 615-616.

0058 "El Catolicismo . . . comenta artículo sobre la Iglesia en América Latina." Noticias Aliadas 26 (April 2, 1966): 2.

0059 "El CELAM y el documento de trabajo." Revista Javeriana 346 (July, 1968): 5-74.

0060 Centro Intercultural de Documentación. "Desde hace seis años, para la América Latina quinientos misioneros de un tipo nuevo han pasado por Cuernavaca." Informaciones Católicas Internacionales 292 (July 22, 1967): 21-23.

0061 CEPEDA, ALFREDO. "La nueva Iglesia." El Día, April 20, 1966.

0062 CHAMBERLAIN, FRANCIS P. "Catholic Education in Latin America." America 116 (May 20, 1967): 750-753.

0063 CHAPELA, GONZALO. "El movimiento tradicionalist católica." Novedades, October 21-23, 1965.

0064 "The Church in Latin America." Magnificat 113 (May, 1964): 49-51.

0065 CLEARY, EDWARD L., ed. Shaping a New World, an Orientation to Latin America. Maryknoll, New York: Orbis Books, 1970. 319 pp.

0066 CLISSOLD, STEPHEN. The Saints of South America. London: C. Knight, 1972. 217 pp.

0067 "Colombian Cardinal Seeks to Stem Tide of Reform." Christian Century 83 (September 28, 1966): 1168.

General

0068   COLONNESE, LOUIS MICHAEL. "The Church in Latin America:
        Imperialism or Servanthoo ." American Ecclesiastical
        Review 161 (August, 1969): 100-113.

0069   COMBLIN, GIBELLINI JOSÉ. "Teología: queale servizio?" In
        La nuova fronteira della teologia in America Latina, edited
        by Rosino Gibellini, pp. 93-121. Brescia, Italy: Queri-
        niana, 1975.

0070   Comisión Episcopal de Acción Social. Signos de renovación
        recopilación de documentos post-conciliares de la Iglesia
        en América Latina. Lima: Editorial Universitaria, 1969.
        282 pp.

0071   Comisión Pontificia Justitia Et Pax. La Iglesia los derechos
        del hombre. Santiago, Chile: I.CH.E.H., 1976. 85 pp.

0072   "Conclusions of the Medellin Congress." Living Light 6 (Fall,
        1969): 127-133.

0073   CONDAL, ELÍAS. "El Vaticano y el tercer mundo." In La
        Iglesia, el subdesarrollo y la revolución, edited by
        Bernardo Castro Villagrana, pp. 170-179. México: Nuestro
        Tiempo, 1968.

0074   Conferencia General del Episcopado Latinoamericano, 2d. La
        Iglesia a la luz del concilio. Santiago, Chile: Paulinas,
        1969. 2 v.

0075   CONGAR, YVES. Christians Active in the World. New York:
        Herder and Herder, 1968. 227 pp.

0076   Congreso Católico Interamericano para el Desarrollo Integral
        del Hombre, 1st. Caracas: Unión de Hombres de Acción
        Catolica, 1971. 418 pp.

0077   Consejo Episcopal Latinoamericano. Antropología y evangeliza-
        ción: Un problema de Iglesia en América Latina. Bogotá:
        Indo-American Press Service, 1972. 142 pp.

0078   _____. Los católicos y la educación en América Latina.
        Bogotá: Consejo Episcopal Latinoamericano, 1967.

0079   _____. Iglesia y religiosidad popular en América Latina.
        Buenos Aires: Patria Grande, 1976.

0080   CONSIDINE, JOHN JOSEPH. New Horizons in Latin America. New
        York: Dodd, Mead, 1958. 379 pp., bibl.

0081   CRUZ, ORLANDO. "A América Latina, 1972." Brotéria 5 (May, 1972): 606-615.

0082   CUAS, JORGE, and OSSA, S. J. MANUEL. "Inserción de la Iglesia en el mundo." Mensaje 16 (November, 1967): 542-546.

0083   CULHANE, EUGENE K. "The Caldron to the South." U.S. Catholic 29 (September, 1963): 43-47.

0084   _____. "The FERES Study of Latin America." America 111 (September 26, 1964): 345-347.

0085   CUSHING, R. "The Church in Latin America." Extension 58 (March, 1964): 10.

0086   CUSSIANOVICH, ALEJANDRO. "Evangelización concientizadora: tensión entre evangelización y concientización." Documentación, Secretariado Nacional de Pastoral Social 6 (April, 1971): 7-17.

0087   DAVIS, A. "The Church Grows Up in Latin America." Our Sunday Visitor 61 (November 26, 1972): 1+.

0088   DEEDY, JOHN G. "Games CELAM Plays: Latin American Bishops Conference." Commonweal 98 (April 13, 1973): 122.

0089   DEELEN, GODOFREDO J. A sociología a serviço da pastoral. Petrópolis, Brazil: Centro de Estadistica Religiosa e Investigações, 1966. 117 pp.

0090   _____. A sociología a serviço da pastoral; a prática dominical. Petrópolis, Brazil: Editora Vozes, 1967. 140 pp.

0091   DE KADT, EMANUEL. "Paternalism and Populism: Catholicism in Latin America." Journal of Contemporary History 2 (October, 1967): 89-106.

0092   _____. "The Latin American Church and Pope Paul's Visit." World Today 24 (September, 1968): 387-392.

0093   DÍAZ ALVAREZ, MANUEL. "Análisis del proceso de secularización en América Latina." Nuevo Mundo 62 (1975): 83-89.

0094   _____. "La Iglesia latinoamericana retrocede?" Nuevo Mundo 69 (May/June, 1976): 132-137.

General

0095 "Diez años por nuevos caminos: mensaje pastoral en ocasión
del décimo aniversario de la Palabra de Dios." Catequesis
Latinoamericana 8 (1976): 81-94.

0096 DOMBROWSKY, J. "A Catholic Continent Awakening." Triumph 4
(August, 1969): 11-14.

0097 DREKONJA, GERHARD. "Subversive Christians: The Transformation
of the Church in Latin America." Worship 44 (April, 1970):
226-237.

0098 DU PLESSI GRAY, FRANCINE. Divine Disobedience: Profiles in
Catholic Radicalism. New York: Knopf, 1970. 322 pp.

0099 DUSSEL, ENRIQUE D. "América Latina: un continente en busca
de su alma." Informaciones Católicas Internacionales 235
(March 7, 1963): 31-32.

0100 _____. Hipótesis para una historia de la Iglesia en América
Latina. Barcelona: Editora Estela, 1967. 219 pp.

0101 _____. Historia de la Iglesia en América Latina: coloniaje
y liberación, 1492-1973. Barcelona: Editorial Nova Terra,
1974. 466 pp.

0102 _____. "La teología dall'America Latina." In La nuova fronteira della teología in America Latina, edited by Rosino
Gibellini, pp. 273-312. Brescia, Italy: Queriniana,
1975.

0103 EGUREN, JUAN A. El concilio a tu alcance: cuestiones con-
ciliares. Bogotá: Ediciones Paulinas, 1962. 98 pp.

0104 EINAUDI, LUIGI; MAULLIN, R.; SEPAN, A.; and FLEET, A. Latin
American Institutional Development: The Changing Catholic
Church. Santa Monica, California: Rand Corporation, 1969.

0105 EPPS, DWAIN C. "Latin America: Present Situation and Pro-
jected Priorities." IDOC-International 32 (September 25,
1971): 2-20.

0106 "Estudios; celebrando los 20 años del CELAM: symposium."
Catequesis Latinoamericano 8 (1976): 59-81.

0107 FALS BORDA, ORLANDO. "Una estrategía para la Iglesia, en la
transformación de América Latina." Cristianismo y Sociedad
6 (October, 1964): 31-39.

0108   FONSECA, JAIME. Latin America: A Challenge to Catholics.
        Washington, D.C.: National Catholic Welfare Conference,
        1960. 37 pp.

0109   FOYACA DE LA CONCHA, MANUEL. "Crise em nossa America."
        Estudos 1 (January/March, 1964): 20-39.

0110   FRAILE DELGADO, LUIS. Cristo y Latino América, 1966.
        Salamanca: Ediciones Sígueme, 1966. 243 pp.

0111   FREIRE, PAULO. "Cultural Freedom in Latin America." In Human
        Rights and the Liberation of Man in the Americas, edited by
        Louis M. Colonnese, pp. 162-179. Notre Dame, Indiana:
        University of Notre Dame Press, 1970.

0112   FURTER, PIERRE. "Qual será o futuro do cristianismo na
        América Latina?" Paz e Terra 2 (April, 1968): 21-33.

0113   GALILEA, SEGUNDO. Hacia una pastoral vernácula: artículos de
        pastoral latinoamericano. Santiago, Chile: Dilapsa, 1966.
        124 pp.

0114   _____. Introducción a la religiosidad latinoamericana.
        Jalapa, México: Editora de Servir, 1967. 39 pp.

0115   _____. "La urbanización y la Iglesia." Christus 30 (April,
        1965): 315-325.

0116   GALL, NORMAN. "Latin America: The Church Militant."
        Commentary 49 (April, 1970): 25-37.

0117   GANNON, THOMAS M. "CICIP 1970: Prelude to Conscientization."
        America 122 (February 28, 1970): 214-218.

0118   GARCÍA ELORRIO, JUAN. "La limosna del Papa." Cristianismo y
        Revolución 13 (April, 1969): 2.

0119   GEYER, GEORGIE ANNE. "Catholic Church in Latin America in New
        Role: The Revolutionary." New York Post, April 24, 1968.

0120   _____. "The Church in Latin America." Critic 31 (March/April,
        1973): 50-57.

0121   GHEERBRANT, ALAIN. La Iglesia rebelde de América Latina.
        México: Siglo Veintiuno, 1970. 319 pp.

0122   GIBELLINI, ROSINO. La nuova fronteira della teologia in
        America Latina. Brescia, Italy: Queriniana, 1975.

General

0122A GIBSON, CHARLES. "Colonial Institutions and Contemporary
       Latin America: Social and Cultural Life." Hispanic
       American Historical Review 43 (August, 1963): 380-389.

0123   GÓMEZ PÉREZ, RAFAEL. "La Iglesia en América Latina: de
       Medellín a hoy." Nuestro Tiempo 21/22 (1974): 55-63.

0124   GONZÁLEZ-RUIZ, JOSÉ MARÍA. Marxismo y cristianismo frente al
       hombre nuevo. Madrid: Ediciones Marova, 1971. 232 pp.

0125   GORDON, PAULUS. "Die religiöse Lage Lateinamerikas in
       katholischer Sicht." Lutherische Rundschau 11 (November,
       1961): 278-291.

0126   _____. "Katholisches Brasilien? Die Kirche in Lateinamerika:
       Klischee und Wirklichkeit I." Wort und Wahreit 12 (July,
       1957): 405-420.

0127   GOROSITO, J. C., and DE ZAN, T. Tercer Mundo, compromiso
       cristiano. Paraná, Argentina: Librería Selecta, 1970.

0128   "Gott oder Mammon: Julio de Santa Ana, Genf, zur Situation der
       Kirche in Lateinamerika." Standpunkt 4 (April, 1977): 101.

0129   GRABENDORFF, WOLF. Lateinamerika--Wohin? Informationen und
       Analysen. München, Germany: Deutschen Taschenbuch Verlag,
       1970. 189 pp.

0130   GREMILLION, JOSEPH B. "The Church in Latin America."
       Commonweal 68 (May 23, 1958): 202-205.

0131   _____. "Renewal in Latin America: Porto Alegre, Brazil
       Conference Sponsored by CELAM." Perspectives 9 (September/
       October, 1964): 151-154.

0132   _____. "The Task of the Church in Inter-American Relationships."
       In Cultural Factors in Inter-American Relations, edited by
       Samuel Shapiro, pp. 200-201. Notre Dame, Indiana:
       University of Notre Dame, 1968.

0133   GROSS, LEONARD. "Catholic Church in Latin America." Look 26
       (October,9, 1962): 27-35.

0134   GUERRA, ALOÍSIO. O catolicismo ainda é Cristão? São Paulo:
       Editora Fulgor, 1963. 103 pp.

0135   GUTIÉRREZ, GUSTAVO MERINO. "Das Kontestationsphänomen in
       Lateinamerika." Concilium. Internationale Zeitschrift für
       Theologie 7 (1971): 550-555.

0136   _____. Líneas pastorales de la Iglesia en América Latina: análisis teológico. Lima: Editora Universitaria, 1970. 88 pp.

0137   GUTIÉRREZ-GIRARDOT, RAFAEL. "Katholizimus in Lateinamerika." Liberal. Beiträge zur Entwicklung einer Freiheitlichen Ordnung 14 (1972): 365-379.

0138   HALPERÍN DONGHI, TULIO. The Aftermath of Revolution in Latin America. New York: Harper and Row, 1973. 149 pp., bibl.

0139   HARPER, CHARLES. "Los derechos humanos y la respuesta cristiana en América Latina." Educación Boletín 2 (1975): 37-42.

0140   HARRIOT, JOHN. "Latin America: The Seed of the Church." Tablet 230 (November 6, 1976): 1066.

0141   HASCHE, RENATO. "'Gaudium et spes' y la cultura en América Latina." Mensaje 15 (October, 1966): 569-578.

0142   HERBERT, KART. "Wandlungen der Kirchen in Südamerika." Die Evangelische Diaspora 36 (1965): 1-9.

0143   HEVIA, PATRICIO, comp. América Latina: crisis de la Iglesia Católico, junio-septiembre de 1968: reacciones de prensa. México: Centro Intercultural de Documentación, 1969. 423 pp.

0144   HILLEKAMPS, KARL HEINZ. "Ist Lateinamerika noch der Katholische Kontinent?" Aussenpolitik. Zeitschrift für Internationale Wirtschaftsbeziehungen 17 (1966): 695-699.

0145   NO ENTRY

0146   HITZ, P. "Pastoral Reflections and Impressions." Lumen Vitae 20 (June, 1965): 340-362.

0147   HOEFFNER, JOSEF CARD. "La Iglesia en la sociedad moderna." El Catolicismo, no. 2,130 (April 30, 1972), pp. 8-9.

0148   HOFFACKER, PAUL. "Die Aktion Adveniat." Stimmen der Zeit 182 (December, 1968): 361-370.

0149   HOFFMAN, RONAN. "Latin America in the Church's Global Mission: What Priority?" America 114 (January 15, 1966): 68-70.

General

0150 _____, and MAGNER, JAMES A. Latin America: Pattern for the Sixties. Cincinnati, Ohio: Catholic Students' Mission Crusade, 1961. 75 pp., bibl.

0151 HOINACKI, CESLAUS. "The Latin America Church and Renewal." Catholic World 206 (October, 1967): 27-31.

0152 HOURTON, JORGE. Iglesia y democracia: la enseñanza de Pio XII. Santiago, Chile: Ediciones Aconcagua, 1976. 115 pp.

0153 HOUTART, FRANÇOIS. La Iglesia latinoamericana en la hora del concilio. Friburg, Switzerland: Oficina Internacional de Investigaciones Sociales de FERES, 1963. 62 pp.

0154 _____. "Present-day Trends in the Roman Catholic Church of Latin America." Student World 1 (1964): 67-76.

0155 _____. "Problemes posés à l'Eglise par L'Amérique Latine." Choisir 73 (1965): 11.

0156 HUBNER GALLO, JORGE IVAN. "Catholic Social Justice, Authoritarianism, and Class Stratification." In The Conflict Between Church and State in Latin America, edited by Frederick B. Pike, pp. 197-207. Notre Dame, Indiana: University of Notre Dame, 1964.

0157 HUFF, RUSSELL. On Wings of Adventure: Some Personal Experiences with the Catholic Church in Latin America. Notre Dame, Indiana: Dujarie Press, 1967. 86 pp.

0158 ILLICH, IVAN. "The Seamy Side of Charity." America 116 (January 21, 1967): 88-91.

0159 _____, and CUSHING, RICHARD J. "Se reinicia controversia entre Monseñor Illich y el Cardenal Cushing." Noticias Aliadas 18 (March 4, 1967): 1.

0160 El imperio y las iglesias. Buenos Aires: Editora Guadelupe, 1974. 155 pp.

0161 INTERDONATO, FRANCISCO. "Desacralizar la lucha de clases en la teología latinoamericana." Revista Teológica Limense 1 (January/April, 1976): 3-29.

0162 "Isms and the Vacuum." Christian Century 77 (February 3, 1960): 124-125.

0163   JOHANSSON, KJELL A. Kyrkan i Latinamerika. Stockholm:
       Utrikespolitiska Institutet, 1969. 32 pp.

0164   NO ENTRY

0165   JOHNSON, JOHN J., ed. Continuity and Change in Latin America.
       Stanford, California: Stanford University Press, 1964.
       282 pp.

0166   KAUFMANN, LUDWIG. "L'Eglise en Amérique Latine." Choisir
       124 (1970): 25.

0167   KENNEDY, JOHN J. "The Force of the Church." In Explosive
       Forces in Latin America, edited by John J. TePaske,
       pp. 43-57. Columbus: Ohio State University Press, 1964.

0168   KIRCHGASSNER, ALFONS. Im Katholischen Kontinent. Frankfurt
       am Main: Knecht, 1963. 129 pp.

0169   KLOPPENBURG, BOAVENTURA. A eclesiologia do Vaticano II.
       Petrópolis, Brazil: Editora Vozes, 1971. 291 pp.

0170   KOSSOK, MANFRED. Revolution in Freiheit: Bürgerlicher
       Reformismus und Christlich-Demokratische Parteien in
       Lateinamerika. Leipzig: Die nationale Befreiungsbewegung,
       Karl-Marx Universität, 1965.

0171   KRUMWIEDE, HEINRICH W. "Katholische Kirche und Soziopoliti-
       scher Wandel in Lateinamerika." In Lateinamerika: Kon-
       tinent in der Krise, edited by Wolf Grabendorff. Hamburg:
       Hoffman and Capte Verlag, 1973.

0172   KUEHNELT-LEDDIHN, ERIK MARIA RITTER VON. Lateinamerika:
       Geschichte eines Scheiterns? Osnabrück, Germany: A. Fromm,
       1967. 194 pp.

0173   LAJE, ENRIQUE J. La autoridad de la Iglesia. Buenos Aires:
       Asociación de los Profesionales de la Acción Católica,
       1977.

0174   LALIVE D'EPINAY, CHRISTIAN. "La nuit de l'Amérique Latine."
       Choisir 99 (1968): 4.

0175   LATAPI, PABLO. "Private and Public Schools." In Integration
       of Man and Society in Latin America, edited by Samuel
       Shapiro, pp. 61-67. Notre Dame, Indiana: University of
       Notre Dame, 1967.

General

0176   "Latin America: New Spirit in the Church." Time 82 (August
        23, 1963): 20.

0177   "Latin American Church Must Be in Vanguard, Bishops Say."
        Our Sunday Visitor 63 (March 23, 1975): 1.

0178   LATORRE CABAL, HUGO. La revolución de la Iglesia latino-
        americana. México: Editorial Joaquín Mortíz, 1969.
        158 pp.

0179   LATOURETTE, KENNETH SCOTT. Christianity in a Revolutionary
        Age: The Twentieth Century Outside Europe: the Americas,
        the Pacific, Asia, and Africa. New York: Harper and Row,
        1962. 568 pp., bibl.

0180   LAURENTIN, RENÉ. Flashes sur l'Amérique Latine: suivis de
        documents rassemblés et présentés par José de Broucker.
        Paris: Editions du Seuil, 1968. 141 pp.

0181   LAVRETSKII, IOSIF RAMUAL'DOVICH. Ten'Vatikana nad Latinskoi
        Amerikoi. Moscow: Izdatel'stvo Akademii Nauk SSSR, 1961.

0182   LEHNER, GUNTHAR, ed. Lateinamerika Heute: Ein Subkontinent
        im Umbruch. München: Kosel, 1972. 167 pp.

0183   LENS, SIDNEY. "Latin Left, Rise of the Social Christians."
        Commonweal 85 (October 14, 1966): 52-55.

0184   LINNENBRINK, GÜNTHER. "Die Kirchen im Umbruch Lateinamerikas."
        Junge Kirche 27 (1966): 144-151.

0185   LITTWIN, LAWRENCE. Latin America: Catholicism and Class
        Conflict. Encino, California: Dickenson Publishing Co.,
        1974. 127 pp.

0186   LLERAS, ALBERTO. "La Iglesia combiante en Latinoamérica."
        Visión 28 (December, 1964): 20-26.

0187   LOMBARDI, RICARDO. "El problema social no es solamente
        económico." Revista Javeriana 288 (September, 1962):
        286-290.

0188   LÓPEZ, SALVADOR. ¿La Iglesia es aliada del capitalismo como
        afirman los comunistas? Bogotá: Ediciones Paulinas, 1962.
        72 pp.

0189   LÓPEZ TRUJILLO, A. "CELAM--Five Years Later; Medellín and the
        Assembly of CELAM in Sucre." L'Osservatore Romano,
        February 28, 1974, pp. 9-10.

0190 MC CARRICK, THEODORE E. "Top Priority: A Reply." America
114 (January 15, 1966): 70-71.

0191 MC CORMACK, ARTHUR. "The Catholic Church in South America."
Wiseman 238 (Fall, 1964): 226-260.

0192 MAC EOIN, G. "Post Conciliar Church: Varieties of Catholicism."
Commonweal 98 (June 15, 1973): 332-336.

0193 MC GRATH, MARK G. "Algunas preguntas sobre el CELAM."
Criterio 41 (February 15, 1968): 70-72.

0194 _____. "Development for Peace." America 118 (April 27, 1968):
562-567.

0195 _____. "Obispos en América Latina: un hombre para el porvenir, Mons. . . ." Informaciones Católicas Internationales
288 (May 22, 1967): 8-9.

0196 _____. "The Latin American Crisis." Jubilee 11 (June, 1963):
9-12.

0197 _____. "The Teaching Authority of the Church: The Situation
in Latin America." In Religion, Revolution and Reform:
New Forces for Change in Latin America, edited by William V.
D'Antonio, pp. 41-47. New York: Praeger, 1964.

0198 _____. "Theological Reflections on Inter-American Relations."
In Cultural Factors in Inter-American Relations, edited by
Samuel Shapiro, pp. 183-199. Notre Dame, Indiana:
University of Notre Dame, 1968.

0199 MAGNI, ROBERTO, and ZANOTTI, LUCIO. América Latina: la
chiesa si contesta. Roma: Editori Riuniti, 1969. 272 pp.

0200 MALLEY, FRANÇOIS. Inquiétante Amérique Latine. Paris: Les
Editions du Cerf, 1963. 175 pp.

0201 MALLON, P. "The Church in Latin America." Furrow 15 (April,
1964): 254-256.

0202 MARISCAL, NICOLÁS. "La renovación de la Iglesia latinoamericana." Razón y Fé 886 (November, 1971): 351-362.

0203 MARKIEWICZ, STANISLAW. Katolicysm w Ameryce Lacinskiej. Wyd
1. Warsaw: Ludowa Poldzielnia Wydawnicza, 1969. 396 pp.

General

0204   MARTÍNEZ, DIEGO. "¿Qué significa 'orientación cristiana' en
        los movimientos de orientación cristiana?" Documentación,
        Secretariado Nacional de Pastoral Social 10 (August, 1971):
        1-6.

0205   MARTÍNEZ ARONA, GALO. "Die Umast in der Kirche Lateinamerikas."
        Orientierung. Katholische Blätter für Weltanschauliche
        Information 34 (1970): 10-11.

0206   MARTZ, JOHN D. "Doctrine and Dilemnas of the Latin American
        New Left." World Politics 22 (January, 1970): 171-196.

0207   "Medellín: la Iglesia nueva." Cuadernos de Marcha, no. 17,
        September, 1968.

0208   MEJÍA, JORGE. "Intercambio entre la Iglesia y el mundo."
        Mensaje 15 (October, 1966): 503-508.

0209   _____. "La reunión interamericana de Mar del Plata."
        Criterio 48 (1975): 270-272.

0210   _____. "Religious Freedom in Latin America." In Human Rights
        and the Liberation of Man in the Americas, edited by Louis M.
        Colonnese, pp. 206-212. Notre Dame, Indiana: University
        of Notre Dame Press, 1970.

0211   MEJIDO, MANUEL, and FERREIRA, ANGEL T. Paulo VI en Latino-
        américa. México: Francisco Casas Perís, 1969. 170 pp.

0212   "El mensaje esencial de Medellín." Pasos 62 (August 6, 1973):
        1-9.

0213   MERCIER, LOUIS. "Les eglises latino-américaines et le siécle."
        Interrogations 8 (September, 1976): 31-44.

0214   MÍGUEZ-BONINO, JOSÉ. "Vatican II and Latin America."
        Christian Century 30 (December, 1964): 1616-1617.

0215   "Les militants d'origine chrétienne." Esprit 1 (April/May,
        1977): 3-231.

0216   MIRO, LORENZO. Coexistenicia pacífica y división de la
        Iglesia. Buenos Aires: Huemul, 1965. 41 pp.

0217   MISCHE, G. F. "Christianity in Latin America; Left or Right?"
        Direction 8 (May, 1962): 28-32.

0218   "Misión urbana y rural de la Iglesia." Respuesta 20 (1975):
        5-44.

0219   MUCKERMAN, N. "CICOP: Christian Concern for Latin America."
       Liguorian 4 (May, 1966): 28-32.

0220   MUTCHLER, DAVID E. "Adaptations of the Roman Catholic Church
       to Latin American Development: The Meaning of Internal
       Church Conflict." Social Research 36 (Summer, 1969):
       231-252.

0221   NEVINS, A. "Latin America's Rising Third Force." Sign 46
       (August, 1966): 7-10.

0222   "No hay crisis dentro de la Iglesia." El Tiempo (May 21, 1967):
       17-21.

0223   NOBMAC'H, ALBERT. Du Mexique a la terre de feu, une Eglise en
       colére. Paris: Bordas, 1973. 127 pp.

0224   NOONAN, DANIEL D. "Latin America, Awakening Giant." World-
       mission 14 (Fall, 1963): 13-16.

0225   "Los obispos y su siesta." Cristianismo y Revoluvión 15
       (May, 1969): 10.

0226   ODELL, LUIS E. "Iglesia y sociedad en América Latina."
       Cristianismo y Sociedad 1: 61-68.

0227   OLIVA, FRANCISCO DE P. "Movimiento de sacerdotes para el
       tercer mundo." Ceniap, November 15, 1971, 8.

0228   OSSA, MANUEL. "Cristianismo y sentido de la historia."
       Mensaje 153 (October, 1966): 539-551.

0229   OVIEDO, VÍCTOR. La revolución en la Iglesia: en busca del
       mensaje. Buenos Aires: Punto Crítico, 1971. 117 pp.

0230   OVIEDO CAVADA, CARLOS. "Un año después del Concilio."
       Mensaje 16 (January, 1967): 47-49.

0231   PADILLA, C. R. "Rome and the Bible: CELAM Conference."
       Christianity Today 19 (October 25, 1974): 53-54.

0232   PAOLI, ARTURO. "La pasión de América Latina." Nuevo Mundo
       61 (1975): 31-37.

0233   PAPE, CARLOS. Katholizismus in Lateinamerika. Siegburg:
       Steyler, 1963. 262 pp.

General

0234   Pasión de Cristo en Cuba. Santiago, Chile: Departmento de
       Publicaciones del Secretariado de Difusión, 1962.   76 pp.

0235   PATTEE, RICHARD. Catholicism in Latin America. Washington:
       National Catholic Welfare Conference, 1945.

0236   PAVLO TENORIO, JESÚS. "Contemplan a Dios en la imagen suya
       que son todos los pobres." Christus 36 (September, 1971):
       33-35.

0237   PETRAS, JAMES, and ZEITLIN, MAURICE. Latin America: Reform
       or Revolution? Greenwich, Connecticut: Fawcett Publishers,
       1968.   511 pp., bibl.

0238   PIKE, FREDERICK B., ed. Freedom and Reform in Latin America.
       Notre Dame, Indiana: University of Notre Dame Press, 1959.
       308 pp.

0239   PIRONIO, EDUARDO F. "Al sínodo." Víspera 3 (September, 1969):
       32-34.

0240   _____. Compromisos y esperanzas de nuestra Iglesia. Bogotá:
       Indo-American Press Service, 1970.   47 pp.

0241   _____. "El verdadero sentido de la conferencia de Medellín."
       Criterio 39 (December, 1973/January, 1974): 44-45.

0242   _____. "En el Cristo vivo." Víspera 3 (February, 1969):
       29-31.

0243   _____. "En el espíritu de Medellín: años después de Medellin."
       Christus 39 (December, 1973/January, 1974): 44-45.

0244   _____. "La Iglesia ante el cambio." In Compromisos y esper-
       anzas de nuestra Iglesia, edited by Eduardo F. Pironio,
       pp. 29-40. Bogotá: Indo-American Press Service, 1970.

0245   _____. La Iglesia que nace entre nosotros. Bogotá: Indo-
       American Press Service, 1970.   75 pp.

0246   _____. "Líneas teológico-pastorales del CELAM." Criterio 48
       (1975):   30-35.

0247   _____. "Naturaleza, misión y espiritualidad del CELAM."
       Christus 38 (March, 1973):   41-45.

0248 _____. "Reflexión teológica sobre la Iglesia: su presencia en el mundo latinoamericano." In Compromisos y esperanzas de nuestra Iglesia, edited by Eduardo F. Pironio, pp. 13-28. Bogotá: Indo-American Press Service, 1970.

0249 PIXLEY, JORGE V. "La sistematización en la teología latino-americana." Pasos 3 (May 29, 1972): 1-8.

0250 POBLETE, RENATO. "Conferencia del CELAM en Medellín." Mensaje 17 (October, 1968): 495-500.

0251 _____. "Pastoral Work Among the Masses and the Religious Elite." In Cultural Factors in Inter-American Relations, edited by Samuel Shapiro, pp. 235-249. Notre Dame, Indiana: University of Notre Dame, 1968.

0251A POPE JOHN XXIII. "To the Spanish Hierarchy on Apostolic Assistance to Latin America." Nouvelle Revue Theologique 85 (February, 1963): 192-193.

0251B POTASH, ROBERT A. "Colonial Institutions and Contemporary Latin America: A Commentary on Two Papers." Hispanic American Historical Review 43 (August, 1963): 390-394.

0252 PROAÑO, LEONIDAS. "Hacia una Iglesia pobre." NADOC 76 (July 30, 1969): 43-60.

0253 _____. "Visión global de América Latina." Búsqueda 3 (1975): 43-60.

0254 PROTOPAPAS CHOUINARD, J. Los cristianos y los cambios sociales en Latinoamérica. Santiago, Chile: Editorial del Pacífico, 1974. 124 pp.

0255 "Punto de partida para un estudio equipo de reflección teológico pastoral del CELAM." Christus 36 (July, 1971): 36-38.

0256 RAMA, CARLOS M. La religión en América Latina. Havana: Casa de las Américas, 1966.

0257 _____. "Pasado y presente de la religión en América Latina: primera parte." Cuadernos Americanos 153 (July/August, 1967): 25-43.

0258 _____. "Pasado y presente de la religión en América Latina: segunda parte." Cuadernos Americanos 154 (September/ October, 1967): 28-36.

General

0259   RAMONDETTI, MIGUEL N. "Sacerdotes para el III mundo."
        Cristianismo y Revolución 18 (July, 1969): 1-2.

0260   RASHKE, R. "Maverick Jesuit Aims at Latin Left." National
        Catholic Reporter 13 (October 17, 1977): 1+.

0261   "Reflecciones sobre los documentos justicia y paz de Medellín."
        Documentación CELAM 5 (September/October, 1976): 283-309.

0262   REPGES, WALTER. "Hacia una pastoral del compromiso temporal:
        la Iglesia latinoamericana entre Rio de Janeiro (1955) y
        Medellín (1968)." Anales de la Facultad de Teología 1
        (1972): 1-55.

0263   As responsabilidades da Igreja na America Latina. Petrópolis,
        Brazil: Vozes, 1966. 166 pp.

0264   "Respuesta del Movimiento para el Tercer Mundo a la Comisión
        Permanente." In Polémica en la Iglesia, edited by Obispos
        Argentinos, pp. 44-123. Avellaneda: Ediciones Búsqueda,
        1970.

0265   "Revista católica criticada: de un memorándum de la
        Nunciatura Apostólica del Perú, Lima, Julio 26, 1964."
        CIDOC Informa 1 (September 16, 1964): 13-14.

0266   RIBEIRO DE OLIVEIRA, PEDRO A. "Le catholicisme populaire en
        Amérique Latine." Social Compass 19 (1972): 567-584.

0267   RIGO, PIERRE. "Los derechos humanos en América Latina."
        Medellín 1 (1975): 207-215.

0268   ROSSI, JUAN JOSÉ, ed. Iglesia latinoamericana: ¿protesta o
        profecía? Avellaneda: Búsqueda, 1969. 462 pp.

0269   RUBIO ANGULO, JAIME. "Filosofía latinoamericana." Revista
        Javeriana 482 (September, 1976): 75-79.

0270   RUÍZ GARCÍA, ENRIQUE. El tercer mundo. Madrid: Alianza,
        1969. 284 pp.

0271   RYCROFT, W. STANLEY. "Latin America: The Church's Task."
        Christian Century 79 (May 2, 1962): 563-565.

0272   Los Sacerdotes para el Tercer Mundo y la actualidad nacional.
        Buenos Aires: Mundo Nuevo, 1973. 136 pp.

0273   SALVATIERRA, ANGEL MARÍA. "Religiosidad popular y ateísmo
        en América Latina." Ateísmo e Diálogo 4 (March, 1976):
        25-33.

0274   SANDERS, THOMAS GRIFFIN. Catholic Innovation in a Changing
        Latin America. Cuernavaca, México: Centro Internacional
        de Documentación, 1969.

0275   _____. "Church in Latin America." Foreign Affairs 48
        (January, 1970): 285-299.

0276   SCHETTE, HEINZ ROBERT. "The Problem of Ideology and Christian
        Belief." Concilium 6 (May, 1965): 107-132.

0277   SCHMITT, KARL MICHAEL, ed. The Roman Catholic Church in Modern
        Latin America. New York: Alfred A. Knopf, 1972. 225 pp.

0278   SEGUNDO, JUAN LUIS. De la sociedad a la teología. Buenos
        Aires: Ediciones C. Lohlé, 1970. 180 pp.

0279   _____. Evolution and Guilt. Maryknoll, New York: Orbis
        Books, 1974. 148 pp.

0280   _____. Grace and the Human Condition. Maryknoll, New York:
        Orbis Books, 1973. 213 pp.

0281   _____. Our Idea of God. Maryknoll, New York: Orbis Books,
        1974. 206 pp., bibl.

0282   _____. "Pastoral latinoamericana: hora de la decisión."
        Mensaje 127 (March/April, 1964): 74-82.

0283   _____. Teología abierta para el laico adulto. Buenos Aires:
        Ediciones C. Lohlé, 1968. 1,038 pp., bibl.

0284   _____. "The Church: A New Direction in Latin America."
        Catholic Mind 65 (March, 1967): 43-47.

0285   _____. The Community Called Church. Maryknoll, New York:
        Orbis Boosk, 1973. 172 pp.

0286   _____. The Sacraments Today. Maryknoll, New York: Orbis
        Books, 1974. 154 pp., bibl.

0287   _____. "Wealth and Poverty as Obstacles to Development." In
        Human Rights and the Liberation of Man in the Americas,
        edited by Louis M. Colonnese, pp. 23-31. Notre Dame,
        Indiana: University of Notre Dame Press, 1970.

The Catholic Left in Latin America

General

0288   SERGEEV, K. "Vatikan i Latinskaia America." Moskovskii
        Propagandist 16 (August, 1959): 60-65.

0289   SHAULL, RICHARD. "Nicolau Berdiaev: perspectiva cristã da
        revolucão social." Paz e Terra 1 (1966): 180-194.

0290   SIGMUND, PAUL E. "Latin American Catholicism's Opening to the
        Left." Review of Politics 35 (January, 1973): 61-76.

0291   SILVERT, KALMAN H. The Conflict Society: Reaction and
        Revolution in Latin America. New Orleans: The Hauser
        Press, 1966. 289 pp., bibl.

0292   "A situação economica, social cultural e religiosa na América
        Latina." Revista Eclesiástica Brasileira 28 (1968):
        432-442.

0293   "La situación de la Iglesia en América Latina." CIDOC Informa
        1 (May, 1964): 9-15.

0294   SMITH, T. LYNN. "Changing Image of Latin America." Catholic
        World 192 (February, 1961): 272-277.

0295   SOBRINO, J. "Cuaderno: los cristianos y el conflicto
        symposium: la conflictividad dentro de la Iglesia."
        Christus 41 (December, 1976): 18-41.

0296   SOUZA, HERBERT JOSÉ. "Capitalismo y miseria." Informaciones
        Católicas Internacionales 215 (May 7, 1964): 26-27.

0297   _____, ed. Cristianismo hoje. Rio de Janeiro: Editorial
        Universitário, 1962. 108 pp.

0298   STORRS, PETER. "The Church in South America." Bank of London
        and South America Review 4 (September, 1970): 478-486.

0299   STROGNOWSKI, J. "The Catholic Church in the 'Third World.'"
        Novoe Vremia 23 (August, 1965): 10-14.

0300   SWEEZY, PAUL M., and HUBERMAN, LEO, eds. Whither Latin
        America? New York: Monthly Review Press, 1963. 144 pp.

0301   SYWULKA, S. R. "Latin Ferment: Catholic Churchmen Expelled
        by Government." Christianity Today 20 (September 10, 1976):
        68.

0302   Les taches de l'église en Amérique Latine: aspects théologi-
        ques et sociologiques. Bogotá: FERES, 1963. 117 pp.

0303 TE PASKE, JOHN J.; FISHER, SYDNEY; and NETTLETON, FISHER, eds. Explosive Forces in Latin America. Columbus: Ohio State University Press, 1964. 196 pp.

0304 "Theology's Visionary Role." America 118 (June 8, 1968): 746-747.

0305 TOMIC, RADOMIRO. "Issues of Justice in Latin America." IDOC-International 53 (May, 1973): 7-24.

0306 TOMIC ROMERO, DRAGOMIR. Sobre el sistema interamericano. Santiago, Chile: Editorial del Pacífico, 1963. 59 pp.

0307 TOTH, CSANAD. "Obstacles to the Realization of Human Rights in the Americas." In Human Rights and the Liberation of Man in the Americas, edited by Louis M. Colonnese, pp. 15-22. Notre Dame, Indiana: University of Notre Dame Press, 1970.

0308 "Toward a Third World Theology: Reaction to Humanae Vitae." America 122 (January 31, 1970): 90.

0309 TRABER, M. "The Third World and Church Renewal." St. Anthony Messenger 77 (October, 1969): 20-30.

0310 "La última esperanza para América Latina." Mensaje 10 (July, 1961): 301-302.

0311 VALERI, GIANCARLO ELÍA. Fuerzas armadas e Iglesia en la transformación de América Latina. Madrid: Nacional, 1971.

0312 VALLIER, IVÁN. "Las élites religiosas in América Latina: catolicismo, dirección y transformación social." Espejo 5 (April/September, 1968): 185-200.

0313 VEKEMANS, ROGER. "La paz, obra de justicia." Mensaje 15 (October, 1966): 601-605.

0314 _____. "Solidaridad internacional." Mensaje 10 (September, 1961): 414-418.

0315 _____, and HUFF, R. "Is the Church Losing Latin America?" Ave Maria 91 (January 9, 1960): 5-10.

0316 VELÁZQUEZ, H. "Cinco años después de la populorum progressio." Christus 37 (April, 1972): 13-18.

General

0317   VELEZ CORREA, JAIME. "Un apóstol social en América Latina."
        Revista Javeriana 353 (April, 1969): 292-301.

0318   VERGARA T., IGNACIO. "Desarrollar un evangelismo de conquista
        humana." Mensaje (July, 1966): 314-316.

0319   VETRANO, VICENTE O. "Crónica de la X Asamblea del CELAM en
        Mar del Plata." Criterio 40 (June 22, 1967): 423-437.

0320   WEIGEL, GUSTAVE. "A Theologian Looks at Latin America."
        Review of Politics 20 (October, 1958): 419-430.

0321   WELTE, BERNARD. "El amor cristiano al próximo en la era
        tecnológica." Acta Científica 6 (1975): 115-131.

0322   WILLIAMS, RAYMOND. "New Left Catholics." New Blackfriars 48
        (November, 1966): 74-77.

0323   WYSE, A. "Dissidents in Latin America." Worldmission 8
        (Winter, 1957): 42-49.

AGRARIAN REFORM

0324   ALEMÁN, JOSÉ LUIS. "La reforma agraria y la doctrina social
        de la Iglesia." Estudios Sociales 30 (July/September):
        121-130.

0325   BERTON, NORBERTO. "La tarea inconclusa en la obra rural en la
        América Latina." Cristianismo y Sociedad 1 (January 4,
        1963): 28-35.

0326   BOCKLET, RICHARD J. "Land Reform in Latin America." America
        115 (October 15, 1966): 458-460.

0327   BRANDO, AVELAR. "Justicia y paz en favor de la reforma agraria
        en América Latina." Informaciones Católicas Internacionales
        293-294 (August, 1967): 12.

0328   CÂMARA, HÉLDER. "Presença da igreja no desenvolvimento da
        América Latina: sugestões fraternas." Vozes 1 (January,
        1967): 5-24.

0329   CARROLL, THOMAS F. "Land Reform as an Explosive Force in
        Latin America." In Explosive Forces in Latin America,
        edited by J. J. TePaske and S. N. Fisher, [n.p.]: Ohio
        University Press, 1964.

Agrarian Reform

0330 _____. Land Tenure and Land Reform in Latin America.
Washington: Inter-American Development Bank, Economic
Development Division, 1962. 256 pp., bibl.

0331 CHONCHOL, JACQUES. "La reforma agraria." Mensaje 123
(October, 1963): 563-571.

0332 _____. La reforma agraria en América Latina. Santiago,
Chile: Universidad de Chile, 1962. 31 pp.

0333 _____. "Reforma agraria en América Latina." Cuadernos
Latinoamericanos de Economía Humana 6 (1963): 139-171.

0334 "The Church in Ecuador Undertakes Agrarian Land Reform."
Reportaje DESAL 1 (July/December, 1968): 3.

0335 DELGADO, OSCAR. Bibliografía latinoamericana sobre reforma
agraria y tenencia de la tierra. México: [n.p.], 1962.
37 pp.

0336 Episcopado Ecuatoriano. "Reforma agraria en Ecuador: carta
pastoral colectiva." Mensaje 10 (May, 1961): 187-188.

0337 "La Iglesia católica y la reforma agraria." La Prensa,
October 31, 1964.

0338 JAVIER, FRANCISCO. El humanismo de Jorge Fernández Pradel.
Santiago, Chile: Instituto Chileno de Estudios Humanísticos
(ICHEH), 1976. 68 pp.

0339 QUIJANO, ANIBAL. "Contemporary Peasant Movements." In Elites
in Latin America, edited by Seymour M. Lipsetand Aldo Solari,
pp. 301-340. New York: Oxford University Press, 1967.

0340 SILVA HENRÍQUEZ, R. "Success of Church's Own Land Reforms in
South America." U.S. Catholic 29 (February, 1964): 56.

0341 STAVENHAGEN, RODOLFO, ed. Agrarian Problems and Peasant
Movements in Latin America. Garden City, New York: Anchor,
1970. 583 pp.

CÂMARA, HÉLDER

0342 BROUKER, JOSÉ DE. Dom Hélder Câmara: la violence d'pacifique.
Paris: Fayard, 1969. 223 pp.

0343 CÂMARA, HÉLDER. Iglesia y desarrollo. Buenos Aires: Búsqueda,
1968. 74 pp.

Câmara, Hélder

0344   "Collision in Latin America." Time 95 (February 9, 1970): 44.

0345   CULHANE, EUGENE K. "Nonviolence in Latin America." America
       120 (March 22, 1969): 331.

0346   GONZÁLEZ, JOSÉ. Hélder Câmara el "Arzobispo Rojo". Barcelona:
       Esplugas de Llobregat Ediciones, 1972. 315 pp.

0347   GOULET, DENIS. "Brief of a Brave Bishop." Catholic World 210
       (January, 1970): 180-181.

0348   "Interview with Dom Hélder Câmara." IDOC-International 54
       (Summer, 1973): 15-19.

0349   NUTE, BETTY RICHARDSON. Helder Camara's Latin America.
       London: Friends Peace and International Relations Committee,
       1974. 26 pp.

0350   "O que pretende dom Hélder." Hora Presente 7 (October, 1970):
       48-62.

CATHOLIC CHURCH AND SOCIAL CHANGE

0351   ADAMS, RICHARD N. The Second Sowing: Power and Secondary
       Development in Latin America. San Francisco: Chandler
       Publishing Co., 1967. 288 pp., bibl.

0352   _____, et al. Social Change in Latin America Today. New
       York: Vintage Books, 1960. 353 pp.

0353   AHUMADA, CORRIPIO, et al. "El compromiso cristiano ante las
       opciones sociales y la política." Documentación Social
       Latinoamericana 14 (June, 1974): 13-23.

0354   ALBERIONE, SANTIAGO. Elementos de sociología cristiana.
       Florida, Argentina: Ediciones Paulinas, 1961. 216 pp.

0355   ALEMÁN, JOSÉ LUIS. "La reforma agraria y la doctrina social
       de la Iglesia." Estudios Sociales 30 (July/September):
       121-130.

0356   ALLAZ, TOMÁS G. "El derecho de los postergados." In La
       Iglesia, el subdesarrollo y la revolución, edited by
       Bernardo Castro Villagrana et al., pp. 200-238. México:
       Editorial Nuestro Tiempo, 1968.

Catholic Church and Social Change

0357   ALVAREZ CALDERÓN, CARLOS. Pastoral y liberación humana.
        Quito: Instituto Pastoral Latinoamericano, 1968. 84 pp.

0358   ALVES, RUBEM. "El pueblo de Dios y la búsqueda de un nuevo
        order social." Cristianismo y Sociedad, no. 26-27 (1971),
        pp. 5-28.

0359   _____. "La muerte de la Iglesia y el futuro del hombre."
        Cristianismo y Sociedad, no. 16-17 (1968), pp. 3-20.

0360   AMBROGGIO, LUIS. Latin America Man and His Revolution.
        Washington: Division for Latin America, United States
        Catholic Conference, 1970.

0361   AMENGUAL, ATALIVA, et al. "Los marxistas cristianos o la
        nostalgia del integrismo." Política y Espíritu 333 (June,
        1972): 22-37.

0362   "América Latina en el umbral del Concilio." Criterio 35
        (October 11, 1962): 729-736.

0363   America Latina: parole come armi. Milan, Italy: Jaca Book
        Edizioni, 1968. 219 pp.

0364   AMOR, EMMANUEL. "La Iglesia y el pueblo." Cuestiones Actuales,
        February, 1968.

0365   ANDRADE VALDERRAMA, VICENTE. "La invasión de tierras."
        Revista Javeriana 50 (November, 1963): 406-410.

0366   ARAÚJO SALES, EUGENIO DE. "A igreja na América Latina e a
        promoção humana." Revista Eclesiástica Brasileira 28
        (1968): 537-554.

0367   ARCUSA, EDUARDO. Tiempo de diálogo: ensayo. La Paz: Nuevas
        Estructuras, 1968. 326 pp., bibl.

0368   ARROYO, GONZALO. "Christians for Socialism: A Christian
        Response." IDOC-International 53 (May, 1973): 54-56.

0369   _____. "Doctrina, utopía y subversión." Mensaje 161
        (August, 1967): 340-347.

0370   ARRUPE, PEDRO. "A los provinciales de América Latina: los
        Jesuitas y la justicia social." Informaciones Católicas
        Internacionales 281 (February 7, 1967): 26-27.

Catholic Church and Social Change

0371 _____. Compromiso social de la compañía de Jesús. Bogotá:
Centro de Investigación y Acción Social, 1971. 42 pp.

0372 ASSMAN, HUGO. "Medellín: a desilusão que nos amadure ceu."
Cuadernos do Ceas 38 (July/August, 1975): 51-57.

0373 BARASH, MEYER. "The Role of Traditional Religion in a
Developing Nation." Archives de Sociologie des Religions
12 (January/June, 1967): 37-40.

0374 BASAURE AVILA, LUZ. "Religión y subdesarrollo: un estudio
sobre la realidad religiosa en Latinoamérica." Oiga,
April 30, 1965.

0375 BECKMAN, JOSEPH F. "Material and Religious Poverty in Latin
America." Homiletic and Pastoral Review 75 (July, 1975):
28-32.

0376 BENHAM, J. "New Rebels: Clerics in Latin America." U.S.
News and World Report, December 14, 1970, pp. 92-95.

0377 BERNARDIN, JOSEPH L. "Derechos humanos y reconciliación."
CELAM, no. 95 (1975), pp. 8, 17.

0378 BERRYMAN, PHILIP E. "Popular Catholicism in Latin America."
Cross Currents 21 (Summer, 1971): 284-301.

0379 Between Honesty and Hope: Documents From and About the Church
in Latin America. Maryknoll, New York: Maryknoll Publications, 1970. 247 pp.

0380 BIGO, PIERRE. "Discernimiento espiritual." In Conflicto
social y compromiso cristiano en América Latina, edited by
the Consejo Episcopal Latinoamericano, pp. 33-37. Bogotá:
Consejo Episcopal Latinoamericano, 1976.

0381 BILHEIMER, ROBERT. "Justice, Development, and Peace, Our Joint
Christian Concern." In Integration of Man and Society in
Latin America, edited by Samuel Shapiro, pp. 215-223.
Notre Dame, Indiana: University of Notre Dame, 1967.

0382 BISHOP M., JORDAN. "Sprouting Slums." Commonweal 86
(April 28, 1967): 172-173.

0383 BOJORGE, HORACIO. "Exodo y liberación." Víspera 19-20
(October/December, 1970): 33-37.

0384 BONINO-MIGUEZ, JOSÉ. "The Church and the Latin Social American
Revolution." Perspective 9 (Fall, 1968): 213-232.

Catholic Church and Social Change

0385 _____. "Vatican II and Latin America." Christian Century 81
(December 30, 1964): 1616-1617.

0386 BONO, AGOSTINO. "Social Action Fades in Latin America."
National Catholic Reporter 10 (November 9, 1973): 1.

0387 BORNEWASSER, HANS. "State and Politics from the Renaissance
to the French Revolution." Concilium 47 (1969): 73-92.

0388 BORRAT, HÉCTOR. "Crisis y renovación: a siete meses de
Medellín." Cuadernos de Marcha, April, 1969, pp. 3-10.

0389 _____. "La Iglesia, ¿para qué?" Cristianismo y Sociedad,
no. 22 (1970), pp. 7-29.

0390 _____. "La revolución de mensaje." Cristianismo y Sociedad,
no. 7 (1965), pp. 26-36.

0391 _____. "Para una cristología de la vanguardia." Víspera 17
(June, 1970): 26-31.

0392 "Both Marx and Jesus." Time, June 5, 1972, p. 57.

0393 BOZA MASVIDAL, EDUARDO. Revolución cristiana en Latinoamerica.
Santiago, Chile: Pacífico, 1963. 90 pp.

0394 BRAVO, CARLOS. "Comprensión teológica de la historia y compromiso cristiano." In Conflicto social y compromiso
cristiano en América Latina, edited by the Consejo Episcopal
Latinoamericano, pp. 233-239. Bogotá: Consejo Episcopal
Latinoamericano, 1976.

0395 BRUNEAU, THOMAS C. "Power and Influence: Analysis of Church
in Latin America and the Case of Brazil." Latin American
Research Review 8 (Summer, 1973): 25-52.

0396 BÜNTIG, ALDO J. "Modelados del catolicismo popular."
Catequesis Latinoamericana 1 (May/June, 1969): 57-74.

0397 _____, and BERTONE, C. A. Hechos, doctrinas sociales y
liberación. Buenos Aires: Editorial Guadalupe, 1971.
275 pp.

0398 CABAL, LATORRE. The Revolution of the Latin American Church.
Norman, Oklahoma: University of Oklahoma Press, 1978.
192 pp.

Catholic Church and Social Change

0399   CABRERA, ILDEFONSO. "Integration of the Rural Population."
In Integration of Man and Society in Latin America, edited
by Samuel Shapiro, pp. 46–58. Notre Dame, Indiana:
University of Notre Dame, 1967.

0400   CALDERÓN, RICARDO ARIAS. "The Intellectual Challenge to
Religion in Latin America." In The Religious Dimension in
the New Latin America, edited by John J. Considine, pp. 58–
68. Notre Dame, Indiana: Fides Publishers, 1966.

0401   _____. "The Universities." In Integration of Man and Society
in Latin America, edited by Samuel Shapiro, pp. 68–73.
Notre Dame, Indiana: University of Notre Dame, 1967.

0402   CALVANI, ARÍSTIDES. "The Christian Ethos in Socioeconomic
Development." In Cultural Factors in Inter-American Rela-
tions, edited by Samuel Shapiro, pp. 227–234. Notre Dame,
Indiana: University of Notre Dame, 1968.

0403   CÂMARA, HÉLDER. "A Igreja nas Américas: suas possibilidades,
seus deveres, sua missão." Vozes 7 (July, 1968): 590–594.

0404   _____. "Ação não-violenta na América Latina." Vozes 8
(August, 1968): 701–711.

0405   _____. "Challenge to Latin America." America, May 2, 1964,
p. 590.

0406   _____. "Conflictos socio-políticos en América Latina:
situación actual y perspectivas en una visión pastoral."
In Conflicto social y compromiso cristiano en América
Latina, edited by the Consejo Episcopal Latinoamericano,
pp. 347–352. Bogotá: Consejo Episcopal Latinoamericano,
1976.

0407   _____. Dom Hélder Câmara vous parle: le combat mondial pour
la justice et la paix: message de dom Hélder Câmara et
résponses aux questions. Lyon, France: Palais des Sports,
1970. 23 pp.

0408   _____. Iglesia y desarrollo. Buenos Aires: Ediciones
Búsqueda, 1966. 74 pp.

0409   _____. Pobreza, abundancia y solidaridad. Algorta, Spain:
Zero, 1970. 56 pp.

0410   _____. Spiral of Violence. London: Sheed and Ward, 1971.
83 pp.

Catholic Church and Social Change

0411 _____. The Desert Is Fertile. Maryknoll, New York: Orbis Books, 1974. 61 pp.

0412 _____. "Towards Peace and Justice Between the Americas." IDOC-International 37 (December 11, 1971): 44-51.

0413 CAMPBELL, B., and HINDE, P. "Latin America: War Against the Poor." Catholic Worker 43 (September, 1977): 3-4.

0414 CAMPOS MENÉNDEZ, HERNANDO. Concepto cristiano del desarrollo. Buenos Aires: Consejo Superior de los Hombres de la Acción Católica Argentina, 1963. 126 pp.

0415 "Carta de los sacerdotes latinoamericanos al Sínodo de Obispos." Víspera 24-25 (December, 1971): 125-130.

0416 CASALDÁLIGA, PEDRO. "Más allá de Medellín." SIC 403 (March, 1978): 100-102.

0417 CASTILLO CARDENAS, GONZALO. Christians and the Struggle for a New Social Order in Latin America. New York: Latin American Committee, 1966. 8 pp.

0418 _____. "Christians and the Struggle for a New Social Order in Latin America." In The Religious Situation: 1968, edited by Donald R. Cutler, pp. 498-517. Boston: Beacon Press, 1968.

0419 _____. "Los cristianos y la lucha por un nuevo orden social en América Latina." Cristianismo y Sociedad 4 (1966): 84-96.

0420 CASTRO VILLAGRANA, BERNARDO. "Introducción: la Iglesia y el cambio social." In La Iglesia, el subdesarrollo y la revolución, edited by Bernardo Castro Villagrana et al., pp. 9-14. México: Editorial Nuestro Tiempo, 1968.

0421 _____, et al. La Iglesia, el subdesarrollo y la revolución. México: Nuestro Tiempo, 1968. 247 pp., bibl.

0422 Los católicos y la educación en América Latina: nuevas perspectivas para el planeamiento. Bogotá: Consejo Episcopal Latinoamericano, Departamento de Educación, 1969. 91 pp.

0423 CAVALLI, FIORELLO. "Studi sulle condizioni religiose e sociali dell 'America Latina.'" La Civiltá Cattolica 113 (June, 1962): 567-570.

Catholic Church and Social Change

0424 _____. "Un organismo episcopale per il coordinamento dell'
apostolato cattolico nell'America Latina." Civiltà
Cattolica 108 (April, 1957): 160-175.

0425 Centro Catequístico Paulino. Construyamos una patria nueva:
estudio de la doctrina social de la Iglesia, libro II.
Cali: Editora Norma, 1962. 208 pp.

0426 Centro de Información y Documentación para América Latina.
Documento que presentará el Episcopado Latinoamericano en
su reunión con Paulo VI el 26 de agosto de 1968, en Medellín.
Caracas: Centro de Información y Documentación para América
Latina, 1968. 54 pp.

0427 Centro de Investigación y Educación Popular. ¿Iglesia en
conflicto? Bogotá: Centro de Investigación y Educación
Popular, 1976. 133 pp.

0428 Centro para el Desarrollo Económico y Social de América Latina.
Iglesia, paz y desarrollo. Santiago, Chile: Centro para
el Desarrollo Económico y Social de América Latina, 1969.
17 pp.

0429 "Changing Role of the Church in Latin America." U.S. News and
World Report 63 (October 16, 1967): 94-95.

0430 CHARBONNEAU, PAUL EUGENE. Cristianismo, sociedade e revolução.
São Paulo: Editôra Herder, 1967. 584 pp.

0431 CHARTIER, RICARDO. "Modos de relación entre la Iglesia y la
sociedad." Cristianismo y Sociedad 1 (1963): 5-13.

0432 The Christian Challenge in Latin America: A Symposium.
Maryknoll, New York: Maryknoll Publications, 1964. 86 pp.

0433 CLARK, ROBERT. "I Failed in Puno: Church and Social Justice
in Latin America." America 112 (January 2, 1965): 7.

0434 COBO, SERGIO. "Justicia evangélica: religiosidad y justicia
social: una catequesis de la religiosidad popular en el
sermón del monte." Pastoral Popular 26 (1975): 4-15.

0435 COLAIANNI, JAMES F. The Catholic Left: The Crisis of Radicalism Within the Church. Philadelphia: Chilton, 1968.
233 pp.

0436 COLEMAN, WILLAIM JACKSON. Latin American Catholicism: A
Self-Evaluation. Maryknoll, New York: Maryknoll Publications, 1958. 106 pp.

Catholic Church and Social Change

0437   COLONNESE, LOUIS MICHAEL. "North American Perceptions of the
        Influence and Inspiration of the Post-Medellin Latin Ameri-
        can Church." In Conscientization for Liberation, edited by
        Louis M. Colonnese, pp. 93-102. Washington, D.C.: Division
        for Latin America, U.S. Conference, 1971.

0438   _____, ed. Conscientization for Liberation: New Dimensions
        in Hemispheric Realities. Washington, D.C.: Division for
        Latin America, U.S. Catholic Conference, 1971. 304 pp.

0439   COMBLIN, JOSEPH. "La Iglesia latinoamericana desde el Vaticano
        II: diez años que hacen historia." SIC 389 (November,
        1976): 425-431.

0440   _____. "Medellín: problemas de interpretación." Pasos 64
        (August 20, 1973): 1-5.

0441   "Conclusões da Mar del Plata sôbre a prença activa de Igreja
        no desenvolvimento e na integração de América Latina."
        Revista Eclesiástica Brasileira 27 (1967): 453-466.

0442   Conference on Church and Society in Latin America. Social
        Justice and the Latin American Churches: Church and
        Society in Latin America. Richmond, Virginia: John Knox
        Press, 1969. 137 pp.

0443   Conferencia Episcopal Cubana. "El desarrollo y la conciencia
        cristiana." Criterio 42 (July 6, 1969): 412-414.

0444   Conferencia Episcopal de Colombia. La Iglesia ante el cambio.
        Bogotá: Secretariado Permanente del Episcopado Colombiano,
        1969. 160 pp.

0445   Conferencia General del Episcopado Latinoamericano, 2d. A
        Igreja na atual transformação da América Latina à luz do
        Concílio: conclusões de Medellín. Petrópolis, Brazil:
        Editôra Vozes, 1970. 182 pp.

0446   _____. Conclusiones. Santiago, Chile: Ediciones Paulinas,
        1968.

0447   _____. Conclusões de Medellín: II Conferência Geral do
        Episcopado Latinoamericano. Porto Alegre: Secretariado
        Regional Sul 3 da C.N.B.B., 1968. 111 pp.

0448   _____. Documento final. Medellín: Imecso, 1968. 246 pp.

Catholic Church and Social Change.

0449 _____. Documento que presentará el Episcopado Latinoamericano de 1968, en Medellín. Caracas: Centro de Información y Documentación para América Latina, 1968. 54 pp.

0450 _____. La Iglesia en la actual transformación de América Latina a la luz del Consilio. Santiago, Chile: Ediciones Paulinas, 1969.

0451 _____. Misión del religioso en América Latina. Bogotá: Confederación Latinoamericana de Religiosos, Secretariado General, 1967. 18 pp.

0452 _____. The Church in the Present-Day Transformation of Latin America in the Light of the Council. Bogotá: General Secretariat of Conferencia Episcopal Latinoamericana, 1970. 2 v.

0453 Congreso Latino Americano dos Secretariados Nacionais de Opinião Publica. Igreja e meios de comunicação na América Latina. Lima: Editora Vozes, 1969. 69 pp.

0454 Consejo Episcopal Latinoamericano. Conflicto social y compromiso cristiano en América Latina. Bogotá: Secretariado General del Consejo Episcopal Latinoamericano, 1976. 386 pp.

0455 _____. "El CELAM y el desarrollo." Criterio 39 (October 27, 1966): 763-768.

0456 _____. Iglesia y universidad en América Latina. Bogotá: Secretariado General del Consejo Episcopal Latinoamericano, 1976. 143 pp.

0457 _____. Igreja na América Latina: desenvolvimento integração: Assembléia Extraordinária do CELAM em Mar del Plata, 11 a 16 de outubro de 1966. Petrópolis, Brazil: Editôra Vozes, 1968. 263 pp.

0458 _____. "Presencia activa de la Iglesia en el desarrollo e integración de América Latina." Informaciones Católicas Internacionales 289 (June 7, 1967): 24-26.

0459 _____. Presencia activa de la Iglesia en el desarrollo y la integración de América Latina. Salvador, Brazil: Departamento de Acción Social, 1967. 43 pp.

0460 _____. "Presencia activa de la Iglesia en el desarrollo y la integración de América Latina." CIAS 167 (October, 1967): 21-35.

Catholic Church and Social Change

0461 _____. "Presencia de la Iglesia en el proceso de cambio de
América Latina." Signos (November, 1969): 37-40.

0462 CONSIDINE, JOHN JOSEPH. "Aid to the Latin American Church."
America 117 (September 30, 1967): 352-354.

0463 _____. "Christian Gains in Today's Latin America." Shield
36 (March, 1957): 12-14.

0464 _____. "Church on the March of Latin America." Ave Maria 97
(June 22, 1963): 5-8.

0465 _____. "Latin America Today: The Socio-Religious Factor."
Social Order 12 (January, 1962): 13-19.

0466 _____. New Horizons in Latin America. New York: Dodd, Mead,
1958. 379 pp.

0467 _____. Social Revolution in the New Latin America. Notre
Dame, Indiana: Fides Publishers, 1965. 245 pp.

0468 _____. "The Papal Program for Latin America." American
Ecclesiastical Review 154 (March, 1966): 153-169.

0469 _____. The Religious Dimension in the New Latin America.
Notre Dame, Indiana: Fides Publishers, 1966. 238 pp.

0470 _____, ed. The Church in the New Latin America. Notre Dame,
Indiana: Fides Publishers, 1964. 240 pp., bibl.

0471 _____, ed. The Missionary's Role in the Socio-Economic
Betterment. Maryknoll, New York: Newman Press, 1970.

0472 Construir una patria nueva: estudio de doctrina social de la
Iglesia: Ultimos años de bachillerato. Cali: Editora Norma,
1961. 207 pp.

0473 CONTERIS, HIBER. "El rol de la Iglesia en el cambio social de
América Latina." Cristianismo y Sociedad 7 (1965): 50-60.

0474 _____. Hombre, ideología y revolución en América Latina.
Montevideo: Iglesia y Sociedad en América Latina, 1965.
133 pp.

0475 CORREA, HECTOR. "Structure dû pouvoir et development social
en Amérique Latine." Tiers Monde 6 (October/December, 1965):
915-937.

Catholic Church and Social Change

0476   COTTIER, GEORGES. "Why Communism Appeals to Developing
        Countries." Concilium 3 (February, 1965): 76-87.

0477   CRAIG, ALEXANDER. "Revolution in the Church." Contemporary
        Review 214 (February, 1969): 57-66.

0478   "Crise et christianisme." Esprit 1 (April/May, 1977): 196-200.

0479   Cristianismo: doctrina social y revolución: antología.
        Buenos Aires: Centro Editor de América Latina, 1972. 176
        pp., bibl.

0480   Los cristianos en la universidad. Bogotá: Consejo Episcopal
        Latinoamericano, Departamento de Educación y de Pastoral
        Universidad, 1967. 61 pp.

0481   Los cristianos y el socialismo: primer encuentro latinoameri-
        cano. Buenos Aires: Siglo Veintiuno, 1973. 274 pp.

0482   CULHANE, EUGENE K. "Feres Study of Latin America." America
        111 (September 26, 1964): 345-347.

0483   _____. "They Call It Conscientization." America 131
        (December 28, 1974): 423-425.

0484   D'ANTONIO, WILLIAM V. and PIKE, FREDERICK B. Religion, Revo-
        lution, and Reform: New Forces for Change in Latin America.
        New York: Praeger, 1964. 276 pp.

0485   DAY, EDWARD. The Catholic Church Story: Changing and Change-
        less. Liguori, Missouri: Liguori Publications, 1975.
        187 pp., bibl.

0486   "De Medellín a Puebla." SIC 403 (March, 1978): 105-106.

0487   DEALY, GLEN CAUDILL. The Public Man: An Interpretation of
        Latin American and Other Catholic Countries. Amherst: The
        University of Massachusetts Press, 1977. 133 pp.

0488   "Declaración del CELAM sobre la Iglesia y la integración de
        América Latina." In La Iglesia y la integración andina,
        edited by the Seminario de la Iglesia y el Proceso de
        Integración Andina, pp. 128-129. Bogotá: Secretariado
        General de Consejo Episcopal Latinoamericano. 1976.

0489   "Declaración final: obstáculos de la integración." In La
        Iglesia y la integración andina, edited by the Seminario de
        la Iglesia y el Proceso de Integración Andina, pp. 105-110.
        Bogotá: Secretariado General de Consejo Episcopal Latino-
        americano, 1976.

Catholic Church and Social Change

0490   DEHAINAUT, RAYMOND K. Faith and Ideology in Latin American
        Perspective. Cuernavaca, México: Centro Intercultural de
        Documentación, 1972.

0491   DE KADT, EMANUEL. "Changing Church and Society in Latin
        America." Theology Digest 20 (Fall, 1972): 238-242.

0492   _____. "Church and Society in Latin America, a Survey of
        Change." Clergy Review 56 (October, 1971): 755-771.

0493   _____. "Church, Society and Development in Latin America."
        Journal of Development Studies 8 (October, 1971): 23-43.

0494   DE ROUX, RODOLFO. "Iglesia y sociedad: los problemas de un
        cambio." Theologica Xaveriana 3 (1976): 273-280.

0495   DE SANTA ANA, JULIO. "Notas para una ética de la liberación
        (a partir de la biblia)." Cristianismo y Sociedad 8 (1970):
        43-60.

0496   "Discurso de Mons. Sergio Méndez Arceo, Obispo de Cuernavaca
        (México), pronunciado en la sesión inaugural, el 23 de
        abril de 1972." In Cristianos por el socialismo: con-
        secuencia cristiana o alienación política?, edited by
        Instituto de Estudios Políticos, pp. 166-172. Santiago,
        Chile: Editorial de Pacífico, 1972.

0497   DREKONJA, GERHARD. "Kirche und Sozialer Umsturz in Latein-
        amerika." Wort und Wahreit 24 (November/December, 1969):
        496-505.

0498   _____. "Religion and Social Change in Latin America." Latin
        American Research Review 6 (Spring, 1971): 53-72.

0499   DUFAY, E., et al. Comunismo y religion. Santiago, Chile:
        Editorial del Pacífico, 1963. 186 pp.

0500   DUSSEL, ENRIQUE D. "Coyuntura de la praxis cristiana en
        América Latina." SIC 403 (March, 1978): 103, 137-141.

0501   _____. "Historia de la fe cristiana y cambio social en
        América Latina." In América Latina: dependencia y libera-
        ción, edited by Enrique D. Dussel, pp. 193-228. Buenos
        Aires: Fernando García Cambeiro, 1973.

0502   _____. "Relaciones de la Iglesia y Estado en las formaciones
        sociales periféricas latinoamericanas." Christus 41
        (December, 1976): 18-41.

Catholic Church and Social Change

0503   EINAUDI, LUIGI, et al. Latin American Institutional Develop-
        ment: The Changing Catholic Church. Santa Monica,
        California: Rand Corporation, 1969.

0504   _____, et al. Latin American Institutional Development: The
        Changing Catholic Church. Santa Monica, California: Rand
        Corporation, 1969. 81 pp.

0505   ELIAS, JOHN LAWRENCE. A Comparison and Critical Evaluation
        of the Social and Educational Thought of Paulo Freire and
        Ivan Illich. Philadelphia: Temple University, 1974.
        210 pp., bibl.

0506   "En paises pobres la Iglesia debe ser parte de las masas,
        afirma." Noticias Aliadas, July 10, 1971, p. 14.

0507   Encuentro Continental de Misiones en América Latina. La
        pastoral en las misiones de América Latina: documento
        final. Bogotá: Consejo Episcopal Latinoamericano,
        Departamento de Misiones, 1968. 46 pp.

0508   Encuentro "Cristianismo e ideologías en América Latina a la
        luz de la Octogésima Adveniens." Cristianismo e ideologías
        en América Latina a la luz de la "Octogésima Adveniens."
        Bogotá: Secretariado General de Consejo Episcopal Latino-
        americano, 1974. 115 pp.

0509   Encuentro Latinoamericano de Cristianos por el Socialismo, 1st.
        Los cristianos y el socialismo: primer encuentro latino-
        americano. Buenos Aires: Siglo Veintiuno Argentina, 1973.
        274 pp.

0510   Encuentro Regional Andino de Justicia y Paz, 1st. Primer
        Encuentro Regional Andino de Justicia y Paz, Lima, 7-12 de
        mayo, 1970. Lima: Comisión Episcopal de Acción Social de
        Perú, 1970. 170 pp.

0511   Encuentro sobre teología y pastoral de los ministerios,
        Cumbaya, Ecuador 1974. Ministerios eclesiales en América
        Latina: reflexión teológico-pastoral. Bogotá: Consejo
        Episcopal Latinamericano, Secretariado General de CELAM,
        1976. 223 pp.

0512   ERRÁZURIZ, MANUEL LARRAÍN. "We Must Know the Signs of the
        Times." In The Religious Dimension in the New Latin
        America, edited by John J. Considine, pp. 215-224. Notre
        Dame, Indiana: Fides Publishers, 1966.

Catholic Church and Social Change

0513   FALS BORDA, ORLANDO. "Una estrategía para la Iglesia en la
       transformación de América Latina." Cristianismo y Sociedad
       2 (1964): 31-39.

0514   Federación de la Juventud Católica del Uruguay. Violando la
       clausura: congreso protestante de pocitos . . . resumido
       y criticado por la FJCU. Montevideo: Gómez, 1975. 445 pp.

0515   "Felici Cautions Latins on Social Reform Push." National
       Catholic Reporter 5 (August 6, 1969): 6.

0516   FETSCHER, IRING. "Developments in the Marxist Critique of
       Religion." Concilium 16 (May, 1966): 131-155.

0517   FIGUEROA TORRES, JESÚS. Jesucristo comunista? México:
       Costa-Amic, 1975.

0518   FLEENER, CHARLES J., and CARGAS, HARRY. Religious and
       Cultural Factors in Latin America. St. Louis, Missouri:
       St. Louis University Press, 1970. 159 pp.

0519   FONSECA, JAIME. "Latin America: A Challenge to Catholics."
       Worldmission 11 (September, 1960): 15-31.

0520   _____. "Latin America's Vocation Shortage Causes Concern for
       Church's Future in that Area." Catholic Messenger 82
       (March 26, 1964): 8.

0521   _____. "The Church in Latin America: A Major Force for Change."
       Catholic Mind 67 (April, 1969): 38-42.

0522   FONTAINE, PABLO. "Decir a Cristo, luchar." Víspera 24-25
       (December, 1971): 69-70.

0523   FOY, FELICIAN A. "Latin American Report." Worldmission 11
       (September, 1960): 78-85.

0524   FREI MONTALVA, EDUARDO. "Notes on the Catholic Church and
       Development." In Latin America: Evolution or Explosive?,
       edited by Mildred Adams, pp. 191-200. New York: Dodd,
       Mead, 1963.

0525   FREIRE, PAULO. "La Misión educativa de las iglesias en
       América Latina." In La desmitificación y otros escritos,
       edited by Paulo Freire, pp. 95-141. Bogotá: Editorial
       América Latina, 1975.

Catholic Church and Social Change

0526 _____. Las iglesias en América Latina: educación para el cambio social. Buenos Aires: Tierra Nueva, 1974. 162 pp.

0527 _____. Las iglesias en América Latina: su papel educativo. Caracas: Laboratorio Educativo, 1975. 60 pp., bibl.

0528 FRINGS, JOSÉ. "Preocupación por América Latina: llamado pastoral de los obispos alemanes." Mensaje 11 (March 4, 1962): 99-100.

0529 GAETE, ARTURO. "Evangelio y cristianismo." Mensaje 194 (November, 1970): 511-520.

0530 GALILEA, SEGUNDO. ¿A los pobres, se les anuncia el evangelio? Bogotá: Consejo Episcopal Latinoamericano, [n.d.] 38 pp.

0531 _____. "Iglesia local latinoamericana y pluralismo." Catequesis Latinoamericana 1 (July/September, 1969): 21-26.

0532 _____. "La eucaristía como protesta." Víspera 21 (January/February, 1971): 48-50.

0533 GALL, NORMAN. "La reforma católica." Mundo Nuevo 48 (June, 1970): 20-43.

0534 GALVAN, LUIS ARMANDO. "El hecho social como fuente del pensamiento filosófico." In Conflicto social y compromiso cristiano en América Latina, edited by Consejo Episcopal Latinoamericano, pp. 125-170. Bogotá: Consejo Episcopal Latinoamericano, 1976.

0535 GARCÍA, JESUS. Paz y justicia. San Antonio, Texas: Mexican American Cultural Center, 1972. 242 pp.

0536 GARCÍA-HUIDOBRO, JUAN EDUARDO. "Los educadores cristianos y la liberación latinoamericana." Educación Hoy 21 (January/February, 1972): 5-39.

0537 General Conference of Latin American Bishops, 2d. The Church in the Present-Day Transformation of Latin America in the Light of the Council. Washington, D.C.: Division for Latin America, United States Catholic Conference, 1973.

0538 "General Declaration, Fifth National Meeting of MPTW." NADOC 268 (September, 1972): 4-5.

0539 GEYER, GEORGIE ANNE. "Catholic Revolution in Latin America." Progressive 32 (July, 1968): 33-36.

Catholic Church and Social Change

0540   GLEICH, ALBRECHT VON. "Soziale Probleme in Lateinamerika."
       Überseeundschau: Latein-Amerika, Afrika, Asien, Australien
       18 (1966): 18-20.

0541   GODOY, HORACIO H. "La Iglesia y la integración de América
       Latina." Anuario de Sociología de los Pueblos Ibéricos 3
       (1967): 161-180.

0542   Golconda: el libro rojo de los "curas rebeldes". Bogotá:
       MUNIPROC, 1969. 200 pp.

0543   GONZÁLEZ, GUILLERMO. "La violencia no es evangélica."
       Revista Javeriana 359 (October, 1969): 404-414.

0544   GONZÁLEZ RUÍS, JOSÉ MARÍA. "The Public Character of the
       Christian Message and of Contemporary Society." Concilium
       36 (May, 1968): 54-62.

0545   GOZZER, GIOVANNI. Religión y revolución en América Latina.
       Madrid: Taurus Ediciones, 1969. 360 pp.

0546   _____. Religione e rivoluzione in America Latina. Milan:
       Bompiani, 1968. 243 pp.

0547   GREGORY, ALFONSO. "Elementos para una teoría del conflicto
       social." In Conflicto social y compromiso cristiano en
       América Latina, edited by Consejo Episcopal Latinoamericano,
       pp. 39-45. Bogotá: Consejo Episcopal Latinoamericano, 1976.

0548   _____. "Strengthening the City Church: A Pastoral View." In
       The Religious Dimension in the New Latin America, edited by
       John J. Considine, pp. 177-185. Notre Dame, Indiana: Fides
       Publishers, 1966.

0549   GREINACHER, NORBERT. "A Community Free of Rule." Concilium
       63 (1971): 87-107.

0550   GUTIÉRREZ, GUSTAVO MERINO. "A Latin American Perception of a
       Theology of Liberation." In Conscientization for Libera-
       tion, edited by Louis M. Colonnese, pp. 57-80. Washington,
       D.C.: Division for Latin America, U.S. Catholic Conference,
       1971.

0551   _____. "¿Crece o declina la Iglesia Latinoamericana?" In
       Liberación: opción de la Iglesia latinoamericana en la
       década del 70, edited by Simposio Sobre Teología de la
       Liberación, pp. 3-24. Bogotá: Editorial Presencia, 1970.

Catholic Church and Social Change

0552   _____. "Contestation in Latin America." Concilium 68 (1971):
         40-52.

0553   _____. "De la Iglesia colonial a Medellín." Víspera 16
         (April, 1970): 3-8.

0554   HARPER, CHARLES. "Los derechos humanos y la respuesta
         cristiana en América Latina." Diálogo 26 (1975): 41-44.

0555   HELLMUT GNADT, VITALIS. The Significance of Changes in Latin
         American Catholicism Since Chimbote, 1953. México: Centro
         Intercultural de Documentación, 1969. 342 pp.

0556   HEMPSTONE, SMITH. "Changing Role of the Church." Nation 203
         (September 12, 1966): 216-219.

0557   HERNÁNDEZ, E. JAVIER ALONSO. Teología y desarrollo. Lima:
         Centro Arquidiocesana de Pastoral, 1969-1970. 2 v.

0558   "Le heurt de l'Eglise et des pouvoirs en Amérique Latine."
         Terre Entiere 42-43 (July/October, 1970): 35-67.

0559   HEVIA, PATRICIO. América Latina: crisis de la Iglesia
         católica, junio-septiembre de 1968: reacciones de prensa.
         Cuernavaca, México: Centro Intercultural de Documentación,
         1969.

0560   HINKELAMMERT, FRANZ JOSEPH. "Instituciones cristians y
         sociedad." In Liberación: opción de la Iglesia latino-
         americana en la década del 70, edited by Simposio sobre
         Teología de la Liberación, pp. 74-92. Bogotá: Ediciones,
         [n.d.]

0561   HOFFMAN, RONAN. "Latin America: The Church Meets the
         Challenge of Change." Catholic World 197 (June, 1963):
         164-171.

0562   HOUSLEY, JOHN B. "The Role of the Churches in U.S., Latin
         American Relations." In Prospects for Latin America,
         edited by David S. Smith, pp. 1-34. New York: Columbia
         University, 1970.

0563   HOUTART, FRANÇOIS. "Les èffects du changement social sur la
         religion catholique en Amérique Latine." Archives de
         Sociologie de Religions 6 (July/December, 1961): 63-73.

0564   _____. "The Latin American Church and the Development of
         Socio-Religious Research." Concilium 9 (October, 1965):
         159-164.

Catholic Church and Social Change

0565   _____, and PIN, EMILE. L'Eglise a l'heure de l'Amerique
      Latine. Tournai, France: Casterman, 1965. 265 pp., bibl.

0566   _____, and _____. The Church and the Latin American Revolu-
      tion. New York: Sheed and Ward, 1965. 264 pp.

0567   HUIZING, PETER. "The Church and Contestation." Concilium 68
      (September/October, 1971): 96-104.

0568   "La Iglesia en Latinoamérica y el desarrollo de la investiga-
      ción socio-religiosa." Concilium 9 (November, 1965):
      143-147.

0569   Iglesia, población y familia: estudios doctrinales. Santiago,
      Chile: DESAL-CELAP, 1967. 262 pp.

0570   Iglesia y Sociedad en América Latina. Hombre, ideología y
      revolución de América Latina. Montevideo: Iglesia y
      Sociedad en América Latina, 1965. 133 pp.

0571   _____. La responsabilidad social del cristiano, guía de
      estudios. Montevideo: Iglesia y Sociedad en América
      Latina, 1964. 140 pp., bibl.

0572   ILLICH, IVAN D. Retooling Society III. Cuernavaca, México:
      Centro Intercultural de Documentación, 1973.

0573   Instituto di Studi Americani Pro Deo. La situazione socio-
      religiosa in America Latina: tavola rotonda. Rome:
      Instituto di Studi Americani Pro Deo, 1968. 71 pp.

0574   Instituto Fe y Secularidad. Fe cristiana y cambio en América
      Latina: encuentro del El Escorial, 1972. Salamanca:
      Ediciones Sígueme, 1973. 428 pp., bibl.

0575   Instituto Latino Americano de Doctrina y Estudios Sociales.
      Documentos sociales de la Iglesia: síntesis cronólogica e
      indices analíticos. Santiago, Chile: Ilades, 1976. 53 pp.

0576   JIMÉNEZ, ROBERTO. "El Conflicto en la teología de la
      Liberación: evaluación de algunos aspectos positivos."
      In Conflicto social y compromiso en América Latina, edited
      by Consejo Episcopal Latinoamericano, pp. 359-381. Bogotá:
      Consejo Episcopal Latinoamericano, 1976.

0577   JOHNSON, DALE L. The Sociology of Change and Reaction in
      Latin America. New York: Bobbs-Merrill, 1973. 57 pp.

Catholic Church and Social Change

0578   JOHNSON, H. "A Priest Speaks to North American Catholics:
        Warning on the Repetition of Conditions Among Latin
        American Catholics." Social Justice Review 55 (December,
        1962): 265.

0579   Justicia y paz. Caracas: Comisión Venezolana de Justicia y
        Paz, 1968. 471 pp., bibl.

0580   KASPER, WALTER. "Politische Utopie und Christliche Hoffnung."
        Frankfurter Hefte 24 (August, 1969): 563-572.

0581   KENNEDY, JOHN J. "Dichotomies in the Church." The Annals of
        the American Academy of Political and Social Science 334
        (March, 1961): 54-62.

0582   KEVANE, RAYMOND A. "Different Cultures but a Common Ideal;
        Lay Volunteers Forming International Bond of Charity."
        America 114 (March 5, 1966): 326-328.

0583   KLOPPENBURG, BOAVENTURA. "Cuestiones pendientes en la acción
        cristiana por la liberación." In Conflicto social y com-
        promiso cristiano en América Latina, edited by Consejo
        Episcopal Latinoamericano, pp. 353-358. Bogotá: Consejo
        Episcopal Latinoamericano, 1976.

0584   LAGE PESOA, FRANCISCO. "Brasil: la Iglesia y el movimiento
        revolucionario." In La Iglesia, el subdesarrollo y la
        revolución, edited by Bernardo Castro Villagrana, pp. 153-
        169. México: Nuestro Tiempo, 1968. 247 pp., bibl.

0585   LALIVE D'EPINAY, CHRISTIAN. "La Iglesia evangélica y la
        revolución latinoamericana." Cristianismo y Sociedad 16-17
        (1968): 21-30.

0586   LANDSBERGER, HENRY A., ed. The Church and Social Change in
        Latin America. Notre Dame, Indiana: University of Notre
        Dame Press, 1970. 240 pp., bibl.

0587   LARIN, U. "Latinskaju Amerika: social'noe mnogoobrazie i
        puti razvitija." Mirovaja Ekonomika i Mezhdunarodnye
        Otnosenija 3 (1971): 93-105.

0588   LARRAIN ERRÁZURIZ, MANUEL, and SILVA HENRÍQUEZ, R. "For a
        Christian Life a Man Needs Dignity." Maryknoll 58
        (October, 1964): 51-55.

0589   "Latin America Calls, But Not for Achilles: Catholic Inter-
        American Cooperation Program." Ave Maria 105 (February 18,
        1967): 4-5.

Catholic Church and Social Change

0590 "Latin American Bishops Anti-Communist, But Push More Social Projects." Our Sunday Visitor 64 (April 11, 1976): 3.

0591 "Latin American Bishops Concerned Over Youth." Our Sunday Visitor 65 (August 29, 1976): 3.

0592 "Latin American Bishops Say Conditions Deteriorating." Our Sunday Visitor 64 (March 21, 1976): 1.

0593 "Latin Social Reform: Recent Catholic Statements." America 106 (November 4, 1961): 139.

0594 LATORRE CABAL, HUGO. La Revolución de la Iglesia Latino-americana. México: Editora Joaquín Moritz, 1969. 158 pp.

0595 LAURENTIN, ANDRÉ. Amérique Latine a l'heure de l'enfantement. Paris: Seuil, 1969. 278 pp.

0596 LAZOS E., HÉCTOR. "Las iglesias en la América Latina frente a los problemas sociales." SIC 31 (May, 1968): 231-233.

0597 LENKERSDORF, KARL. "Iglesias y liberación del pueblo." Cristianismo y Sociedad 9 (1971): 52-54.

0598 LEPARGNEUR, FRANCOIS H. "The Church's Role as It Affects Human Rights." In Human Rights and the Liberation of Man in the Americas, edited by Louis M. Colonnese, pp. 42-49. Notre Dame, Indiana: University of Notre Dame Press, 1970.

0599 LITTWIN, LAWRENCE. Latin America: Catholicism and Class Conflict. Encino, California: Dickenson, 1974. 135 pp.

0600 LONGARZO, L. "The Catholic Church in the Social Revolution of Latin America." Catholic Charities Review 50 (April, 1966): 14-17.

0601 LÓPEZ TRUJILLO, ALFONSO. "Balance de la vida del CELAM desde la asamblea de Sucre." CELAM 8 (1975): 11-17.

0602 _____. "La conflictualidad, el compromiso cristiano y la reconciliación." In Conflicto social y compromiso cristiano en América Latina, edited by Consejo Episcopal Latinoameri-cano, pp. 9-20. Bogotá: Consejo Episcopal Latinoamericano, 1976.

0603 _____. "Líneas de pastoral social en América Latina." CELAM 8 (1975): 16-21.

Catholic Church and Social Change

0604   LORA, CECILIO DE, and GONZÁLEZ ANLEO, JUAN. <u>Nuestra doctrina</u>
        <u>social cristiana</u>. Bogotá: Feres América Latina, 1966.
        311 pp.

0605   LOZANO, JAVIER. "Compromiso cristiano en los conflictos
        sociales en América Latina." In <u>Conflicto social y com-</u>
        <u>promiso cristiano en América Latina</u>, edited by Consejo
        Episcopal Latinoamericano, pp. 241-273. Bogotá: Consejo
        Episcopal Latinoamericano, 1976.

0606   MC CORMACK, ARTHUR. "The Catholic Church in South America."
        <u>Wiseman Review</u> 501 (Autumn, 1964): 226-260.

0607   MC GRATH, MARK G. "A Living Theology in Latin America." <u>The</u>
        <u>Review of Politics</u> 33 (April, 1971): 163-171.

0608   _____. "The Church and Social Revolution in Latin America."
        <u>Perspectives</u> 10 (January/February, 1965): 4-10.

0609   _____. "The Church's Socio-Economic Role in Latin America."
        <u>American Ecclesiastical Review</u> 158 (January, 1968): 1-18.

0610   MACI FIORDALISI, GUILLERMO A. "Aspectos sociológicos del
        cristianismo en el contexto de los cambios sociales en
        América Latina." <u>Ecclesia</u> 7 (August/December, 1963):
        2-23.

0611   MC KEON, WILLIAM. "A Reply to Monsignor Illich." <u>American</u>
        <u>Ecclesiastical Review</u> 156 (March, 1967): 145-150.

0612   MC MAHON, F. E. "Latin America's Struggle Toward Social
        Justice." <u>Work</u> 18 (October, 1960): 4.

0613   MC MAHON, THOMAS F. "Mass Religious Education through Audio-
        Visuals." In <u>The Religious Dimension in the New Latin</u>
        <u>America</u>, edited by John J. Considine, pp. 195-204. Notre
        Dame, Indiana: Fides Publishers, 1966.

0614   MC NASPY, C. J. "From a South American Diary." <u>America</u> 119
        (October 5, 1968): 293.

0615   MADERO, C. "La tierra de un pueblo, riqueza de pocos."
        <u>Christus</u> 40 (May, 1975): 16-23.

0616   MADURO, OTTO. "¿Cómo es marxista un cristiano?" <u>SIC</u> 402
        (February, 1978): 71-73.

0617   MAGNER, JAMES A. "Religion in Latin America." <u>America</u> 106
        (January 13, 1962): 472-473.

Catholic Church and Social Change

0618   MALLON, VINCENT T. "Medellin Guidelines: Latin American
        Episcopal Conference Statement." America 122 (January 31,
        1970): 92-96.

0619   El Manifiesto de los obispos del tercer mundo: una respuesta
        al clamor de los pobres. Buenos Aires: Ediciones Búsqueda,
        1968. 61 pp.

0620   MARÍN LEÓN, JOSÉ MARÍA. Tecnificación administrativa de la
        acción pastoral: teorización y tecnología. Bogotá:
        Secretariado General del Consejo Episcopal Latinoamericano,
        1975. 344 pp.

0621   MARINS, JOSÉ. "Iglesia y conflictividad social en América
        Latina." In Conflicto social y compromiso cristiano en
        América Latina, edited by Consejo Episcopal Latinoamericano,
        pp. 275-345. Bogotá: Consejo Episcopal Latinoamericano,
        1976.

0622   MEDINA, CARLOS ALBERTO, and FURTADO, DIMAS. Participacão e
        Igreja. Cuernavaca, México: Centro Intercultural de
        Documentación, 1971. 212 pp.

0623   MEJÍA, JORGE. "Church and Culture in Latin America." In
        Cultural Factors in Inter-American Relations, edited by
        Samuel Shapiro, pp. 212-226. Notre Dame, Indiana:
        University of Notre Dame, 1968.

0624   _____. "The Growth of Ecumenism in Latin America." In The
        Religious Dimension in the New Latin America, edited by
        John J. Considine, pp. 69-76. Notre Dame, Indiana: Fides
        Publishers, 1966.

0625   "Mensaje de la X Asamblea Ordinaria del CELAM sobre integración
        latinoamericana." In La Iglesia y la integración andina,
        edited by Seminario de la Iglesia y el Proceso de Inte-
        gración Andina, pp. 130-132. Bogotá: Secretariado General
        del Consejo Episcopal Latinoamericano, 1976.

0626   METHOL FERRÉ, ALBERTO. "Actualidad de la Iglesia en América
        Latina." In Conflicto social y compromiso cristiano en
        América Latina, edited by Consejo Episcopal Latinoamericano,
        pp. 201-231. Bogotá: Consejo Episcopal Latinoamericano,
        1976.

0627   MÉTRAUX, ALFRED. "Fêtes religieuses et développement com-
        munautaire dans la région andine." Archives de Sociologie
        des Religions 7 (January/June, 1962): 121-126.

Catholic Church and Social Change

0628   MÍGUEZ BONINO, JOSÉ. Ama y haz lo que quieras: una ética
        para el hombre nuevo. Buenos Aires: Escatón, 1972. 133 pp.

0629   MILLER, JOHN, and GAKENHEIMER, RALPH A., eds. Latin American
        Urban Policies and the Social Sciences. Beverly Hills,
        California: Sage Publications, 1971. 398 pp.

0630   "Modest Proposal: Church's Wealth and Cardinal Maurer."
        Commonweal 95 (October 1, 1971): 2.

0631   MOLINA, P. MANUEL. El progresismo religioso: orígenes,
        desarrollo y crítica. México: Tradición, 1975. 244 pp.

0632   NO ENTRY

0633   MORAO, A. "Algunas reflexões sobre a função religiosa da
        razão." Brotéria 86 (1968): 853-858.

0634   MORENO, FERNANDO. Conflicto y tendencias socio-políticas en
        América Latina. Santiago, Chile: Ilades, 1973. 35 pp.

0635   MUÑOZ, RONALDO. "El servicio de la Iglesia al hombre."
        Pastoral Popular 145 (July/Sugust/September, 1976):
        601-612.

0636   _____. Nueva conciencia de la Iglesia en América Latina.
        Salamanca: Ediciones Sígueme, 1974. 394 pp.

0637   NEGRE RIGOL, PEDRO. "Biblia y liberación." Cristianismo y
        Sociedad 8 (August, 1970): 69-80.

0638   _____. "El cristianismo y el cambio político." Diálogo
        Social 74 (December 9, 1975): 36s.

0639   New Perspectives on Latin America. Political and Social
        Change. New York: MSS Information, 1976. 298 pp.

0640   NÚÑEZ, DAVID. Los invasores: la Iglesia Católica inflitrada
        por velados enemigos. Buenos Aires: [n.p.], 1969. 25 pp.

0641   NÚÑEZ, M. SECUNDINO. "Nueva imagen del sacerdote rural."
        Revista Paraguaya de Sociología 5 (April, 1968): 93-96.

0642   Obispos del Tercer Mundo. Una respuesta al clamor de los
        pobres: el manifesto de los obispos del tercer mundo.
        Avellanada, Argentina: Búsqueda, 1968. 60 pp.

Catholic Church and Social Change

0643   O'GARA, JAMES. "Crisis to the South: Condition of the Poor
        in Latin America." Commonweal 81 (March 12, 1965):   754.

0644   O'GORMAN, ONESIMO. "Continental Program for Religious Educa-
        tion." In The Religious Dimension in the New Latin America,
        edited by John J. Considine, pp. 186-194. Notre Dame,
        Indiana: Fides Publishers, 1966.

0645   OLAYA, NOEL. "Ciencias sociales y teología." In Liberación
        en América Latina, pp. 55-67. Bogotá: Servicio Colombiano
        de Comunicación Social, 1971.

0646   _____. "Unidad cristiana y lucha de clases." Cristianismo y
        Sociedad 8 (August, 1970):   61-69.

0647   OLIVOS, LUIS, and DELGADO, OSCAR. Bibliografía sobre la
        Iglesia y el cambio social en América Latina. Washington:
        Union Panamericana, 1966.   66 pp.

0648   ORTEGA, BENJAMÍN. Repertorio para el estudio de las iglesias
        en la sociedad de América Latina: 1960-1969. Cuernavaca,
        México: Centro Intercultural de Documentación, 1970.
        208 pp.

0649   OSSA, MANUEL. "El compromiso de la Iglesia en lo social a un
        año de Medellín." Mensaje 18 (September, 1969):   401-410.

0650   OZÁN, URBANO J. Cristianismo y realidad social. Buenos Aires:
        Ediciones Troquel, 1967.   109 pp.

0651   PALAGI, D. W. "Wegweiser für Lateinamerika?" Ungeloste
        Sozialprobleme trotz Wirtschaftswunder." Die Volkswirt 20
        (1966):   315-316.

0652   PARADA, HERNÁN. Crónica de Medellín: segunda conferencia
        general del espiscopado latinoamericano, Bogotá, 24 de
        agosto, Medellín, agosto 26-septiembre 6, Colombia, 1968.
        Bogotá: Indo-American Press Service, 1975.   280 pp.

0653   _____. "Hace 5 años . . . en Medellín.... Marco histórico
        de un gran momento." Pasos 59 (July 16, 1973):   1-8.

0654   NO ENTRY

0655   PAYSEE GONZÁLEZ, EDUARDO. "La Iglesia Católica y las fuerzas
        políticas en América Latina." Cristianismo y Sociedad 9-10
        (1965/1966):   44-70.

Catholic Church and Social Change

0656   PÉREZ, MARÍA DEL CARMEN. "El religioso ante la exigencia de
       la justicia y la caridad." In 5a semana social de Chile
       1976: caridad y justicia, edited by Instituto Chileno de
       Estudios Humanísticos, pp. 223-227. Santiago, Chile:
       E.CH.E.C., 1976.

0657   PÉREZ RAMÍREZ, GUSTAVO. "Family Planning and Latin American
       Problems: Perspectives in 1965." Concilium 10 (November,
       1965): 142-164.

0658   _____. "International Religious Cooperation." In Integration
       of Man and Society in Latin America, edited by Samuel Shapiro,
       pp. 160-169. Notre Dame, Indiana: University of Notre
       Dame, 1967.

0659   _____. "The Church and the Social Revolution in Latin America."
       Concilium 36 (June, 1968): 124-135.

0660   _____. "The Trek to the Cities: A Sociological View." In
       The Religious Dimension in the New Latin America, edited
       by John J. Considine, pp. 161-176. Notre Dame, Indiana:
       Fides Publishers, 1966.

0661   PIKE, FREDERICK B. "Discussing the Issues, II: Spiritual and
       Secular Forces in Latin America." In Religious, Revolution
       and Reform: New Forces for Change in Latin America, edited
       by William V. D'Antonio, pp. 227-265. New York: Praeger,
       1964.

0662   _____. "The Catholic Church and Modernization in Peru and
       Chile." Journal of International Affairs 20 (1966):
       272-288.

0663   PIN, EMILE. Elementos para una sociología del catolicismo
       latinoamericano. Bogotá: Oficiana Internacional de
       Investigaciones Sociales de FERES, 1963. 120 pp.

0664   PINAY, MAURICE. The Plot Against the Church. Los Angeles:
       St. Anthony Press, 1967. 110 pp.

0665   PIRONIO, EDUARDO. La ayuda del personal exterior a la iglesia
       latinoamericano, 1969. 34 pp.

0666   _____. "Reflexiones en torno a la reconciliación." In Con-
       flicto social y compromiso cristiano en América Latina,
       edited by Consejo Episcopal Latinoamericano, pp. 47-65.
       Bogotá: Consejo Episcopal Latinoamericano, 1976.

Catholic Church and Social Change

0667   POBLETE, RENATO. "Algunas consideraciones acerca del con-
       flicto social en América Latina." In Conflicto social y
       compromiso cristiano en América Latina, edited by Consejo
       Episcopal Latinoamericano, pp. 47-65. Bogotá: Consejo
       Episcopal Latinoamericano, 1976.

0668   _____. "Aspectos sociológicos de la religiosidad popular."
       Catequesis Latinoamericana 1 (May/June, 1969):   3-17.

0669   _____. "La Iglesia y la integración latinoamericana."   In
       La Iglesia y la integración andina, edited by Seminario de
       la Iglesia y el Proceso de Integración Andina, pp. 57-66.
       Bogotá: Secretariado General del Consejo Episcopal Latino-
       americano, 1976.

0670   _____. "The Religious Action of the Church in the New Latin
       America." Catholic Messenger 82 (January 30, 1964):   8.

0671   _____. "Vocations in a Social Revolution." Catholic Mind 64
       (January, 1968):   36-41.

0672   POLLINGER, KENNETH J. "On Thinking in Latin America." America
       113 (August 28, 1965):   214-21.

0673   Pontificium Consilium pro America Latina. Consiglio General.
       Colaboración intraeclesial: documentos. Bogotá: Consejo
       Episcopal Latinoamericano, 1976.   132 pp.

0674   POPE PAUL VI. "Address to the Faithful About Economic and
       Social Changes in Latin America." La Documentation Catho-
       lique 71 (December 1, 1974):   1002-1003.

0674A _____. "Presencia de la Iglesia en el desarrollo y la inte-
       gración de América Latina." Mensaje 15 (December, 1966):
       708-710.

0675   "O primeiro relatório do grupo misto de trabalho entre a
       Igreja Católica e o conselho ecumênico das ingrajas."
       Revista Eclesiástica Brasileira 26 (1966):   441-447.

0676   "¿Qué es el proyecto MISUR?" Carta de ISAL 2 (May, 1969):
       3-4.

0677   "15 obispos hablen en pro del tercer mundo." SIC 300
       (December, 1967):   501.

0678   QUINN, WILLIAM. "The Church in Latin America." American
       Benedictine Review 15 (June, 1964):   206-214.

Catholic Church and Social Change

0679   RAHNER, KARL. "Christianity and Ideology." Concilium 6
        (May, 1965): 41-58.

0680   "Reappraising Aid to Latin America." Herder Correspondence
        4 (June, 1967): 178-179.

0681   "Revolutionary Cardinal." Newsweek, August 26, 1963, p. 69.

0682   REYES MATTA, FERNANDO. Hélder Câmara: universidad y revo-
        lución. Santiago, Chile: Ediciones Nueva Universidad,
        1969. 108 pp.

0683   ROGEL, ISAAC, ed. Documentos sobre la realidad de la Iglesia
        en América Latina, 1968-1969. Cuernavaca, México: Centro
        Intercultural de Documentación, 1970. 266 pp.

0684   ROPER, CHRISTOPHER. "The Revolutionary Church in Latin
        America." New Blackfriars 52 (June, 1971): 245-249.

0685   ROSSI, JUAN JOSÉ. ¿Cambia la Iglesia? Reflexión y perspec-
        tivas pastorales para nuestro tiempo. Buenos Aires:
        Ediciones Búsqueda, 1965. 148 pp.

0686   ROUQUETTE, ROBERT. "Father Arrupe on Social Justice." Month
        37 (May, 1967): 226-270.

0687   RUIZ GARCÍA, SAMUEL. "The Latin American Church Since
        Medellin: Expectations and Accomplishments." In Con-
        scientization for Liberation, edited by Louis M. Colonnese,
        pp. 81-92. Washington, D.C.: Division for Latin America,
        United States Catholic Conference, 1971.

0688   _____. "The Quest for Justice as Latin Americans Live It."
        IDOC-International 53 (May, 1973): 46-52.

0689   RUIZ-TAGLE, JAIME. "¿División en la Iglesia Católica? El
        caso de los miristas prófugos." Mensaje 245 (December,
        1975): 543-546.

0690   Sacerdotes para el tercer mundo: historia, documentos,
        reflexión. Buenos Aires: Editorial del Movimento, 1970.
        160 pp.

0691   Sacerdotes para el Tercer Mundo. Sacerdotes para el tercer
        mundo. Buenos Aires: Publicaciones del Movimiento
        Sacerdotes para el Tercer Mundo, 1970. 158 pp.

Catholic Church and Social Change

0692   SACHERI, CARLOS A. La Iglesia clandestina. Buenos Aires:
        Ediciones Cruzamante, 1970. 158 pp.

0693   SANDERS, THOMAS. "The Church in Latin America." Mind 68
        (June, 1970): 31-43.

0694   SANTA ANA, JULIO DE. "Reflexiones sobre el sentido de la
        acción cristiana en América Latina." Cristianismo y
        Sociedad, January 4, 1963.

0694A   SANTOS, JOHN. "Personal Values." In Integration of Man and
        Society in Latin America, edited by Samuel Shapiro, pp. 3-
        11. Notre Dame, Indiana: University of Notre Dame, 1967.

0695   SAVAGE, F. "Latin America, Our Neighbor: Social Problems
        and Solutions." Catholic Charities Review 48 (December,
        1964): 19-22.

0696   SCANNONE, JUAN CARLOS. "Hacia una dialéctica de la liberación."
        Stromata 27 (January/March, 1971): 23-60.

0697   _____. "La Iglesia y los derechos humanos en América Latina:
        la teología en perspectiva latinoamericana, sus intenciones,
        sus corrientes, sus aportes." Actualidad Pastoral 100-101
        (1976): 176-177.

0698   SCHUMACHER, JOHN. "The 'Third World' and the Self-Understand-
        ing of the Twentieth Century Church." Concilium 67 (1971):
        102-111.

0699   SCHUTZ, ROGER. "Latin America: Testing Ground of Ecumenism."
        Catholic World 197 (April, 1963): 28-35.

0700   SEGUNDO, R. "The Future of Christianity in Latin America."
        Cross Currents 13 (Summer, 1963): 273-281.

0701   SELONG, GABRIEL. "The Church in Latin America." Commonweal
        77 (January 11, 1963): 413.

0702   Seminario de la Iglesia y el Proceso de Integración Andina.
        La Iglesia y la integración andina. Bogotá: Secretariado
        General del Consejo Episcopal Latinoamericano, 1976.
        256 pp.

0703   SETIÉN, JOSÉ MARÍA. La Iglesia y lo social ¿intromisión o
        mandato? Madrid: Guadarrama, 1963. 325 pp.

0704   Shaping a New World: An Orientation to Latin America. Mary-
        knoll, New York: Orbis Books, [n.d.]. 319 pp., bibl.

Catholic Church and Social Change

0705 SHAPIRO, SAMUEL, ed. Integration of Man and Society in Latin America. Notre Dame, Indiana: Univeristy of Notre Dame, 1968.

0706 NO ENTRY

0707 SHAULL, RICHARD. "A Theological Perspective on Human Liberation." In Cultural Factors in Inter-American Relations, edited by Samuel Shapiro, pp. 3-15. Notre Dame, Indiana: University of Notre Dame, 1968.

0708 _____. "La forma de la Iglesia en la nueva diáspora." Cristianismo y Sociedad 2 (1964): 3-17.

0709 SHEREFF, R. "Latin Bishops Eye Social Issues: First Time Since Slavery Days." National Catholic Reporter 4 (September 18, 1968): 1.

0710 Simposio sobre Teología de la Liberación. Liberación: opción de la Iglesia latinoamericana en la década del 70. Bogotá: Editorial Presencia, 1970. 111 pp.

0711 SMITH, B. H. "Religion and Social Change: Classical Theories and New Formulations in the Context of Recent Developments in Latin America." Latin American Research Review 10 (Summer, 1975): 3-34.

0712 SMITH, EARL M. "Latin American Revolution: It Has Brought Catholics and Protestants Together on Behalf of Oppressed and Dispossessed." Christian Century 86 (May 14, 1969): 674-677.

0713 SMITH, ROBERT FREEMAN. "Social Revolucion in Latin America: The Role of the United States Policy." International Affairs 41 (October, 1965): 637-649.

0714 "Social Reform in Latin America." Tablet 219 (December 4, 1965): 1367-1368.

0715 "Society and Church in Latin America." IDOC-International 1 (April 4, 1970): 37-38.

0716 SORGE, BARTOLOMÉ. "¿Está superado el concepto tradicional de doctrina social de la Iglesia?" Criterio 41 (June 27, 1968): 414-420.

Catholic Church and Social Change

0717   SUENENS, LEON JOSEF. "Latin America and the Universal Church."
        In Integration of Man and Society in Latin America, edited
        by Samuel Shapiro, pp. 317-352. Notre Dame, Indiana:
        University of Notre Dame, 1967.

0718   TALBOT, J. F. "Latin America's Own Work Corps: 180,000
        Religious." America 124 (April 3, 1971): 343-344.

0719   Las tareas de la Iglesia en América Latina: aspectos teológicos
        y sociológicos. Friburg, Switzerland: FERES, 1964. 87 pp.

0720   TORRES CALVO, ANGEL, ed. Diccionario de textos sociales
        pontificos. Madrid: Compañía Bibliográfica Española, 1956.
        1172 pp., bibl.

0721   TORRES RESTREPO, CAMILO. Camilo Torres, 1956-1966. Cuernavaca,
        México: Centro Intercultural de Documentación, 1966. 377
        pp.

0722   _____. "Encruzilhadas da Igreja na América Latina." Paz e
        Terra 6 (1968): 117-137.

0723   _____. La revolución: imperativo cristiano. Bogotá: Edici-
        ones del Caribe, 1965. 58 pp., bibl.

0724   _____. "Mensaje a los cristianos." Frente Unido 1 (August 24,
        1965): 3.

0725   _____. Revolutionary Priest: The Complete Writings and
        Messages of Camilo Torres. New York: Random House, 1971.
        460 pp.

0726   TURNER, FREDERICK C. Catholicism and Political Development
        in Latin America. Chapel Hill: University of North
        Carolina Press, 1971. 272 pp., bibl.

0727   _____. "Roman Catholic Church." In Latin American Scholarship
        Since World War II: Trends in History, Political Science,
        Literature, Geography, and Economics, edited by Roberto
        Esquenazi-Mayo and Michael C. Mayer, pp. 173-184. Lincoln,
        Nebraska: University of Nebraska Press, 1971.

0728   "Uso y abuso de la doctrina social de la Iglesia." Criterio
        38 (September 23, 1965): 683-687.

0729   VALDA PALMA, ROBERTO. Obispos "rojos" de Latinoamérica.
        Madrid: Propaganda Popular Católica, 1971. 157 pp.

Catholic Church and Social Change

0730   VALLIER, IVAN. Catholicism, Social Control and Modernization
        in Latin America. Santa Cruz: University of California
        Press, 1970. 172 pp., bibl.

0731   _____. "Las elites religiosas en América Latina: catolicismo,
        liderazgo y cambio social." In Elites y desarrollo en
        América Latina, edited by Seymour M. Lipset and Aldo Solari,
        pp. 150-189. Buenos Aires: Paidos, 1967.

0732   _____. "Religious Elites in Latin America: Catholicism,
        Leadership and Social Change." América Latina 8 (October/
        December, 1965): 93-115.

0733   VEGA, GUILLERMO, and BETANCOURT, OCTAVIO. Brillante camino.
        Medellín: Editorial Impresos Jiménez, 1970. 208 pp.

0734   VEKEMANS, ROGER. "La reforma social o la reforma de las
        reformas." Mensaje 123 (October, 1963): 505-513.

0735   VICHUVAIB, ALEX. "El obispo do los pobres: entrevista de
        monseñor Leonidas E. Proaño." Certeza 15 (October/December,
        1975): 119-121.

0736   VIGIL, GABRIEL. "El contexto social de la autoridad de la
        Iglesia." Christus 41 (September, 1976): 23.

0737   VILLALAZ, M. "La fe en la biblia." Catequesis Latinoamericana
        1 (May/June, 1969): 35-50.

0738   VILLEGAS-MATHIEU, BELTRAN. "En torno al concepto de signos
        de los tiempos." Teología y Vida 17 (1976): 289-299.

0739   VIOLA, R. "Las grandes tensiones de la catequesis latino-
        americana." Catequesis Latinoamericana 3 (April/June,
        1971): 171-181.

0740   VITALIS, HELLMUT GNADT. The Significance of Changes in Latin
        American Catholicism Since Chimbote, 1953. Cuernavaca,
        México: Centro Intercultural de Documentación, 1969.

0741   WANDELL, R. "Problems of the Church in Latin America."
        Social Justice 56 (June, 1963): 76-80.

0742   WARD, BARBARA. "Haves and Have-Nots: The Spiritual Factor."
        In The Religious Dimension in the New Latin America, edited
        by John J. Considine, pp. 3-18. Notre Dame, Indiana: Fides
        Publishers, 1966.

Catholic Church and State

0743   WYSSENBACH, JEAN PIERRE. "La Biblia de Puebla." SIC 403
        (March, 1978): 113-116.

0744   ZAFFARONI, JUAN CARLOS. Sacerdocio y revolución en América
        Latina. Buenos Aires: Editora América Latina, 1968.
        128 pp.

0745   ZAÑARTU, MARIO. Desarrollo, económica y moral católica.
        Cuernavaca, México: Centro Intercultural de Documentación,
        1969.

0746   _____. "La pastoral: su contenidio y reacciones." Mensaje
        11 (November, 1962): 534-538.

0747   _____. "Religión y desarrollo." Mensaje 123 (October, 1963):
        645-651.

0748   _____. "Religious Values in Latin America: An Appraisal."
        In The Religious Dimension in the New Latin America, edited
        by John J. Considine, pp. 19-42. Notre Dame, Indiana:
        Fides Publishers, 1966.

CATHOLIC CHURCH AND STATE

0749   ALFONZO RAVARD, FRANCISCO. Los católicos frente a la cuestión
        social. Caracas: Artes Gráficas, 1943. 134 pp., bibl.

0750   ALLAZ, TOMÁS G. ¿Hambre o revolución? La Iglesia contra la
        pared. México: Editora Nuestro Tiempo, 1971. 244 pp.

0751   ASSMANN, HUGO. "Medellín: a desilusão que nos amadure ceu."
        Cadernos do Ceas 38 (July/August, 1975): 51-57.

0752   _____. Opresión-liberación: desafío a los cristianos.
        Montevideo: Tierra Nueva, 1971. 208 pp.

0753   BARASH, MEYER. "The Role of Traditional Religion in a Develop-
        ing Nation." Archives de Sociologie des Religions 12
        (January/June, 1967): 37-40.

0754   BARNADAS, JOSEP. "Christian Faith and the Colonial Situation
        in Latin America." In Power and the Word of God, edited by
        Frank Bockle and Jacques-Marie Pohier, pp. 129-138. New
        York: Herder and Herder, 1973.

0755   BERRYMAN, PHILLIP E. "Popular Catholicism in Latin America."
        Cross Currents 21 (Summer, 1971): 284-301.

Catholic Church and State

0756   BIGO, PIERRE. "La Deuxième Conférence Générale de l'Épiscopat
        Latin-Américain a Medellín." Études 329 (December, 1968):
        748-754.

0757   BORRAT, HÉCTOR. "La revolución de mensaje." Cristianismo y
        Sociedad 3 (1965): 26-36.

0758   _____, and BUNTIG, ALDO. El imperio y las iglesias. Buenos
        Aires: Guadalupe, 1973. 115 pp.

0759   BROCKMAN, JAMES R. "A Chronicle of Persecution." America
        135 (September 25, 1976): 167-169.

0760   BRUNEAU, THOMAS C. "Power and Influence: Analysis of the
        Church in Latin America and the Case of Brazil." Latin
        American Research Review 8 (Summer, 1973): 25-51.

0761   CARROLL, THOMAS F. "Land Reform as an Explosive Force in
        Latin America." In Explosive Forces in Latin America,
        edited by J. J. TePaske and S. N. Fisher, pp. 81-125.
        Athens, Ohio: Ohio University Press, 1964.

0762   "Church and State in Latin America." Ave Maria 104 (September
        17, 1966): 6.

0763   "Church and State in Latin America: Remarks of Bishop Méndez
        Arceo." Tablet 218 (February 1, 1964): 140.

0764   "The Church Embattled." Economist 228 (August 24, 1968):   23.

0765   "Church-State Conflicts in Latin America." Our Sunday Visitor
        63 (April 27, 1975): 4.

0766   COMBLIN, JOSEPH. "La Iglesia y el sistema de la seguridad
        nacional." In Conflicto social y compromiso cristiano en
        América Latina, edited by Consejo Episcopal Latinoamericano,
        pp. 62-86. Bogotá: Consejo Episcopal Latinoamericano,
        1976.

0767   CONCATTI, ROLANDO. Sacerdotes para el Tercer Mundo: nuestra
        reflección: carta a los obispos argentinos, versión
        definitiva en torno a la declaración de la comisión perma-
        nente del episcopado argentino del día 12 de agosto de 1970.
        Buenos Aires: [n.p.], 1970. 94 pp., bibl.

Catholic Church and State

0768   Confederación Latinoamericana de Religiosos. "Fe y política."
        Vida religiosa y situación socio-política en América Latina:
        grandes problemas socio-políticos de América Latina, edited
        by Confederación Latinoamericana de Religiosos, pp. 8-14.
        Bogotá: Indo-American Press Service, 1972.

0769   Consulta Latinoamericana de Iglesia y Sociedad, 2d. América
        hoy: acción de Dios y responsabilidad del hombre.
        Montevideo: Iglesia y Sociedad en América Latina, 1966.
        132 pp.

0770   "Cristianos perseguidos en nuestra América: documentos."
        SIC 378 (1975): 340-344, 377-384.

0771   "Cross and Sword in Latin America." Christianity Today 14
        (December 5, 1969): 26-27.

0772   CUSHING, R. "The Church in Latin America." Marist Missions
        19 (January/February, 1963): 14-16.

0773   DUSSEL, ENRIQUE D. "Church-State Relations in Peripheral
        Latin American Formations." The Ecumenical Review 29
        (January, 1977): 28-38.

0774   FONSECA, JAIME. "Latin America: A Challenge to Catholics."
        Worldmission 11 (September, 1960): 15-31.

0775   GOMEZ, LINO. "Iglesia y Estado en la historia de Latino-
        américa." Medellín 9 (March, 1977): 44-54.

0776   GREINACHER, NORBERT. "A Community Free of Rule." Concilium
        63 (1971): 87-107.

0777   HILLEKAMPS, KARL HEINZ. Religion, Kirche und Stadt in Latein-
        amerika. Munich: Kösel, 1966. 185 pp.

0778   HOUTART, FRANÇOIS. "Les éffets du changement social sur la
        religion catholique en Amérique Latine." Archives de
        Sociologie des Religions 6 (July/December, 1961): 63-73.

0779   _____. "The Latin American Church and the Development of
        Socio-Religious Research." Concilium 9 (October, 1965):
        159-164.

0780   "Kerk en Staat in Latinjns-Amerika." Alternatief 18 (May/June,
        1977): 13-20.

Catholic Church and State

0781   LAVRETSKII, IOSIF RAMUAL'DOVICH. Kolonizatori ukhodiat-
        missionery ostaiutsia. Moscow: Izdatel'stvo Akademii
        Nauk SSSR, 1963. 162 pp.

0782   MADARIAGA, SALVADOR DE. Latin America Between the Eagle and
        the Bear. New York: Praeger, 1962. 192 pp.

0783   MELADY, T. P. "Church, State, and Schools in Guyana."
        America 135 (August 7, 1976): 49-50.

0784   "Mensaje fraterno a los religiosos y a las religiosas de
        América Latina." Christus 1 (February, 1976): 58-60.

0785   MORÃO, A. "Algunas reflexões sobre a função religiosa."
        Brotéria 86 (1968): 853-858.

0786   MUTCHLER, DAVID E. The Church as a Political Factor in Latin
        America. New York: Praeger, 1971. 461 pp., bibl.

0787   OLIVEIRA, PLINIO CORREA DE. A liberdade da Igreja no estado
        comunista: a Igreja, o decálogo e o direito de propriedade.
        São Paulo: Editora Vera Cruz, 1965. 44 pp.

0788   PIKE, FREDERICK B. The Conflict Between Church and State in
        Latin America. New York: Knopf, 1964. 240 pp.

0789   PROAÑO, LUIS E. Iglesia, política y libertad religiosa.
        Quito: Editorial Ecuatoriana, 1968. 167 pp., bibl.

0790   "Religious Freedom in Latin America." America 135 (February 7,
        1976): 84.

0791   "Religious Persecution." America 135 (September 4, 1976): 88.

0792   "The Role of Priests in a World of Revolution." Concilium
        42 (1969): 116-134.

0793   RUÍZ GARCÍA, SAMUEL. Los cristianos y la justicia en América
        Latina. Lima: Centro de Documentación del MIEC-JECI,
        1972. 27 pp.

0794   RYCROFT, W. STANLEY. "The Protestant Churches and Religious
        Freedom in Latin America." A Journal of Church and State
        8 (Spring, 1966): 264-273.

0795   SEGUNDO, JUAN LUIS. "Christianity and Violence in Latin
        America." Christianity and Crisis 28 (March 4, 1968):
        31-34.

0796   Seminario sobre Comunidad Educativa en América Latina. *Educación liberadora: dimensión sociológica.* Buenos Aires: Ediciones Búsqueda, 1973. 108 pp.

0797   TURNER, FREDERICK C. "Catholicism and Nationalism in Latin America." *American Behavioral Scientist* 17 (July, 1974): 845–864.

0798   VALLIER, IVAN. *Catholicism, Social Control and Modernization in Latin America.* Englewood Cliffs, New Jersey: Prentice-Hall, 1970. 172 pp.

0799   VEKEMANS, ROGER. *Doctrina, ideología y política.* Santiago, Chile: DESAL/CELAP, 1970. 101 pp.

0800   VIDALES, RAÚL. *La Iglesia latinoamericana y la política después de Medellín.* Bogotá: Ediciones Paulinas, 1972. 170 pp., bibl.

0801   WESTHUES, KENNETH. "Curses Versus Blows: Tactics in Church-State Conflict." *Sociological Analysis* 36 (Spring, 1975): 1–16.

0802   WILLIAMS, EDWARD J. "The Emergence of the Secular Nation-State and Latin American Catholicism." *Comparative Politics* 5 (January, 1973): 261–277.

CATHOLIC CLERGY

0803   "Acción y no palabras: mensaje cristiano para el mundo de hoy." *Mensaje* 159 (June, 1967): 204–208.

0804   AIZCORBE, ROBERTO. "La nueva iglesia de los pobres." *Primera Plana* 4 (October 11–17, 1966): 34–35.

0805   ARROYO, GONZALO. "Católicos de izquierda en América Latina." *Mensaje* 191 (August, 1970): 369–372.

0806   _____. "Represión a la Iglesia latinoamericana: las purgas armadas y la CIA." *Contacto* 12 (October, 1975): 19–27.

0807   BECKMAN, JOSEPH F. "The Priesthood of the Future in Latin America." *Saint Anthony* 82 (May, 1975): 20–25.

0808   BENHAM, J. "New Rebels: Clerics in Latin America." *U.S. News and World Report*, December 14, 1970, pp. 92–95.

Catholic Clergy

0809   BOUCHARD, PAUL. "La religión en América Latina." Revista de
       las Indias 21 (January/March, 1961): 151-157.

0810   BULNES ALDUNATE, JUAN. Sacerdocios y dominación. Cuernavaca,
       México: Centro Intercultural de Documentación, 1971.

0811   BUNTING, A. "Modelados del catolicismo popular." Catequesis
       Latinoamericana 1 (May/June, 1969): 57-74.

0812   "Carta de los sacerdotes latinoamericanos al Sínodo de Obispos."
       Víspera 24-25 (December, 1971): 125-130.

0813   CASTILLO, ALFONSO. "Rasgos del sacerdote latinoamericano."
       Christus 39 (May, 1974): 5-8.

0814   CASTRO PALLARES, SALVADOR. "El sacerdote ante las ideologías
       actuales." Servir 36 (December, 1971): 651-663.

0815   "Catholic Mission Council Praises Latin Bishops." Our Sunday
       Visitor 66 (August 21, 1977): 2.

0816   "Colaboración con el Departamento de Ecumenismo del CELAM."
       Catequesis Latinoamericana 1 (May/June, 1969): 153-155.

0817   Conferencia dos Religiosos do Brasil. Vida religiosa y
       desarrollo latinoamericano. Bogotá: Secretariado General
       de la CLAR, 1969. 57 pp.

0818   Consejo Episcopal Latinoamericano. Directorio para el
       ministerio pastoral de los obispos. Bogotá: Secretariado
       General del Consejo Episcopal Latinoamericano, 1975. 182 pp.

0819   _____. "El ministerio de los sacerdotes en la Iglesia toda
       ella ministerial." Búsqueda 3 (1975): 61-66.

0820   _____. "Teologia e situazione del sacerdozio nell'America
       Latina." Il Regno 231 (1971): 496-504.

0821   "Continent of the Godfathers." Month 6 (October, 1973): 323-
       324.

0822   COULTER, C. "Saving South America: Volunteer Priests."
       Priest 20 (April, 1974): 338-343.

0823   Encuentro Continental de Misiones en América Latina, 1st. La
       Pastoral de América Latina: documento final. Bogotá:
       Consejo Episcopal Latinoamericano, Departamento de Misiones,
       1968. 46 pp.

Catholic Clergy

0824   Encuentro de Escrituristas de América Latina, 1st. Exégesis,
        evangelización y pastoral: primer Encuentro de Escrituristas
        de América Latina. Bogotá: Consejo Episcopal Latinoameri-
        cano, Secretariado General del Consejo Episcopal Latino-
        americano, 1976. 106 pp.

0825   Encuentro sobre Teología y Pastoral de los Ministerios,
        Cumbayá, Ecuador, 1974. Ministerios eclesiales en América
        Latina: reflexión teológico-pastoral. Bogotá: Consejo
        Episcopal Latinoamericano, Secretariado General, 1976.
        223 pp.

0826   ¿Entiendes el mensaje? Charles sobre el sentido y contenido
        de la Biblia, para entenderla y compartirla. Bogotá:
        Ediciones Paulinas, 1976. 119 pp.

0827   FRAGOSO, ANTONIO. "The Bishop's Part in Development." Con-
        cilium 71 (1972): 106-111.

0828   GAETE, ARTURO. "Catolicismo social marxismo en la primera
        mitad del Siglo XX: aún no es posible el diálogo."
        Mensaje 215 (December, 1972): 706-716.

0829   GALILEA, SEGUNDO. "Para un concepto de 'Misiones' en América
        Latina." In Antropología y evangelización: un problema
        de Iglesia en América Latina, edited by Consejo Episcopal
        Latinoamericano, pp. 35-47. Bogotá: Indo-American Press
        Service, 1972.

0830   COLAN, CARLOS. "¿Quiénes son los curas del Tercer Mundo?"
        Cristina 917 (November, 1971): 38-39.

0831   GONZÁLEZ-RUIZ, JOSÉ MARÍA. "The Political Meaning of Jesus in
        the Christian Community's Political Commitment." Concilium
        4 (1973): 31-38.

0832   GOULET, G. "Congrès des Supérieurs des Séminaires Latino-
        Américains." Relations 22 (July, 1962): 194-195.

0833   GUTIÉRREZ, GUSTAVO MERINO. Líneas pastorales en América
        Latina. Lima: Consejo Episcopal Peruano, 1976. 75 pp.

0834   HICKS, FREDERIC. "Politics, Power, and the Role of the Village
        Priest in Paraguay." Journal of Inter-American Studies and
        World Affairs 9 (April, 1967): 273-282.

0835   HOFFMAN, RONAN. "United Front Is Latin America Bishops Pro-
        gram." Shield 39 (March, 1960): 4-5.

Catholic Clergy

0836   HOORNAERT, EDUARDO. "A Igreja, a Europa e a América Latina."
       Revista Eclesiástica Brasileira 24 (1964): 352-358.

0837   Igreja na América Latina: desenvolvimento e intergração:
       assembleia extraordinária de CELAM em Mar del Plata, 11 a
       16 de Outubro de 1966. Petrópolis, Brazil: Editora Vozes
       1966. 263 pp.

0838   "Informe: obispos de la patria grande." Víspera 2 (July,
       1968): 52-100.

0839   Instituto de Estudios Políticos. Cristianos por el socialismo:
       ¿Consecuencia cristiana o alienación política? Santiago,
       Chile: Pacífico, 1972. 438 pp.

0840   JIMÉNEZ CADENA, GUSTAVO. Sacerdote y cambio social. Bogotá:
       Ediciones Tercer Mundo, 1967. 296 pp.

0841   _____. The Role of the Rural Parish Priest as an Agent of
       Social Change in Central Colombia. Madison: University
       of Wisconsin, 1965. 235 pp.

0842   NO ENTRY

0843   KLOPPENBURG, BOAVENTURA. "El contexto histórico de la actual
       situación en la Iglesia." Catequesis Latinoamericana 1
       (July/September, 1969): 15-20.

0844   "Kongress der Lateinamerikanischen Bischofskonferenz, III."
       Herder Korrespondence 13 (January, 1959): 180-182.

0845   KUEHNELT-LEDDIHN, ERIK MARIA RITTER VON. "Catholics in Latin
       America." Commonweal 74 (June 23, 1961): 322-325.

0846   LERNOUX, PENNY. "Priests for the People: Latin America's
       Insurgent Church." Nation 222 (May 22, 1976): 612-613,
       618-625.

0847   "Letter from the Latin American Bishops." Catholic Mind 65
       (May, 1967): 8-10.

0848   "Lucha de clases y evangelio." NADOC 265 (August 16, 1971):
       1-4.

0849   MAC EOIN, GARY. Catholic Leaders Defend Latin American
       Guerrillas. New York: Universal Press Syndicate, 1968.
       2 pp.

Catholic Clergy

0850 _____. "Los misioneros americanos víctimas de la C.I.A."
Contacto 12 (1976): 53-66.

0851 MAGNET, ALEJANDRO. El Padre Hurtado. Santiago, Chile:
Editorial del Pacífico, 1954. 366 pp.

0852 MARTINA, GIACOMO. "The Contribution of Liberalism and Socialism to a Better Self-Conception of the Church." Concilium
67 (1971): 93-101.

0853 MAZA, ENRIQUE. "Obispos, sacerdotes, Iglesia divididos."
Christus 37 (March, 1972): 5-7.

0854 MEJÍA, JORGE. "Integration of Priests." In Integration of
Man and Society in Latin America, edited by Consejo Epis-
copal Latinoamericano, pp. 149-159. Notre Dame, Indiana:
University of Notre Dame, 1967.

0855 MEJIDO, MANUEL, and FERREIRA, ANGEL T. Pablo VI en Latinoamérica: reportaje de la visita de Su Santidad a Colombia
y el texto íntegro de Sus alocuciones. México: Francisco
Casas Peris, 1969. 140 pp..

0856 "Movimentos sacerdotaís da América Latina." Brotéria 38
(July/August, 1975): 46-50.

0857 Movimientos Sacerdotales de América Latina. "Resúmen de los
apuntes del encuentro de dirigentes." Tierra Nueva 4
(1975): 12-16.

0858 "Objetivos de la evangelización." Catequesis Latinoamericana
3 (January/March, 1971): 14-17.

0859 ORRUPE, PEDRO. "El sacerdote y la política." In Liberación:
opción de la Iglesia latinoamericana en la década del 70,
edited by Simposio sobre Teología de la Liberación, pp. 63-
71. Bogotá: Editorial Presencia, 1970.

0860 OSSA, MANUEL. "El sacerdote en el mundo de hoy." Teología y
Vida 4 (October/December, 1966): 269-282.

0861 PÉREZ, JAVIER. "Cuba, Paraguay, Uruguay y la Iglesia."
Actualidad Pastoral 4 (June, 1971): 123-126.

0862 PIRONIO, EDUARDO. "Priests and Religious for Latin America."
In Proceedings and Conclusions of the First Inter-American
Conference of Major Superiors: Mexico City, February 8-12,
1971. Washington, D.C.: United States Catholic Conference,
Division for Latin America, 1971.

Catholic Clergy

0863   POBLETE, R. "Aspectos sociológicos de la religiosidad
        popular." Catequesis Latinoamericana 1 (May/June, 1969):
        3-17.

0863A   POPE JOHN XXIII. "Importance, Responsibility of Bishops'
        Program." Acta Apostolicae Sedis 50 (December, 1958):
        997-1005.

0864   "Priest Corps." Commonweal 81 (February 19, 1965):   652.

0865   "O primeiro relatório do grupo misto de trabalho entre a
        Igreja católica oe conselho ecumênico das igrejas."
        Revista Eclesiástica Brasileira 26 (1966):   441-447.

0866   PROMPER, WERNER. Priesternot in Lateinamerika. Löwen,
        Belgium: Latein-Amerika-Kolleg der katholischen Universtät,
        1965. 317 pp.

0867   ROCA, BLAS. "La lucha ideológico contra las sectas religiosas."
        Cuba Socialista 3 (June, 1963):   28-41.

0868   RODRÍGUEZ ARIAS BUSTAMENTE, LINO, ed. La democracia cristiana
        y América Latina: testimonios de una posición revolucio-
        naria. Lima: Editorial Universitaria, 1961. 170 pp.

0869   SABATTÉ, A. Crisis sacerdotal en América Latina: análisis y
        reflección sobre la encuesta CELAM. Buenos Aires: Edi-
        torial Guadalupe, 1974. 150 pp.

0870   Sacerdotes para el Tercer Mundo. Sacerdotes para el Tercer
        Mundo: historia, documentos, reflexión. Buenos Aires:
        Editorial del Movimiento, 1970. 160 pp.

0871   SELONG, GABRIEL. "The Church in Latin America." Commonweal
        77 (January 11, 1963): 413.

0872   SHAULL, RICHARD. "La forma de la Iglesia en la nueva dispora."
        Cristianismo y Sociedad 6 (1964):   3-17.

0873   "Spanische Priesterhilfe für Lateinamerika." Herder-Korres-
        pondence 17 (May, 1963): 360-361.

0874   TAMAYO, FRANCISCO E. Crisis sacerdotal en América Latina.
        Salamanca: Ediciones Sígueme, 1967. 184 pp.

0875   "Upsurge in Latin America." America 111 (September 26, 1964):
        343-344.

Christian Democracy

0876   VICHUVAIB, ALEX. "El obispo de los pobres: entrevista de
Monsignor Leonidas E. Proaño." Certeza 15 (October/December, 1975): 119-121.

0877   VIOLA, R. "Las grandes tensiones de la catequesis latinoamericana." Catequesis Latinoamericana 3 (April/June,
1971): 171-181.

0878   YODER, HOWARD W. "The Second Latin American Evangelical
Conference." International Review of Missions 51 (January,
1962): 75-78.

CHRISTIAN DEMOCRACY

0879   El ABC de la democracia cristiana. Lima: Editora Universitaria, 1960. 20 pp.

0880   BOERSNER, DEMETRIO. América Latina y el socialismo democrático.
San José, Costa Rica: Centro de Estudios Democráticos de
América Latina, 1970. 81 pp.

0881   CALDERA RODRÍGUEZ, RAFAEL. Christian Democracy and Social
Reality. Notre Dame, Indiana: Fides, 1965.

0882   _____. Christliche Demokratie: Eine Modelle für Lateinamerika
und... Mainz: Hase und Koehler, 1976.

0883   _____. Democracia cristiana y desarrollo. Caracas: Instituto
de Formación Demócrata Cristiana, 1964. 99 pp.

0884   _____. "Democratic Revolutions: Growth of Christian Democracy." Commonweal 83 (October 29, 1965): 120-124.

0885   _____. El bloque latinoamericano. Santiago, Chile: Editorial
del Pacífico, 1961. 128. pp.

0886   _____. Ideario: la democracia cristiana en América Latina.
Barcelona: Ediciones Aries, 1970. 308 pp.

0887   _____. Latin America: Crucial Test for Christian Civilization.
New York: Center for Christian Democratic Action, 1963.
23 pp.

0888   _____. "The Christian Democrat Idea." America 107 (April 7,
1962): 12-15.

0889   NO ENTRY

Christian Democracy

0890   CASTILLO VELASCO, JAIME. Las fuentes de la democracia
        cristiana. Santiago, Chile: Editorial del Pacífico, 1963.
        103 pp., bibl.

0891   "The Christian Democrats of South America." Catholic Digest
        30 (November, 1965): 69-71.

0892   Congresos Internacionales Demócrata-Cristianos. Santiago,
        Chile: Editorial del Pacífico, 1957. 402 pp.

0893   CÓRDOVA, EFRÉN. "El neosindicalismo cristiano en América
        Latina: CLASC." Revista de Ciencias Sociales 12 (June,
        1968): 255-295.

0894   CORVALAN, SALOMÓN G., and CRUZ, LUCIANO. "Las nacionalizaciones
        y la democracia cristiana." El Siglo 24 (July 7, 1964):
        2.

0895   CULHANE, EUGENE K. "Congress in Caracas." America 107
        (June 9, 1962): 370.

0896   D'ANTONIO, WILLIAM V. "Democracy and Religion in Latin
        America." In Religion, Revolution, and Reform: New Forces
        for Change in Latin America, edited by William V. D'Antonio,
        pp. 243-265. New York: Praeger, 1964.

0897   DECAMILLI, JOSÉ LEOPOLDO. La democracia cristiana ante el
        futuro de Hispanoamérica. Berlin: Círculo Cultural
        Germano Iberoamericano, 1968. 196 pp.

0898   DE KADT, EMANUEL. "Paternalism and Populism: Catholicism in
        Latin America." Journal of Contemporary History 2
        (October, 1967): 89-106.

0899   "La democracia cristiana de Italia analiza la situación
        política de América Latina." El Día, January 7, 1965.

0900   Las democracias cristianas: análisis crítico. Montevideo.
        Uruguay: Sandino, 1968. 190 pp.

0901   EGGERS LAN, CONRADO. Bases para un humanismo revolucionario.
        Buenos Aires: Movimiento Humanista Renovador de Filosofía
        y Letras, 1961. 17 pp.

0902   "Encuentro internacional de Cristianos por el Socialismo."
        Contacto 12 (June, 1975): 48-55.

0903   "An Exuberant Eruption: Group of Latin American Christian
        Democrats in England." Tablet 217 (October 19, 1963): 1124.

0904   FREI MONTALVA, EDUARDO. "Christian Democracy in Latin America."
       Tablet 218 (September 5, 1964): 993-994.

0904A   _____. "Paternalism, Pluralism, and Christian Democratic
       Reform Movements in Latin America." In Religion, Revolu-
       tion, and Reform: New Forces for Change in Latin America,
       edited by William V. D'Antonio, pp. 27-40. New York:
       Praeger, 1964.

0905   GILLY, ADOLFO. "El programa de la democracia cristiana."
       Marcha 26 (September 4, 1964): 16-22.

0906   HUBNER GALLO, JORGE IVAN. Los católicos en la política.
       Santiago, Chile: Zig-Zag, 1959. 107 pp.

0907   "Informe: la DC ante su crisis." Víspera 3 (July, 1969):
       39-80.

0908   JAGUARIBE, HELIO. L'Amérique Latine aujourd'hui et demain:
       politique, développment, révolution, socialisme.
       Cuernavaca, México: [n.p.], 1967. 17 pp.

0909   JARAMILLO, FRANCISO DE PAULA. "La democracia cristiana,
       esperanza de América Latina?" La Nueva Prensa 117 (June
       16, 1964): 48.

0910   Latin America: Crucial Test for Christian Civilization. New
       York: Center for Christian Democratic Action, 1963. 23 pp.

0911   "Latin America Patchwork." Herder Correspondence 5 (January,
       1968): 21-23.

0912   LEGOV, MIGUEL E. "Sinn und Bedeutung der Christlichen
       Mission." Stimmen der Zeit 191 (January, 1973): 62-66.

0913   MC CORMACK, ARTHUR. "Christian Democracy in Latin America."
       Month 33 (May, 1965): 302-310.

0914   MARCHANT, R. "Christian Democracy in Latin America." Social
       Order 11 (June, 1961): 251-258.

0915   MASPERO, EMILIO. "Latin America's Labor Movement of Christian
       Democratic Orientation as an Instrument of Social Change."
       In Religion, Revolution, and Reform: New Forces for Change
       in Latin America, edited by William V. D'Antonio, pp. 163-
       181. New York: Praeger, 1964.

Christian Democracy

0916   MENA, ISMAEL. "Christian Democracy: The Right Solution to
Under-development?" Linacre Quarterly 32 (February, 1965):
33-37.

0917   MIGUEL, BENJAMIN. Democracia Cristiana. La Paz: Talleres
Gráficos de Colegio Don Bono, 1966. 326 pp., bibl.

0918   MOLINA, MANUEL HELIODORO. "Christian Democrats Answer
Charges." Foreign Radio Broadcasts, February 6, 1963,
pp. 1-16.

0919   NO ENTRY

0920   NATALE, REMOLDI. América Latina hoy: esquemas populares
demócratas cristianos. Caracas: Editorial Nuevo Orden,
1964. 111 pp.

0921   "New Political Force." Time, June 2, 1961, p. 28.

0922   OLIVEIRA, PLINIO CORREA DE. A liberdade da Igreja no estado
comunista: A Igreja, o decálogo e o direito de propriedade.
São Paulo: Editora Vera Cruz, 1965. 44 pp.

0923   O'SHAUGHNESSY, HUGH. "Christian Democracy in Latin America."
Catholic Mind 61 (December, 1963): 25-28.

0924   Partido Social Demócrata Cristiano. Declaración de principios.
Bogotá: Editorial Kelly, 1966. 40 pp.

0925   PETRAS, JAMES. Chilean Christian Democracy: Politics and
Social Forces. Berkeley: University of California,
Institute of International Studies, 1967. 61 pp.

0926   REAL DE AZUA, CARLOS. Las democracias cristianas. Montevideo:
Sandina, 1968. 190 pp.

0927   RODRÍGUEZ-ARIAS BUSTAMENTE, LINO. La democracia cristiana y
América Latina: testimonios de una posición revolucionaria.
Lima: Editorial Universitaria, 1961. 170 pp.

0928   SEMENOY, SERGEI IVANOVICH. Khristianskaia Demokratiia i
Revoliutsionnyi Protsess v Latinsko Amerike. Moscow:
Nauka, 1971. 301 pp.

0929   SHAULL, RICHARD. The Church and Revolutionary Change:
Contrasting Perspectives. New York: Office of Student
World Relations, 1966. 13 pp.

0930   SIGMUND, PAUL E.   "Latin American Catholicism's Opening to
        the Left." The Review of Politics 35 (January, 1973):
        61-76.

0931   SZULC, TAD. "Communists, Socialists, and Christian Democrats."
        Annals of the American Academy of Political and Social
        Science 360 (July, 1965): 99-109.

0932   TOMIC ROMERO, DRAGOMIR. Unidad y diversidad de la democracia
        cristiana en el mundo. Santiago, Chile: Imprenta del
        Pacífico, 1962. 32 pp.

0933   WILLIAMS, EDWARD J. "Christian Politics: The Significance
        for Latin America." Duquesne Review 14: 65-83.

0934   _____. Latin American Christian Democratic Parties.
        Knoxville, Tennessee: University of Tennessee Press, 1967.
        305 pp.

COMMUNISM

0935   ANDRONOVA, V. P. "Revoliutsiia Monsen'orov?" Latinskaia
        Amerika. Akademia Nauk SSR, Institut Latinskoi Ameriki 2
        (March/April, 1971): 76-91.

0936   ARÉVALO, JUAN JOSÉ. Anti-Communism in Latin America. New
        York: Lyle Stuart, 1963. 224 pp.

0937   _____. Anticomunismo en América Latina: radiografía del
        proceso hacia una nueva colonización. Buenos Aires:
        Palestra, 1959. 194 pp.

0938   BAEZ CAMARGO, GONZALO. El comunismo, el cristianismo y los
        cristianos. México: Casa Unida de Publicaciones, 1960.
        101 pp.

0939   BARROS, JAIME. "Repudio nacional: fuegos comunistas contra
        la Iglesia." Flecha Roja 2 (June 26, 1964): 5.

0940   BURKS, DAVID D. Survey of the Alliance for Progress: In-
        surgency in Latin America. Washington, D.C.: Government
        Printing Office, 1968. 29 pp.

0941   CARDOSO, JOAQUÍN. El comunismo y la conspiración contra el
        orden cristiano. México: Editorial Buena Prensa, 1950.
        512 pp.

Communism

0942   CARRIZO, EULOGIO D. ¿Puede un católico ser un anticomunista? Buenos Aires: [n.p.], 1964. 15 pp.

0943   CASTILLO VELASCO, JAIME. El problema comunista. Santiago, Chile: Editorial del Pacífico, 1955. 218 pp.

0944   _____. "La comunista: una táctica burda." Flecha Roja 2 (June 5, 1964): 8.

0945   CERUTI CORSA, PEDRO. Catolicismo y comunismo. Montevideo: Ediciones Unidad, 1938. 73 pp.

0946   The Christian Challenge in Latin America: A Symposium. Maryknoll, New York: Maryknoll Publications, 1964. 86 pp.

0947   CLEMENT, MARCEL. Comunismo versis Dios. Santiago, Chile: Editorial Pomaire, 1962. 258 pp.

0948   CLINCH, MINTY. "Catholic and Communist in South America." New Society, December 3, 1970, pp. 995-998.

0949   "Close-Up on Latin America." Worldmission 16 (Summer, 1965): 17.

0950   "Communist or Christian: Excerpts." Tablet 220 (October 29, 1966): 1229.

0951   "Communist Threat to Latin America." Shield 43 (October/November, 1963): 11-13.

0952   Consejo Episcopal Latinoamericano. "América Latina y el comunismo: declaración del . . . reunido en Bogotá." Mensaje 15 (January 2, 1960): 55-56.

0953   NO ENTRY

0954   DAMBORIENCA, P. "Protestantismo e comunismo nell'America Latina." Civilita Católica 57 (February 18, 1956): 382-396.

0955   "Divide and Conquer." America 105 (July 15, 1961): 517.

0956   DOMINGO, PEDRO V. "Activistas de nota en América Latina." Estudios Sobre el Comunismo 6 (January/March, 1958): 87-91.

0957   DONOVAN, JOHN. Red Machete: Communist Infiltration in the Americas. Indianapolis: Bobbs-Merrill, 1962. 310 pp., bibl.

0958   ELIZALDE, ENRIQUE C. Naciones de comunismo para católicos.
       Buenos Aires: Editorial Poblete, 1961. 141 pp.

0959   Encuentro "Cristianismo e Ideologías en América Latina a la
       Luz de la Octogésima Adveniens." Cristianismo e ideologías
       en América Latina a la luz de la "Octogésima adveniens."
       Bogotá: Secretariado General de Consejo Episcopal Latino-
       americano, 1974. 115 pp.

0960   FERLA, SALVADOR. Cristianismo y marxismo. Buenos Aires:
       Peña Lillo, 1970. 359 pp.

0961   GAETE, ARTURO. "Socialismo y comunismo: historia de una
       problemática condenación." Mensaje 200 (July, 1971):
       290-302.

0962   GORBEA, JOSÉ. "El 'impacto' de la pastoral." Mensaje 11
       (November, 1962): 520-521.

0963   HOOK, SIDNEY. Poder político y libertad personal: estudios
       críticos sobre la democracia, el comunismo y los derechos
       civiles. Mexico: UTEHA, 1968. 512 pp.

0964   Infiltración comunista en la Iglesia católica. México:
       Instituto de Investigaciones Sociales Económicas, 1966:
       12 pp.

0965   "Interview with Dom Hélder Câmara." IDOC-International 54
       (Summer, 1973): 15-19.

0966   LAUERHASS, LUDWIG. Communism in Latin America: A Biblio-
       graphy. Los Angeles: Center of Latin American Studies,
       University of California, 1962. 78 pp.

0967   MAC LAURIN, DÁMASO. "Instrumentos de penetración comunista
       en América: institutos culturales." Estudios sobre el
       Comunismo 4 (April/June, 1956): 87-90.

0968   MEINVIELLE, JULIO. El comunismo en la revolución anti-
       cristiana. Buenos Aires: Ediciones Theoris, 1964. 155 pp.

0969   MILLAS, ORLANDO. Los comunistas, los católicos y libertad.
       Santiago, Chile: Editorial Austral, 1964. 215 pp.

0970   NOONAN, DANIEL P. "For the Sick Giant: New Hope." World-
       mission 14 (Winter, 1963/1964): 38-42.

Communism

0971   NÚÑEZ, DAVID. Los invasores: la Iglesia católica infiltrada
       por velados enemigos. Buenos Aires: [n.p.], 1969. 25 pp.

0971A OLIVEIRA, PLINIO CORREA DE. The Freedom of the Church in the
       Communist State: The Church, the Decalogue and the Right
       of Ownership. São Paulo: Boa Imprensa, 1964. 28 pp.

0972   PELYPENKO, ALEJO. Infiltración comunista en las iglesias
       cristianas de América. Buenos Aires: Edition of the
       Author, 1961. 233 pp.

0973   PFLAUM, IRVING PETER. Arena of Decision: Latin America in
       Crisis. Englewood Cliffs, New Jersey: Prentice-Hall,
       1964. 334 pp., bibl.

0974   POPPINO, ROLLIE E. International Communism in Latin America:
       A History of the Movement, 1917-1963. New York: The
       Free Press of Glencoe, 1964. 247 pp., bibl.

0975   RAY, PHILIP ALEXANDER. South Wind Red: Our Hemispheric
       Crisis. Chicago: Regnery, 1962. 242 pp. bibl.

0976   ROBLEDO, J. MANUEL. Religión o comunismo. México: Editora
       Justicia, 1969. 48 pp.

0977   ROSS, STANLEY. Communism in Latin America. New York: New
       Background, 1947. 44 pp.

0978   ROSSELL Y ARELLANO, MARIANO. "A Pastoral Letter on Catholic
       Social Justice and Struggle Against Communism." In Con-
       flict Between Church and State in Latin America, edited
       by Frederick B. Pike, pp. 175-182. New York: Knopf, 1964.

0979   SABLE, MARTIN H., comp. Communism in Latin America: An
       International Bibliography, 1900-1945, 1960-1967. Los
       Angeles: University of California, Latin American Center,
       1968. 220 pp.

0980   Testimonio, R. Hacia las fuentes del comunismo. Florida,
       Argentina: Ediciones Paulinas, 1962. 133 pp.

0981   VELA MONSALVE, CARLOS. Tácticas y directivas contra la farsa
       comunista. Quito: Editora Colón, 1962. 145 pp., bibl.

DOCUMENTS

0982   "A propos de la situatión en Amérique Latine: solidaires
        d'une telle Eglise: déclaration d'évêques français." La
        Documentation Catholique 74 (March 20, 1977): 259-260.

0983   ABALOS, DAVID. "The Medellin Conference." Cross Currents 19
        (Spring, 1968): 113-132.

0984   ABBOT, WALTER. The Documents of Vatican II. London: Guild
        Press, 1966. 792 pp.

0985   Acción Católica Mexicana. "México: la acción católica se
        preocupa de las responsibilidades políticas de los cris-
        tianos." Informaciones Católicas Internacionales 234
        (February 22, 1967): 11.

0986   "Asamblea del Departamento de Ecumenismo del CELAM, Bogotá.
        19 al 23 de enero de 1970." Catequesis Latinoamericana 2
        (July/September, 1970): 409-412.

0987   AVILA P., RAFAEL. Elementos para una evangelización liberadora.
        Salamanca: Sígueme, 1971. 160 pp.

0988   _____. La liberación. Bogotá: Voluntad, 1971. 187 pp.

0989   Bishops' Commission for Social Action, Lima. Between Honesty
        and Hope: Documents from and about the Church in Latin
        America. Maryknoll, New York: Maryknoll Publications,
        1970. 247 pp.

0990   CAFFERRATA, C. "Declaration, 22nd May, 1969." IDOC-Inter-
        national 1 (April 4, 1970): 49-50.

0991   CASTER, M. VAN. "Latin America: International Catechetical
        Week, Medellin, August 11-17, 1968." Lumen Vitae 24
        (March, 1969): 142-146.

0992   CAVALLI, FIORELLO. "Documenti pontificé per la regresa
        religiosa dell' America Latina." La Civilat Cattolica 3
        (1965): 248-256.

0993   Centro Intercultural de Documentación. El 'entredicho' del
        CIDOC: índice de algunos documentos. Cuernavaca, México:
        Centro Intercultural de Documentación, 1969. 64 pp.

0994   "Chronicle." Worldmission 21 (Fall, 1970): 30-32.

Documents

0995   "The Church and Its Mission Among the Indians of Latin America:
        The Asuncion Statement." Worldmission 23 (Winter, 1973/
        1973): 26-29.

0996   COMBLIN, JOSEPH. "Notas sobre el documento básico para la II
        Conferencia General del CELAM." Cuadernos de Marcha 17
        (September, 1968): 47-57.

0997   Comisión Episcopal de Acción Social. Signos de renovación:
        recopilación de documentos post-conciliares de la Iglesia
        en América Latina. Lima: Editorial Universitaria, 1969.
        282 pp.

0998   COMPARATO, FABIO KONDER. "A miséria na América Latina:
        fatalidad ou pecado? Aos padres conciliares de Vaticano
        II." Paz e Terra 1 (August, 1967): 27-41.

0999   Confederación Latinoamericana de Sindicatos Cristianos.
        "Carta abierta de trabajordores latinoamericanos al Papa
        Paulo VI, abogado de los pueblos pobres, en su tercera
        visita a América Latin." Mensaje 17 (September, 1968):
        434-440.

1000   Conferencia Episcopal Cubana. "El desarrollo y la conciencia
        cubana." Criterio 42 (July 6, 1969): 412-414.

1001   Conferencia Evangélica Latinoamericana, 3d. "Conclusiones."
        Criterio 42 (September 25, 1969): 659-663.

1002   Conferencia General del Episcopado Latinoamericano, 2d. The
        Church in the Present-Day Transformation of Latin America
        in the Light of the Council. Bogotá: General Secretariat
        of Consejo Episcopal Latinoamericano, 1970. 2 v.

1003   _____. Conclusões de Medellín: II Conferência Geral do
        Epsicopado Latino-Americano. Porto Alegre: Secretariado
        Regional Sul 3 da C.N.B.B., 1968. 111 pp.

1004   _____. Documento final. Medellín: Imesco, 1968. 246 pp.

1005   _____. Documentos de Medellín. San José: Costa Rica:
        Editora Metropolitano, 1969. 99 pp.

1006   _____. La Iglesia en la actual transformación de América
        Latina a la luz del Concilio. Bogotá: Consejo Episcopal
        Latinoamericano, Secretariado General, 1970. 284 pp.

1007 Consejo Episcopal Latinoamericano. Departamento de Acción
      Social, Salvador, Brasil. Presencia activa de la Iglesia
      en el desarrollo y en la integración de América Latina.
      Bogotá: Ediciones Paulinas, 1967. 48 pp.

1008 _____. "La Iglesia en la actual transformación en América
      Latina a la luz del Concilio Vaticano II." Criterio 41
      (October 24, 1968): 757-804.

1009 _____. "Pobreza de la Iglesia." Mensaje 17 (October, 1968):
      522-524.

1010 _____. "Presencia activa de la Iglesia en el desarrollo y en
      la integración de América Latina." CIAS 167 (October,
      1967): 21-35.

1011 _____. Responsibilidad y posición de la Iglesia ante la labor
      presente y la evolución real y jurídica de las instituciones
      panamericanas. Bogotá: Editora Pío X, 1958. 55 pp.

1012 "Declaration Issued by the Group of Priests for the Third
      World, 1st-3rd March, 1969." IDOC-International 1 (April
      4, 1970): 42-45.

1013 DOMERGUE, RAYMOND. "Por una presencia de la conciencia
      cristiana en la búsqueda socialista." Documentación 4
      (February, 1971): 10-16.

1014 EAGLESON, JOHN. Christians for Socialism: Documentation of
      the Christians for Socialism Movement in Latin America.
      Maryknoll, New York: Orbis Books, 1975. 246 pp.

1015 "Encuentro internacional de cristianos por el socialismo."
      Contacto 12 (June, 1975): 48-55.

1016 Episcopado Argentino. "La Iglesia en el período post-
      conciliar." Criterio 39 (June 9, 1966): 417-421.

1017 Episcopado Colombiano. "Reforma agraria: declaración del...."
      Mensaje 9 (December, 1960): 554-557.

1018 Episcopado Paraguayo. Las exigencias de la doctrina social
      cristiana ante el insuficiente desarrollo del país.
      Asunción: Conferencia Episcopal Paraguaya, 1963. 32 pp.

1019 FABRES RIVAS, JULIO. América Latina: ¿Colapso de un mensaje
      o integración social? Santiago, Chile: Zig-Zag, 1964.
      92 pp.

Documents

1020   "First Latin American Encounter of Christians for Socialism."
        IDOC-International 48 (November, 1972):   53-58.

1021   GALILEA, SEGUNDO, ed. Documentos sobre la pastoral, 1965-
        1967. Cuernavaca, México: Centro Intercultural de Docu-
        mentación, 1968. 456 pp.

1022   "The Golconda Declaration." Catholic Mind 68 (March, 1970):
        48-53.

1023   La Iglesia en América Latina: testimonios y documentos, 1969-
        1973. Navarra: Verbo Divino, 1975. 650 pp.

1024   "Una iglesia vitalmente incorporada en el actual contexto
        social: exhortación del episcopado cubano a los sacerdotes,
        religiosos, religiosas y fieles." Mensaje Iberoamericano
        115 (1975): 9.

1025   Iglesia y la comunidad política: documentos colectivos de
        los episcopados católicos de todo el mundo, 1965-1975.
        Madrid: Biblioteca de Autores Cristianos, 1975. 759 pp.,
        bibl.

1026   ILLICH, IVAN D. "Mgr. Illich's Letter to Cardinal Seper."
        Herder Correspondence 6 (April, 1969): 115-117.

1027   "Informe del Departamento de Catequesis del CELAM, November
        20, 1969-March 15, 1971." Catequesis Latinoamericana 3
        (April/June, 1971): 259-266.

1028   Instituto Latino Americano de Doctrina y Estudios Sociales.
        Documentos sociales de la Iglesia: síntesis cronológica e
        índices analíticos. Santiago, Chile: Ilades, 1976. 53 pp.

1029   Instituto para el Desarrollo Económico y Social. Desarrollo
        y promoción del hombre. Caracas: Ediciones Arte, 1965.
        298 pp.

1030   "Die Lateinamerikanische Kirche in der Stunde des Konzils."
        Herder-Korrespondence 17 (January, 1963): 167-169.

1031   "Latin America: International Catechetics Week in Medellin,
        August 11-17, 1968." Lumen Vitae 24 (June, 1969): 343-347.

1032   "Latin American Panel: Aspects of the Church's Life Discussed
        at the 20th National CSMC Convention." Shield 42 (March,
        1963): 6-7.

1033   "Letter to the Synod." IDOC-International 38 (December 25, 1971): 2-14.

1034   LÓPEZ TRUJILLO, ALFONSO. "Declaración del Secretariado General del CELAM." CELAM 108 (August, 1976): 7.

1035   _____. "El compromiso político del sacerdote." Tierra Nueva 4 (1975): 17-53.

1036   "Manifiesto de Obispos del Tercer Mundo." Cristianismo y Revolución 6-7 (April, 1968): 42-46.

1037   "La misión de la Universidad Católica en América Latina: resultado del seminario de Buga, Colombia (12-18 de febrero de 1967)." Mensaje 16 (August, 1967): 385-391.

1038   Notiziario della Pontificia Commissione per L'America Latina. Tercera sesión del consejo general de la Comisión Pontificia para América Latina. Rome: [n.p.], 1966. 22 pp.

1039   "Los obispos de América Latina hacen examen de conciencia." Revista Javeriana 349 (October, 1968).

1040   "Los obispos se lavan las manos." Cristianism y Revolución 15 (May, 1969): 6.

1041   "Options and Strategies." IDOC-International 51 (March, 1973): 21-37.

1042   "The Pope in Latin America." The Pope Speaks 13 (Winter, 1968): 229-260.

1043   POPE JOHN XXIII. "Importance, Responsibility of Bishops' Program." Acta Apostolicae Sedis 50 (December, 1958): 997-1005.

1044   POPE PAUL VI. "Address at the Conclusion of the 15th Assembly of the Latin American Episcopal Council." Acta Apostolicae Sedis 66 (November 30, 1974): 640-643.

1045   _____. "Letter to the Bishops Attending the Meeting of CELAM (the Latin American Bishops' Council) in Mar del Plata, Argentina: The Church Should Contribute to the Solution of the Grave Contemporary Problems with the Resources that are Proper to It." Tablet 220 (October 22, 1966): 1196.

1046   QUEVEDO, A.; QUINN, R.; and POZO, L. "Conclusiones sobre los institutos del CELAM." Catequesis Latinoamericana 3 (January/March, 1971): 111-112.

Documents

1047   "Reunión de la Comisión Episcopal de CLAF: Colombia."
       Catequesis Latinoamericana 3 (October/December, 1971):
       106-111.

1048   "Reunión nacional de delegados diocesanos de catequesis del
       Perú, Lima (October 27-30, 1970)." Catequesis Latino-
       americana 3 (October/December, 1971): 99-102.

1049   ROGEL, ISAAC. Documentos sobre la realidad de la Iglesia en
       América Latina, 1968-1969. Cuernavaca, México: Centro
       Intercultural de Documentación, 1970. 278 pp.

1050   Sacerdotes Latinoamericanos. "El documento de los sacerdotes
       latinoamericanos contra la violencia, la de los poderosos."
       OIGA 287 (August 23, 1968): 31-36.

1051   "Sacerdotes para el Tercer Mundo." Cristianismo y Revolución
       19 (August, 1969): 16-17.

1052   Sacerdotes para el Tercer Mundo. "Documento del V Encuentro
       Nacional 19 de Octubre de 1972." Pasos 25 (October 30,
       1972): 10.

1053   _____. "La hora de la acción: compromiso de Navidad."
       Cristianismo y Revolución 12 (March, 1968): 16-17.

1054   "II consulta latinoamericana de la Iglesia y sociedad."
       Cristianismo y Sociedad 3-4: 83-102.

1055   Signos de liberación: testimonios de la Iglesia en América
       Latina, 1969-1973. Lima: Centro de Estudios y Publica-
       ciones, 1973. 294 pp.

1056   "A Statement Issued by the Inter-American Bishops' Conference."
       Catholic Mind 68 (May, 1970): 62-64.

1057   VELÁZQUEZ, H. "El documento episcopal sobre fe y política."
       Christus 39 (April, 1974): 13-14.

ECONOMIC DEVELOPMENT

1058   ADAMS, RICHARD N. The Second Sowing: Power and Secondary
       Development in Latin America. San Francisco: Chandler
       Publishing Co., 1967. 288 pp., bibl.

1059   ALVES, RUBEM. "Apuntes para un programa de reconstrucción en
       la teología." Cristianismo y Sociedad 7 (1969): 21-31.

Economic Development

1060 ANDER-EGG, EZEQUIEL. <u>Acerca de la revolución de América</u>
<u>Latina</u>. Córdoba, Argentina: Centro de Estudios Políticos,
1970. 80 pp.

1061 ANDERSON, CHARLES W. <u>Politics and Economic Change in Latin</u>
<u>America</u>. Princeton, New Jersey: Van Nostrand, 1967.
388 pp.

1062 "Aspectos prioritarios de la contribución de la Iglesia para
el desarrollo e integración de América Latina." <u>CIAS</u> 174
(July, 1968): 50-52.

1063 "Ayuda internacional, ¿Mito o realidad?" <u>Reportaje-DESAL</u> 2
July/December, 1969): 5-8.

1064 BASAURE AVILA, LUZ. "Efectos mútuos del desarrollo y de la
religión en América Latina." <u>América Latina</u> 3 (July/
September, 1968): 97-104.

1065 BETANCUR, BELISARIO. "Cristo del desarrollo." <u>Revista</u>
<u>Javeriana</u> 348 (September, 1968): 301-306.

1066 CALVEZ, JEAN-YVES. "El cristiano frente al desarrollo."
<u>Mensaje</u> 115 (December, 1962): 708-717.

1067 CÂMARA, HÉLDER. "A igreja nas Américas: suas possibilidades,
seus deveres, sua missão." <u>Vozes</u> 7 (July, 1968): 590-594.

1068 _____. "La América Latina y la opción de la no-violencia."
<u>Comunidad</u>, October, 1973, pp. 567-575.

1069 "CELAP: Seeking an Overall Solution." <u>Reportaje-DESAL</u> 1
(1967): 6.

1070 Centro para el Desarrollo Económico y Social de América
Latina. "Tipología socio-económica latinoamericana."
<u>Mensaje</u> 123 (October, 1963): 557-577.

1071 CHONCHOL, JACQUES. "Reforma agraria en América Latina."
<u>Cuadernos Latinoamericanos de economía humana</u> 6 (1963):
139-171.

1072 CLAPS, GERALDO. "El cristiano frente a la revolución violenta."
<u>Mensaje</u> 115 (December, 1962): 708-717.

1073 Consejo Episcopal Latinoamericano. "Presencia activa de la
Iglesia en el desarrollo y en la integración de América
Latina." <u>CIAS</u> 167 (October, 1967): 21-35.

Economic Development

1074 _____. Presencia activa de la Iglesia en el desarrollo y en
       integración de América Latina. Bogotá: Consejo Episcopal
       Latinoamericano, 1967.

1075 _____. "Reflexión teológica sobre el desarrollo (conclusiones
       de Itopoan)." CIAS 174 (1968): 29-57.

1076 CÓRDOVA, EFRÉN. "El neosindicalismo cristiano en la América
       Latina: CLASC." Caribbean Studies 12 (June, 1968): 255-
       295.

1077 COTTIER, GEORGES. "Why Communism Appeals to Developing
       Countries." Concilium 3 (February, 1965): 76-87.

1077A COWLEY B., PERCIVAL. El humanismo de los padres de la
       Iglesia. Santiago, Chile: Instituto Chileno de Estudios
       Humanísticos, 1976. 266 pp.

1078 DANCZYK, FRANCIS. "Banking Human Dignity." Worldmission 17
       (Fall, 1966): 12-14.

1079 DANILIEVICH, MARIA, and KONDRATIEVA, ADELINA. "El movimiento
       obrero en América Latina." Historia y Sociedad 7 (Fall,
       1966): 45-68.

1080 "Declaración del CELAM sobre la Iglesia y la integración de
       América Latina." In La Iglesia y la integración andina,
       edited by Seminario de la Iglesia y el Proceso de Integra-
       ción Andina, pp. 128-129. Bogotá: Secretariado General
       del Consejo Episcopal Latinoamericano, 1976.

1081 DELMAS, GLADYS. "Latin Labor's Alarming Christians." The
       Reporter 32 (February 25, 1965): 27-30.

1082 DESROCHE, HENRI CHARLES. "Religion et developpement: le
       theme de Leurs rapports reciproques it ses variations.
       Archives de Sociologie de Religions 6 (July/December, 1961):
       3-34.

1083 "Documentos del primer congreso del movimiento 'Sacerdotes
       para el Pueblo.'" Pasos 41 (December 3, 1973): 1-6.

1084 FALS BORDA, ORLANDO. Subversion and Development: The Case
       of Latin America. Geneva: Europe Third World Center Under
       Auspices of the Foyer John Knox Association, 1970. 17 pp.

1085 FRAGOSO, ANTONIO. "The Bishop's Part in Development."
       Concilium 71 (1972): 106-111.

1086   FRANK, ANDRE GUNDER. Latin America: Underdevelopment or
        Revolution. New York: Monthly Review Press, 1970. 409
        pp., bibl.

1087   GUTIÉRREZ, GUSTAVO MERINO. "Liberation and Development."
        Cross Currents 21 (Summer, 1971): 243-256.

1088   HAHN, J. "The Quit Revolution: Fr. Beausoleil Establishes
        Credit Unions." Maryknoll 57 (November, 1963): 2-7.

1089   HOUTART, FRANÇOIS, and VETRANO, VICENTE O. Hacia una teología
        del desarrollo. Buenos Aires: Editorial Latinoamericana,
        1967. 126 pp.

1090   IGLESIAS, ENRIQUE V. "Money, Markets, and Power." IDOC-
        International 53 (May, 1973): 37-39.

1091   LARRAÍN ERRÁZURIZ, MANUEL. Desarrollo, éxisto o fracaso en
        América Latina: llamado de un obispo a los cristianos.
        Santiago, Chile: Editorial Universidad Católica, 1965.
        46 pp.

1092   MAC EOIN, GARY. "Latin America: Who is to Blame?" Common-
        weal 94 (June 25, 1975): 331-336.

1093   MC GRATH, MARK G. "Development for Peace." America 118
        (April 27, 1968): 562-567.

1094   _____. "Los fundamentos teológicos de la presencia de la
        Iglesia en el desarrollo socio-económico de América Latina."
        Víspera 1 (May, 1967): 30-37.

1095   _____. "The Church's Socio-Economic Role in Latin America."
        American Ecclesiastical Review 158 (January, 1968): 1-18.

1096   MARTÍNEZ, HORACIO. "Iglesia y desarrollo integral según el
        magisterio de Pablo VI." Revista Javeriana 428 (September,
        1976): 51-62.

1097   MASSARD A., CARLOS, and HOFFMAN L., RODOLFO. "La integración
        económica de América Latina." Mensaje 123 (October, 1963):
        584-588.

1098   MEDINA ECHAVARRÍA, JOSÉ. "Teoría del cambio de estructuras."
        Mensaje 123 (October, 1963): 497-504.

1099   MÉNDEZ ARCEO, SERGIO. "Desacralización para el desarrollo."
        In La Iglesia, el subdesarrollo y la revolución, edited by
        Bernardo Castro Villagrana, pp. 239-247. México: Editorial
        Nuestro Tiempo, 1968.

Economic Development

1100   "Mensaje de la X Asamblea Ordinaria del CELAM sobre integración
latinoamericana." In <u>La Iglesia y la integración andina</u>,
edited by Seminario de la Iglesia y el Proceso de Integración Andina, pp. 130–132. Bogotá: Secretariado General
del Consejo Episcopal Latinoamericano, 1976.

1101   MOLINA, SERGIO. "La reforma fiscal." <u>Mensaje</u> 123 (October,
1963): 533–544.

1102   MOLTMANN, JÜRGEN. "¿Esperanza sin fe?: en torno a un
humanismo escatológico sin Dios." <u>Concilium</u> 16 (May, 1966):
25–40.

1103   MOYANO LLERENA, CARLOS. "Los supuestos económicos de
Medellín." <u>Criterio</u> 42 (August 28, 1969): 562–569.

1104   MUNÁRRIZ, MIKEL. "Capitalismo internacional e Iglesia Latinoamericana: resignación o liberación." <u>SIC</u> 403 (March,
1978): 107–110.

1105   Notiziario de la Pontificia Commissione per L'America Latina.
<u>Tercera sesión del consejo general de la comisión ponti-</u>
<u>ficia para América Latina</u>. Rome: [n.p.], 1966. 22 pp.

1106   PELLEGRINI, VICENTE. "La teología del desarrollo." <u>CIAS</u> 16
(October, 1976): 7–10.

1107   _____. "¿Mercado común latinoamericano?" <u>Mensaje</u> 9 (September, 1960): 368–372.

1108   NO ENTRY

1109   PÉREZ MORALES, R. OVIDIO. "Fe y desarrollo." Caracas:
Ediciones Paulinas, 1971. 59 pp.

1110   _____. "Teología del desarrollo." In <u>La Iglesia: Sacramento</u>
<u>de unificación universal</u>, edited by Ovidio R. Pérez
Morales. Salamanca: Sígueme, 1971.

1111   PETRAS, JAMES. <u>Latin America: From Dependence to Revolution</u>.
New York: John Wiley and Sons, 1973. 274 pp., bibl.

1112   PIÑOL, JOSEP MARIA. <u>Iglesia y liberación en América Latina:</u>
<u>diálogos con la vanguardia católica latinoamericana</u>.
Madrid: Marova, 1972. 269 pp.

Economic Development

1113 POBLETE, RENATO. "La Iglesia y la integración latinoamericana."
      In La Iglesia y la integración andina, edited by Seminario
      de la Iglesia y el Proceso de Integración Andina, pp 57-
      66. Bogotá: Secretariado General del Consejo Episcopal
      Latinoamericano, 1976.

1114 "Presencia activa de la Iglesia en el desarrollo y en la
      integración de América Latina." CIAS 15 (October, 1967):
      21-35.

1115 "¿Qué es el proyecto MISUR?" Carta de ISAL 2 (May, 1969):
      3-4.

1116 "Reflexión teológica sobre el desarrollo." CIAS 174 (July,
      1968): 33-37.

1117 RUÍZ GARCÍA, ENRIQUE. El Tercer Mundo. Madrid: Alianza
      Editorial, 1967. 281 pp.

1118 SCHIFFELBEIN, ERNESTO. "Estructura democrática de la plani-
      ficación." Mensaje 123 (October, 1963): 607-617.

1119 SEGUNDO, JUAN LUIS. "Desarrollo y subdesarrollo: polos
      teológicos." Perspectivas de Diálogo 43 (May, 1970): 76-
      80.

1120 Seminario de la Iglesia y el Proceso de Integración Andina.
      La Iglesia y la integración andina. Bogotá: Secretariado
      General del Consejo Episcopal Latinoamericano, 1976. 256
      pp.

1121 SHAULL, RICHARD. "National Development and Social Revolution."
      Christianity and Crisis 29 (February 3, 1969): 9-12.

1122 STANGANA, B., ed. Le tiers monde: L'occident et l'Eglise.
      Paris: Editions du Cerf, 1967. 327 pp.

1123 TOMIC ROMERO, DRAGOMIR. Sobre el sistema interamericano.
      Santiago, Chile: Editorial del Pacífico, 1963. 59 pp.

1124 TORRES RESTREPO, CAMILO. La revolución: imperativo cristiano.
      Bogotá: Ediciones del Caribe, 1965. 58 pp., bibl.

1125 VALLIER, IVAN. "Church Development in Latin America: A Five-
      Country Comparison." The Journal of Developing Areas 1
      (July, 1967): 461-476.

Economic Development

1126   VEKEMANS, ROGER. "Economic Development, Social Change, and Cultural Mutation in Latin America." In Religion, Revolution and Reform: New Forces for Change in Latin America, edited by William V. D'Antonio, pp. 131-142. New York: Praeger, 1964.

1127   _____. "La reforma y el ethos cultural." Mensaje 123 (October, 1963): 637-644.

1128   _____, and VENEGAS, R. Marginalidad, integración, promoción popular latinoamericano. Santiago, Chile: Centro para el Desarrollo Económico y Social de América Latina, 1970. 84 pp.

1129   VELIZ, CLAUDIO, ed. Obstacles to Change in Latin America. London: Oxford University Press, 1965. 263 pp.

1130   VENEGAS CARRASCO, RAMÓN. "Organizaciones de base y cuerpos intermedios." Mensaje 123 (October, 1963): 627-636.

1131   _____. "The Problems of Economic and Social Development in Latin America: Policy to Obtain a New Order." World Justice 5 (Summer, 1963): 55-77.

1132   ZAÑARTU, MARIO. Desarrollo económico y moral católica. Cuernavaca, México: Centro Intercultural de Documentación, 1969.

1133   _____. "Economía y cristianismo." Mensaje 134 (November, 1964): 567-573.

1134   _____. "La tarea común del cambio económico en América Latina." Mensaje 15 (October, 1966): 591-599.

EDUCATION

1134A   Alternatives in Education. Cuernavaca, México: Centro Intercultural de Documentación, 1972.

1134B   BETANCUR MEJÍA, GABRIEL. "La reforma de la educación." Mensaje 123 (October, 1963): 572-582.

1134C   Bishops of Latin America. "Catholic Universities in Latin America." Catholic Mind 66 (April, 1968): 19-30.

1134D   Consejo Episcopal Latinoamericano. Juventud y cristianismo en América Latina. Bogotá: Indo-American Press Service, 1969. 54 pp.

1134E DELOBELLE, ANDRE. Die katholische Universität in Lateinamerika. Cuernavaca, México: Centro Intercultural de
Documentación, 1968. 98 pp.

1134F DÍAZ CASANOVA, MÁXIMO. Religiosidad y actitudes ante el
cambio social de los universitarios latinoamericanos en
Madrid. Cuernavaca, México: Centro Intercultural de
Documentación, 1969.

1134G ILLICH, IVAN D. The Dawn of Epimethean Man and Other Essays.
Cuernavaca, México: Centro Intercultural de Documentación,
1970.

1134H KING, MARTIN LUTHER. "El tiempo de la justicia y de la
rebelión." Cristianismo y Sociedad 2 (1964): 18-30.

1134I MAC LAURIN, DÁMASO. "Instrumentos de penetración comunista
en América: institutos culturales." Estudios sobre el
comunismo 4 (April/June, 1956): 87-90.

1134J REIMER, EVERETT. An Essay on Alternatives in Education.
Cuernavaca, México: Centro Intercultural de Documentación,
1976.

HUMANISM

1135 ALFARO JIMÉNEZ, JUAN. Hacia una teología del progreso humano.
Barcelona: Editorial Herder, 1969. 117 pp., bibl.

1136 ALVES, RUBEM. A Theology of Human Hope. Washington, D.C.:
Corpus Books, 1969. 199 pp.

1137 _____. "La muerte de la Iglesia y el futuro del hombre."
Cristianismo y Sociedad 5 (1964): 3-20.

1138 _____. Religión: opio o instrumento de liberación?
Montevideo: Ediciones Tierra Nueva, 1970. 196 pp.

1139 ARROYO, GONZALO. "Le chrétien face à la pauvreté en Amérique
Latine." Revue Nouvelle 36 (December, 1962): 514-521.

1140 ASSMANN, HUGO. "Fe y promoción humana." Perspectivas de
Diálogo 36 (1969): 177-185.

1141 BISHOP M., JORDAN. Secularización y América Latina: la
mediación de la Iglesia en una sociedad secularidad.
Cochabamba, Bolivia: [n.p.], 1968. 13 pp., bibl.

Humanism

1142   CÂMARA, HÉLDER. "Que faria S. Tomás de Aquino, o comentador
        de Aristóteles, diante de Karl Marx?" Cadernos do Ceas 37
        (May/June, 1975): 52-59.

1143   COTTO, AUGUSTO. "Teología para América Latina." Cristianismo
        y Sociedad 14 (1976): 15-35.

1144   DEL MONTE, CARLOS. "Revisión del pensamiento social de Calvino."
        Cristianismo y Sociedad 3 (1965): 96-114.

1145   ELIAS, JOHN LAWRENCE. A Comparison and Critical Evaluation
        of the Social and Educational Thought of Paulo Freire and
        Ivan Illich. Philadelphia: Temple University, 1974.
        210 pp., bibl.

1146   "En América Latina: la Iglesia prefiere los caminos del amor
        a los de la violencia." Informaciones Católicas Inter-
        nacionales 303 (January 1, 1968): 16.

1147   Encuentro de Profesores de Teología y Filosofía sobre el
        Tratado de Dios. Dios: problemática de la no-creencia en
        América Latina. Bogotá: Secretariado General del Consejo
        Episcopal Latinoamericano, 1974. 360 pp.

1148   FLORES CABALLERO, LUIS. Humanismo y revolución en América
        Latina. Lima: Unión Latinoamericana de Escritores y
        Artistas, 1968. 69 pp.

1149   FREIRE, PAULO. Ação cultural para a liberdade e outros
        escritos. Rio de Janeiro: Paz e Terra, 1976. 149 pp.

1150   _____. La desmitificación de la concientización y otros
        escritos. Bogotá: Editorial América Latina, 1975. 141 pp.

1151   _____. "La misión educativa de las iglesias en América
        Latina." In La desmitificación de la concientización y
        otros escritos, edited by Paulo Freire, pp. 95-141. Bogotá:
        Editorial América Latina, 1975.

1152   _____. Las iglesias en América Latina: su papel educativo.
        Caracas: Laboratorio Educativo, 1975. 60 pp., bibl.

1153   _____. Las iglesias: la educación y el proceso de liberación
        humana en la historia. Buenos Aires: La Aurora, 1974.

1154   _____. Pedagogía del oprimido. Montevideo: Tierra Nueva,
        1970. 250 pp.

1155 _____; ILLICH, IVAN; and FURTER, PIERRE. Educación para el cambio social. Buenos Aires: Tierra Nueva, 1974. 162 pp.

1156 GIRARDI, GIULIO. Educación integradora y educación liberadora. Caracas: Laboratorio Educativo, 1974.

1157 HÖRGEL, CHARLOTTE. "Christian and Marxist Humanity." Concilium 23 (February, 1971): 172-179.

1158 HORNUNG, WARREN GEORGE. Paulo Freires' Contribution to the Theological Education of the Protestant Laity in Chile. Claremont, California: School of Theology at Claremont, 1974. 347 pp., bibl.

1159 JOLIF, JEAN-YVES. "Marxism and Humanism." Concilium 6 (1973): 111-117.

1160 KING, MARTIN LUTHER. "El tiempo de la justicia de la rebelión." Cristianismo y Sociedad 6 (1964): 18-30.

1161 LAMBERT, BERNARD. "Quand un paysan chrétien devient marxiste." Esprit 1 (April/May, 1977): 70-75.

1162 ORREGO VICUÑA, CLAUDIO. "Humanismo cristiano, capitalismo y socialismo marxista." In Cristianos por el Socialismo: ¿consecuencia cristiana o alienación política?, edited by Instituto de Estudios Políticos, pp. 331-334. Santiago, Chile: Editorial Pacífico, 1972.

1163 SANDERS, THOMAS G. "Education as Liberation." ICA News 8 (January/February, 1969): 2, 7-8.

1164 SANTA ANA, JULIO DE, ed. Hombre, ideología y revolución en América Latina. Montevideo: Federación de Iglesias Evangélicas del Uruguay, 1965. 133 pp.

1165 SEGUNDO, JUAN LUIS. "Evangelización y humanización." Perspectivas de Diálogo 41 (March, 1970): 9-17.

1166 TORRES RESTREPO, CAMILO. "Carta latinoamericana." Christianisme Social 74 (September/October, 1966): 549-551.

1167 ZAMBRANO CAMADER, RAÚL. "Iglesia y desarrollo." In Lo que importa es el hombre, pp. 152-160. Bogotá: Ediciones Tercer Mundo, 1968.

Labor and Laboring Classes

LABOR AND LABORING CLASSES

1168   ALEXANDER, ROBERT JACKSON. "Latin America's Secular Labor
        Movement as an Instrument of Social Change." In Religion,
        Revolution and Reform: New Forces for Change in Latin
        America, edited by William V. D'Antonio, pp. 145-160. New
        York: Praeger, 1964.

1169   _____. Organized Labor in Latin America. New York: Free
        Press, 1965. 274 pp.

1170   ANDRADE VALDERRAMA, VICENTE. "La invasión de tierras."
        Revista Javeriana 50 (November, 1963): 406-410.

1171   BASTIDE, R. "Contributions a une sociologie des religions en
        Amérique Latine: les publications du CIDOC, Mexique
        (1968/1971)." Archives de Sciences Sociales des Religions
        18 (1973): 139-150.

1172   BONILLA, ADOLFO. "Trade Union Movements." In Integration of
        Man and Society in Latin America, edited by Samuel Shapiro,
        pp. 86-100. Notre Dame, Indiana: University of Notre
        Dame, 1967.

1173   Congreso Latinoamericano de Vocaciones, 1st. La pastoral de
        las vocaciones en América Latina. Bogotá: Consejo Episcopal
        Latinoamericano, Departamento de Vocaciones, 1967. 62 pp.

1174   FLORIDI, ULISSE ALESSIS, and STIEFBOLD, ANNETTE E. The
        Uncertain Alliance: The Catholic Church and Labor in Latin
        America. Miami, Florida: Center for Advanced Inter-
        national Studies, University of Miami, 1973. 108 pp.

1175   FREIRE, PAULO. "Cultural Liberty in Latin America." ICA News
        8 (January/February, 1969): 3-6.

1176   Instituto Nacional de Estudios Sindicales. Introducción al
        sindicalismo cristiano. Caracas: Fracción Parlamentaria
        de COPEI, 1962. 140 pp.

1177   "Marginalidad." Reportaje-DESAL 1 (July, 1966): 4-5.

1178   MEDINA ECHAVARRÍA, JOSÉ. "Teoría del cambio de estructuras."
        Mensaje 123 (October, 1963): 497-504.

1179   POBLETE TRONCOSO, MOISÉS. The Rise of the Latin American
        Labor Movement. New Haven, Connecticut: College and
        University Press, 1969. 179 pp., bibl.

1180 POZAS, CARMELO. "Presente y futuro de la fe cristiana en el mundo obrero." Sal Terrae 63 (1975): 794-801.

1181 ROBAYO RODRÍGUEZ, JAIME. Las organizaciones de trabajadores a la luz de las doctrinas sociales de la Iglesia católica. Bogotá: Universidad Javeriana, 1962. 140 pp.

1182 Sacerdotes para el Tercer Mundo. Sacerdotes para el Tercer Mundo. Buenos Aires: Publicaciones del Movimiento Sacerdotes para el Tercer Mundo, 1950. 158 pp.

1183 ZABALA, E. DE. El problem social obrero: capitalismo, marxismo, doctrina social de la Iglesia. Caracas: Editorial Sucre, 1959. 195 pp., bibl.

LIBERATION

1184 ALGORTA DEL CASTILLO, JUAN MANUEL M. Por una moral responsable. Montevideo: Bosco Canelones, 1973. 89 pp.

1185 ARIAS, MORTIMER. Salvación es liberación. Buenos Aires: Editorial La Aurora, 1973. 183 pp., bibl.

1186 ARROYO, GONZALO. "Represión a la Iglesia latinoamericana: las purgas armades y la CIA." Contacto 12 (October, 1975): 19-27.

1187 ASSMANN, HUGO. "El aporte cristiano al proceso de liberación de América Latina." Contacto 8 (June, 1971): 12-27.

1188 _____. "Implicaciones socio-analíticas e ideológicas del lenguaje de liberación." In Encuentro teología de la Liberación. Montevideo: Iglesia y Sociedad en América Latina, 1971.

1189 _____. "La dimensión política de la fe como praxis de la liberación histórica del hombre." Vida Pastoral 21 (April, 1970): 16-25.

1190 _____. "Liberación: notas sobre las implicacias de un nuevo lenguaje teológico." Stromata 28 (January/June, 1972): 161-181.

1191 _____. Opresión-liberación: desafío a los cristianos. Montevideo: Tierra Nueva, 1971. 208 pp.

1192 _____. "Reflexión teológica a nivel estratégico-táctico." In Liberación en América Latina, pp. 69-81. Bogotá: América Latina, 1971.

Liberation

1193 _____. Teología de la liberación. Montevideo: Centro de Documentación MIEC-JECI, 1970. 55 pp.

1194 AVILA P., RAFAEL. "Profecía, interpretación y reinterpretación." In Liberación en América Latina, pp. 113-130. Bogotá: América Latina, 1971.

1195 _____. Teología, evangelización y liberación. Bogotá: Ediciones Paulinas, 1973. 111 pp., bibl.

1196 BELDA, RAFAEL. "Los 'Cristianos por el Socialismo' ante el ateísmo marxista." Iglesia Viva 52-53 (July/October, 1974): 401-416.

1197 BENETTI, SANTOS. Jesús y la liberación. Buenos Aires: Paulinas, 1972. 96 pp.

1198 BERRYMAN, PHILLIP E. "Latin American Liberation Theology." In Theology in the Americas, edited by Sergio Torres and John Eagleson, pp. 20-83. New York: Orbis Books, 1976.

1199 _____. "Latin American Liberation Theology." Theological Studies 34 (September, 1973): 357-395.

1200 BISHOP M., JORDAN. "Prudencia y revolución." Víspera 5 (April, 1968): 3-6.

1201 BOFF, LEONARDO. "La liberazione di Gesù Cristo attraverso il cammino dell'oppressione." In La nuova fronteira della teologia in America Latina, edited by Rosino Gibellini, pp. 156-201. Brescia, Italy: Queriniana, 1975.

1202 BOJORGE, HORACIO. "Exodo y liberación." Víspera 19-20 (October/December, 1970): 33-37.

1203 BONINO MÍGUEZ, JOSÉ. "Theology and Theologians of the New World: Latin America: Five Theses Towards an Understanding of the Theology of Liberation." Expository Times 87 (April, 1976): 196-200.

1204 BORRAT, HÉCTOR. "Hacia una teología de la liberación." Cuadernos de Marcha 1 (January 8, 1971): 15.

1205 _____. "Liberación ¿cómo?" Stromata 28 (January/June, 1972): 7-43.

1206 _____. "Liberation Theology in Latin America." Dialog 13 (Summer, 1974): 172-176.

1207   BUNTIG, ALDO J.   "Catolicismo popular y aporte a la liberación." Mensaje Iberoamericano 111 (1975): 8-11.

1208   CÂMARA, HÉLDER.   "Human rights and the Liberation of Man in the Americas: Reflections and Responses." In Human Rights and the Liberation of Man in the Americas, edited by Louis M. Colonnese, pp. 259-268. Notre Dame, Indiana: University of Notre Dame Press, 1970.

1209   CARVAJAL, RAFAEL TOMÁS, et al. América Latina: movilización popular y fe cristiana. Montevideo: Iglesia y Sociedad en América Latina, 1971. 172 pp.

1210   CASTILLO, CARLOS. "Chemins de libération en Amérique Latine." Parole et Pain 58 (September/October, 1973): 318-323.

1211   CASTRILLON, DARÍO. "Exposé sur le développement de la théologie de la libération en Amérique Latine." Dial 304 (May 13, 1976): 10.

1212   Centro Arquidiocesano de Pastoral. Hombre, paz, liberación. Lima: Centro Arquidiocesano de Pastoral, 1970. 95 pp.

1213   Centro de Estudios para el Desarrollo e Integración de América Latina. Iglesia y liberación. Bogotá: Centro de Estudios para el Desarrollo y Integración de América Latina, 1976.

1214   COLONNESE, LOUIS MICHAEL. Conscientization for Liberation. Washington: Division for Latin America, United States Catholic Conference, 1971. 305 pp.

1215   _____. Human Rights and the Liberation of Man in the Americas. Notre Dame, Indiana: University of Notre Dame Press, 1970. 278 pp.

1216   COMBLIN, JOSEPH. "La liberación en el pensamiento cristiano latinoamericano." Servir 49 (January/February, 1974): 11-30.

1217   _____. "Le theme de la libération dans la pensée chrétienne latinoaméricaine." La Revue Nouvelle 55 (May/June, 1972): 560-574.

1218   Conferencia Episcopal de Colombia. Cuestiones actuales de teología. Bogotá: Secretariado Permanente del Episcopado Colombiano, 1974.

1219   CONWAY, JAMES F. Marx and Jesus: Liberation Theology in Latin America. New York: Carleton Press, 1973.

Liberation

1220   COTTO, AUGUSTO. "Teología para América Latina." Cristianismo
        y Sociedad 14 (1976): 15-35.

1221   CROATTO, JOSÉ SEVERIANO. Liberación y libertad: pautas
        hermenéuticas. Buenos Aires: Ediciones Mundo Nuevo, 1973.
        150 pp.

1222   CULHANE, EUGENE K. "New Mood in Latin America." America 126
        (April 29, 1972): 449-450.

1223   CUSSIANOVICH, ALEJANDRO. Nos ha liberado. Lima: Centro de
        Estudios y Publicaciones, 1972. 173 pp.

1224   DE BOVIS, A. "Fe y compromiso temporal." Selecciones de
        Teología 2 (1963): 295-300.

1225   DE LORA, CECILIO. "Liberación y concentrización: un desafío
        educativo en América Latina." Sal Terrae 8-9 (August/
        September, 1976): 583-592.

1226   DEL VALLE, LUIS G. "El papel de la teología en América
        Latina." In Liberación en América Latina, pp. 17-33.
        Bogotá: América Latina, 1971.

1227   DERISI, O. N. "El sentido cristiano de la liberación del
        hombre." Veritas 15 (1971): 207-211.

1228   DE SANTA ANA, JULIO. "Notas para una ética de la liberación
        (a partir de la Biblia)." Cristianismo y Sociedad 8 (1970):
        43-60.

1229   DRI, RUBÉN R. "Alienación y liberación." Cristianismo y
        Revolución 24 (April, 1970): 59-64.

1230   DUSSEL, ENRIQUE D. Caminos de liberación y Latinoamerica.
        Buenos Aires: Latinoamérica Libros, 1972. 174 pp.

1231   _____. "Para una fundamentación dialéctica de la liberación
        latinoamericana." Stromata 28 (January/June, 1972): 53-
        89.

1232   ECHEGARAY, HUGO. "'Tierra nueva' y la teología de liberación:
        críticas desde el orden establecido." Páginas 2 (May,
        1977): 5-19.

1233   "Education for Liberation in Latin America." IDOC-Inter-
        national 26 (March 13, 1971): 53-58.

1234 Encuentro Latinoamericano de Espiritualidad, 3d. Hacia una
espiritualidad latinoamericana: teología, espiritualidad
de la liberación. Quito: Editorial Kelly, 1974. 268 pp.,
bibl.

1235 Encuentro Latinoamericano de Teología. Comité Organizador.
Liberación y cautoverio: debates en torno al método de la
teología en América Latina. México: Encuentro Latinoamericano de Teología, 1975. 658 pp.

1236 "Estrategias sociales para el proceso de liberación: con-
clusiones de tres encuentros promovidos por 'Justicia y
Paz' en América Latina." Servir 45-46 (May-June/July-
August, 1973): 265-278.

1237 FÁREZ JIMÉNEZ, ROBERTO. La teología de la liberación: visión
global. Santiago, Chile: Ilades, 1975. 25 pp., bibl.

1238 FLORES, PATRICIO. Colección mestiza americana: The Bible,
the Past, the Present, the Problem, the Response. San
Antonio, Texas: Mexican American Cultural Center, 1975.
118 pp.

1239 FLORISTAN, CASIANO. Los sacramentos de la iniciación cristiana:
momentos del proceso de liberación. San Antonio, Texas:
Mexican American Cultural Center, 1974. 80 pp., bibl.

1240 FOX, T. "Liberation Theology Tests U.S. Conscience."
National Catholic Reporter 11 (August 16, 1975): 1.

1241 FREIRE, PAULO. Ação cultural para a liberdade e outros
escritos. Rio de Janeiro: Paz e Terra, 1976. 149 pp.

1242 _____. Conciencia, crítica y liberación: pedagogía del
oprimido. Bogotá: Ediciones Camilo, 1971. 237 pp.

1243 _____. Educação e conscientização: extensionismo rural.
Cuernavaca, México: Centro Intercultural de Documentación,
1968.

1244 _____. La desmitificación de la concientización y otros
escritos. Bogotá: Editorial América Latina, 1975. 141 pp.

1245 _____. Las iglesias: la educación y el proceso de liberación
humana en la historia. Buenos Aires: La Aurora, 1974.

1246 GALAT NOUMER, JOSÉ, and ORDOÑEZ NORIEGA, FRANCISCO. Liberación
integral. Bogotá: Ediciones Paulinas, 1976. 78 pp.

Liberation

1247   GALILEA, SEGUNDO. "La teología de la liberación como crítica
        de la actividad de la Iglesia en América Latina." <u>Christus</u>
        37 (May, 1972): 53-56.

1248   _____. "Situación pastoral de América Latina." <u>Christus</u> 36
        (May, 1971): 54-58.

1249   _____. <u>Teología de la liberación: ensayo de síntesis.</u>
        Bogotá: Indo-American Press Service, 1976. 55 pp.

1250   _____. "Teología della liberazione e nuove esigenze cristiane."
        In <u>La nuova fronteira della teologia in America Latina,</u>
        edited by Rosino Gibellini, pp. 245-272. Brescia, Italy:
        Queriniana, 1975.

1251   GARCÍA G., JESÚS. "Del desarrollo a la liberación." <u>Contacto</u>
        8 (1972): 29-44.

1252   GARCÍA-HUIDOBRO, JUAN EDUARDO. "Los educadores cristianos y
        la liberación latinoamericana." <u>Educación Hoy</u> 2 (January/
        February, 1972): 5-39.

1253   GERA, P. LUCIO. "Teología de liberación." <u>Pasos</u> 42 (March
        19, 1973): 1-10.

1254   _____. "Teología de liberación." <u>Pasos</u> 42 (March 26, 1973):
        1-16.

1255   _____. <u>Teoología de la liberación.</u> Lima: Centro de Docu-
        mentación del MIEC-JECI, 1972. 49 pp.

1256   GIRARDI, GIULIO. <u>Educación integradora y educación liber-
        tadora.</u> Caracas: Laboratorio Educativo, 1974-1975.

1257   GUTIÉRREZ, GUSTAVO MERINO. "A Latin American Perception of a
        Theology of Liberation." In <u>Conscientization for Libera-
        tion,</u> edited by Louis M. Colonnese, pp. 57-80. Washington:
        Division for Latin America, United States Catholic Con-
        ference, 1971.

1258   _____. <u>A Theology of Liberation: History, Politics, and
        Salvation.</u> Maryknoll, New York: Orbis Books, 1973. 323
        pp.

1259   _____. "Apuntes para una teología de la liberación." In
        <u>Liberación: opción de la Iglesia latinoamericana en la
        década del 70,</u> edited by Simposio sobre Teología de la
        Liberación, pp. 25-62. Bogotá: Editorial Presencia, 1970.

1260 _____. "Apuntes para una teología la liberación." Cristian-
      ismo y Sociedad 24-25 (1970): 6-22.

1261 _____. Hacia una teología de la liberación. Bogotá: Indo-
      American Press Service, 1971. 81 pp.

1262 _____. "Liberation and Development." Cross Currents 21
      (Summer, 1971): 243-256.

1263 _____. "Notes for a Theology of Liberation." Theological
      Studies 31 (June, 1970): 243-261.

1264 _____. "Prassi di liberazione e fede cristiana." In La Nuova
      fronteira della teologia in America Latina, edited by Rosino
      Gibellini, pp. 15-58. Brescia, Italy: Queriniana, 1975.

1265 _____. Praxis de liberación y fe cristiana. Lima: Centro
      de Documentación del MIEC-JECI, 1972. 28 pp.

1266 _____. Teología de la liberación: perspectivas. Lima:
      Centro de Estudios y Publicaciones, 1971. 374 pp.

1267 _____. Teología desde el reverso de la historia. Lima:
      Centro de Estudios y Publicaciones, 1977. 59 pp.

1268 _____, and SHAULL, RICAHARD. Liberation and Change. Atlanta:
      Knox Press, 1977. 184 pp.

1269 HAMILTON, WILLIAM. "A Note on Radical Theology." Concilium
      29 (October, 1967): 85-97.

1270 HERNÁNDEZ, E. JAVIER ALONSO. "Esboso para una teología de la
      liberación." In Aportes para la liberation, edited by
      Simposio sobre Teología de la Liberación, pp. 37-59.
      Bogotá: Presencia, 1970.

1271 HERRARA, CESAR. Liberación y crisis. Bogotá: Hispana, 1971.

1272 HOUTART, FRANÇOIS. "Les conditions sociales de la pastorale
      dans les grandes villes de l'Amérique Latine." Social
      Compass 5 (Winter, 1958): 181-199.

1273 Iglesia y liberación humana: los documentos de Medellín.
      Barcelona: Editorial Nova Terra, 1969. 419 pp.

Liberation

1274   JIMÉNEZ, ROBERTO. "El conflicto en la teología de la libera-
       ción: evaluación de algunos aspectos positivos." In
       Conflicto social y compromiso en América Latina, edited by
       Consejo Episcopal Latinoamericano, pp. 359-381. Bogotá:
       Consejo Episcopal Latinoamericano, 1976.

1275   KLOPPENBURG, BOAVENTURA. "Cuestiones pendientes en la acción
       cristiana por la liberación." In Conflicto social y
       Compromiso cristiano en América Latina, edited by Consejo
       Episcopal Latinoamericano, pp. 353-358. Bogotá: Consejo
       Episcopal Latinoamericano, 1976.

1276   LAJE, ENRIQUE J. Apuntes sobre Iglesia y liberación. Buenos
       Aires: Instituto de Enseñanza General GRAM Editora, 1975.
       146 pp.

1277   _____. "La Iglesia y el proceso latinoamericano de liberación."
       Stromata 28 (April/June, 1971): 163-187.

1278   LEÑERO, VICENTE. "Teología de la liberación: la Iglesia con
       los opresores." Christus 40 (October, 1975): 69-70.

1279   LERNOUX, PENNY. "Priests for the People: Latin America's
       Insurgent Church." Nation 222 (May 22, 1976): 612-613,
       618-625.

1280   LESBAUPIN, IVO. "The Latin American Bishops and Socialism."
       In Christianity and Socialism, edited by Johann-Baptist
       Metz, pp. 113-123. New York: Seabury Press, 1977.

1281   Liberación: diálogos en el CELAM. Bogotá: Secretariado
       General del Consejo Episcopal Latinoamericano, 1974. 442
       pp.

1282   Liberación en América Latina: encuentro teologico, julio de
       1971. Bogotá: Editorial América Latina, 1971. 208 pp.

1283   "Liberación, si, marxismo, no." El Catolismo 2,230 (October
       31, 1976): 1-14.

1284   "Liberation of Men and Nations." America 125 (August 7, 1971):
       53-54.

1285   LONDOÑO, ALEJANDRO. Dinámica de la concientización. Buenos
       Aires: Ediciones Paulinas, 1974. 106 pp., bibl.

1286   LÓPEZ TRUJILLO, ALFONSO. "La liberación y las liberaciones."
       Tierra Nueva 1 (April, 1972): 5-26.

1287 _____. "Las teologías de la liberación en América Latina."
Ateísmo y Diálogo 3 (September, 1975): 96-102.

1288 _____. ¿Liberación o revolución? Bogotá: Ediciones Paulinas,
1974. 144 pp.

1289 _____. Teología liberadora en América Latina. Bogotá: Ediciones Paulinas, 1974. 197 pp., bibl.

1290 LOZANO BARRACAN, JAVIER. "El compromiso de la Iglesia en la
liberación de América Latina." In Simposio sobre teología
de la liberación: aportes para la liberación, pp. 88-115.
Bogotá: Presencia, 1970.

1291 MC GRATH, MARK G. "A Living Theology in Latin America."
Review of Politics 33 (April, 1971): 163-171.

1292 MALDO, JUAN CARLOS. "Un ensayo sobre la teología de la liberación: primera parte." Política y Espírtu 332 (May, 1972):
42-45.

1293 MARTÍNEZ SAEZ, SANTIAGO. "Teología y liberación." Istmo 74
(May/June, 1971): 9-21.

1294 MIGUEZ BONINO, JOSÉ. "Teología y liberación." Actualidad
Pastoral 3 (1970): 83.

1295 MONTES, FERNANDO. "Teología de la liberación: un aporte de
la teología latinoamericana: revisión bibliográfica."
Mensaje 208 (May, 1972): 277-283.

1296 MUÑOZ VEGA, PABLO. "Hora del cambio de estructuras y justicia
social." NADOC 171 (September 13, 1970): 5.

1297 NEGRE RIGOL, PEDRO. "Biblia y liberación." Cristianismo y
Sociedad 8 (August, 1970): 69-80.

1298 NIEUWENHOVE, JACQUES VAN. "The Theological Project of Gustavo
Gutierrez: Reflections on His Theology of Liberation."
Lumen Vitae 28 (September, 1973): 398-432.

1299 NUÑEZ, ENRIQUE. Notas para una teología de la liberación.
México: Secretariado Social Mexicano, 1971.

1300 OCHAGAVIA, JUAN. "Liberación de Cristo y cambio de estructuras."
Mensaje 188 (May, 1970): 181-188.

1301 _____. "Primer encuentro latinoamericano de cristianos por el
socialismo." Mensaje 209 (June, 1973): 356-366.

Liberation

1302 OLAYA, NOEL. "Ciencias sociales y teología." In Liberación
      en América Latina, pp. 55-67. Bogotá: Servicio Colombiano
      de Comunicación Social, 1971.

1303 OLIVEROS, ROBERTO. "Liberación y teología: génesis y creci-
      mento de una reflexión, 1966-1976." Páginas 2 (May, 1977):
      53-54.

1304 _____. "Teología liberadora en América Latina." Páginas 5-6
      (September, 1976): 64-65.

1305 PADILLA, C. RENE. "Theology of Liberation." Christianity
      Today 18 (November 9, 1973): 69-70.

1306 PANTELIS, JORGE. "Implications of the Theologies of Liberation
      for the Theological Training of the Pastoral Ministry of
      Latin America." International Review of Mission 261
      (January, 1977): 14-21.

1307 "Paulo VI habla sobre América Latina y la liberación." El
      Catolicismo 2,137 (August 13, 1972): 16.

1308 PAVLO TENORIO, JESÚS. "Los teólogos de la liberación, no son
      los teólogos del marxismo." Christus 41 (August, 1976):
      57-59.

1309 PÉREZ ESCLARÍN, ANTONIO. Ateismo y liberación. Caracas:
      Editorial Fuentes, 1974. 267 pp., bibl.

1310 PIÑOL, JOSEP MARÍA. Iglesia y liberación en América Latina.
      Madrid: Fontanella Marova, 1972. 269 pp.

1311 PINTO, JOÃO BOSCO. "Hacia una pedogogía de liberación." In
      Simposio sobre teología de la liberación: aportes para la
      liberación, pp. 23-36. Bogotá: Presencia, 1970.

1312 PIRONIO, EDUARDO. "Reflección teológica en torno a la libera-
      ción." In La Iglesia que nace entre nosotros, edited by
      Eduardo Pironio, pp. 43-69. Bogotá: Indo-American Press
      Service, 1970.

1313 PONGUTÁ, SILVESTRE. "Terminología bíblica sobre la liberación."
      In Amor, violencia, liberación, edited by Fernando Urrea
      et al., pp. 49-70. Bogotá: Centro de Pastoral Juvenil,
      1970.

1314 "PPI Stance on the Priests' Task of Liberation." Impact 6
      (June, 1972): 207.

1315   QUIGLEY, THOMAS F., ed. Freedom and Unfreedom in the Americas:
        Towards a Theology of Liberation. New York: IDOC-North
        America, 1971. 140 pp.

1316   RADFORD RUETHER, ROSEMARY. "Latin America and the Theology of
        Revolution/Liberation." In Freedom and Unfreedom in the
        Americas: Towards a Theology of Liberation, edited by
        Thomas E. Quigley, pp. 76-80. New York: IDOC, 1971.

1317   RAMA, CARLOS M. Revolución social y facismo en el siglo XX.
        Buenos Aires: Editorial Palestra, 1962. 346 pp., bibl.

1318   "La réponse de l'Eglise d'Amérique Latine a la pauvreté et a
        la misere." La Documentation Catholique 73 (September 5-19,
        1976): 765-768.

1319   REYERO, M. ARIAS. "Teología y liberación." Iglesia de San-
        tiago, January/February, 1978, pp. 5-9.

1320   RICHARD, PABLO. "La theologie de la libération dans la situation
        politique actuelle en Amérique Latine." Foi et Développe-
        ment 42 (December, 1976): 6.

1321   _____. "Teología de la liberación latinoamericana: un aporte
        crítico a la teología europea." Páginas 3 (July, 1976):
        1-12.

1322   ROGEL, ISAAC, ed. Documentos sobre la realidad de la Iglesia
        en América Latina, 1968-1969. Cuernavaca, México: Centro
        Intercultural de Documentación, 1970. 266 pp.

1323   RUÍZ GARCÍA, SAMUEL. Los cristianos y la justicia en América
        Latina. Lima: Centro de Documentación del MIEC-JECI,
        1972. 27 pp.

1324   SCANNONE, JUAN CARLOS. "Hacia una dialéctica de la liberación."
        Stromata 27 (January/March, 1971): 23-60.

1325   _____. "La liberación latinoamericana, ontología del proceso
        auténticamento liberador." Stromata 28 (January/June,
        1972): 107-150.

1326   SEGUNDO, JUAN LUIS. "Education, Communication, and Liberation:
        A Christian Vision." IDOC-International 35 (November 13,
        1971): 63-96.

1327   _____. Grace and the Human Condition. Maryknoll, New York:
        Orbis Books, 1973. 213 pp.

Liberation

1328 _____. "Instrumentos de la teología latinoamericana." In
Liberación en América Latina, pp. 35-54. Bogotá: América
Latina, 1971.

1329 _____. Liberación de la teología. Buenos Aires: Ediciones
Carlos Lohle, 1975. 270 pp.

1330 _____. "Liberación: fe e ideología." Mensaje 208 (May, 1972):
248-254.

1331 _____. Our Idea of God. Maryknoll, New York: Orbis Books,
1974. 206 pp.

1332 SENDOYA, LUIS. "Teología y proceso de liberación del hombre
latinoamericano." Estudios Ecuménicos 9 (1971): 2-9.

1333 SHAULL, RICHARD. "Consideraciones teológicos sobre la liberación del hombre." IDOC 68 (April 28, 1968): 1-11.

1334 Signos de liberación: testimonios de la Iglesia en América
Latina. Lima: Centro de Estudios y Publicaciones, 1973.
294 pp.

1335 Simposio sobre Teología de la Liberación. Aportes para la
liberación: conferencias. Bogotá: Editorial Presencia,
1970. 143 pp.

1336 _____. Liberación: opción de la Iglesia latinoamericana en
la década del 70. Bogotá: Editorial Presencia, 1970.
111 pp.

1337 "Theology of Liberation." IDOC-International 14 (November 28,
1970): 66-78.

1338 UGALDE, LUIS. "La ambigüedad de la esperanza de los cristianos,
la utopía y la transformación de la realidad latinoamericana." In Liberación en América Latina, pp. 83-112.
Bogotá: América Latina, 1971.

1339 VAILLANCOURT, Y. "Les politises chretiens e la liberation."
Relations 371 (May, 1972): 141, 143-145.

1340 VALENZUELA MONGES, RODOLFO. De la dependencia a la teología
de la liberación: notas bibliográficas. Cuernavaca,
México: Centro Intercultural de Documentación, 1973. 45
pp.

1341 VANDERHOFF, FRANCISCO. "Teología de la liberación y ecle-
siología práctica." Servir 55 (January/February, 1975):
62-81.

1342 VEKEMANS, ROGER. "Antecedentes para el estudio de la teología
de la liberación: comentario bibliográfico, primera parte."
Tierra Nueva 2 (July, 1972): 5 23.

1343 _____. "Antecedentes para el estudio de la teología de la
liberación: comentario bibliográfico, segunda parte."
Tierra Nueva 3 (October, 1972): 5-20.

1344 _____. "El papel de la Iglesia en el proceso de liberación
latinoamericana." Tierra Nueva 19 (September, 1976): 80-
88.

1345 _____. "La reforma y el ethos cultural." Mensaje 123
(October, 1963): 637-644.

1346 VERGES, SALVADOR. Jalones para una teología de la liberacion.
Bilbao: Mensajero, 1972.

1347 VIDALES, RAUL. Cuestiones en torno al método en la teología
de la liberación. Lima: Centro de Documentación de MIEC-
JECI, 1972. 27 pp., bibl.

1348 _____. "Cuestioni sul metodo della teologia del la libera-
zione." In La nueva fronteira della teologia in America
Latina, edited by Rosino Gibellini, pp. 59-62. Brescia,
Italy: Queriniana, 1975.

1349 WOODIS, JACK. El saqueo del tercer mundo: introducción al
neocolonialismo. Buenos Aires: Granica, 1972. 142 pp.

1350 YRARRÁZAVAL, DIEGO. "Religión del pueblo y teología de la
liberación: hipótesis." Pasos 61 (July 30, 1973): 1-5.

1351 ZENTENO, ARNALDO. Liberación social y Cristo: apuntes para
teología de la liberación. México: Secretariado Social
Mexicano, 1971. 87 pp.

1352 _____. "Liberación y magisterio." In Liberación en América
Latina, pp. 131-162. Bogotá: América Latina, 1971.

MARXISM

1353 "A Dios se le puede hablar con lenguaje marxista." Carta de
ISAL 2 (May, 1969): 1-4.

Marxism

1354   ADURIZ, JOAQUÍN. Hombre, marxismo y cristianismo. Buenos
       Aires: Editorial Heróica, 1961. 118 pp.

1355   AGUILAR LEON, LUIS E., ed. Marxism in Latin America. New
       York: A. A. Knopf, 1968. 271 pp.

1356   AGÚNDEZ, M. "Hombre y religión en la óptica marxista actual."
       Estudios de Deusto 18 (1970): 11-35.

1357   ALBA, PEDRO DE. "El socialismo cristiano." La Nueva Demo-
       cracia 32 (January, 1952): 24-28.

1358   AMENGUAL, ATALIVA et al. "Los marxistas cristianos o la nos-
       talgia del integrismo." Política y Espíritu 333 (June,
       1972): 22-37.

1359   AMORIN DA COSTA, A. "Cristianismo e marxismo: colaboração
       ou oposicão?" Brotéria 10 (October, 1974): 289-304.

1360   ARROYO, GONZALO. "Doctrina, utopía y subversión." Mensaje
       161 (August, 1967): 340-347.

1361   "Beneath the Surface of the Revolution." Reportaje-DESAL 2
       (January, 1969): 7.

1362   BERRYMAN, PHILLIP E. "Christian Delegates, Marxist Language."
       Commonweal 96 (June 16, 1972): 324-325.

1363   BIGO, PIERRE. "Meditación sacerdotal sobre el marxismo."
       Política y Espíritu 332 (May, 1972): 46-53.

1364   BISHOP M., J. "Latin America: Marxist-Christian Goals."
       Listening 4 (Fall, 1969): 174-185.

1365   BORRAT, HÉCTOR. "Presencia cristiana en la revolución latino-
       americana." Marcha, October 9, 1964.

1366   BOUCHARD, PAUL. "Religion in Latin America." American Eccle-
       siastical Review 144 (April, 1961): 231-239.

1367   BRÖKER, W. "A 'Dialogue' Between Christian and Marxist
       Scholars." Concilium 7 (August, 1965): 171-172.

1368   CÂMARA, HÉLDER. "Que faria S. Tomás de Aquino, o comentador
       de Aristóteles, diante de Karl Marx?" Cadernos do Ceas 37
       (May/June, 1975): 52-59.

1369   CASTILLO S., IGNACIO. "Asumir la historia, hacer la historia."
       SIC 402 (February, 1978): 68-70.

1370   CEPEDA, ALFREDO. "Cristianismo y marxismo." El Día, January
        22, 1966.

1371   COTTIER, GEORGE. "¿Cuál es el valor del 'análisis marxista'?"
        Tierra Nueva 3 (October 3, 1972): 21-32.

1372   "Cristianismo y marxismo." SIC 403 (February, 1978): 57.

1373   Diálogo entre católicos y marxistas. Buenos Aires: Tres
        Américas, 1974. 10 pp.

1374   DOGNIN, PAUL DOMINIQUE. "El colectivismo de marx." Teología
        y vida 13 (1972): 283-298.

1375   DUSSEL, ENRIQUE D. "Marx ante el pasado y el porvenir de la
        huminidad." Teología y vida 13 (1972): 207-226.

1376   _____. "Para una fundamentación dialéctica de la liberación
        latinoamericana." Stromata 28 (January/June, 1972): 53-89.

1377   ECHENIQUE, M. R. "Marxist Infiltration in the Church in Latin
        America." Social Justice Review 66 (September, 1975):
        163-171.

1378   EGGERS LAN, CONRADO. "Acerca de marxismo o cristianismo:
        respuesta a la derecha marxista." Pasado y Presente 1
        (January/March, 1964): 322-328.

1379   _____. "O Cristianismo: retorno ás fontes." Paz e Terra 1
        (July, 1966): 39-51.

1380   Encuentro de Profesores de Teología y Filosofía sobre el
        Tratado de Dios, Lima, 1974. Dios: Problemática de la
        No-Creencia en América Latina. Bogotá: Secretariado
        General del Consejo Episcopal Latinoamericano, 1974. 360
        pp.

1381   ESCOBAR, SAMUEL. Diálogo entre Cristo, Marx y otros ensayos.
        Lima: Publicaciones AGEUP, 1967. 303 pp.

1382   FETSCHER, IRING. "Developments in the Marxist Critique of
        Religion." Concilium 16 (May, 1966): 131-155.

1383   FLORES OLEA, VICTOR. Marxismo y democracia socialista.
        México: Unam, 1968. 321 pp.

Marxism

1384   FLORIA, CARLOS ALBERTO. "Sobre el conflicto político." In
        Conflicto social y compromiso cristiano en América Latina,
        edited by Consejo Episcopal Latinoamericano, pp. 87-101.
        Bogotá: Consejo Episcopal Latinoamericano, 1976.

1385   GAETE, ARTURO. "Catolicismo social y marxismo en el siglo
        XIX: un diálogo imposible." Mensaje 205 (December, 1971):
        588-602.

1386   _____. "Catolicismo social y marxismo en la primera mitad del
        siglo XX: aún no es posible el diálogo." Mensaje 215
        (December, 1972): 706-716.

1387   _____. "El largo camino del diálogo del cristiano-marxista."
        Mensaje 17 (June, 1968): 209-219.

1388   _____. "Los cristianos y el marxismo: de Pio XI a Paulo VI."
        Mensaje 209 (June, 1972): 328-341.

1389   GARAYDY, ROGER. "Marxismo y cristianismo en diálogo." Selec-
        ciones de Teología 7 (1968): 76-82.

1390   GINES ORTEGA, JESUS. "El fondo de la polémica cristiano-
        marxista: los discursos inaugurales del encuentro de
        Cristianos por el Socialismo." In Cristianos por el
        Socialismo: ¿consecuencia cristiana o alienación política?,
        edited by Instituto de Estudios Políticos, pp. 355-372.
        Santiago, Chile: Pacífico, 1972.

1391   GIRARDI, GIULIO. "Cristianismo y marxismo." Pasos 19
        (September, 1972): 11.

1392   GONZÁLIZ E., GERARDO. "El diálogo cristiano marxista ¿imprés-
        cindible o imposible?" In Diálogo hoy, pp. 29-59. Santiago,
        Chile: Corporación de Desarrollo y Promoción Juvenil, 1972.

1393   GOZZINI, MARIO et al. El diálogo de la epoca: católicas y
        marxistas. Buenos Aires: Editorial Platina, 1965. 317
        pp., bibl.

1394   HERRERA, FELIPE. Nacionalismo latinoamericano. Santiago,
        Chile: Editorial Universitaria, 1967. 224 pp.

1395   HÖRGL, CHARLOTTE. "Christian and Marxist Humanity." Concilium
        23 (February, 1967): 172-179.

1396   HROMADKA, JAMES L. Evangelio para los ateos. Montevideo:
        Tierra Nueva, 1970. 107 pp.

1397   Instituto para el Desarrollo Económico y Social. Desarrollo
        y promoción del hombre. Caracas: Ediciones Arte, 1965.
        298 pp.

1398   JOLIF, JEAN-YVES. "Marxism and Humanism." Concilium 6 (1973):
        111-117.

1399   KINNEN, EDUARDO. "¿De qué marxismo nos hablan?" Política y
        Espíritu 322 (June, 1971): 55-58.

1400   KONDER, LEANDRO. "Marxismo e cristianismo: pressupostos de
        um dialogo." Estudos Sociais 6 (March, 1963): 332-340.

1401   LAMBERT, BERNARD. "Quand un paysan chrétien devient marxiste."
        Esprit 1 (April/May, 1977): 70-75.

1402   LEGOV, MIGUEL E. "Sinn und Bedeutung der Christlichen
        Mission." Stimmen der Zeit 191 (January, 1973): 62-66.

1403   LENDERSDORF, KARL et al. "Fe cristiana y marxismo." Cuadernos
        de Cristianismo y Sociedad 1 (1965): 9-78.

1404   LEÑERO, VICENTE. "Teología de la liberación y marxismo:
        parentesco quizá ineludible." Christus 40 (October, 1975):
        64-66.

1405   "Liberación, sí, marxismo, no." El Catolicismo 2,230 (October
        31, 1976): 1-14.

1406   LODGE, GEORGE CABOT. "The Campesinos." In Integration of Man
        and Society in Latin America, edited by Samuel Shapiro,
        pp. 34-45. Notre Dame, Indiana: University of Notre Dame,
        1967.

1407   LÓPEZ, SALVADOR. ¿La religión es el opio del pueblo? Bogotá:
        Ediciones Paulinas, 1962. 38 pp.

1408   LÓPEZ TRUJILLO, ALFONSO. "El análisis marxista en el documento
        del 'Primer Encuentro Latinoamericano de Cristianos por el
        Socialismo.'" Tierra Nueva 4 (January, 1973): 31-39.

1409   _____. Liberación marxista y liberación cristiana. Madrid:
        B.A.C., 1974. 276 pp.

1410   MAC EOIN, GARY. "Marx with a Latin Beat." Cross Currents 21
        (Summer, 1971): 269-275.

1411   MADURO, OTTO. "¿Cómo es marxista un cristiano?" SIC 402
        (February, 1978): 71-73.

Marxism

1412　"Marxismo e cristianismo." Tabloide-UAP 1 (August, 1963): 7.

1413　MUÑOZ, FREDDY. "Socialismo, marxismo, cristianismo." Servicio Europeo de Universitarios Latinoamericanos 70-71 (June/ July, 1976): 26-30.

1414　MUSTO, OSVALDO. Tercer mundo. Buenos Aires: Ediciones Paulinas, 1975. 112 pp.

1415　"No se puede ser cristiano y marxista." Cristianidad 540 (February, 1976): 34-37.

1416　ORREGO VICUÑA, CLAUDIO. "Humanismo cristiano, capitalismo y socialismo marxista." In Cristianos por el socialismo: ¿consecuencia cristiana o alienación política?, edited by Instituto de Estudios Políticos, pp. 331-334. Santiago, Chile: Pacífico, 1972.

1417　ORTIZ, EDUARDO J. "El marxismo en los Documentos Pontificios." SIC 402 (February, 1978): 58-60.

1418　PAOLI, ARTURO. Diálogo entre católicos y marxistas. Buenos Aires: Latinoamérica-Libros, 1966. 12 pp.

1419　PAVEZ BRAVO, JORGE. "Jesucristo y la violencia." Mensaje 14 (January/February, 1965): 17-22.

1420　PAVLO TENORIO, JESÚS. "Los teólogos de la liberación, no son los teólogos del marxismo." Christus 41 (August, 1976): 57-59.

1421　PEARSON, NEALE J. "Latin American Peasant Pressure Groups and the Modernization Process." Journal of International Affairs 20 (1966): 309-317.

1422　"Un peligro terrible para la Iglesia y la evangelización del mundo: el marxismo." Cristo al Mundo 20 (1975): 346-354.

1423　PÉREZ ESCLARÍN, ANTONIO. Ateismo y liberación. Caracas: Editorial Fuentes, 1974. 267 pp., bibl.

1424　_____. La revolución con Marx y con Cristo. Caracas: Monte Avila, 1974. 292 pp., bibl.

1425　PETULLA, JOSEPH M. Christian Political Theology: A Marxian Guide. Maryknoll, New York: Orbis Books, 1972. 256 pp., bibl.

1426   ROCHE, D. J. "Christ to Marx Step by Step: Why a Latin
        American Left the Church for the Communist Party." Sign,
        June, 1962, pp. 23–26.

1427   ROSALES, JUAN. Los cristianos, los marxistas, y la revolución.
        Buenos Aires: Ediciones Silaba, 1970. 449 pp.

1428   _____. "Revolution, Socialism, Theology." World Marxist
        Review 18 (June, 1975): 80–90.

1429   RUEDA GÓMEZ, LUIS. "Cristianismo con metodología marxista."
        Revista Javeriana 355 (June, 1969): 505–509.

1430   RUETHER, ROSEMARY. "Monks and Marxists: A Look at the
        Catholic Left." Christianity and Crisis 33 (April 30,
        1973): 75–79.

1431   SANTUC, VINCENT. "El problema de la religión en Marx y sus
        interrogantes." In Diálogo hoy, pp. 5–28. Santiago,
        Chile: Corporación de Desarrollo y Promoción Juvenil, 1972.

1432   SAUTER, GERHARD. "The Future: A Question for the Christian-
        Marxist Dialogue." Concilium 41 (1969): 125–134.

1433   SCANNONE, J. C. "La liberación latinoamericana, ontología
        del proceso auténticamente liberador." Stromata 28
        (January/June, 1–72): 107–150.

1434   SEGUNDO, JUAN. "Los caminos del desarrollo político latino-
        americano." Mensaje 115 (December, 1962): 701–707.

1435   _____. "Liberación: fe e ideología." Mensaje 208 (May,
        1972): 248–254.

1436   SOSA A., ARTURO. "La mediación marxista de la fe cristiana."
        SIC 402 (February, 1978): 64–67.

1437   "Sugerencias sobre el tema 'lucha de clases y evangelio de
        Jesucristo." Pasos 16 (August 28, 1972): 1–4.

1438   TERRA, JUAN PABLO. "El desafío marxista." Mensaje 115
        (December, 1962): 726–732.

1439   TRIGO, PEDRO. "El cristianismo en las relaciones entre
        marxistas y cristianos." SIC 389 (November, 1976): 414–
        416.

1440   "The Truth About Latin America." America 115 (November 19,
        1966): 638–639.

Marxism

1441   VALLE, RAFAEL HELIODORO. "¿Podrán entenderse católicos y
        marxistas?" La Nueva Democracia 26 (July, 1945): 27-29.

1442   VELEZ CORREA, JAIME. "Análisis filosófico del conflicto
        social." In Conflicto social y compromiso cristiano en
        América Latina, edited by Consejo Episcopal Latinoamericano,
        pp. 171-199. Bogotá: Consejo Epsicopal Latinoamericano,
        1976.

1443   VERRET, MICHEL. "Marxista ante la Iglesia católica." Cultura
        Boliviana 2 (November, 1965).

1444   _____. "Un marxista diante da Igreja católica: o diálogo de
        marxistas e católicos." Paz e Terra 1 (July, 1966): 163-
        179.

1445   VIANA, MIKEL. "De la ortodoxia a la heterodoxia: la crítica
        de los marxismos a la religión." SIC 402 (February, 1978):
        61-63.

1446   ZAFFARONI, JUAN CARLOS. Marxismo y cristianismo. Montevideo:
        Ediciones A. P., 1966. 103 pp.

NATIONALISM

1447   ALBA, VICTOR. "Nationalism and Political Reality." America
        118 (April 27, 1968): 571-574.

1448   CASTRO, JOSUÉ; GERASSI, JOHN; and HOROWITS, L., eds.
        Latin American Radicalism: A Documentary Report on Left
        and National Movements. New York: Vintage, 1969. 658 pp.

1449   DUNCAN, W. RAYMOND, and GOODSELL, JAMES NELSON, eds. The
        Quest for Change in Latin America: Sources for a Twentieth
        Century Analysis. New York: Oxford University Press, 1970.
        562 pp.

1450   KENNEDY, JOHN J. "Dichotomies in the Church." In The Dynamics
        of Change in Latin American Politics, edited by John D.
        Martz, pp. 276-283. Englewood Cliffs, New Jersey: Prentice-
        Hall, 1965.

1451   SMITH, DAVID S., ed. Prospects for Latin America. New York:
        Columbia University, 1970. 384 pp.

1452   TURNER, FREDERICK. "Catholicism and Nationalism in Latin
        America." American Behavioral Scientist 17 (July, 1974):
        845-864.

1453   ZEA, LEOPOLDO. Latin America and the World. Norman: Univer-
        sity of Oklahoma Press, 1969. 105 pp.

PEASANTRY

1454   FREIRE, PAULO. Pedagogy of the Oppressed. New York: Herder
        and Herder, 1970. 186 pp.

1455   FRIAS, PEDRO J. "Iglesia y Estado: las relaciones pactadas
        después del Vaticano II." Criterio 48 (1975): 297-299.

1456   HUIZER, GERRIT. "Peasant Organizations in the Process of Poli-
        tical Modernization: The Latin American Experience." In
        City and Country in the Third World: Issues in the Moderni-
        zation of Latin America, edited by Arthur J. Field, pp. 49-
        62. Cambridge, Massachusetts: Schenkman Publishing Com-
        pany, 1970.

1457   _____. The Revolutionary Potential of Peasants in Latin
        America. Lexington, Massachusetts: D. C. Heath, 1972.
        237 pp., bibl.

1458   LANDSBERGER, HENRY A., ed. Latin American Peasant Movements.
        Ithaca, New York: Cornell University Press, 1969. 476 pp.

1459   _____, and CANITROT, FERNANDO. Iglesia, clase media y el
        movimiento sindical campesino. Santiago, Chile: Editorial
        del Pacífico, 1967.

1460   MÉTRAUX, ALFRED. "Fêtes religieuses et développement com-
        munautaire dans la région andine." Archives de Sociologie
        des Religions 7 (January/June, 1962): 121-126.

1461   MIGUENS, JOSÉ ENRIQUE. "Iglesia y Estado en América Latina:
        ¿un enfrentamiento por el control social?" Criterio 50
        (April 14, 1977): 160-165.

1462   "New Help for the Campesinos: Cultural Self-Help Projects in
        Latin America." Catholic Digest 31 (August, 1967): 41-44.

1463   RODRÍGUEZ, E. "Upsurge of the Peasant Movement in Latin Amer-
        ican Countries." Mirovaia Ekonomika i Mezhdunarodnye
        Otnosheniia 10 (1963): 41-54.

1464   SINGELMANN, PETER MARIUS. Peasant Movements, Social Exchange,
        and Poverty in Latin America: Explorations of a Theoretical
        Model. Austin: University of Texas Press, 1972. 385 pp.,
        bibl.

Peasantry

1465   UNDURRAGA, A. "Evaluación de la religiosidad popular de
        Latinoamérica." Catequesis Latinoamericana 1 (May/June,
        1969): 18-34.

POLITICS

1466   ADIE, ROBERT F. Latin America: The Politics of Immobility.
        Englewood Cliffs, New Jersey: Prentice-Hall, 1974. 278
        pp., bibl.

1467   AHUMADA, CORRIPIO, et al. "El compromiso cristiano ante las
        opciones sociales y la política." Documentación Social
        Latinoamericana 14 (June, 1974): 13-23.

1468   ALBARRAN, ANTONIO. "¿Sacerdotes en política? Interrogantes
        y evaluación provisional de una experiencia." Sal Terrae
        762 (November, 1976): 794-803.

1469   ALEXANDER, ROBERT JACKSON. Prophets of the Revolution: Pro-
        files of Latin American Leaders. New York: Macmillan,
        1962. 322 pp.

1470   ALFARO JIMÉNEZ, JUAN. "Las esperanzas intramundanas y la
        esperanza cristiana." Concilium 59 (1970): 352-363.

1471   ANDERSON, CHARLES W. Politics and Economic Change in Latin
        America. Princeton, New Jersey: D. Van Nostrand Company,
        1967. 388 pp.

1472   ANTONCICH, RICARDO. "Experiencia latinoamericana de la dimen-
        sión política de la fe." Sal Terrae 8-9 (August/September,
        1976): 593-600.

1473   ARIAS CALDERÓN, RICARDO. "Hacia una perspectiva cristiana de
        la política." Mensaje 16 (July, 1967): 217-227.

1474   ARRUPE, PEDRO. "El clero y la política." Política y Espíritu
        322 (May, 1971): 70-72.

1475   ASSANDRI, ANDRÉS. "El compromiso de la Iglesia y el cuestiona-
        miento de sus estructuras." Perspectivas de Diálogo 51
        (March, 1971): 14-22.

1476   ASSMANN, HUGO. Iglesia y política: Iglesia proyecto histórico.
        Montevideo: Centro de Documentación MIEC-JECI, 1971. 11
        pp.

1477   _____. "La dimensión política de la fe como praxis de la liberación histórica del hombre." Vida Pastoral 21 (April, 1970): 16-25.

1478   _____. "Teología política." Perspectivas de Diálogo 50 (December, 1970): 306-312.

1479   AVILA P., RAFAEL. Teología, evangelización y liberación. Bogotá: Ediciones Paulinas, 1973. 111 pp., bibl.

1480   "Ayuda internacional, ¿mito o realidad?" Reportaje-DESAL 2 (July/December, 1969): 5-8.

1481   BARBIERI, LÁZARO. La integración de Latinoamérica. Buenos Aires: Editora Troquel, 1961. 183 pp., bibl.

1482   BARNADAS, JOSEP. "Christian Faith and the Colonial Situation in Latin America." In Power and the Word of God, edited by Frank Bockle and Jacques-Marie Pohier, pp. 129-138. New York: Herder and Herder, 1973.

1483   BARREIRO, JULIO, et al. El destino de Latinoamérica: la lucha ideológica. Montevideo: Editorial Alfa, 1969. 146 pp.

1484   BERMUDEZ, LUIS A. Colombia hacia la revolución. Caracas: Editorial Domingo Fuentes, 1971. 128 pp.

1485   BIANCHI, E. "Radical Faith Goes With Radical Politics." National Catholic Reporter 9 (April 6, 1973): 13.

1486   BISHOP M., JORDAN. "Politics and Latin American Catholicism." International Review of Mission 60 (April, 1971): 206-211.

1486A   BORAH, WOODROW. "Colonial Institutions and Contemporary Latin America: Political and Economic Life." Hispanic American Historical Review 43 (August, 1963): 371-379.

1487   BORRAT, HÉCTOR. "Apertura eclesial y oclusión política en América Latina." Misiones Extranjeras 33 (May/June, 1976): 219-238.

1488   BOUCHARD, PAUL. "Religion in Latin America." In The Latin Americas: The Twenty-Ninth Annual Couchiching Conference edited by Douglas Hamlin. Toronto: The Canadian Institute on Public Affairs, 1960.

Politics

1489   CARVAJAL, RAFAEL TOMÁS. América Latina: movilización popular
        y fe cristiana. Montevideo: Iglesia y Sociedad en América
        Latina, 1971. 172 pp.

1490   CASTILLO, ALFONSO. "Problema eclesial y político: la laguna
        en efervescencia." Christus 41 (December, 1976): 6-8.

1491   CASTILLO-CARDENAS, GONZALO. "Theological the Political Task
        of the Church: From Protest to Revolutionary Commitment."
        IDOC-International 23 (April 10, 1971): 19-32.

1492   CETRULO, RICARDO. "Teoría y prática de la política de desar-
        rollo de la Iglesia." Perspectivas de Diálogo 46 (May,
        1970): 182-186.

1493   _____. "Utilización política de la Iglesia." Perspectivas
        de Diálogo 4 (April, 1969): 40-44.

1494   COMBLIN, JOSÉ. "La nueva práctica de la Iglesia en el sistema
        de seguridad nacional: exposición de sus principios teó-
        ricos." Christus 40 (October, 1975): 46-51.

1495   _____. "Latin America's Version of National Security." America
        132 (February 21, 1976): 137-139.

1496   "El compromiso cristiano ante las pociones sociales y la polí-
        tica: mensaje del episcopado mexicano al pueblo de México."
        Christus 39 (February, 1974): 48-62.

1497   Confederación Latinoamericana de Religiosos. "Vida religiosa
        y situación socio-política en América Latina." Servir,
        no. 50/51, March/June, 1974, pp. 271-294.

1498   _____. Vida religiosa y situación socio-política en América
        Latina: grandes problemas socio-políticos de América Latina.
        Bogotá: Indo-American Press Service, 1972. 26 pp.

1499   Consejo Episcopal Latinoamericano. Comisión Episcopal de
        Departamento de Acción Social. "La instrumentalización
        política de la Iglesia en América Latina." El Catolicismo
        2,138 (August 27, 1972): 1-2.

1500   Consulta Latinoamericana de Iglesia y Sociedad. América hoy:
        acción de Dios y responsabilidad del hombre. Montevideo:
        Iglesia y Sociedad en América Latina, 1966. 132 pp.

1501   CÓRDOVA, EFRÉN. "El neosindicalismo cristiano en América
        Latina: CLASC." Revista de Ciencias Sociales 12 (June,
        1968): 255-295.

1502　DE KADT, EMANUEL.　"Church and Politics in Latin America."
　　　New York:　Oxford University Press, 1969.

1503　DEL MONTE, CARLOS.　"Revisión del pensamiento social de
　　　Calvino."　Cristianismo y Sociedad 3 (1965):　96-114.

1504　DEL VALLE, LUIS G.　"Iglesia y poder."　Christus 41 (November,
　　　1976):　39-45.

1505　"Democratic Left."　Time, May 11, 1962, p. 35.

1506　DÍAZ ALVAREZ, MANUEL.　"Opciones socio-políticas de Iglesia
　　　latinoamericana."　Naturaleza y Gracia 1 (September/Decem-
　　　ber, 1974):　409-438.

1507　DUFF, ERNEST A., and MC CAMANT, JOHN F.　Violence and Repres-
　　　sion in Latin America.　New York:　Free Press, 1976.　322
　　　pp., bibl.

1508　DUMAS, BENOIT A.　Los dos rostros alienados de la Iglesia:
　　　ensayo de teología política.　Buenos Aires:　Latinoamérica
　　　Libros, 1971.　255 pp.

1509　EDELMANN, ALEXANDER T.　Latin American Government and Politics:
　　　The Dynamics of a Revolutionary Society.　Homewood, Illinois:
　　　Dorsey Press, 1965.　511 pp.

1510　Equipo de Reflexión Teológico-Pastoral de Consejo Episcopal
　　　Latinoamericano.　Iglesia y política:　Documento preparado
　　　para la VII Reunión Interamericana de Obispos, Montréal,
　　　15-19 de mayo de 1972.　Bogotá:　Consejo Episcopal Latino-
　　　americano, 1972.　12 pp.

1511　FLANNERY, HARRY W., ed.　"Pope's Plan for Latin America:
　　　Interviews."　Catholic World 193 (July, 1961):　233-238+.

1512　FLORIA, CARLOS ALBERTO.　"Sobre el conflicto político."　In
　　　Conflicto social y compromiso cristiano en América Latina,
　　　edited by Consejo Episcopal Latinoamericano, pp. 87-101.
　　　Bogotá:　Consejo Episcopal Latinoamericano, 1976.

1513　FONSECA, JAIME.　"Catholic Leaders in Latin America Losing
　　　Faith in Capitalism as a Cure."　National Catholic Reporter
　　　5 (February 5, 1969):　1+.

1514　FREI MONTALVA, EDUARDO.　"Catholic Social Justice, Democracy
　　　And Pluralism."　In The Conflict Between Church and State
　　　in Latin America, edited by Frederick B. Pike, pp. 208-217.
　　　Notre Dame, Indiana:　University of Notre Dame, 1964.

Politics

1515   FREIRE, PAULO. <u>Las iglesias en América Latina: educación</u>
        <u>para el cambio social</u>. Buenos Aires: Tierra Nueva, 1974.
        16 pp.

1516   FURTER, PIERRE. "L'Amérique Latine: jeunesse et politiques."
        <u>Choisir</u> 107 (1968): 10.

1517   GALILES, SEGUNDO, ed. <u>Vertiente política de la pastoral</u>.
        Quito: IPLA, 1970. 117 pp.

1518   GERASSI, JOHN. <u>The Great Fear: The Reconquest of Latin</u>
        <u>America by Latin Americans</u>. New York: Macmillan, 1963.
        457 pp.

1519   GINES ORTEGA, JESÚS. "Esperanza cristiana y acción política."
        <u>Política y Espíritu</u> 325 (1971): 40-43.

1520   GIRALDO, ALBERTO. <u>Líneas de búsqueda para ubicar al sacerdote</u>
        <u>frente a la problemática socio-política del país</u>. Bogotá:
        Conferencia Episcopal Colombiana, 1971. 12 pp.

1521   GONZÁLEZ-RUÍZ, JOSÉ MARÍA. "¿Sacerdotes en política? anota-
        ciones a una presencia de pastor y cuidadano." <u>Sal Terrae</u>
        762 (November, 1976): 785-793.

1522   _____. "The Political Meaning of Jesus in the Christian
        Community's Political Commitment." <u>Concilium</u> 4 (1973):
        31-38.

1523   GUICHARD, JEAN. "Ideologies and Power." In <u>Power and the</u>
        <u>Word of God</u>, edited by Franz Bockle and Jacques-Marie
        Pohier, pp. 89-96. New York: Herder and Herder, 1973.

1524   GUTIÉRREZ, GUSTAVO, and SHAULL, RICHARD. <u>Liberation and</u>
        <u>Change</u>. Atlanta: John Knox Press, 1977. 184 pp.

1525   GUZMÁN CAMPOS, GERMÁN. "La rebeldía clerical en América
        Latina." <u>Revista Mexicana de Sociología</u> 32 (March/April,
        1970): 357-394.

1526   HAMILTON, WILLIAM. "A Note on Radical Theology." <u>Concilium</u>
        29 (October, 1967): 85-97.

1527   HODGES, DONALD CLARK. <u>Latin America Revolution: Politics</u>
        <u>and Strategy from Apro-Marxism to Guevarism</u>. New York:
        William Morrow, 1974. 287 pp.

1528   HOROWITZ, IRVING LOUIS; CASTRO, JOSUÉ DE; and GERASSI, JOHN. Latin American Radicalism. New York: Random House, 1969. 653 pp.

1529   HUBNER GALLO, JORGE IVÁN. Los católicos en la política. Santiago, Chile: Zig-Zag, 1959. 107 pp.

1530   HUMPHREY, HUBERT H. "Alliance for Progress: The Role of the Church." Vital Speeches 30 (March 1, 1964): 307-311.

1530A   IBAÑEZ LANGLOIS, JOSÉ MIGUEL. Iglesia y política. Pamplona: Eunsa, 1975. 32 pp.

1531   Iglesia y la comunidad política: documentos colectivos de los episcopados católicos de todo el mundo, 1965-1975. Madrid: Biblioteca de Autores Cristianos, 1975. 759 pp., bibl.

1532   "Iglesia y política en América Latina." CIDOC Informa 1 (May, 1964): 8-11.

1533   JOHNSON, DALE L. The Sociology of Change and Reaction in Latin America. New York: Bobbs-Merrill, 1973. 57 pp.

1534   JOHNSON, JOHN J. Political Change in Latin America: The Emergence of the Middle Sectors. Stanford: Stanford University Press, 1958. 272 pp., bibl.

1535   KASPER, WALTER. "Politische Utopie und Christliche Hoffnung." Frankfurter Hefte 24 (August, 1969): 563-572.

1536   KRUMWEIDE, HEINRICH W. "Der Wandel der sozialverantwortlichen Rolle der katholischen Kirche in Lateinamerika." In Politik in Lateinamerika: interne und externe Faktor en einer Konfliktorientierten Entwicklung, edited by Klaus Lindenberg, pp. 82-98. Hannover: Verlag für Literatur und Zeitgeschehen, 1971.

1537   LAMBERG, ROBERT F. "Der lateinamerikanische Populismus als Element politischer Dynamik." Kulturarbeit 19 (1967): 23-24.

1538   "Latin American Patchwork." Herder 5 (January, 1968): 21-23.

1539   LEVINE, DANIEL H. "Religion and Politics." Journal of Interamerican Studies and World Affairs 16 (November, 1974): 497-507.

Politics

1540 _____, and WILDE, ALEXANDER W. "The Catholic Church, Politics and Violence: The Colombian Case." Review of Politics 39 (April, 1977): 220-249.

1541 LLANO CIFUENTES, RAFAEL. "La actuación del cristiano en la vida política." Istmo 77 (November/December, 1971): 32-44.

1542 LOMBARDO TOLEDANO, VICENTE. "El documento político mas audáz en la historia de la Iglesia católica: la encíclica de Paulo VI sobre el desarrollo de los pueblos." Siempre 72 (April, 1967): 26-29, 69.

1543 LOPEZ, MAURICIO. "The Political Dynamics of Latin American Society Today." In The Church Amid Revolution, edited by Harvey Cox, pp. 129-150. New York: Association Press, 1967.

1544 LOPEZ TRUJILLO, ALFONSO. "El compromiso político del sacerdote." Tierra Nueva 4 (1975): 17-53.

1545 _____. "El cristiano ante la política." El Catolicismo 2,126 (February 27, 1972): 8-11.

1546 MAC EOIN, GARY. "El clero frente a la política y los problemas sociales: la nueva 'Imagen' del sacerdote en América Latina." Life en Español 28 (September, 1966): 5-6.

1547 MC GRATH, MARK G. "A Living Theology in Latin America." The Review of Politics 33 (April, 1971): 163-171.

1548 MAC KINNON, KENNETH P. "New Leaven, New Mentality." Linacre 32 (May, 1965): 107.

1549 MADARIAGA, SALVADOR DE. Latin America Between the Eagle and the Bear. New York: Praeger, 1962. 192 pp.

1550 MARTZ, JOHN D., ed. The Dynamics of Change in Latin American Politics. Englewood Cliffs, New Jersey: Prentice-Hall, 1965. 283 pp.

1551 "Marx's Three Revolutions." Reportaje-DESAL 1 (July/December, 1968): 7.

1552 MEINVIELLE, JULIO. Concepción católica de la política. Buenos Aires: Ediciones Theoria, 1961. 74 pp.

1553   MENDES DE ALMEIDA, CANDIDO. "The Exercise of Power in Deve-
        loping Countries." In Power and the Word of God, edited
        by Frank Bockle and Jacques-Marie Pohier, pp. 104-117.
        New York: Herder and Herder, 1973.

1554   MÍGUEZ BONINO, JOSÉ. "Christians and the Political Revolution."
        Motive 27 (1966): 37-40.

1555   MONTEFORTE TOLEDO, MARIO. Partidos políticos de Iberoamérica.
        México: Instituto Nacional de Investigaciones Sociales,
        Universidad de México, 1961. 145 pp., bibl.

1556   MORENO, FERNANDO. "Análisis político del conflicto social en
        América Latina y compromiso cristiano." In Conflicto social
        y compromiso cristiano en América Latina, edited by Consejo
        Episcopal Latinoamericano, pp. 102-124. Bogotá: Consejo
        Episcopal Latinoamericano, 1976.

1557   MORENO, FRANCISCO JOSÉ, and MITRANI, BARBARA, eds. Conflict
        and Violence in Latin American Politics: A Book of Read-
        ings. New York: T. Crowell, 1971. 452 pp.

1558   MUTCHLER, DAVID E. The Church as a Political Factor in Latin
        America. New York: Praeger, 1971. 460 pp., bibl.

1559   New Perspectives on Latin America: Political and Social
        Change. New York: MSS Information, 1976. 298 pp.

1560   ORREGO VICUÑA, CLAUDIO. "Libertad política de los cristianos."
        In Cristianos por el socialismo: ¿Consecuencia cristiana
        o alienación política?, edited by Instituto de Estudios
        Políticos, pp. 339-342. Santiago, Chile: Pacífico, 1972.

1561   ORRUPE, PEDRO. "El sacerdote y la política." In Liberación:
        opción de la Iglesia latinoamericana en la decada del 70,
        edited by Simposio sobre Teología de la Liberación, pp. 63-
        71. Bogotá: Editorial Presencia, 1970.

1562   OSSA, MANUEL. "Cristianismo y política." Mensaje 187 (April/
        May, 1970): 103-107.

1563   PACHECO GÓMEZ, MAXIMO. "Política y santidad." Mensaje 105
        (January, 1962): 13-19.

1564   PADILLA, C. R. "Church and Political Ambiguity." Christian-
        ity Today 18 (June 26, 1974): 41-42.

Politics

1565   "Pastorales de los obispos latinamericanos sobre cuestiones
        político-sociales." Boletín Bibliográfico Iberoamericano
        (1975), número extraordinario.

1566   PAYSSE GONZÁLEZ, EDUARDO. "La Iglesia católica y las fuerzas
        políticas en América Latina." Cristianismo y Sociedad 3
        (September/December, 1965): 44-70.

1567   PÉREZ RIVAS, MARCELO. "Algunas reflexiones teológicas sobre
        la participación del cristiano en la política." Cristian-
        ismo y Sociedad 2 (May 4, 1964): 3-10.

1568   PINTO, FRANCISCO. "La reforma del régimen político." Mensaje
        123 (October, 1963): 514-522.

1569   POWELL, JOHN DUNCAN. Political Mobilization of the Venezuelan
        Peasant. Cambridge: Harvard University Press, 1971. 259
        pp.

1570   "Priests in Politics." Senior Scholastic 97 (October 19,
        1970): 20-21.

1571   QUIJANO, ANIBAL. "Contemporary Peasant Movements." In Elites
        in Latin America, edited by Seymour M. Lipset and Aldo
        Solari, pp. 301-340. New York: Oxford University Press,
        1967.

1572   RAMA, CARLOS M. "La política vaticanista en América Latina."
        Cuadernos Americanos 5 (September/October, 1969): 31-41.

1573   "El religioso latinoamericano en la política latinoamericana."
        In Vida religiosa y situación socio-político en América
        Latina: grandes problemas socio-políticos de América
        Latina, edited by Confederación Latinoamericana de Reli-
        giosos, pp. 15-19. Bogotá: Indo-American Press Service,
        1972.

1574   REYES MATTA, FERNANDO, comp. Hélder Câmara: universidad y
        revolución. Santiago, Chile: Ediciones Nueva Universidad,
        1969. 108 pp.

1575   RIAS CALDERÓN, RICARDO. "Hacia una perspectiva cristiana de
        la política." Mensaje 159 (June, 1967): 217-227.

1576   RODRÍQUEZ, C. R. "La révolution démocratique bourgeoise en
        Amérique Latine." La Nouvell Critique 42 (March, 1971):
        32-35.

1577 ROSIER, IRENAEUS. Het Volk Gelooft Niet Meer in Beloften: een Situatieschets van Latijns Amerika. Hilversum: Uitgeverij Paul Brand, 1968. 143 pp.

1578 SCHIFFELBEIN, ERNESTO. "Estructura democrática de la planificación." Mensaje 123 (October, 1963): 607-617.

1579 SCHMITT, KARL MICHAEL. Evolution or Chaos: Dynamics of Latin American Government and Politics. New York: Praeger, 1963. 308 pp., bibl.

1580 SEGUNDO, JUAN LUIS. "Education, Communication, and Liberation: A Christian Vision." IDOC-International 35 (November 13, 1971): 63-96.

1581 _____. "Los caminos del desarrollo político latinoamericano." Mensaje 115 (December, 1962): 701-707.

1582 SIGMUND, PAUL E. "Latin American Catholicism's Opening to the Left." The Review of Politics 35 (1973): 61-76.

1583 SILVA BASCUNAN, ALEJANDRO. "Relaciones entre comunidades políticas." Mensaje 119 (May, 1963): 240-243.

1584 SMITH, DAVID S., ed. Prospects for Latin America. New York: Columbia University, 1970. 384 pp.

1585 SZULC, TAD. The Winds of Revolution: Latin America Today and Tomorrow. New York: Praeger, 1963. 308 pp.

1586 TOMIC ROMERO, DRAGOMIR. Unidad y diversidad de la democracia cristiana en el mundo. Santiago, Chile: Imprenta del Pacífico, 1962. 32 pp.

1587 TORRES RESTREPO, CAMILO. Camilo, el cura revolucionario: sus obras. Buenos Aires: Ediciones Cristianismo y Revolucion, 1968. 313 pp.

1588 _____. Camilo Torres, His Life and His Message: The Text of His Original Platform and All His Messages to the Colombian People. Springfield, Illinois: Templegate Publishers, 1968. 128 pp.

1589 _____. Camilo Torres, 1956-1966. Cuernavaca, México: Centro Internacional de Documentación, 1966. 377 pp.

1590 _____. Con las armas en la mano. México: Editorial Diogenes, 1971. 183 pp.

Politics

1591   _____. Cristianismo y revolución. México: Ediciones Era,
        1970. 611 pp.

1592   _____. "Por qué no voy a las elecciones." Frente Unido 1
        (August 26, 1965): 1, 8.

1593   TURNER, FREDERICK C. Catholicism and Political Development
        in Latin America. Chapel Hill: University of North
        Carolina Press, 1971. 272 pp., bibl.

1594   VAILLANCOURT, Y. "Les politises chrétiens et la libération."
        Relations 371 (May, 1972): 141, 143-145.

1595   VEKEMANS, ROGER. "Iglesia y política." Ateísmo y Diálogo 4
        (December, 1976): 160-166.

1596   VELA MONSALVE, CARLOS. Tácticas y directivas contra la farsa
        comunista. Quito: Editora Colón, 1962. 145 pp., bibl.

1597   VELÁSQUEZ, H. "El documento episcopal sobre fe y política."
        Christus 39 (April, 1974): 13-14.

1598   VELIZ, CLAUDIO. The Politics of Conformity in Latin America.
        New York: Oxford University Press, 1967. 292 pp.

1599   WIARDA, HOWARD J., ed. Politics and Social Change in Latin
        America: The Distinct Tradition. Amherst: University of
        Massachusetts Press, 1974. 297 pp.

1600   WILLIAMS, EDWARD J. "Christian Politics: The Significance
        for Latin America." Dusquesne Review 14 (1969): 65-83.

1601   _____. "Latin American Catholicism and Political Integration."
        Comparative Political Studies 2 (October, 1969): 327-348.

1602   WIPLER, WILLIAM L. "The Current Roman Catholic Challenge to
        Government in Latin America." South East Latin Americanist
        16 (September, 1972): 1-4.

1603   WOODIS, JACK. El saqueo del tercer mundo: introducción al
        neocolonialismo. Buenos Aires: Granica, 1972. 142 pp.

1604   ZAZPE, VICENTE. "Conciencia política y compromiso cristiano."
        Consejo Episcopal Latinoamericano 61 (September, 1972):
        14-15.

REFERENCE

1605   ALONSO, ISIDORO. "Les statistiques religieuses en Amérique
        Latine." Social Compass 14 (1967):   365-370.

1606   BINGAMAN, JOSEPH W. Latin America: A Survey of Holdings at
        the Hoover Institution on War, Revolution, and Peace.
        Stanford: Stanford University, Hoover Institution, 1972.
        96 pp.

1607   BRUNN, STANLEY D. Urbanization in Developing Countries: An
        International Bibliography. East Lansing: Michigan State
        University, 1971. 693 pp.

1608   Centro de Estudios para el Desarrollo e Integración de América
        Latina. Desarrollo y revolución, Iglesia y liberación.
        Bogotá: Centro de Estudios para el Desarrollo e Integración
        de América Latina, 1973.

1609   Centro Intercultural de Documentación. Catálogo de adquisi-
        ciones de los archivos, Centro Intercultural de Documenta-
        ción. Cuernavaca, México: Centro Intercultural de Docu-
        mentación, 1967.

1610   _____. Catálogo de adquisiciones no. 1: items clasificados
        y catalogados en los archivos CIDOC entre el 15 de junio
        y el 1 de diciembre de 1966. Cuernavaca, México: Centro
        Intercultural de Documentación, 1966. 265 pp.

1611   _____. Catálogo de adquisiciones, religión: clase 2 CDU.
        Cuernavaca, México: Centro Intercultural de Documentación,
        1967.

1612   _____. Catálogo de publicaciones. Cuernavaca, México:
        Centro Intercultural de Documentación, 1966.

1613   _____. Indice a CIDOC Dossier nos. 1-37, 1966-1971. Cuerna-
        vaca, México: Centro Intercultural de Documentación, 1971.

1614   CHILCOTE, RONALD H. Revolution and Structural Change in Latin
        America: A Bibliography on Ideology, Development, and the
        Radical Left, 1930-1965. Stanford: Stanford University,
        The Hoover Institution on War, Revolution, and Peace, 1970.
        2 v.

1615   Consejo Episcopal Latinoamericano. Secretariado General.
        Directorio católico latinoamericano, 1968. Bogotá: Indo-
        American Press, 1968. 586 pp.

Reference

1616   DELGADO, OSCAR. Bibliografía latinamericana sobre reforma
        agraria y tenencia de la tierra. México: [n.p.], 1962.
        37 pp.

1617   DELPAR, HELEN, comp. The Borzoi Reader in Latin American
        American History, vol. II: The Nineteenth Century and
        Twentieth Century. New York: Knopf, 1972. 304 pp., bibl.

1618   NO ENTRY

1619   GEOGHEGAN, ABEL RODOLFO. Obras de referencia de América
        Latina. Buenos Aires: UNESCO, 1965. 280 pp.

1620   GROPP, ARTHUR E. A Bibliography of Latin American Biblio-
        graphies. Metuchen: Scarecrow Press, 1958. 515 pp.

1621   Instituto Superior Evangélico de Estudios Teológicos de la
        Asociación Interconfesional de Estudios Teológicos. Bib-
        liografía teólogica comentada del área iberoamericana.
        Buenos Aires: Publicaciones El Escudo, 1973.

1622   LABELLE, YVAN, and ESTRADA, ADRIANA. Latin America in Maps,
        Charts, Tables, no. 2: Socio-Religious Data (Catholicism).
        Cuernavaca, México: Center of Intercultural Information,
        1965.

1623   Latin America in Maps, Charts, and Tables, no. 3: Socio-
        Educational Data. Cuernavaca, México: Centro Inter-
        cultural de Documentación. 294 pp., bibl.

1624   North American Congress on Latin America. NACLA's Biblio-
        graphy on Latin America. Berkeley: North American Congress
        on Latin America, 1973. 47 pp.

1625   OKINSHEVICH, LEO, comp. Latin America in Soviet Writings: A
        Bibliography: vol. II, 1959-1964. Baltimore: Johns
        Hopkins Press, 1966. 311 pp.

1626   OLIVOS, LUIS, and DELGADO, OSCAR. Bibliografía sobre la
        Iglesia y el cambio social en América Latina. Washington,
        D.C.: Unión Panamericana, 1966. 66 pp.

1627   ORTEGA, BENJAMÍN, comp. Repertorio para el estudio de las
        iglesias en la sociedad de América Latina: 1960-1969.
        Cuernavaca, México: Centro Intercultural de Documentación,
        1970.

1628   PROMPER, WERNER. "Amérique Latine." Eglise Vivante 18 (May/
        June, 1966): 329-338.

1629 _____. "Amérique Latine 1967." Eglise Vivante 20 (May/June, 1968): 292-303.

1630 RUSSELL, CHARLES A.; MILLER, JAMES A.; and HILDNER, ROBERT E. "The Urban Guerrilla in Latin America: A Select Bibliography." Latin American Research Review 9 (Spring, 1974): 37-79.

1631 RYAN, EDWIN. The Church in the South American Republics. New York: Bruce Publishing Company, 1932. 119 pp., bibl.

1632 SABLE, MARTIN H. Latin American Urbanization: A Guide to the Literature, Organizations and Personnel. Metuchen: Scarecrow Press, 1971. 1077 pp., bibl.

1633 SINCLAIR, JOHN H., ed. Protestantism in Latin America: A Bibliographical Guide. South Pasadena: William Carey Library, 1976. 414 pp.

1634 TORRES CALVO, ANGEL, ed. Diccionario de textos sociales pontificios. Madrid: Compañia Bibliográfica Española, 1956. 1172 pp., bibl.

1635 VAUGHAN, DENTON P., comp. Urbanization in Twentieth Century Latin America: A Working Bibliography. Austin: University of Texas, Institute of Latin American Studies, Population Research Center, 1970. 122 pp., bibl.

1636 ZAMARRIEGO, TOMAS. Enciclopedia de orientación bibliográfica. Barcelona: Juan Flores Editores, 1964.

REVOLUTION

1637 "A la paz por la revolución." Concilium 35 (May, 1968): 149-178.

1638 Acción Católica Mexicana. "México: en declaración solemne, la Acción Católica reconoció los aspectos positivos de la revolución mexicana." Informaciones Católicas Internacionales 218 (June 22, 1964): 12.

1639 ADLER, GERHARD. Revolutionares Lateinamerika: Eine Dokumentation. Paderborn: Schoningh, 1970. 216 pp., bibl.

1640 ALDUANTE L., JOSÉ. "El deber moral ante la situación revolucionaria." Mensaje 115 (December, 1962): 667-676.

Revolution

1641   America Latina: parole come armi. Milan: Jaca Book Edizioni,
       1968.   219 pp.

1642   ANDER-EGG, EZEQUIEL.   Acerca de la revolución de América
       Latina.   Córdoba, Argentina: Centro de Estudios Políticos,
       1970.   80 pp.

1643   ANDRÉ-VICENT, P. I.   "Les théologies de la libéracion."
       Nouvelle Revue Theologique 98 (February, 1976):   109-125.

1644   ANDRONOVA, V. P.   "Revoliustsiia monsen'orov?" Latinskaia
       Amerika: Adademia Nauk SSSR, Institut Latinskoi Ameriki
       2 (March/April, 1971):   76-91.

1645   ARENAS, JAIME.   La guerrilla por dentro: análisis del ELN
       colombiano.   Bogotá: Ediciones Tercer Mundo, 1971.   204 pp.

1646   ARROYO, GONZALO.   "Doctrina, utopía y subversión."   Mensaje
       161 (August, 1967):   340-347.

1647   ASSMANN, HUGO.   "Caracterização de uma teologia de revolução."
       Ponto Homen 4 (1968):   6-58.

1648   _____.   "Los cristianos revolucionarios: aliados estratégicos
       en la construcción del socialismo."   Hechos y Dichos 426
       (February, 1972):   31-39.

1649   _____.   "Elementos para uma ética da opção e praxis revolu-
       cionária."   Ponto Homen 4 (1968):   46-59.

1650   _____.   "Reflexión teológica a nivel estratégico-táctico."
       In Liberación en América Latina, pp. 113-130.   Bogotá:
       América Latina, 1971.

1651   AVILA P., RAFAEL.   "Profecía, interpretación y reinterpreta-
       ción."   In Liberación en América Latina, pp. 113-130.
       Bogotá: América Latina, 1971.

1652   BARREIRO, JULIO.   Ideologías y cambios sociales.   Montevideo:
       Editorial Alfa, 1971.   146 pp.

1653   "Beneath the Surface of the Revolution."   Reportaje-DESAL 2
       (January/June, 1969):   7.

1654   BERRIGAN, DANIEL, and STEVENSON, ALDON J.   "The Church at the
       Edge."   Jesuit Missions 40 (September, 1966):   13-19.

1655   BESSIERE, GERARD. "Do Revolutionaries Pray? Testimonies
        from South America." In The Prayer Life, edited by
        Christian Fuquoc and Claude Gellré, pp. 109-116. New York:
        Herder and Herder, 1972.

1656   BIGO, PIERRE. "Cristianismo y revolución en la época contem-
        poránea." Mensaje 115 (December, 1962): 594-604.

1657   BISHOP M., JORDAN. "Cristianisme et révolution en Amérique
        Latine." Esprit 39 (January, 1971): 16-30.

1658   _____. "Prudencia y revolución." Víspera 5 (April, 1968):
        3-6.

1659   _____. "La última revolución y el tercer mundo." CIDOC 8
        (1968).

1660   BORRAT, HÉCTOR. "Presencia cristiana en la revolución latino-
        americana." CIDOC 7 (1968): 1-7.

1661   BRILLA, RUDOLF. "Die Christen in Lateinamerika und die Revo-
        lution." Orientierung. Katholische Blätter Für Weltan-
        schauliche Information 32 (1968): 190-192.

1662   BRÖKER, W. "A 'Dialogue' Between Christian and Marxist
        Scholars." Concilium 7 (August, 1965): 171-172.

1663   BUSTON, ISMAEL. "El Estado y las reformas revolucionarias."
        Mensaje 123 (October, 1963): 618-626.

1664   CABERO, JUAN A. "Fermento revolucionario del catolicismo
        latinoamericano." Nueva Sociedad 13 (July/August, 1974):
        3-26.

1665   CÂMARA, HÉLDER. "Presença da Igreja no desenvolvimento da
        América Latina: sugestões fraternas." Vozes 1 (January,
        1967): 5-24.

1666   NO ENTRY

1667   "Cardinal Cushing Christian Revolution for Latin America."
        Catholic Messenger 82 (January 23, 1964): 1.

1668   CASTELNUOVO, ELÍAS. Jesucristo: montonero de Judea. Buenos
        Aires: La Técnica Impresora, 1971. 137 pp.

1669   CASTRO, EMILIO. "Church in a Revolutionary Situation." IDOC
        Bulletin 18 (April, 1974): 5-9.

Revolution

1670   CASTRO, JOSUÉ DE; GERASSI, JOHN; and HOROWITZ, IRVING, eds.
        Latin American Radicalism: A Documentary Report on Left
        and National Movements. New York: Vintage, 1969. 658 pp.

1671   CASTRO VILLAGRANA, BERNARDO, et al. La Iglesia, el subdesar-
        rollo y la revolución. México: Nuestro Tiempo, 1968. 247
        pp., bibl.

1672   CAVILLIOTTI, MARTA, comp. Cristianismo: doctrina social y
        revolución: antología. Buenos Aires: Centro Editor de
        America Latina, 1972. 176 pp.

1673   CAZES, DANIEL. Los revolucionarios. México: Grijalbo, 1973.
        390 pp.

1674   Centro para el Desarrollo Económico y Social de América Latina.
        Iglesia, paz y desarrollo. (n.p.): Centro para el Desar-
        rollo Económico y Social de América Latina, 1969. 17 pp.

1675   CHAPMAN, JOSEPH. "Guerrilla Priests." Spectator, August 23,
        1968, pp. 252-253.

1675A   CHARBONNEAU, PAUL EUGENE. Cristianismo, sociedade e revolução.
        São Paulo: Editora Herder, 1967. 584 pp.

1676   CHARLESWORTH, M. "Behind the Slogans: Latin America and
        Revolution." Tablet 219 (April 17, 1965): 431-433.

1677   CHILCOTE, RONALD H., and MAC BEAN, SALLY V. "Latin America's
        Left and the Causes of Revolution." Hispanic American
        Report 16 (February, 1963): 197-216.

1678   CHONCHOL, JACQUES. "Los factores de aceleración revolucion-
        aria." Mensaje 115 (December, 1962): 662-666.

1679   CLARK, GERALD. The Coming Explosion in Latin America. New
        York: McKay, 1963. 436 pp.

1680   "Comes the Revolution." America 108 (June 1, 1963): 796-797.

1681   CONTERIS, HIBER. Hombre, ideología y revolución en América
        Latina. Montevideo: Iglesia y Sociedad en América Latina,
        1965. 133 pp.

1682   _____, et al. Conciencia y revolución: contribución al
        proceso de consientización del hombre en América Latina.
        Montevideo: Tierra Nueva, 1969. 117 pp.

1683   NO ENTRY

1684   COULMAS, PETER. "Weder Reform noch Revolution." Moderne
        Welt 9 (1968): 339–345.

1685   CRAHAN, MARGARET E. "Latin American Church: Reluctant Revo-
        lution." America 133 (August 30, 1975): 90–93.

1686   D'ANTONIO, WILLIAM V., and PIKE, FREDERICK B. Religion, Revo-
        lution and Reform: New Forces for Change in Latin America.
        New York: Praeger, 1964. 276 pp.

1687   DEBRAY, REGIS. Strategy for Revolution: Essays on Latin
        America. New York: Monthly Review Press, 1967. 256 pp.

1688   DEEDY, JOHN G. "Rand and the Church." Commonweal 96 (April
        21, 1972): 154.

1689   DEL VALLE, LUIS G. "El papel de la teología en América
        Latina." In Liberación en América Latina, pp. 17–33.
        Bogotá: América Latina, 1971.

1690   DOMINGO, PEDRO V. "Activistas de nota en América Latina."
        Estudios sobre el Comunismo 6 (January/March, 1958): 87–
        91.

1691   DUNCAN, W. RAYMOND, and GOODSELL, JAMES NELSON, eds. Quest
        for Change in Latin America: Sources for a Twentieth
        Century Analysis. New York: Oxford University Press, 1970.
        562 pp.

1692   EDMONSTONE, W. E. "Revelation in the Revolution?" Anglican
        Dialogue 5 (Winter, 1967): 20–23.

1693   "Education for Liberation in Latin America." IDOC-Interna-
        tional 21 (March 31, 1964): 53–58.

1694   EINAUDI, LUIGI. Changing Contexts of Revolution in Latin
        America. Santa Monica: Rand Corporation, 1966.

1695   FALS-BORDA, ORLANDO. Marginality and Revolution in Latin
        America, 1809–1969. New Brunswick: Rutgers University,
        1970–1971. 91 pp.

1696   _____. Las revoluciones inconclusas en América Latina, 1809–
        1969. México: Editores Siglo Veintiuno, 1968. 82 pp.

Revolution

1697 _____. Subversion and Development: The Case of Latin America.
Geneva: Europe Third World Centre, under auspices of the
Foyer John Knox Association, 1970. 17 pp.

1698 FERNÁNDEZ CABRELI, ALFONSO. Artigas y los curas rebeldes.
Montevideo: Ediciones Grito de Asencio, 1968. 165 pp.

1699 FLORES OLEA, VICTOR. "América Latina: los caminos de la
revolución." In La Iglesia, el subdesarrollo y la revolución, edited by Bernardo Castro Villagrana et al., pp. 105-
141. México: Editorial Nuestro Tiempo, 1968.

1700 FRANCO, R. "La estrategia del enfrentamiento." Christus 39
(February, 1974): 6-15.

1701 FRANK, ANDRÉ GUNDER. Latin America: Underdevelopment or
Revolution? New York: Monthly Review Press, 1970. 409
pp., bibl.

1702 FURTER, PIERRE. L'imagination creatrice, la violence et le
changement social: une interpretation. Cuernavaca, México:
Centro Intercultural de Documentación, 1968. 211 pp.

1703 GALILEA, SEGUNDO. "Un cristiano para tiempos de revolución."
Mensaje 201 (August, 1971): 332-337.

1704 GALL, NORMAN. "Latin America: the Church Militant." Commentary 49 (April, 1970): 25-37.

1705 _____. "La reforma católica." Mundo Nuevo 48 (June, 1970):
20-43.

1706 GANNON, FRANCIS X. "Catholicism, Revolution and Violence in
Latin America: Lessons of 1968 Guatemala Maryknoll Episode."
Orbis, Winter, 1969, pp. 1204-1225.

1707 GARCÍA ELORRIO, JUAN. "Definición, deber y desafío."
Cristianism y Revolución 5 (November, 1967): 1-2.

1708 _____. "La misma guerra." Cristianismo y Revolución 6-7
(April, 1968): 1-2.

1709 _____. "El pueblo no elige la violencia, lucha por la justicia." Cristianismo y Revolución 20 (September, 1969):
2-3.

1710 _____. "'Tiempo Social' con 'Estado de Sitio.'" Cristianismo
y Revolución 18 (July, 1969): 24-25.

1711   GARCÍA G., JESÚS. "Los obstáculos al desarrollo en América
       Latina." In La Iglesia, el subdesarrollo y la revolución,
       edited by Bernardo Castro Villagrana et al., pp. 54-80.
       México: Editorial Nuestro Tiempo, 1968.

1712   GARCÍA LIZARRALDE, RENÉ. "Cristianismo y revolución." Revista
       Javeriana 355 (July, 1969): 502-504.

1713   GERASSI, JOHN. The Great Fear: The Reconquest of Latin
       America by Latin Americans. New York: Macmillan Company,
       1963. 457 pp.

1714   GEYER, GEORGIE ANNE. "Latin America: the Rise of a New Non-
       Communist Left." Catholic Mind 65 (November, 1967): 19-
       26.

1715   GHEERBRANT, ALAIN. La Iglesia rebelde de América Latina.
       México: Siglo Veintiuno Editores, 1970. 319 pp.

1716   GOLDRICH, DANIEL. "Toward an Estimate of the Probability of
       Social Revolutions in Latin America: Some Orienting Concepts
       and a Case Study." The Centennial Review 7 (Summer, 1962):
       394-408.

1717   GONZÁLEZ RUIZ, JOSÉ MARÍA. "El cristiano y la revolución"
       Cuadernos de Ruedo Ibérico 2 (February/March, 1967): 4-17.

1718   GOSS MAYR, HILDEGERO. "Une révolution non-violente." Con-
       cilium 35 (1968): 153-165.

1719   GOTT, RICHARD. Guerrilla Movements in Latin America. Garden
       City: Doubleday, 1971. 452 pp., bibl.

1720   _____. "Revolution in Latin America." Guardian (June 11,
       1965): 12.

1721   GOZZER, GIOVANNI. Religión y revolución en América Latina.
       Madrid: Taurus, 1969. 360 pp.

1722   GREMILLION, JOSEPH B. "Church Sees Revolution in Latin
       America." Catholic Messenger 82 (April 30, 1964): 12.

1723   GUICHARD, JEAN. "Ideologies and Power." In Power and the
       Word of God, edited by Franz Bockle and Jacques Marie
       Pohier, pp. 89-96. New York: Herder and Herder, 1973.

1724   GUZMÁN CAMPOS, GERMÁN. Camilo: el cura guerrillero. Bogotá:
       Servicios Especiales de Prensa, 1967. 257 pp., illus.

Revolution

1725   HIRSHFIELD, R.   "Padre Bolo: Popular Revolutionary, Still
        Learning How."   National Catholic Reporter 3 (June 28,
        1967):   2.

1726   _____.   "Voice of Revolution."   Jubilee 13 (January, 1966):
        24-27.

1727   HODGES, DONALD CLARK.   Latin American Revolution: Politics
        and Strategy from Apro-Marxism to Guevarism.   New York:
        Morrow, 1974.   287 pp.

1728   Hombre, ideología y revolución en América Latina.   Montevideo:
        Centro de Estudios de la Federación de Iglesias Evangélicas
        del Uruguay, 1965.   133 pp.

1729   HOUTART, FRANÇOIS, and PIN, EMILE.   The Church and the Latin
        American Revolution.   New York: Sheed and Ward, 1965.
        264 pp., bibl.

1730   HUFF, RUSSELL.   "Christian Revolution in Latin America."   Ave
        Maria 99 (April 18, 1964):   5-7.

1731   HUIZER, GERRIT.   The Revolutionary Potential of Peasants in
        Latin America.   Lexington, Massachusetts: D. C. Heath,
        1972.   237 pp., bibl.

1732   Iglesia católica y revolución.   Havana: Impresora Universita-
        ria "Andre Voisin", 1969.   241 pp.

1733   Iglesia y Sociedad en América Latina.   Hombre, ideología y
        revolución en América Latina.   Montevideo: Talleres
        Gráficos de la Comunidad del Sur, 1965.   133 pp.

1734   "The Ingredients of Pre-Revolution."   Reportaje-DESAL 1 (July/
        December, 1968):   6.

1735   ¿Una izquierda cristiana?   debate.   Lima: Centro de Estudios
        y Publicaciones, 1972.   50 pp.

1736   JARLOT, GEORGES.   "Riforme o rivoluzione nella America Latina."
        La Civiltá Cattolica 10 (1964):   353-359.

1737   Justicia y paz.   Caracas: Comisión Venezolana de Justicia y
        Paz, 1968.   471 pp., bibl.

1738   KARCZAG, GABOR.   Latin Amerika a Kubai Forradalom Utan.
        Budapest: Kossuth Konyvkaido, 1968.   203 pp.

1739   LAGARRIGUE, JAVIER. "Génesis de la revolución latinoamericano."
       Mensaje 115 (December, 1962): 610-617.

1740   LARA-BRAUD, JORGE. "Latin America: The Crisis and Signs of
       Hope." Catholic World 204 (February, 1967): 290-295.

1741   _____, ed. Our Claim on the Future. New York: Friendship
       Press, 1970. 128 pp.

1742   LEIDEN, CARL, and SCHMITT, KARL M. The Politics of Violence:
       Revolution in the Modern World. Englewood Cliffs:
       Prentice-Hall, 1968. 244 pp.

1743   LEÑERO, VICENTE. "Revolución en la Iglesia durante los sesenta."
       Espejo 9 (October/December, 1969): 21-37.

1744   LENKERDORF, KARL. "Religión y revolución." In La Iglesia,
       el subdesarrollo y la revolución, edited by Bernardo
       Castro Villagrana et al., pp. 142-152. México: Editorial
       Nuestro Tiempo, 1968.

1745   LÓPEZ OLIVA, ENRIQUE. El camilismo en la América Latina.
       Havana: Casa de las Américas, 1970. 97 pp., bibl.

1746   _____. Los católicos y la revolución latinoamericana.
       Havana: Editorial de Ciencias Sociales, 1970. 186 pp.

1747   LÓPEZ TRUJILLO, ALFONSO. ¿Liberación e revolución? Bogotá:
       Ediciones Paulinas, 1975. 144 pp.

1748   "Lucha de clases, compromiso político, cristianismo." Mensaje
       209 (June, 1972): 301-309.

1749   MAC EOIN, GARY. Revolution Next Door: Latin America in the
       1970's. New York: Holt, Rinehart, and Winston, 1971.
       243 pp., bibl.

1750   MAC KAY, JOHN A. "Latin America and Revolution: The New
       Mood in the Churches." Christian Century 82 (November 24,
       1965): 1439-1443.

1751   MADURO, OTTO. Revelación y revolución. Mérida: Ediciones
       del Rectorado, Universidad de los Andes, Departamento de
       Publicaciones, 1970. 133 pp.

1752   MAGNET, ALEJANDRO. "Génesis de una situación prerrevolucionaria."
       Mensaje 123 (October, 1963): 485-496.

Revolution

1753   MANSIR, JEAN. "Revolution dans l'Eglise catholique." La
        Lettre 128 (April, 1969): 13-16.

1754   MARTÍNEZ ARONA, GALO. "Lateinamerikanisches Dilemna. Die
        Christen und die Revolution." Orientierung. Katholische
        Blätter für Weltanschauliche Information 32 (1968): 93-96.

1755   "Marx's Three Revolutions." Reportaje-DESAL 1 (July/December,
        1968): 7.

1756   MASPERO, EMILIO. "Latin America's Labor Movement of Christian
        Democratic Orientation as an Instrument of Social Change."
        In Religion, Revolution, and Reform: New Forces for Change
        in Latin America, edited by William V. D'Antonio, pp. 163-
        181. New York: Praeger, 1964.

1757   MAULLIN, RICHARD L. Soldiers, Guerrillas, and Politics in
        Columbia. Lexington, Massachusetts: Lexington Books,
        1973. 168 pp., bibl.

1758   MENDOZA MIAZ, AVARO. La revolución de los profesionales e
        intelectuales en Latinoamerica. México: Instituto Nacional
        de Investigaciones Sociales de la Universidad Nacional
        Autonoma de México, 1962. 178 pp.

1759   MERCADER, MANUEL. Cristianismo y revolución en América Latina.
        Mexico: Diogenes, 1974. 145 pp.

1760   MÍQUEZ BONINO, JOSÉ. Ama y haz lo que quieras: una ética
        para el hombre nuevo. Buenos Aires: Escatón, 1972. 133
        pp.

1761   MOLNAR, T. "Iglesia y revolución." Triumph 3 (June, 1968):
        15-16.

1762   MOLTMANN, JÜRGEN. "Dios en la revolución." Cristianismo y
        Revolución 20 (September/October, 1969): 19-24.

1763   MOSS, ROBERT. Urban Guerrillas in Latin America. London:
        Institute for the Study of Conflict, 1970. 15 pp.

1764   OJEDA, GONZALO. "Algo más sobre revolución en libertad."
        Rebeldía 2 (June 12, 1964): 2.

1764A   OLIVEIRA, PLINIO CORREA DE. Revoluçaõ e contra revolução.
        Rio de Janeiro: Editora Boa Imprensa, 1959. 58 pp.

1765   ORREGA VICUÑA, CLAUDIO. "A proposito del social-cristianismo
       y el cristianismo revolucionario." In Cristianos por el
       Socialismo. ¿Consecuencia cristiana o alienación política?,
       edited by Instituto de Estudios Políticos, pp. 383-398.
       Santiago, Chile: Pacífico, 1972.

1766   ORTEGA, BENJAMÍN, comp. El Che Guevara: reacción de la prensa
       del continente americano con motivo de su muerte, octubre-
       noviembre, 1967. Cuernavaca, México: Centro Intercultural
       de Documentación, 1968. 446 pp.

1767   OVIEDO, VÍCTOR. La revolución en la Iglesia. Buenos Aires:
       Punto Crítico, 1971.

1768   PACHECO GÓMEZ, MÁXIMO. "Revolución, justicia y derecho."
       Mensaje 115 (December, 1962): 676-680.

1769   PÉREZ ESCLARÍN, ANTONIO. "Theology of Revolution for the
       Third World." Catholic World 213 (September, 1971): 277-
       282.

1770   PÉREZ GARCÍA, ANTONIO. "Reflexiones pacíficas sobre la revo-
       lución." Víspera 4 (January, 1968): 13-21.

1771   PÉREZ RAMÍREZ, GUSTAVO. "Revolution: A Challenge to Christians
       in Latin America." Canadian Forum 47 (December, 1967):
       194-198.

1772   PETRAS, JAMES, ed. Latin America: From Dependence to Revo-
       lution. New York: John Wiley and Sons, 1973. 274 pp.,
       bibl.

1773   POWELSON, JOHN P. Latin America: Today's Economic and Social
       Revolution. New York: McGraw-Hill, 1964. 303 pp.

1774   "Presencia cristiana en la revolución latinoamericana."
       Criterio 37 (December 24, 1964): 948-952.

1775   PUHLE, HANS-JÜRGEN. Revolution und Reformen in Latein Amer-
       ika. Gottingen: Vandenhoeck, 1976. 281 pp.

1776   QUINN, R. M. "A Planned Social Revolution Is in Progress."
       Maryknoll 56 (April, 1962): 52-56.

1777   RADFORD RUETHER, ROSEMARY. "Latin America and the Theology of
       Revolution Liberation." In Freedom and Unfreedom in the
       Americas: Towards a Theology of Liberation, edited by
       Thomas E. Quigley, pp. 76-80. New York: International
       Documentation, 1971.

Revolution

1778 RAMA, CARLOS M. Revolución social y fascismo en el siglo XX.
      Buenos Aires: Editorial Patestra, 1962. 346 pp., bibl.

1779 "Reformas revolucionarias en América Latina." Mensaje 123
      (October, 1963): 481-484.

1780 "Revolución en América Latina." Mensaje 115 (December, 1962):
      589-726.

1781 ¿Revolución violenta? Bogotá: Editorial Andes, 1965. 157
      pp.

1782 "Revolution in the Universities: The Moral Problem." Con-
      cilium 45 (1969): 151-172.

1783 RIAS CALDERÓN, RICARDO. "Hacia una perpectiva cristiana de
      la polítice." Mensaje 159 (June, 1967): 217-227.

1784 RODRIGUEZ, C. R. "La révolution démocratique bourgeoise en
      Amérique Ñatine." La Nouvelle Critique 42 (1971): 32-35.

1785 ROSA, M. "El drama de los cristianos revolucionarios."
      Christus 37 (November, 1972): 42-47.

1786 SANTA ANA, JULIO DE. Cristianismo sin religion: ensayo.
      Montevideo: Editorial Alfa, 1969. 137 pp.

1787 _____, ed. Hombre, ideología y revolución en América Latina.
      Montevideo: Federación de Iglesias Evangelicas del Uruguay,
      1965. 133 pp.

1788 SANTAMARIA ANSA, CARLOS. "Crisis actual del pacifismo y de la
      revolución." Cuadernos para el Diálogo 57-58 (June/July,
      1968): 12-14.

1789 SCHUURMAN, LAMBERTO. El cristiano, la Iglesia y la revolucion.
      Buenos Aires: Junta de Publicaciones de las Igles Refor-
      madas, 1970. 198 pp.

1790 SEGUNDO, JUAN LUIS. "Christianity and Violence in Latin
      America." Cristianity and Crisis 28 (March 3, 1968):
      31-34.

1791 _____. "Instrumentos de la teología latinoamericana." Liber-
      ación en América Latina, pp. 35-54. Bogotá: América
      Latina, 1971.

1792 _____. "Social Justice and Revolution." America 118 (April
      27, 1968): 574-578.

1793   Shaping a New World: An Orientation to Latin America.
        Maryknoll: Orbis Books, 1970. 319 pp., bibl.

1794   SHAULL, RICHARD. "A Christian Participation in the Latin
        American Revolution." Christianity Amid Rising Men and
        Nations, edited by Creighton Lacy, pp. 91-118. New York:
        Association Press, 1965.

1795   _____. "Desafío revolucionario a la Iglesia y la teología."
        Cristianismo y Revolución 2-3 (October/November, 1966):
        34-38.

1796   _____. "National Development and Social Revolution: What
        Paths Will Latin America Follow?" Christianity and Crisis
        28 (January 20, 1969): 347-348.

1797   _____. "Nicolau Berdiaev: perpectiva cristã da revolução
        social." Paz e Terra 1 (July, 1966): 180-194.

1798   _____. "O novo espírito revolucionário da América Latina."
        Paz e Terra 1 (August, 1967): 103-119.

1799   _____. The New Revolutionary Mood in Latin America. New
        York: National Council of the Churches of Christ in the
        U.S.A. (n.d.)

1800   SHEERIN, JOHN B. "Irresistible Revolution in Latin America."
        Catholic World 191 (July, 1960): 200-204.

1801   "El signo revolucionario." Cristianismo y Revolución 1
        (September, 1966): 2, 23.

1802   SMITH, EARL M. "Latin American Revolution." Christian Cen-
        tury 86 (May 14, 1969): 674-677.

1803   SMOLIK, JOSEP. "Revolution and Desacralization." Concilium
        47 (1969): 163-180.

1804   SNOEK, C. JAIME. "Tercer mundo: revolución y cristianismo."
        Concilium 15 (May, 1966): 34-53.

1805   STAHLI, MARTIN JOHANN. Reich Gottes und Revolution. Hamburg:
        Evangelischer Verlag, 1976. 161 pp., bibl.

1806   SUMMERLIN, SAM. Latin America: Land of Revolution. London:
        F. Watts, 1973.

1807   SWOMLEY, JOHN M. "Justiçia, revolucão e violência." Paz e
        Terra 2 (April, 1968): 59-72.

Revolution

1808 TAGLE, FERNANDO. "Rebeldía cristiana y 'comunidades de protesta.'" Mensaje 168 (May, 1968): 132.

1809 TOMIC ROMERO, DRAGOMIR. Es necesaria la revolución en América
Latina. Bogotá: Ediciones Paulinas, 1962. 23 pp.

1810 TORRES RESTREPO, CAMILO. "Latin America: Some Problems of
Revolutionary Strategy." In Latin America Radicalism, pp.
499-531. New York: (n.p.), 1969.

1811 ____, et al. Cristianismo y revolución. México: Ediciones
Era, 1970. 611 pp.

1812 TURNER, FREDERICK W. The Church in Latin America: A Bibliography. Storrs: University of Connecticut, 1972. 40 pp.

1813 UGALDE, LUIS. "La ambigüedad de la esperanza de los cristianos:
la utopia y la transformacion de la realidad latinoamericana." In Liberación en América Latina, pp. 83-112.
Bogotá: América Latina, 1971.

1814 VAILLANCOURT, Y. "Les chrétiens révolutionnaires en Amérique
Latine." Relations 360 (May, 1971): 139-144.

1815 VALLIER, IRAN. "Radical Priest and the Revolution." Academy
of Political Science Proceedings 30 (August, 1972): 15-26.

1816 VAN LEEUWEN, AREND THEODOR. Desarrollo y revolución. Buenos
Aires: Aurora, 1967.

1817 VEKEMANS, ROGER. "Analisis psico-social de la situación pre-
revolucionaria de América Latina." Mensaje 115 (December,
1962): 647-655.

1818 ____. La pre-revolución latinoamericana. Santiago, Chile:
Centro para el Desarrollo Económico y Social de América
Latina, 1969. 88 pp.

1819 VENEGAS CARRASCO, R. "The Revolution in Latin America."
Shield 43 (February/March, 1964): 16.

1820 VILLELA, HUGO. "Los cristianos en la revolución: ¿Posibilidad
de una praxis revolucionaria?" Cuadernos de la Realidad
Nacional 9 (September, 1971): 29-44.

1821 "Viva la Revolución: Statements of Cardinal Landázuri
Ricketts." Tablet 220 (June 11, 1966): 685.

1822   WISSOW, BOTHO V. "Südamerika—Reform oder Revolution."
        Moderne Welt 10 (1969): 77–83.

1823   YUTZIS, MARIO. "The Revolutionary Process and Latin American
        Christianity." Lutheran Quarterly 22 (1970): 11–28.

1824   ZENTENO, ARNALDO. "Liberación y magisterio." In Liberación
        en América Latina, pp. 131–163. Bogotá: América Latina,
        1971.

SOCIALISM

1825   ALBA, PEDRO DE. "El socialismo cristiano." La Nueva Demo-
        cracia 32 (January, 1952): 24–28.

1826   ARCE MARTÍNEZ, SERGIO. "Misión de la Iglesia en una sociedad
        socialista." Cristianismo y Revolución 6–7 (April, 1968):
        47–55.

1827   ARCE MOSTAJO, JUAN. Doctrina social cristiana y democracia.
        La Paz: Empresa Editora Urquizo, 1972. 309 pp.

1828   ASSMANN, HUGO. "El cristianismo, su plusvalía ideológica y
        el costo social de la revolución socialista." Cuadernos
        de la Realidad Nacional 12 (April, 1972): 154–179.

1829   _____. "Los cristianos revolucionarios: aliados estraté
        gicos en la construcción del socialismo." Hechos y Dichos
        426 (February, 1972): 31–39.

1830   _____, et al. Cristianos por el socialismo: exigencias de
        una opción. Montevideo: Tierra Nueva, 1973. 165 pp.

1831   BARBEITO, JOSÉ. Introducción al pensamiento social cristiano.
        Buenos Aires: Los Andes, 1976. 119 pp.

1832   BARNDT, JOSEPH R. "Revolutionary Christians Confer in San-
        tiago." Christian Century 89 (June 14, 1972): 691–692.

1833   BELDA, RAFAEL. "Los 'Cristianos por el Socialismo' ante el
        ateísmo marxista." Iglesia Viva 52–53 (July–October, 1974):
        401–416.

1834   BLANQUART, PAUL. Los cristianos y el socialismo: conferencia
        de inauguración de los diálogos universitarios. Santiago,
        Chile: Universidad Católica de Chiel, 1971. 15 pp.

Socialism

1835   BUSTOS, ISMAEL. "Cristianismo y socialismo." Política y
       Espíritu 320 (1-71): 17-21.

1836   CALVEZ, JEAN-YVES. "El cristiano frente al desarrollo."
       Mensaje 115 (December, 1962): 708-717.

1837   "Carta de S.Em. el Cardenal Raul Silva Henríquez al P. Gonzalo
       Arroyo, s.j., en repuesta a la invitación al 'Primer
       Encuentro Latinoamericano de Cristianos por el Socialismo'
       Santiago, 2 de marzo de 1972." Documentación, Secretariado
       Nacional de Pastoral Social 15 (April, 1972): 26-31.

1838   CASTILLO CÁRDENAS, GONZALO. "Los cristianos y la lucha por
       un nuevo orden social en América Latina." Cristianismo y
       Sociedad 4 (1966): 84-96.

1839   Centro Catequístico Paulino. Construyamos una patria nueva:
       estudio de la doctrina social de la Iglesia, libro II.
       Cali: Editora Norma, 1962. 208 pp.

1840   Centro de Estudios para el Desarrollo e Integración de América
       Latina. Cristianos latinoamericanos y socialismo. Bogotá:
       Centro de Estudios para el Desarrollo e Integración de
       América Latina, 1972.

1841   Centro de Investigación y Acción Social. Socialismo y cris-
       tianismo. Bogotá: Centro de Investigación y Acción Social,
       1971. 48 pp.

1842   "Christianity Between Capitalism and Socialism." Social
       Justice 69 (June, 1976): 77-80.

1843   Comisión Redactora. "Primer encuentro latinoamericano de
       Cristianos por el Socialismo, Santiago, 23 al 30 de abril
       de 1972 (invitación redactada en Santiago de Chile en
       diciembre de 1971)." Documentación, Secretariado Nacional
       de Pastoral Social 15 (April, 1972): 16-25.

1844   Conselho Episcopal Latinoamericano. América Latina: ação e
       pastoral sociais: conclusões de Mar del Plata. Petrópolis.
       Editora Vozes, 1968. 45 pp.

1845   Construyamos una patria nueva: estudio de la doctrina social
       de la Iglesia: texto para los últimos años de bachillerato.
       Cali: Editora Norma, n.d. 208 pp.

1846   Cristianos latinoamericanos y socialismo. Bogotá: Ediciones
       Paulinas, 1972. 296 pp.

1847   Cristianos por el socialismo. Buenos Aires: Mundo Nuevo,
        1973. 40 pp.

1848   "Cristianos por el socialismo: documento final." NADOC 253
        (May 17, 1972): 1-11.

1849   Los cristianos y el socialismo: primer encuentro latinoameri-
        cano. Buenos Aires: Siglo XXI, 1973. 274 pp.

1850   DARQUIER, HAROLD. "La doctrina social cristiana y su aplica-
        ción: el papel de la universidad y de los univeristarios."
        Prólogo 1 (August, 1962): 5-12.

1851   "Discurso de Monseñor Méndez Arceo, Obispo de Cuernavaca
        (México) pronunicado en la sesión inaugural, el 23 de abril
        de 1972." In Cristianos por el Socialismo. ¿Consecuéncia
        cristiana o alienación política?, edited by Instituto de
        Estudios Politico, pp. 166-172. Santiago, Chile: Pacífico,
        1972.

1852   DOMERGUE, RAYMOND. "Por una presencia de la conciencia cris-
        tiana en la búsqueda socialista." Documentación, Secre-
        tariado Nacional de Pastoral Social 4 (February, 1971):
        10-16.

1853   DURAN CANO, RICARDO. Hombres y libros de América. Buenos
        Aires: Ediciones Líbera, 1975. 153 pp.

1854   EAGLESON, JOHN. Christians for Socialism: Documentation of
        the Christians for Socialism Movement in Latin America.
        Maryknoll: Orbis Books, 1975. 246 pp.

1855   ECHEVERRI, J. A. Catecismo de la doctrina social cristiana.
        Medellín: Editora Bedout, 1962. 126 pp.

1856   "L'Eglise et le socialisme." La Documentation Catholique 68
        (July 4, 1971): 636-637.

1857   Encuentro Latinoamericano de Cristianos por el Socialismo, 1st.
        "Discurso Inaugural pronunciado por Gonzalo Arroyo, s.j."
        In Cristianos por el Socialismo. ¿Consecuencia cristiana
        o alienación política?, edited by Instituto de Estudios
        Políticos, pp. 155-166. Santiago, Chile: Pacífico, 1972.

1858   ____. Los cristianos y el socialismo: primer encuentro
        latinoamericano. Buenos Aires: Siglo Veintiuno Argentina
        Editores, 1973. 274 pp.

Socialism

1859   Episcopado Peruano. "Socialismo y poder poular." Contacto
        13 (August, 1976): 59-65.

1860   FERRANDO, MIGUEL ANGEL. "El Primer Encuentro Latinoamericano
        'Cristianos por el Socialismo'." Teología y Vida 13 (1972):
        118-123.

1861   "First Latin American Encounter of Christians for Socialism."
        IDOC-International 48 (November, 1972): 53-85.

1862   FRIELING, REINHARD. "Lateinamerika: Christen für und gegen
        den Sozialismus." Materialdienst des Konfessions Kindlichen
        Instituts 24 (1973): 24-26.

1863   GAETE, ARTURO. "Eucaristia y lucha de clases." Mensaje 196
        (January/February, 1971): 56-60.

1864   _____. "Socialismo y comunismo: historia de una problemática
        condenación." Mensaje 200 (July, 1971): 290-302.

1865   GARCIA NIETO, JUAN N. "CPS (Cristianos por el Socialismo):
        interrogantes sobre su indentidad y objetivos." Sal Terrae
        762 (November, 1976): 774-784.

1866   Hacia un futuro mejor: cartilla introductoria al estudio de
        la doctrina social de la Iglesia, preparada por un comité
        para los primeros años de bachillerato. Cali: Editora
        Norma, 1963. 127 pp.

1867   HURTADO, ALBERTO. Cristianos por el socialismo: primer en-
        cuentro latinoamericano. Lima: Centro de Estudios y
        Publicaciónes, 1972.

1868   Instituto de Estudios Politicos. Cristianos por el socialismo.
        ¿Consecuencia cristiana o alienación política? Santiago,
        Chile: Pacífico, 1972. 438 pp.

1869   ¿Una izquierda cristiana?: debate. Lima: Centro de Estudios
        y Publicaciones, 1972. 50 pp.

1870   "El justicialismo y la doctrina social cristiana." Nuevo
        Mundo 4 (January/February, 1974): 100-109.

1871   KORB, GEORGE M. "Latin American Church Support." America
        114 (April 2, 1966): 440-442.

1872   LENS, SIDNEY. "Latin Left: Rise of the Social Christians."
        Commonweal, October 14, 1966, pp. 52-55.

1873   LESBAUPIN, IVO. "The Latin American Bishops and Socialism." In Christianity and Socialism, edited by Johann–Baptist Metz, pp. 113–123. New York: Seabury Press, 1977.

1874   LEVI, VIRGILIO. "Cristianos para el Socialismo: una respuesta equivocada." CELAM 8 (1975): 21–22.

1875   LLONA, CHRISTIAN. "Carta a un amigo sacerdote: cristianos y socialismo." In Cristianos por el Socialismo. ¿Consecuencia cristiana o alienación política?, edited by Instituto de Estudios Políticos, pp. 309–330.

1876   LÓPEZ TRUJILLO, ALFONSO. "El análisis marxista en el documento del Primer Encuentro Latinoamericano de Christianos por el socialismo." Tierra Nueva 4 (January, 1973): 31–39.

1877   _____. "Socialismo en America Latina: un estudio del equipo de reflexión teológico-pastoral del CELAM." CELAM 9 (August, 1976): 2–4.

1878   "Luces y sombras de 'Cristianos por Socialismo.'" Iglesia Viva 52–53 (July/October, 1974): 453–463.

1879   "Lucha de clases, compromiso político, cristianismo." Mensaje 209 (June, 1972): 301–309.

1880   MAC EOIN, GARY. "Latin America: Who Is to Blame?" Commonweal June 25, 1975, pp. 331–336.

1881   MARTINA, GIACOMO. "The Contribution of Liberation and Socialism to a Better Self-Conception of the Church." Concilium 67 (1971): 93–101.

1882   MONTEFORTE TOLEDO, MARIO. "El enigma de los social-cristianos en la América Latina." Siempre 653 (December 29, 1965): 28.

1883   MONTES, FERNANDO. "Primer Encuentro Latinoamericano de Cristianos por el Socialismo." Mensaje 209 (June, 1972): 347–352.

1884   MUÑOZ, FREDDY. "Socialismo, marxismo, cristianismo." Servicio Europeo de Universitarios Latinoamericanos 70–71 (June/July, 1976): 26–30.

1885   MUÑOZ VEGA, PABLO. La Iglesia ante el reto entre capitalismo y socialismo. Quito: Vita Católica, 1971. 24 pp.

Socialism

1886　"No se puede combatir unos males con otros, dice un documento
del CELAM sobre 'los Cristianos para el Socialismo.'" <u>ICIA</u>
120 (May 1, 1976): 2.

1887　OCHAGAVIA, JUAN. "Primer Encuentro Latinoamericano de Cristianos por el Socialismo: presentación del documento,
notas al pie de página y evaluación global." <u>Mensaje</u> 209
(June, 1972): 356-366.

1888　ORREGA VICUNA, CLAUDIO. "Cristianismo, historia y cambia
social." In <u>Cristianos por el socialism. ¿Consecuencia
cristiana o alienación política?</u>, edited by Instituto de
Estudios Políticos, pp. 335-338. Santiago, Chile:
Pacifico, 1972.

1889　_____. "Evangelio, política y socialismos." In <u>Cristianos
por el socialismo. ¿Consecuencia cristiana o alienación
política?</u>, edited by Instituto de Estudios Políticos, pp.
343-346. Santiago, Chile: Pacifico, 1972.

1890　PALCIOS R., SERGIO. "Alcance y precisiones a los 'Cristianos
por el Socialismo.'" <u>Política y Espíritu</u> 336 (September,
1972): 43-48.

1891　"¿Por qué decimos no a 'Cristianos para el Socialismo'?"
<u>L'Osservatore Romano</u>, January 9, 1977, p. 10.

1892　PRELLWITZ, J. "Koloss auf tonernen Füssen: Ursachen und
Therapie die sozialen Krankheit Lateinamerikas." <u>Wort
Wahreit</u> 16 (September, 1961): 509-524.

1893　"Primer encuentro 'Cristianos por el Socialismo': documento
final." <u>Servir</u> 39 (May/June, 1972): 323-338.

1894　RIBERO, DARCY. <u>El dilema de América Latina: estructura del
poder y fuerzas insurgentes</u>. México: Siglo Veintiuno,
1971. 358 pp., bibl.

1895　RICCIARDI, RENZO. <u>La tercera solución: bosquejo histórico
de las doctrinas sociales</u> . Buenos Aires: Ediciones
Paulinas, 1963. 213 pp.

1896　Sacerdotes de la Parroquia Universitaria. "El presente de
Chile y el evangelio." <u>Mensaje</u> 196 (January/February,
1971): 36-41.

1897　SANTOS, THEOTONIO DOS. <u>Socialismo o fascismo: dilema latino-
americano</u>. Santiago, Chile: Ediciones Prensa Latinoamericana, 1969. 194 pp.

Camilo, Torres

1898　SEGUNDO, JUAN LUIS. "Capitalismo-socialismo, crux theologica."
In La nuova fronteira della teologia in America Latina,
edited by Rosino Gibellini, pp. 351-376. Bresica, Italy,
Queriniana, 1975.

1899　SHAULL, RICHARD. "Hacia una perspectiva cristiana de la
revolución social." Cristianismo y Sociedad 3: 6-16.

1900　_____. "National Development and Social Revolution: What
Paths Will Latin America Follow?" Christianity and Crisis
28 (January 20, 1969): 347-348.

1901　SORGE, BARTOLOMEO. "Opciones y tesis de los Cristianos por
el Socialismo a la luz de la enseñanza de la Iglesia."
Tierra Nueva 5 (April, 1976): 34-62.

1902　TORRES, SERGIO. "Utopía de los Cristianos por el Socialismo."
Mundo 72 46 (May 18-31, 1972): 24-31.

1903　"Uso y abuso de la doctrina social de la Iglesia." Criterio
38 (September, 23, 1965): 683-687.

1904　VEKEMANS, ROGER. "El 'Primer Encuentro Latinoamericano de
Cristianos por el Socialismo', la jerarquía chilena y la
'Octogesima Adveniens': estudio sinóptico." Tierra Nueva
4 (January, 1973): 44-62.

1905　VERGARA ACEVES, J. "Los cristianos por el Socialismo: una
opción acertada?" Christus 37 (August, 1972): 47-50.

1906　VILLAIN, JEAN. La enseñanza social de la Iglesia. Madrid:
Aguilar, 1961. 502 pp.

TORRES, CAMILO

1907　ALVARE GARCÍA, JOHN, and RESTREPO CALLE, CHRISTIAN. Camilo
Torres: His Life and His Message. Springfield: Templegate Publishers, 1968. 128 pp.

1908　ANDRADE, VICENTE. "The Death of Camilo Torres." America 114
(March,12, 1966): 355.

1909　CÂMARA, HÉLDER. "Ação não-violenta na América Latina." Vozes
8 (August, 1968): 701-711.

1910　CAYCEDO, OLGA DE. El padre Camilo Torres o la crisis de
maduréz de América. Barcelona: Ediciones Aura, 1972. 462
pp., bibl.

Torres, Camilo

1911 CLAPS, GERALDO. "El cristiano frente a la revolución vio-
      lenta." Mensaje 115 (December, 1962): 708-717.

1912 "Frente Unido del Pueblo." Frente Unido 1 (August 26, 1965):
      4-5.

1913 FUNK, RICHARD HARRIES. Camilo Torres Restrepo and the Christian
      Left in the Tradition of Colombian Church-State Relations.
      [n.p.], 1972.

1914 HOURDIN, GEORGE. "A justa violencia dos oprimodos." Paz e
      Terra 2 (April, 1968): 73-88.

1915 LÓPEZ OLIVA, ENRIQUE. El camilismo en la América Latina.
      Havana: Casa de las Américas, 1970. 97 pp., bibl.

1916 MALDONADO PIEDRAHITA, RAFAEL. Conversaciones con un sacerdote
      colombiano: puntos de choque con la Iglesia. Bogotá:
      Antares, 1957. 102 pp.

1917 PÉREZ GARCÍA, ANTONIO. "Reflexiones pacíficas sobre la revo-
      lución." Víspera 4 (January, 1968): 13-21.

1918 SMITH, ROBERT FREEMAN. "Till We Have Built Jerusalem."
      Nation 208 (June 30, 1969): 829-830.

1919 WOMACK, JOHN. "Priest of Revolution." The New York Review
      of Books (October 23, 1969): 13-16.

VIOLENCE

1920 ANDRADE, VICENTE. "La Iglesia en la lucha contra la vio-
      lencia." El Catolicismo 2236 (February 27, 1977): 5.

1921 ARCUSA, EDUARDO. ¿Violencia o diálogo? Bogotá: Ediciones
      Paulinas, 1972. 293 pp.

1922 ARENAS AMIGO, VALENTÍN. "Reformas en la Populorum Progressio:
      la violencia como alternativa." SIC 31 (May, 1968): 236-
      237.

1923 ARROYO, GONZALO. "Violencia institucionalizada en América
      Latina." Mensaje 174 (November, 1968): 534-544.

1924 BARREIRO, JULIO. Violencia y política en América Latina.
      México: Siglo Veintiuno Editores, 1971. 205 pp.

1925   BIGO, PIERRE. "Enseñanza de la Iglesia sobre la violencia."
        Mensaje 17 (November, 1968): 574-578.

1926   BOSC, ROBERT. La violencia y la no violencia en el pensa-
        miento de la Iglesia. Buenos Aires: Faculdade de Filo-
        sofía y Teologia en San Miguel, 1968. 23 pp.

1927   CÂMARA, HÉLDER. "Acão não violência na América Latina."
        Vozes 8 (August, 1968): 701-711.

1928   _____. "La América Latina y la opción de la no-violencia."
        Comunidad 8 (October, 1973): 567-575.

1929   _____. "Violence of the Peaceful." IDOC-International 18
        (January 30, 1971): 42-46.

1930   CASABO, JOSÉ MARÍA. "Nota acerca de la violencia." Documen-
        tación Secretariado Nacional de Pastoral Social 4 (February,
        1971): 1-15.

1931   CASALIS, GEORGE, and HOWARD YODER, JOHN. "Es posible la no
        violencia? diálogo entre dos teólogos comprometidos."
        Testimonium 11 (April, 1976): 28-38.

1932   Centro para el Desarrollo Económico y Social de América Latina.
        Iglesia, paz y desarrollo. n.p.: Centro para el Desar-
        rollo Económico y Social de América Latina, 1969. 17 pp.

1933   Consejo Epsicopal Latinoamericano. "Equipo del Instituto
        Pastoral Violencia y Opresión Moral." Vida Pastoral 78
        (1975): 12-17.

1934   _____. "The Problem of Violence in Latin America." Impact
        12 (December, 1969): 12.

1935   CULHANE, EUGENE R. "Nonviolence in Latin America." America
        120 (March 22, 1969): 331.

1936   DORFMAN, ARIEL. Imaginación y violencia en América Latina:
        ensayos. Santiago, Chile: Editorial Universitario, 1970.
        224 pp., bibl.

1937   DUFF, ERNEST A., and MC CAMANT, JOHN F. Violence and Repres-
        sion in Latin America. New York: Free Press, 1976. 322
        pp., bibl.

1938   FURTER, PIERRE. L'imagination creatrice, la violence et le
        changement social: une interprétation. Cuernavaca, México:
        Centro Intercultural de Documentación, 1968.

Violence

1939   GAETE, ARTURO. "Un cristiano se interroga acerca de la vio-
       lencia." Mensaje 175 (November, 1968):   584-591.

1940   GALEANO, EDUARDO H. Violencia y enajenación. Mexico: Editora
       Nuestro Tiempo, 1971. 118 pp.

1941   GANNON, FRANCIS X. "Catholicism, Revolution and Violence in
       Latin America: Lessons of 1968 Guatemala Maryknoll Episode."
       Orbis (Winter, 1968):   1204-1225.

1942   GARCÍA ELORRIO, JUAN. "Carta abierta al padre Gardella."
       Cristianismo y Revolución 15 (May, 1969):   3-4.

1943   _____. "El pueblo no elige la violencia, lucha por la justi-
       cia." Cristianismo y Revolución 20 (September 10, 1969):
       2-3.

1944   _____. "El reponso del Cardenal." Cristianismo y Revolución
       15 (May, 1969):   2.

1945   _____. "Tiempo social con 'estado de sitio.'" Cristianismo
       y Revolución 18 (July, 1969):   24-25.

1946   GERASSI, JOHN. Revolutionary Priest: The Complete Writings
       and Messages of Camilo Torres. New York: Random House,
       1971. 460 pp.

1947   GONZÁLEZ, GUILLERMO. "La violencia no es evangélica." Revista
       Javeriana 359 (October, 1969):   404-414.

1948   GOSS-MAYR, HILDEGARD. "Une révolution non-violente." Con-
       cilium 35 (1968):   153-165.

1949   HAERING, BERNHARD; GIRARDI, GIOULIO; and GONZÁLEZ RUIZ, JOSÉ
       MARÍA. La violencia de los cristianos. Salamanca: Sígueme,
       1971. 192 pp.

1950   ILLICH, IVAN D. "Ivan Illich Writes Pope Paul." Commonweal,
       September 4, 1970, pp. 428-429.

1951   _____. "Violencia: espelho para americanos." Paz e Terra 2
       (April, 1968):   175-182.

1952   "The Ingredients of Pre-Revolution." Reportaje-DESAL 1 (July/
       December, 1968):   6.

1953   LAPARGNEUR, FRANÇOIS H. "Introdução a uma teologia da não-
       violência evangélica." Revista Eclesiástica Brasileira 25
       25 (June, 1965):   221-243.

148

1954   LEPARGNEUR, HUBERT. "L'Amérique latine entre la rhétorique et la violence." La Lettre 122 (October, 1968): 1-3.

1955   LEPELEY, JOAQUÍN. "La violencia y el cristiano." Tierra Nueva 1 (April, 1972): 37-50.

1956   _____. "¿Violencia y no violencia?" Tierra Nueva 3 (October, 1972): 33-48.

1957   MASCIALINO, MIGUEL. "Apuntes de..." Cristianismo y Revolución 8 (July, 1968): 14-15.

1958   MORENO, FRANCISCO JOSÉ, and MITRANI, BARBARA. Conflict and Violence in Latin American Politics: A Book of Readings. New York: Thomas Crowell, 1971. 452 pp.

1959   PAVEZ BRAVO, JORGE. "Jesucristo y la violencia." Mensaje 136 (January/February, 1965): 16-22.

1960   PODESTA, JERÓNIMO. La violencia del amor. Buenos Aires: Editorial Plus Ultra, 1968. 238 pp.

1961   SARAVIA, JOSÉ MARIA. Reflexiones sobre la violencia. Buenos Aires: Abelardo-Perrot, 1976. 43 pp.

1962   SEGUNDO, JUAN LUIS. "Christianity and Violence in Latin America." Christianity and Crisis 28 (March 4, 1968): 31-34.

1963   SWONLEY, JOHN M. "Justica, revolução e violência." Paz e Terra 2 (April, 1968): 59-72.

1964   "Toward an Ethics of Violence." Reportaje-DESAL 1 (July/ December, 1968): 8.

1965   WINDASS, STANLEY. El cristianismo frente al la violencia. Barcelona: Fontanella-Marova, 1971.

II Argentina

GENERAL

1966 ALBERIONE, GIACOMO GUISEPPE. Elementos de sociología cristiana. Buenos Aires: Paulinas, 1963. 216 pp.

1967 Bibliografía teológica comentada del área iberoamericana. Año 1975. Volumen 3. Buenos Aires: Instituto Superior Evangélico de Estudios Teológicos Departamento de Bibliografía Teológica Comentada, 1976. 567 pp.

1968 BROCKMAN, JAMES R. "The People That Aren't There." America 134 (April 10, 1976): 309.

1969 BUNTIG, ALDO J. El catolicismo popular en la Argentina. Buenos Aires: Editorial Bonum, 1969. 198 pp.

1970 Conferencia Episcopal Argentina. "Declaración del episcopado 'Biblia latinoamericana." El Catolicismo 2,232 (November 28, 1976): 5.

1971 DEINER, JOHN T. "Radicalism in the Argentine Catholic Church." Government and Opposition 10 (Winter, 1975): 70-89.

1972 DEVOTO, ALBERTO. "Argentina . . . hace a sus fieles testigos de su 'voto' de pobreza." Informaciones Católicas Internacionales 264 (May 22, 1966): 10.

1973 ECHEVERRI, MATIAS. "La Iglesia en la Argentina." Selecciones de Servicio Social 2 (1975): 39-45.

1974 GARCÍA ELORRIO, JUAN. "Carta abierta al episcopado argentino." Cristianismo y Revolución 2-4 (October 11, 1966): 2.

1975 _____. "Los traidores a Medellín." Cristianismo y Revolución 14 (April, 1969): 2.

1976 GAYNOR, J. "The Church in Argentina." Furrow 14 (April, 1963): 203-211.

General

1977   GERA, P. LUCIO, and RODRÍGUEZ, GUILLERMO. "Apuntes para una
       interpretación de la Iglesia argentina." Cristianismo y
       Revolución 25 (September, 1970): 76.

1978   El imperio y las iglesias. Buenos Aires: Editora Guadalupe,
       1974. 155 pp.

1979   MAYOL, ALEJANDRO et al. Los católicos postconciliares en la
       Argentina 1963-1969. Buenos Aires: Galerna, 1970. 407 pp.

1980   NEFFA, J. C. "La evolución de la Iglesia en Argentina." IDOC
       68 (September 15, 1968): 33.

1981   OSSA, MANUEL. "Esperanza en la Iglesia argentina." Mensaje
       15 (July, 1966): 320-322.

1982   REYES, JOSÉ M. "O catolicismo na Argentina." Broteria 68
       (1959): 52-55.

1983   SEGUNDO, JUAN LUIS. Funciones de la Iglesia en la realidad
       rioplatense. Montevideo: Barreiro y Ramos, 1962.

AGRARIAN REFORM

1984   DI TELLA, GUIDO, and ZYMELMAN, MANUEL. Etapas del desarrollo
       económico argentino. Buenos Aires: Departamento de Socio-
       logía, Facultad de Filosofía y Letras, Universidad de
       Buenos Aires, 1961. 540 pp.

CATHOLIC CHURCH AND SOCIAL CHANGE

1985   AMATO, ENRIQUE. La Iglesia en Argentina. Buenos Aires:
       Centro de Investigaciones Sociales y Religiosas, 1965.
       253 pp.

1986   "Argentina: los obispos reclaman con urgencia la amnistía y
       la justicia social." Informaciones Católicas Internacionales
       199 (September 7, 1963): 8-9.

1987   BÜNTIG, P. "Manifestaciones de la religiosidad popular."
       Catequesis Latinoamericana 1 (May/June, 1969): 90-101.

1988   "Los católicos y el cambio político." Criterio 39 (July 28,
       1969): 523-526.

Catholic Church and Social Change

1989   CIRIA, ALBERTO, et al. New Perspectives on Modern Argentina.
        Bloomington: Indiana University Latin American Studies
        Program, 1972. 94 pp.

1990   CLAUSEN, ARNE. Una imagen del hombre argentino. Cuernavaca,
        México: Centro Intercultural de Documentación, 1969.

1991   CULHANE, EUGENE K. "Letter from Argentina." America 129
        (July 21, 1973): 38-39.

1992   DEANE, ALBERT. "Catholicism in Argentina." Worldmission 13
        (September, 1972): 17-23.

1993   DEVOTO, ALBERTO and CÁMARA, HÉLDER. El manifiesto de los
        obispos del Tercer Mundo. Una respuesta al clamor de los
        pobres. Buenos Aires: Ediciones Búsqueda, 1968. 61 pp.

1994   DONINI, ANTONIO. "El catolicismo argentino frente al cambio
        social." Centro de Investigación y Acción Social 13
        (November/December, 1964): 45-55.

1995   EGGERS LAN, CONRADO. Cristianismo y nueva ideología. Buenos
        Aires: Editorial J. Alvarez, 1968. 295 pp., bibl.

1996   El imperio de las iglesias. Buenos Aires: Editorial Guadalupe,
        1973. 115 pp.

1997   LALIVE D'EPINAY, CHRISTIAN. Penetration culturelle et presse
        religieuse: le cas d'une revue protestante argentine.
        Cuernavaca, México: Centro Intercultural de Documentación,
        1971.

1998   LOMBARDI, S. "We Have No Childhood." Saturday Evening Post,
        September 7, 1963, pp. 76-77.

1999   LUCA, JOSÉ N. DE. Situación social y liberación. Cuernavaca,
        México: Centro Intercultural de Documentación, 1969.
        243 pp.

2000   Movimiento de Sacerdotes para el Tercer Mundo. El pueblo,
        ¿dónde está? Buenos Aires: MSTM, 1975. 153 pp.

2001   _____. Los sacerdotes para el Tercer Mundo y la actualidad
        nacional. Buenos Aires: Blindad, 1973. 131 pp.

2002   "National Security vs. Individual Rights: Bishops of Argentina
        Pastoral Message, May 7, 1977." Origins 7 (June 2, 1977):
        20-22.

Catholic Church and Social Change

2003   RICCIARDI, RENZO. La tercera solución. Bosquejo histórico
de las doctrinas sociales. Florida, Argentina: Ediciones
Paulinas, 1963. 213 pp.

2004   Sacerdotes Argentinos. "Declaración de sacerdotes de los
llanos riojanos." Criterio 42 (November 27, 1969): 815–
916.

2005   Sacerdotes para el Tercer Mundo. Buenos Aires: Publicaciones
del Movimiento de Sacerdotes para el Tercer Mundo, 1970.
158 pp.

2006   SCHELTHOFF, ROSALINDE. "Harvesting in the White Fields of
Argentina." Worldmission 15 (Winter, 1965): 75–80.

2007   VIVIANI, GUILLERMO. Doctrinas sociales. Florida, Argentina:
Ediciones Paulinas, 1961–1962. 2 v.

CATHOLIC CHURCH AND STATE

2008   "Argentina: aclaración sobre la actitud de la Iglesia con
relación al nuevo régimen." Informaciones Católicas Internacionales 272 (September 22, 1966): 10.

2009   "Argentina: por un acuerdo 'ejemplar,' el Estado renuncia a
sus privilegios en la designación de obispos." Informaciones
Católicas Internacionales 272 (November 7, 1966): 11–12.

2010   "Confronting Repression." America 135 (August 21, 1976): 68.

2011   "Contestation in Argentina." Herder Correspondence 6 (October,
1969): 313–316.

2012   DEANE, ALBERT. "Catholicism in Argentina." Worldmission 13
(September, 1972): 17–23.

2013   "Death of a Bishop." Christian Century 93 (September 29,
1976): 807.

2014   DEINER, JOHN T. "Radicalism in the Argentine Catholic Church."
Government and Opposition 10 (Winter, 1975): 70–89.

2015   DRINAN, R. "Repression in Argentina: Religious and Political."
Commonweal 104 (February 18, 1977): 103–104.

2016   ESTRADA, SANTIAGO DE. Nuestras relaciones con la Iglesia,
hacia un concordato entre la sede apostólica y el Estado
argentino. Buenos Aires: Editorial Theoria, 1963. 203 pp.

2017   "Forgive and Forget." Newsweek, October 19, 1959, p. 61.

2018   GERA, P. LUCIO. Contexto de la Iglesia argentina: informe
       sobre diversos aspectos de la situación argentina. Buenos
       Aires: Facultad de Teología de la Pontificia Universidad
       Católica Argentina, 1969. 181 pp.

2019   ____, et al. La Iglesia y el país. Buenos Aires: Ediciones
       Búsqueda, 1967. 101 pp.

2020   El imperio de las iglesias. Buenos Aires: Editorial Guadalupe,
       1973. 115 pp.

2021   Latin American Studies Association, Gainesville, Florida.
       Subcommittee on Academic Freedom and Human Rights in Argen-
       tina. Argentina de hoy: un régimen de terror, informe
       sobre la represión desde julio de 1973 hasta diciembre de
       1974; Report and Documentary Supplement. Gainesville,
       Florida: Latin American Studies Association, 1975.

2022   LUCA, JOSÉ N. DE. Situación social y liberación. Cuernavaca,
       México: Centro Intercultural de Documentación, 1969. 243
       pp., bibl.

2023   MARSAL S., PABLO. Perón y la Iglesia. Buenos Aires: Edi-
       ciones Rex, 1955. 154 pp.

2024   Movimiento de Sacerdotes para el Tercer Mundo. Nuestra re-
       flexión. Buenos Aires: Movimiento de Sacerdotes para el
       Tercer Mundo, 1970. 94 pp.

2025   MUGICA, CARLOS. Peronismo y cristianismo. Buenos Aires:
       Editorial Merlin, 1973. 100 pp.

2026   Obispos de Goya-Argentina. "Argentina: el obispo de Goya
       afirma la independencia de la Iglesia con relación al
       régimen." Catolicismo Internacional 271 (September 7,
       1966): 9.

2027   O'MARA, RICHARD. "Church in Argentina." Commonweal 84
       (September 23, 1966): 612-614.

2028   "Society and Church in Latin America." IDOC-International 1
       (April 4, 1970): 37-69.

2029   "Trouble from the Pulpits." Time, August 26, 1966, p. 28.

2030   YACCUZZI, RAFAEL. "La lucha del norte." Cristianismo y Revo-
       lución 18 (July, 1969): 4.

Catholic Clergy

CATHOLIC CLERGY

2031 "Buenos Aires Archdiocese Ordained Two Priests Last Year."
National Catholic Reporter 4 (March 27, 1968): 12.

2032 BUNTIG, P. "Manifestaciones de la religiosidad popular."
Catequesis Latinoamericana 1 (May/June, 1969): 90–101.

2033 "Carta del Tercer Mundo a la conferencia episcopal argentina."
NADOC 229 (December 6, 1972): 1–4.

2034 LOMBARDI, S. "We Have No Childhood." Saturday Evening Post,
September 7, 1963, pp. 76–77.

2035 Movimiento de Sacerdotes para el Tercer Mundo. Nuestra reflexión. Buenos Aires: Movimiento de Sacerdotes para el
Tercer Mundo, 1970. 94 pp.

2036 ROSSI, JUAN JOSÉ. ¿Cambia la Iglesia? Reflexión y perspectivas pastorales para nuestro tiempo. Buenos Aires: Ediciones Búsqueda, 1965. 146 pp., bibl.

2037 Social-Activist Priests: Colombia, Argentina. Washington,
D.C.: Division for Latin America, USCC. [n.d.]. 70 pp.

CHRISTIAN DEMOCRACY

2038 BUSACCA, SALVADOR. La democracia cristiana en busca del país.
Buenos Aires: Ediciones Democrist, 1958. 310 pp.

2039 KENNEDY, JOHN H. Catholicism, Nationalism, and Democracy in
Argentina. Notre Dame, Indiana: University of Notre Dame
Press, 1958. 219 pp.

2040 PARERA, RICARDO GREGORIO. Democracia cristiana el la Argentina: los hechos y las ideas. Buenos Aires: Editorial
Nahuel, 1967. 375 pp., bibl.

2041 Partido Demócrata Cristiano de Argentina. "Manifiesto del
Partido Democrata Cristiano de Argentina." Política y
Espíritu 11 (August 1, 1955): 15–18.

2042 ROGGI, LUIS OSVALDO, comp. Argentina, Confederación General
del Trabajo, 1965: documentos y reacciones de prensa.
Cuernavaca, México: Centro Intercultural de Documentación,
1967. 268 pp., bibl.

Argentina

COMMUNISM

2043   IMAZ, JOSÉ LUIS DE. Los que mandan. Albany: State University of New York Press, 1970. 279 pp.

2044   MEINVIELLE, JULIO. El comunismo en la revolución anticristiana. Buenos Aires: Editorial Theoria, 1964. 155 pp.

2045   SCOTTI, ELVIO JOSÉ. "Infiltración comunista en América y Argentina." Estudios 48 (May, 1959): 212-216.

2046   VOLPI, ALBERTO EZEQUIEL. Radiografía del comunismo. Buenos Aires: Editorial Poblet, 1964. 180 pp., bibl.

DOCUMENTS

2047   "Argentina: Priests for the Third World." IDOC-International 15 (December 12, 1970): 58-96.

2048   Comisión Argentina Justicia y Paz. Bien común y situación actual. Carta Pastoral del Epsicopado Argentino (San Miguel, 15 de mayo de 1976). Buenos Aires: Don Bosco, 1976. 7 pp.

2049   Conferencia Episcopal Argentina. "Argentina: el episcopado abre las puertas al soplo del Concilio." Informaciones Católicas Internacionales 266 (June 22, 1966): 8.

2050   _____. Reflexión cristiana para el pueblo de la patria. Buenos Aires: Conferencia Episcopal, 1977.

2051   "Declaration of the Argentine Episcopate on the Adaptation of the Conclusions of the Second General Conference of the Latin American Episcopate (Medellin, 21st-26th, April 1969) to the Present Reality of the Argentine." IDOC-International 1 (April 4, 1970): 39-42.

2052   "Document from Carlos Paz." IDOC-International 48 (November, 1972): 39-45.

2053   GERA, P. LUCIO, et al. La Iglesia y el país. Buenos Aires: Editora Búsqueda, 1967. 101 pp.

2054   "Lettre des évêques d'Argentine, San Miguel, le 7 mai, 1977." La Documentation Catholique 74 (June 5, 1977): 515-517.

2055   "National Security vs. Individual Rights: Bishops of Argentina Pastoral Message, May 7, 1977." Origina 7 (June 2, 1977): 20-22.

Documents

2056   Obispos Argentinos. "Las relaciones de la Iglesia con lo
       temporal." Criterio 42 (November 27, 1969): 813-814.

2057   Obispos de Goya-Argentina. "Argentina: el obispo de Goya
       afirma la independencia de la Iglesia con relación al
       régimen." Catholicismo Internacional 271 (September 7,
       1977): 9.

2058   Polémica en la Iglesia: documentos de obispos argentinos y
       sacerdotes para el Tercer Mundo, 1969-1970. Avellaneda,
       Argentina: Ediciones Búsqueda, 1970. 125 pp.

2059   Sacerdotes Argentinos. "Declaración de sacerdotes de los
       llanos riojanos." Criterio 42 (November 27, 1969): 815-
       816.

2060   Sacerdotes de Córdoba-Argentina. "Argentina: dos sacerdotes
       se explican sobre su pastoral 'revolucionaria'." Informa-
       ciones Católicas Internacionales 276 (December 22, 1966):
       9.

2061   "Society and Church in Latin America." IDOC-International 1
       (April 4, 1970): 37-69.

2062   TIBALDO, M. "Eduquemos para el diálogo: II encuentro judeo-
       católico, Buenos Aires, Argentina, March 4-5, 1974."
       Catequesis Latinoamericana 6 (April/July, 1974): 229-233.

2063   VETRANO, VICENTE. "Encuentro de directores y dirigentes
       diocesanos de catequesis en Argentina." Catequesis Latino-
       americana 1 (October/December, 1969): 87-90.

ECONOMIC DEVELOPMENT

2064   DI TELLA, GUIDO and ZYMELMAN, MANUEL. Etapas del desarrollo
       económico argentino. Buenos Aires: Departamento de Socio-
       logia, Facultad de Filosofia y Letras, Universidad de
       Buenos Aires, 1961. 540 pp.

2065   VIRASORO, MANUEL. "Desarrollo económico y pensamiento."
       CIAS 130 (December, 1963): 1-22.

EDUCATION

2066   ROGGI, LUIS OSVALDO, comp. Argentina: enseñanza superior,
       1958: documentos reproducidos. Cuernavaca, México: Centro
       Intercultural de Documentación, 1967.

LABOR AND LABORING CLASSES

2067   "Argentina: la Acción Católica Obrera denuncia la actitud
        antisocial del gobierno." Informaciones Católicas Inter-
        nacionales 286 (April 22, 1967): 16-17.

2068   "Argentina: una vigorosa campaña contra la C.G.T. siembra la
        confusión." Informaciones Católicas Internacionales 249
        (October 7, 1965): 29.

2069   PODESTA, JOSÉ JERÓNIMO. "El mundo obrero golpea a la Iglesia
        argentina." Cristianismo y Revolución 5 (November, 1967):
        16-17.

2070   ROGGI, LUIS OSVALDO, comp. Argentina: Confederación General
        del Trabajo, 1965: documentos y reacciones de prensa.
        Cuernavaca, México: Centro Intercultural de Documentación,
        1967. 268 pp., bibl.

2071   "Towards a More Just Society. Declaration Issued by a Group
        of Priests and Trade Union and Student Organizations of
        North-Eastern Argentina, May, 1969." IDOC-International 1
        (April 4, 1970): 45-47.

LIBERATION

2072   LUCA, JOSÉ N. DE. Situación social y liberación: interpre-
        tación teológica de un contexto social específico: un
        área urbana-industrial en el Gran Buenos Aires. Cuernavaca,
        México: Centro Intercultural de Documentación, 1969. 243
        pp.

2073   WOODWARD, KENNETH L., and MOREAU, R. "Battle of the Bible."
        Newsweek, November 8, 1976, p. 110.

MARXISM

2074   ARAMBURU, JUAN CARLOS, and ZASPE, FAUSTINO VICENTE, MONSEÑOR.
        "Dos obispos argentinos declaran que marxismo y cristianismo
        son inconciliables." El Catolicismo 2,234 (January 30,
        1977): 6.

2075   ARES SOMOSA, PAULINO. Marxismo ortodoxo. Buenos Aires:
        Imprenta López, 1964. 207 pp.

2076   EGGERS LAN, CONRADO. Cristianismo, marxismo y revolución
        social. Buenos Aires: Editorial Jorge Alvarez, 1964. 95 pp.

Marxism

2077   "La marxisticación en el cristianismo según un obispo." ICIA
        154 (September 15, 1977): 6.

2078   ROGGI, LUIS OSVALDO, comp. Argentina: Confederación General
        del Trabajo, 1965: documentos y reacciones de prensa.
        Cuernavaca, México: Centro Intercultural de Documentación,
        1967. 268 pp., bibl.

NATIONALISM

2079   BLAKEMORE, H. "John J. Kennedy: Catholicism, Nationalism
        and Democracy in Argentina." Erasmus. Specucum Scientiarum
        15 (1963): 44-46.

2080   GOLDWERT, MARVIN. Democracy, Militarism, and Nationalism in
        Argentina, 1930-1966. Austin: University of Texas Press,
        1972. 253 pp., bibl.

2081   KENNEDY, JOHN J. Catholicism, Nationalism and Democracy in
        Argentina. Notre Dame, Indiana: University of Notre Dame
        Press, 1958. 219 pp.

2082   WHITAKER, ARTHUR P. "Nationalism and Religion in Argentina
        and Uruguay." In Religion, Revolution and Reform. New
        Forces for Change in Latin America, edited by William V.
        D'Antonio, pp. 75-90. New York: Praeger, 1964.

POLITICS

2083   AUZA, NÉSTOR T. Los católicos argentinos. Experiencia polí-
        tica y social. Buenos Aires: Ediciones Diagrama, 1962.
        139 pp.

2084   CENTENO, ANGEL M. Cuatro años de una política religiosa.
        Buenos Aires: Editorial Desarrollo, 1964. 127 pp.

2085   CIRIA, ALBERTO et al. New Perspectives on Modern Argentina.
        Bloomington: Indiana University Latin American Studies
        Program, 1972. 94 pp.

2086   Cristianos de Argentina. "La dictadura enfrenta y persigue a
        los verdaderos cristianos." Cristianismo y Revolución 19
        (August, 1969): 2-3.

2087   DEINER, JOHN T. "Radicalism in the Argentine Church."
        Government and Oppositions 10 (Winter, 1975): 70-89.

2088   "Document from Carlos Paz."   IDOC-International 48 (November,
       1972):   39-45.

2089   FLORIA, CARLOS ALBERTO.   "La Iglesia, los católicos y la
       política."   Criterio 36 (December, 1963):   885-888.

2090   GANDOLFO, MERCEDES.   La Iglesia, factor de poder político en
       Argentina.   Montevideo: Ediciones Nuestro Tiempo, 1969.
       204 pp., bibl.

2091   MEINVIELLE, JULIO.   Concepción católica de la política: los
       tres pueblos bíblicos en su lucha por la dominación del
       mundo; el comunismo en la Argentina.   Buenos Aires: Edi-
       ciones Dictio, 1974.   510 pp.

2092   O'MARA, RICHARD.   "The Church in Argentina."   Commonweal 84
       (September 23, 1966):   612-614.

2093   RAMOS, JORGE ABELANDO.   Revolución y contrarevolución en la
       Argentina: las masas en nuestra historia.   Buenos Aires:
       Editorial Amerindia, 1957.   463 pp., bibl.

REVOLUTION

2094   GANDOLFO, MERCEDES.   La Iglesia, factor de poder político en
       Argentina.   Montevideo: Ediciones Nuestro Tiempo, 1969.
       204 pp., bibl.

2095   GARCÍA ELORRIO, JUAN.   "Carta abierta al Arzobispo de Tucmán
       Monseñor J.C. Aramburu."   Cristianismo y Revolución 4
       (March, 1967):   1.

2096   _____.   "La escalada del miedo."   Cristianismo y Revolución
       15 (May, 1969):   2.

2097   _____.   "Secuestros, torturas y traiciones."   Cristianismo y
       Revolución 11 (November, 1968):   1-2.

2098   RAMOS, JORGE ABELANDO.   Revolución y contrarevolución en la
       Argentina, las masas en nuestra historia.   Buenos Aires:
       Editorial Amerindia, 1957.   463 pp., bibl.

2099   Sacerdotes de Córdoba, Argentina.   "Argentina: dos sacerdotes
       se explican sobre su pastoral 'revolucionaria.'"   Informa-
       ciones Católicas Internacionales 276 (December 22, 1966):
       9.

Revolution

2100   WOODWARD, KENNETH L., and MOREAU, R. "Battle of the Bible."
        Newsweek, November 8, 1976, p. 110.

SOCIALISM

2101   EGGERS LAN, CONRADO. Cristianismo, marxismo y revolución
        social. Buenos Aires: Jorge Alvarez, 1964. 95 pp.

2102   OZAN, URBANO J. Cristianismo y realidad social. Buenos Aires:
        Ediciones Troquel, 1966. 109 pp.

VIOLENCE

2103   "Argentine 3rd World Priest Killed at Church." National
        Catholic Reporter 10 (May 24, 1974): 3.

2104   BETANCOURT, ALFONSO. "Actitud violenta de tercermundistas."
        NADOC 268 (September 6, 1972): 3-4.

2105   "Death of a Bishop." Christian Century 93 (September 29,
        1976): 807.

2106   "Ex-Bishop Flees Argentina After Death Threat." National
        Catholic Reporter 10 (October 18, 1974): 15.

2107   GARCÍA ELORRIO, JUAN. "Secuestros, torturas y traiciones."
        Cristianismo y Revolución 11 (November, 1968): 1-2.

2108   GENTA, JORDAN B. Seguridad y desarrollo: reflexiones sobre
        el terror en Argentina. Buenos Aires: Editorial Cultura
        Argentina, 1970. 117 pp.

2109   HIGGINS, R. "Priest Praises Catholic Defense of Human Rights:
        La Salette Father James M. Weeks Held Prisoner by the
        Argentine Government." Our Sunday Visitor 65 (September
        19, 1976): 3.

2110   ZAZPE, VICENTE F. Paz, cambio, violencia. Buenos Aires:
        Paulinas, 1971. 142 pp.

III Bolivia

GENERAL

2111   MANRIQUE, JORGE. "Bolivia Today." IDOC-International 16
       (December 26, 1970): 47-64.

2112   PIKE, FREDERICK B. The United States and the Andean Republics:
       Peru, Bolivia, and Ecuador. Cambridge: Harvard University
       Press, 1977. 493 pp.

2113   TURRI, CLAUDIANO. Hacia una renovación pastoral (reflexiones
       y propuestas). Canelas: Aiquile, 1974. 148 pp.

2114   ZAREÁSTEGUI, ALFREDO. "Otra universidad católica en América
       Latina: Carta a CIDOC Informa, Sucre, Bolivia, mayo 4 de
       1966." CIDOC Informa (May 15, 1966): 173.

AGRARIAN REFORM

2115   "Bolivian Bishops in Land Reform." America 98 (March 22,
       1958): 716-717.

CATHOLIC CHURCH AND SOCIAL CHANGE

2116   ARROYO, GONZALO. "Rebeldía cristiana y compromiso cristiano:
       a propósito de un viaje a Bolivia." Mensaje 17 (March/
       April, 1968); 78-83.

2117   BISHOP M., JORDAN. "Tremor in Bolivia." Commonweal 83
       (December 17, 1965): 339-342.

2118   "Bolivia acuerdo Iglesia-Estado para ayudar a las familias
       pobres." Informaciones Católicas Internacionales 214
       (April 22, 1964): 9.

2119   BÜNTIG, P. "Manifestaciones de la religiosidad popular."
       Catequesis Latinoamericana 1 (May/June, 1969): 90-101.

Catholic Church and Social Change

2120   JEREZ, FRANCISCO, pseud. "Bolivia: Prayers Before a Coup."
       Commonweal 94 (September 17, 1971): 469-470.

2121   "Manifesto of the Executive Committee ISAL, Bolivia." IDOC-
       International 17 (January 16, 1971): 27-32.

2122   Movimiento Social Evangélico Boliviano. Reto a los evangélicos:
       los propósitos son el de luchar por el bienestar social,
       moral y económico de nuestro pueblo. La Paz: [n.p.],
       1962. 9 pp.

2123   "El secretario general de ISAL visita los países de la zona
       andina." Carta de ISAL 2 (November, 1969): 1-4.

CATHOLIC CHURCH AND STATE

2124   BERRYMAN, PHILIP E. "Banzer Regime Ousts Priests: Bolivia."
       National Catholic Reporter 11 (April 18, 1975): 25.

2125   "Bolivia: After the Coup." IDOC-International 45 (April 15,
       1972): 24-43.

2126   "Bolivia: hay organismos de estado que impiden los cambios
       radicales." Carta de ISAL 3 (April, 1970): 6-7.

2127   "Church-State Tensions Flare, Priest Arrested in Bolivia."
       National Catholic Reporter 11 (February 7, 1973): 15.

2128   LATINO, J. "Repression and Resistance in Bolivia." Christian
       Century 89 (June 7, 1972): 667-669.

2129   "Repression in Bolivia." America 128 (April 17, 1973): 297-
       298.

2130   "Society and Church in Latin America." IDOC-International 1
       (April 4, 1970): 37-69.

2131   "Tensión Iglesia-gobierno, Bolivia." Páginas 52 (1975): 33-
       40.

2132   VALDA PALMA, ROBERTO. "Bolivia: Bishops' Case of Conscience."
       America 128 (January 20, 1973): 37-38.

CATHOLIC CLERGY

2133   BÜNTIG, P. "Manifestaciones de la religiosidad popular."
       Catequesis Latinoamericana 1 (May/June, 1969): 90-101.

2134   GORSKI, J. "Miremos nuestra religiosidad." Catequesis
        Latinoamericana 3 (January/March, 1971): 18-21.

2135   PONCE GARCÍA, JAIME. El clero en Bolivia, 1968. Cuernavaca,
        México: Centro Intercultural de Documentación, 1970.

CHRISTIAN DEMOCRACY

2136   "Christian Party Withdraws from Elections in Bolivia."
        Catholic Messenger 82 (June 4, 1964): 3.

2137   ESTRADA, CARLOS. Siete ensayos. Cochabamba, Bolivia: Edi-
        torial Canelas, 1963. 46 pp.

COMMUNISM

2138   RIGOL, PETER NECRE. "Bolivia: Catholicism or Communism."
        Worldmission 12 (September, 1961): 89-97.

DOCUMENTS

2139   "Case Studies on Human Rights." IDOC-International 51 (March,
        1973): 1-5.

2140   "The Church and the Mining Workers in Bolivia. Conclusions
        of the Oruro Congress, 31st July 1969." IDOC-International
        1 (April 4, 1970): 65-67.

2141   "Declaration Issued by the Bolivian Epsicopate, 10th September,
        1969." IDOC-International 1 (April 4, 1970): 67-69.

2142   Episcopado Boliviano. La Iglesia en Bolivia y el desarrollo
        integral: pastoral colectiva. La Paz: Ediciones Paulinas,
        1968. 64 pp.

2143   "Manifesto of the Executive Committee ISAL, Bolivia." IDOC-
        International 17 (January 16, 1971): 27-32.

2144   "May Day Message of the Bolivian Bishops, 24th April, 1969."
        IDOC-International 1 (April 4, 1970): 62-65.

2145   "Minister Answers 'Gospel and Violence' Statement." IDOC-
        International 51 (March, 1973): 5-6.

Documents

2146   "Nestor Paz: Mystic, Christian, Guerrilla." IDOC-Internation-
       al 23 (April 10, 1971): 33-37.

2147   Obispos de Bolivia. "Paz y fraternidad." CELAM 113 (February,
       1977): 1-19, 21-26.

2148   "El papel del sacerdote en la política. Declaraciones del
       epsicopado boliviano." Servir 27 (June, 1970): 295-298.

2149   "Population Problems: A Pastoral Letter of the Epsicopate of
       Bolivia." L'Osservatore Romano, August 7, 1975, pp. 4-5.

2150   Sacerdotes Bolivianos. "Bolivia: la Iglesia y la situación
       del país." Mensaje 17 (March/April, 1968): 129-130.

2151   _____. "En la religión: ochenta sacerdotes piden revolucionar
       la Iglesia." Oiga 275 (May, 1968): 29-30.

2152   "Society and Church in Latin America." IDOC-International 1
       (April, 1970): 37-39.

2153   "The Violation of Human Rights in Bolivia." IDOC-International
       50 (January/February, 1973): 1-4.

ECONOMIC DEVELOPMENT

2154   La Iglesia en Bolivia y el desarrollo integral. Cochabamba,
       Bolivia: Los Amigos del Libro, [n.d.], 64 pp.

LABOR AND LABORING CLASSES

2155   "Bolivia: hay organismos de estado que impiden los cambios
       radicales." Carta de ISAL 3 (April, 1970): 6-7.

2156   "The Church and the Mining Workers in Bolivia. Conclusions
       of the Oruro Congress, 31st July 1969." IDOC-International
       1 (April 4, 1970): 65-67.

2157   Congreso Nacional de Sacerdotes de los Centros Mineros de
       Bolivia, VI. "La Iglesia y los trabajadores mineros de
       Bolivia." NADOC 81 (August 20, 1969): 1-2.

2158   "Cuestiones sociales en Bolivia: el episcopado toma la defensa
       de los mineros." Informaciones Católicas Internacionales
       296 (September 2, 1967): 8-9.

2159   "Declaración de ISAL, Bolivia." Carta de ISAL 3 (April,
        1970): 8-10.

POLITICS

2160   "Bolivia." Christian Century 86 (June 18, 1969): 849-850.

2161   "El papel del sacerdote en la política. Declaraciones del
        episcopado boliviano." Servir 27 (June, 1970): 295-298.

2162   RIGOL, PETER NEGRE. "Bolivia: Catholicism or Communism."
        Worldmission 12 (September, 1961): 89-97.

REFERENCE

2163   ALONSO, ISIDORO. La Iglesia en Perú y Bolivia: estructuras
        eclesiásticas. Bogotá: Centro de Información y Sociología
        de la Obra de Cooperación Sacerdotal Hispanoamericana,
        1961. 271 pp.

2164   CHILCOTE, RONALD H. "Cambio estructural y desarrollo en
        Bolivia." Desarrollo Económico 6 (January/March, 1967):
        693-708.

2165   PASCUAL, TOMÁS, and AGUILO, FEDERICO. Sociología eclesiástica
        de Bolivia. La Paz: Universidad Católica, 1968. 128 pp.

REVOLUTION

2166   ALGERIA, JOEL, pseud. "Theology of the Coup d'Etat?" Common-
        weal 95 (January, 1972): 340-341.

2167   ARROYO, GONZALO. "Rebeldía cristiana y compromiso comuni-
        tario." Mensaje 167 (March/April, 1968): 78-83.

2168   BISHOP M., JORDAN. "Tremors in Bolivia." Commonweal 83
        (December 17, 1965): 339-342.

2169   "Diario de un guerrillero cristiano, Francisco Néstor Paz
        Zamora." Servicio Colombiano de Comunicación Social 18
        (March, 1973): 21.

2170   GUTIÉRREZ, GRANIER. "En Bolivia: frente a las guerillas un
        obispo pide 'la restauración de la justicia.'" Informa-
        ciones Católicas Internacionales 295 (September, 1967): 7.

Revolution

2171 "La Iglesia en la revolución." Cristianismo y Sociedad 1
      (January 4, 1963): 55-63.

2172 JEREZ, FRANCISCO, pseud. "Bolivia: Prayers Before a Coup."
      Commonweal 94 (September 17, 1971): 469-470.

2173 MORA SÁENS, CLOVIS. "Los cristianos y la revolución en
      Bolivia." Pasos 27 (October 23, 1972): 12.

2174 Movimiento Social Evangélico Boliviano. Reto a los evangélicos
      los propósitos son el de luchar por el bienestar social,
      moral, y económico de nuestro pueblo. La Paz: [n.p.],
      1962. 9 pp.

2175 PAZ, NESTOR. "Death of a Freedom Fighter." Critic 33 (March/
      April, 1975): 42-47.

2176 _____. "Message of Nestor Paz on Leaving to Join the Guer-
      rillas." U.S. Catholic 40 (April, 1975): 23-27.

2177 "Peacemaker in La Paz: Father A. Kennedy." America 111
      (November 14, 1964): 583.

2178 PERROT, ROY. "Quest of the Student Guerrillas." Critic 20
      (September/October, 1971): 38-44.

SOCIALISM

2179 "Declaración del ISAL, Bolivia." Carta de ISAL 3 (April,
      1970): 8-10.

VIOLENCE

2180 "Case Studies on Human Rights." IDOC-International 51 (March,
      1973): 1-5.

2181 "Minister Answers 'Gospel and Violence' Statement." IDOC-
      International 51 (March, 1973): 5-6.

2182 "The Violation of Human Rights in Bolivia." IDOC-International
      50 (January/February, 1973): 1-4.

IV Brazil

GENERAL

2183   "Accusations from Prison." New Blackfriars 51 (December,
       1970): 549-555.

2184   NO ENTRY

2185   AMOROSO LIMA, ALCEU. "Diálogo de Igreja como o mundo moderno."
       Paz e Terra 1 (July, 1966): 11-27.

2186   ANTOINE, CHARLES. "L'Eglise dans la Societé Brésilienne."
       Choisir 186 (1975): 27.

2187   _____. "Où en est l'Eglise du Brésil?" Choisir 135 (1971):
       15.

2188   ANTONIAZZI, A. "Várias Interpretações do catolicismo popular
       no Brasil." Revista Eclesiástica Brasileira 36 (March,
       1976): 82-94.

2189   ANTUNES, MANUEL. "O mundo de hoje e a religião." Brotéria
       78 (1964): 657-670.

2190   Apostolado Positivista do Brasil. Comunismo e positivismo.
       Rio de Janeiro: Jornal do Comércio, 1946. 15 pp.

2191   ARAUJO, FRANCISCO DE. "¿Cuál es el papel de la Iglesia en el
       Brasil?" Mensaje 17 (July, 1968): 303-309.

2192   ARNS, PAULO EVARISTO. A quem iremos, Senhor? Idéias e
       sugestões para a aplicação da pastoral de conjunto. São
       Paulo: Editôra Paulinas, 1968. 222 pp.

2193   AZEVEDO, T. DE. "The Church in Brazil." Furrow 15 (April,
       1964): 222-227.

2194   AZZI, R. "Elementos para a história do catolicismo popular."
       Revista Eclesiástica Brasileira 36 (March, 1976): 95-130.

General

2195   BARROS, RAIMUNDO CARAMURU DE. Brasil: uma Igreja em reno-
        vação: a experiência brasileira de planejamento pastoral.
        Petrópolis: Editôra Vozes, 1967. 206 pp.

2196   BASTOS DE AVILA, FERNANDO. "La Iglesia en Brasil." Mundo
        Nuevo 35 (May, 1969): 23-28.

2197   "Brazil and the Pope." Commonweal 92 (June 12, 1970): 284.

2198   "Brazil Deports Priest for Subversive Activity." National
        Catholic Reporter 5 (January 29, 1969): 3.

2199   "Brazilian Schizophrenia: A Church and People at Odds."
        Herder Correspondence 4 (February, 1967): 48-52.

2200   BRUNEAU, THOMAS C. "How to Demoralize the Laity." America
        118 (June 22, 1968): 789-791.

2201   _____. "The Church Moves Left." Commonweal 87 (February 2,
        1968): 535-536.

2202   CALMON, PEDRO. Brasília: catedral do Brasil; história da
        Igreja no Brasil. Rio de Janeiro: Editora Promoções,
        1970. 251 pp.

2203   CÂMARA, HÉLDER. "Bishops with Capitalistic Mentalities:
        Excerpts." Tablet 218 (October 21, 1964): 1244.

2204   _____. "Brasil: disipados los 'malentendidos' con el
        Estado ... desarrollo a su campaña." Informaciones Cató-
        licas Internacionales 272 (September 22, 1966): 10-11.

2205   _____. "Brasil: los obispos del noreste del país en favor
        de la promoción de las masas." Informaciones Católicas
        Internationales 234 (February 22, 1965): 234.

2206   _____. "Carta a los jóvenes." Criterio 41 (July 11, 1968):
        482-483.

2207   _____. "Carta el episcopado y al pueblo brasileño." Mundo
        72 (August 17/September 6, 1972): 23.

2208   _____. Declaraciones y pastorales. Cuernavaca, México:
        [n.p., n.d.].

2209   _____. Discurso de paraninfo da Escola de Agronomia da Uni-
        versidad Rural. Recife: [n.p.], 1965. 7 pp.

2210 _____. "En América Latina: revolución, ¡sí! violencia, ¡no! socialismo, ¿por qué no?" Informaciones Católicas Internacionales 309 (April 1, 1968): 16-18.

2211 _____. "A encíclica 'Populorum Progressio' e reações." Paz e Terra 2 (April, 1968): 178-180.

2212 _____. Es ist Zeit. Köln: Styria, 1970.

2213 _____. "Face a l'injustice actuelle, les mots ne suffisent plus." La Documentation Catholique 69 (September 2, 1972): 781-785.

2214 _____. Fame e sete di pace com giustizia. Milano: Massimo, 1970.

2215 _____. Gebet für die Reichen. Zürich: Pendo-Verlag, 1972.

2216 _____. "Les hommes meurent, et non les idees." Informations Catholique Internationales 361 (1970).

2217 _____. "Human Rights: Address Given When He Received the World Humanity Award." Tablet 229 (October 25, 1975): 1046-1047.

2218 _____. "Imposições da solidaridade universal." Paz e Terra 1 (October, 1967): 159-168.

2219 _____. "Les juristes chrétiens et le développement." La Documentation Catholique 66 (March 16, 1969): 273-275.

2220 _____. Kapplögning med Tiden. Stockholm: Gummessous Bokforlag, 1970.

2221 _____. "Letter from Brazil." Worldmission 21 (Spring, 1970): 58-59.

2222 _____. "Limosna, no; sino justicia en el comercio internacional." NADOC 47 (April, 1969): 1-3.

2223 _____. "Mensagem aos jovens." Ecclesia 1,337 (February 10, 1968): 21.

2224 _____. Mensaje ... al tomar posesión de la arquidiócesis de Olinda y Recife en abril 12 de 1964. Recife: [n.p.], 1964. 4 pp.

General

2225 _____. "Mensaje fraterno a los religiosos y a las religiosas de América Latina." Misiones Extranjeras 30 (1975): 542-545.

2226 _____. "Les minorités abrahamiques et les structures de l'Eglise." Informationes Catholiques Internationales 417 (1972): 21-24.

2227 _____. "Nous avons présénté un christianisme trop passif." La Documentation Catholique 72 (November 16, 1975): 979-981.

2228 _____. "Nuestros hijos los sacerdotes." Informaciones Católicas Internacionales 205 (December 7, 1963): 34-35.

2229 _____. "El obispo en su diócesis, la Iglesia y el mundo." Criterio 38 (May 14, 1965): 339-342.

2230 _____. Um olhar sobre a cidade. Rio de Janeiro: Editora Civilização Brasileira, 1976. 144 pp.

2231 _____. Opvoeding tot Vrijeheid. Amsterdam: Uitgeverij Orion, 1972.

2232 _____. Para llegar a tiempo. Salamanca: Ediciones Sígueme, 1970. 152 pp.

2233 _____. "Pour un veritable dialogue entre pays riches et pays pauvres." La Documentation Catholique 72 (August 3-17, 1975): 732-735.

2234 _____. "Les pretres, nos fils." Informations Catholiques Internationales 205 (December 7, 1963): 34.

2235 _____. "Projets de développement et changements de structures." La Documentation Catholique 67 (1970): 218-221.

2236 _____. Pronunciamentos de Dom Hélder. Recife: Secretariado Regional, CNBB, [n.d.].

2237 _____. "Os subversivos são os que nos acusam." Informations Catholiques Internationales 328 (January 2, 1969).

2238 _____. "Un Après-Concile à la Hauteur du Vatican II." Informations Catholiques Internationales 254 (December 22, 1965): 17-19.

2239 _____. Universidad y revolución. Santiago, Chile: Universidad Católica de Chile, Ediciones Nueva Universidad, 1969. 108 pp.

2240 _____. "Voice in the Wilderness: Interview by O. Falacci." Sign 55 (July/August, 1976): 9-15.

2241 _____. Vold Losning der Tragedie. Oslo: Dreyer, 1970.

2242 _____. Die Wüste ist Fruchtbar. Köln: Stryria, 1972.

2243 _____. Zullen We Nog op Tijo Komen. Utrecht: Desclée de Brouwer-Orion, 1970.

2244 CÂMARA, JAIME DE BARROS. Problemas. Rio de Janeiro: Editôra Presença, 1963. 241 pp.

2245 CAMPOS, RENATO CARNEIRO. Igreja, política e região. Recife: Instituto Joaquim Nabuco de Pesquisas Socias, 1967. 61 pp., bibl.

2246 CAMPOS, ROBERTO DE OLIVEIRA. Temas e sistemas. Rio de Janeiro: Apec Editôra, 1969. 303 pp.

2247 CARDOZO, MANOEL. "The Brazilian Church and the New Left." Journal of Inter-American Studies 6 (July, 1964): 313-321.

2248 CARREÑO, JOSE. "Entrevista con el padre Pessoa." El Día, February 6, 1966.

2249 CAVALCANTI, JOSE KOSINSKI. "A Igreja em agonia." Visao 32 (April 12, 1968): 66-75.

2250 CEPEDA, ALFREDO. "La Iglesia del Brasil." El Día, June 24, 1965.

2251 "Church in Brazil." Newsweek, August 17, 1970. pp. 94-95.

2252 "The Church in Brazil." Tablet 228 (September 14, 1974): 885.

2253 "Clergy Urge Brazil Action." National Catholic Reporter 11 (December 20, 1974): 5.

2254 CLOIN, TIAGO G. "Perfiles de la revolución pastoral en Brasil." Criterio 39 (March 10, 1969): 163-167.

2255 Comunidade de Vida Crista. Confrontação ou contradição? Recife: Comunidade de Vida Crista, 1969. 258 pp.

General

2256   COSTA, H. E. SERGIO CORREA. "Brazil: A Reply." New Black-
       friars 52 (January, 1971): 5-9.

2257   COSTA CAMPOS, J. "Resumen de las actividades del CLAF, Región
       Brasil, período 1964-1973." Catequesis Latinoamericana 5
       (April/June, 1973): 211-215.

2258   CULHANE, EUGENE K. "Social Minded Archbishop." America 109
       (July 6, 1963): 5.

2259   DALE, ROMEU. "A Igreja católica às vésperas do concílio."
       Revista Eclesiástica Brasileira 21 (1961): 593-600.

2260   DEELEN, GODOFREDO J. Diócese de Ponta Grosa, Paraná. Cuerna-
       vaca, México: Centro Intercultural de Documentación, 1968.
       2 v., bibl.

2261   DE KADT, EMANUEL. Catholic Radicals in Brazil. New York:
       Oxford University Press, 1970. 304 pp., bibl.

2262   _____, and GOTT, RICHARD. "Priests in Protest: Catholic
       Radicals in Brazil." New Society (April 1, 1971): 545-
       546.

2263   DELLA CAVA, RALPH. "Catholicism and Society in Twentieth-
       Century Brazil." Latin American Research Review 11 (August
       13, 1976): 7-50.

2264   ENGEL, OTTO. "Brazil: Church, Army Clash Over Aggiornamento."
       Ave Maria 107 (February 10, 1968): 16-18.

2265   FREIRE, PAULO, et al. Educação e conscientização: exten-
       sionismo rural. Cuernavaca, México: Centro Intercultural
       de Documentación, 1968. 318 pp.

2266   FREITAS, JOSÉ-ITAMAR, ed. Brasil, ano 2000: o futuro sem
       fantasia. São Paulo: Artes Gráficas Gomes de Souza, 1968.
       327 pp.

2267   GLOIN, T. "The Natal Movement in Brazil: Evangelization
       Accompanied by Social-Economic Action." Christian World 8
       (1963): 117-128.

2268   GREGORY, ALFONSO FELIPPE. "La ayuda de la Iglesia y el desar-
       rollo." NADOC 34 (March 12, 1969): 1-4.

2269   _____. A paróquia ontem hoje e amanhã. Petrópolis: Centro
       de Estadística Religiosa e Investigações Sociais, 1967.
       152 pp.

Brazil

2270   GRIGULEVICH, I. "Katholitisizm v Sovremennoi Brazilii."
       Nauki i Religiia 4 (November, 1962): 46-50.

2271   GUERRA, ALOISIO. A Igreja está com o povo? Rio de Janeiro:
       Editora Civilização Brasileira, 1963. 100 pp.

2272   HOORNAERT, EDUARDO. "Para uma historia da Igreja no Brasil."
       Revista Eclesiástica Brasiliera 34 (March, 1974): 123-131.

2273   "La Iglesia de los pobres en el 'nordeste' brasileño: un
       cuento real de Navidad." Informaciones Católicas Inter-
       nacionales 206 (December 22, 1963): 25-34.

2274   "J'ai entendu les cris de mon peuple." Etudes 339 (July,
       1973): 31-47.

2275   JORDAN, J. "Brazil." Furrow 17 (January, 1966): 23-27.

2276   JUNIOR, THEOTONIO. "A luta ideologica no Brasil." Revista
       Brasiliense 39 (January/February, 1962): 100-118.

2277   KIRCHNER, DONNELL L. "Banned in Brasilia: Bishop's Pastoral,
       May 6, 1973." America 129 (December 22, 1973): 479-481.

2278   "Leader with Vision: Brazil." America 114 (February 26,
       1966): 279.

2279   LIENARD, ACHILLE. "A Igreja a luz do concílio." Revista
       Eclesiástica Brasileira 23 (1963): 488-492.

2280   LIMA, ALCEU AMOROSO. "A Igreja para o desenvolvimento."
       Cadernos Brasileiros 10 (March/April, 1968): 3-5.

2281   LIMA VAZ, HENRIQUE C. DE. "The Church and Conscientização."
       America 118 (April 27, 1968): 578-581.

2282   LORSCHEIDER, ALOISIO. "O mistério da Igreja." Revista Ecle-
       siástica Brasileira 23 (1963): 871-882.

2283   MAC EOIN, GARY. "Brazil's Bishops Fight for Human Rights."
       Saint Anthony 81 (November, 1973): 10-19.

2284   _____. "Social Sinners in Brazil." Christian Century 90
       (August 1, 1973): 780-783.

2285   METSCH, GERARDO. "Strukturen und Wandlungen im Katholizismus
       Brasiliens." Stimmen der Zeit 182 (December, 1968): 371-
       387.

General

2286   MONTENEGRO, JOÃO ALFREDO DE SOUSA. Evolução do catolicismo no
       Brasil. Petrópolis: Editôra Voses, 1972. 188 pp.

2286A MOREIRA ALVES, MARCIO. "Brazil: A Country Where Christians
       Are Outlaws." Catholic World 212 (November, 1970): 65-68.

2287   MURPHY, R. "Episode in Natal." Columbia 43 (January, 1963):
       10-11.

2288   MUTCHLER, DAVID E. Roman Catholicism in Brasil. Saint Louis:
       Washington University, Social Science Institute, 1965.
       117 pp.

2289   "Notas da Arquidiocese de Olinda e Recife." SEDOC 2 (1969):
       143.

2290   OLIVEIRA, JORGE MARCOS DE. "Brasil: el obispo de Santo André
       toma el partido de los estudiantes contra el régimen."
       Informaciones Católicas Internacionales 273 (October 7,
       1966): 9.

2291   Partido Demócrata Cristão. "Posição de vanguarda de demo-
       cracia crista para garantir a paz, a seguerança e a pros-
       peridade de família brasileira." Brasil, Urgente 1 (June
       2-8, 1963): 17.

2292   Pastoral de Conjunto: simpósio. Petrópolis: Editôra Vozes,
       1968. 110 pp.

2293   PAULA, FRANCISCO JULIAO ARRUDA DE. "The Declaration of Belo
       Horizonte." In Agrarian Reform in Lation America, edited
       by T. Lynn Smith, pp. 116-122. New York: Knopf, 1965.

2294   PEREIRA CAMARGO DE, CANDIDO P. "Essai de typologie du
       catholicisme bréselien." Social Compass 14 (1967): 399-
       422.

2295   PEREIRA DA CÂMARA. Brasilidade e catolicismo: esboços his-
       toricos. Pôrto Alegre: Libraria Sulina Editôra, 1971.
       388 pp.

2296   POPE JOHN XXIII. "S. Micheal Archangelus in caelestem patronum
       pro tota brasiliana publicae disciplinae ac securitatis
       tuendae militati administratione eligitur." Acta Apostol-
       icae Sedis 53 (March, 1969): 147-148.

2297   "A presença da Igreja no Brasil de hoje." Paz e Terra 8
       (1968): 149-279.

2298 "Les problèmes de l'Eglise au Brésil." Amérique Latine 8 (February, 1968): 12-23.

2299 RAINE, PHILIP. "The Catholic Church in Brazil." Journal of Inter-American Studies and World Affairs 13 (April, 1971): 279-295.

2300 "Red-Baiting in Rio." America 130 (February 9, 1974): 83.

2301 REGAN, DAVID. "The Church in Brazil: An Overview." Worldmission 25 (September, 1974): 17-22.

2302 RÉTIF, ANDRE. "Events and Trends." World Justice 6 (December, 1964): 211-230.

2303 RIBEIRO DE OLIVEIRA, P. "Catolicismo popular e romanização do catolicismo brasileiro." Revista Eclesiástica Brasileira 36 (March, 1976): 131-141.

2304 _____. "Catolicismo popular no Brasil." Revista Eclesiástica Brasileira 36 (March, 1976): 272-280.

2305 ROETT, RIORDAN, ed. Brazil in the Sixties. Nashville: Vanderbilt University Press, 1972. 424 pp.

2306 ROPER, CHRISTOPHER. "Brazil: Assessing the Debate." New Blackfriars 52 (January, 1971): 10-12.

2307 SANDERS, THOMAS G. "¿A dónde van los católicos de Brasil?" ECA 234 (January/February, 1968): 15-17.

2308 "La situación de la Iglesia en Brasil." Cristianismo y Revolución 1 (September, 1966): 3-4.

2309 SOUZA, HERBERT JOSÉ, ed. Cristianismo hoje. Rio de Janeiro: Editôra Universo, 1962. 108 pp.

2310 SOUZA, LUIZ ALBERTO G. DE, comp. Brasil, o confronto de duas geraçoes de cristãos: 1960. Cuernavaca, México: Centro Intercultural de Documentación, 1966. 1 v.

2311 "Support for Brazil Bishops." Tablet 220 (September 3, 1966): 1002.

2312 THIBAULT, GUY. "El problema de la Iglesia en el Brasil." ECA 239 (July, 1968): 215-216.

General

2313   TORRES, JOÃO CAMILO DE OLIVEIRA. História das idéias reli-
       giosas no Brasil (a Igreja e a sociedade brasileira). São
       Paulo: Editôra Grijalbo, 1968. 324 pp.

2314   "Eine Typologie des brasilianischen Katholizismus." Herder
       Korrespondenz 22 (1968): 215-218.

2315   TYSON, BRADY, and LIMA, ALCEU AMOROSO. "Catholicism in
       Brazil." America 110 (May 30, 1964): 764-767.

2316   VAZ, HENRIQUE C. DE LIMA. "Igreja-reflexo vs. Igreja-fonte."
       Cadernos Brasileiros 10 (March, 1968): 17-22.

2317   WANDERLY, LUIZ EDUARDO W. "A Igreja no mundo de hoje." Paz
       e Terra 1 (July, 1966): 28-38.

2318   WEGENER, STEPHAN. Die katholische Kirche und der gessell-
       schaftliche Wandel im brasilianischen Nordosten. Friburg:
       Arnold Bergstraesser-Institut für kulturwissenschaftliche
       Forschung, 1965. 264 pp.

AGRARIAN REFORM

2319   CÂMARA, HÉLDER. "Discurso de paraninfo da Escola de Agronomia
       da Universidade Rural." Mensaje 137 (May/April, 1964).

2320   _____, and OBISPOS DEL NORDESTE. "La piedra del escándolo."
       Cristianismo y Revolución 1 (September, 1966): 6.

2321   CASTRO MAYER, ANTONIO DE, et al. Reforma agrária: questão
       de consciência. São Paulo: Gráfica da "Revista dos Tri-
       bunais," 1960. 387.

2322   CONN, STEPHEN. The Squatters' Rights of Favelados. Cuerna-
       vaca, México: Centro Intercultural de Documentación, 1969.
       1 v.

2323   DE KADT, EMANUEL. Catholic Radicals in Brazil. London:
       Oxford University Press, 1970. 304 pp.

2324   "Dom Hélder ajuda padre Melo na reforma agrária." Centro
       Informativo Católico 911 (December, 1969).

2325   FONSECA, GONDIN DA. Os gorilas, o povo, e a reforma agrária:
       manifestos dos bispos do Brasil. São Paulo: Editôra
       Fulgor, 1963. 77 pp.

2326　FONSECA, JAIME. "Brazilian Catholics Organize for Land Reform." Catholic Messenger 81 (July 4, 1963): 12.

2327　PAULA, FRANCISCO JULIÃO ARRUGA DE. "Brazil: A Christian Country." Monthly Review 14 (September, 1962): 243-250.

2328　____. "The Declaration of Belo Horizonte." In Agrarian Reform in Latin America, edited by T. Lynn Smith, pp. 116-122. New York: Knopf, 1965.

CÂMARA, HÉLDER

2329　"Archbishop Criticized for Demanding Reform." Catholic Messenger 82 (April 30, 1964): 1.

2330　ARRAES, MIGUEL. "Au Brésil." Lettre 135 (November, 1969): 23-25.

2331　ASSMANN, HUGO. "Tarefas e limitações de uma teologia de desenvolvimento." Editôra Vozes 62 (January, 1968): 13-21.

2332　"Autocrítica de dom Hélder Câmara." Manchete, March 25, 1967, pp. 16-18

2333　NO ENTRY

2334　BECKMAN, JOSEPH F. "Dom Hélder Câmara, the Man and His Message." Priest 31 (December, 1975): 16+.

2335　"Bishop Criticizes Câmara." National Catholic Reporter 4 (June 12, 1968): 3.

2336　"Bishop Leaves Palace, Moves into Small House." National Catholic Reporter 4 (April 3, 1968): 5.

2337　"Bishops Need to be Humble: Archbishop Hélder Pessoa Câmara." Tablet 219 (December 11, 1965): 1398.

2338　"Bishops' Reply." Time, September 2, 1966, p. 31.

2339　"Bispos anuncian fim do imperialismo." Última Hora, October 30, 1967.

2340　BLÁQUEZ, CARMONA FELICIANO. Hélder Câmara: el grito del pobre. Madrid: Sociedad de Educación Atenas, 1972.

2341　"Brazil Bishops Attack Problem of Violence." Justice and Peace 1 (February/March, 1977): 1.

Câmara, Hélder

2342   BROUCKER, JOSE DE. Dom Hélder Câmara: The Violence of Peace-
       maker. Maryknoll, New York: Orbis Books, 1970. 154 pp.

2343   BURGEON, ROGER. L'Archevêque des Favelles. Paris: Robert
       Laffont Editions, 1968. 220 pp.

2344   CALLADO, ANTÔNIO. Tempo de arrães, padres e comunistas na
       revolução sem violência. Río de Janeiro: Jose Alvaro
       Editor, 1964. 156 pp.

2345   CÂMARA, HÉLDER. "Inauguração que vale um símbolo." Informa-
       tions Catholiques Internationales 241 (June 7, 1965): 29.

2346   _____. "Is Violence the Only Solution?" U.S. Catholic 34
       (March, 1969): 14-18.

2347   "Câmara and Illich." Commonweal 89 (February 7, 1969): 575-
       576.

2348   "Câmara: Practically Voiceless." National Catholic Reporter
       9 (February 16, 1973): 20.

2349   "Candidatura de Dom Hélder ao Prêmio Nobel da Paz." SEDOC 3
       (1970): 59.

2350   "Cardeal da Bahia fala sobre Dom Hélder Câmara." O Estado de
       São Paulo, October 10, 1967.

2351   "Carta aberta a Dom Hélder." SEDOC 3 (1970): 761.

2352   "Carta do Cardeal Roy a Dom Hélder." SEDOC 4 (1972): 1,187.

2353   CAYUELA, JOSÉ. Hélder Câmara; Brasil: un Vietnam católico.
       Santiago, Chile: Editorial Pomaire, 1969. 280 pp.

2353A _____. Hélder Câmara; Brasil: un Vietnam católico. Madrid:
       Editorial Pomaire, 1970. 280 pp.

2354   "Cineastas procuram Dom Hélder." O Estado de São Paulo, May
       12, 1968.

2355   CLARK, JAMES A. "Religion and Revolution South of the Rio
       Grande." American Ecclesiastical Review 159 (October,
       1968): 256-260.

2356   "Clero de Recife defende Dom Hélder." SEDOC 3 (1970): 640-
       641.

Brazil

Câmara, Hélder

2357 "Collision in Latin America." _Time_, February 9, 1970, p. 44.

2358 "Comentarios al discurso de Dom Hélder Câmara en el palacio de los deportes de París." _Correire Della Sera_, May 15, 1970.

2359 "Comunicado sobre la actuación de Monseñor Hélder Câmara." _L'Osservatore Romano_, July 23, 1969, p. 3.

2360 "Contestation in Brazil." _Herder Correspondence_ 6 (April, 1969): 105-109.

2361 CRAIG, MARY. "Dom Hélder Câmara: Rebel Priest with a Cause." _Impact_ 12 (December, 1969): 13-15.

2362 _____. "In Câmara: Profile of a Bishop." _Month_ 41 (June, 1969): 350-355.

2363 "Críticas a Dom Hélder provocaram tumulto." _O Estado de São Paulo_, July 2, 1968.

2364 "Declaração de Dom Hélder." _SEDOC_ 3 (1970): 635.

2365 "Declaracion de Dom Hélder Câmara el asesinato del padre Henrique." _Mensaje_ 186 (January/February, 1970): 26.

2366 "O desencontro de Dom Hélder com a história." _O Estado de São Paulo_, March 13, 1968.

2367 "Documento de Congregación Vaticana desacredita al Arzobispo Hélder Câmara." _Noticias Aliadas_ 71 (September 12, 1970): 2.

2368 "Dom Avelar defende Dom Hélder." _SEDOC_ 3 (1970): 641-643.

2369 "Dom Helder." _Informaciones Católicas Internacionales_ 244 (July 22, 1965): 2.

2370 "Dom Hélder a seus prosélitos." _O Estado de São Paulo_, December 1, 1967.

2371 "Dom Hélder, al lanzar 'Acción Justicia y Paz', reanuda la lucha de Gandhi." _Informaciones Católicas Internacionales_ 322 (October 2, 1968): 18.

2372 "Dom Helder anuncia a 'pressão moral.'" _O Estado de São Paulo_, July 24, 1968.

Câmara, Hélder

2373   "Dom Hélder Câmara á Paris." Amerique Latine 23 (1975): 3-10.

2374   Dom Hélder Câmara, Bischof und Revolutionär. Berlin: Lahn
        Verlag, 1970.

2375   "Dom Hélder Câmara convidado especial na Alemanha." Centro
        Informativo Católico 952 (October 18, 1970).

2376   "Dom Hélder Câmara en Europa." Misiones Católicas 981 (July,
        1970): 235-239.

2377   "Dom Hélder Câmara: 'hora de liberación.'" NADOC 28 (February
        19, 1969).

2378   "Dom Hélder Câmara interpela a occidente." El Catolicismo,
        June 15, 1970.

2379   "Dom Hélder Câmara: "Limosna, no; sino justicia en el comercio
        internacional.'" NADOC 47 (April 23, 1969).

2380   "Dom Hélder Câmara sprach in Zürich: 'Es gibt keine inneren
        Angelegenheiten.'" Schweiz, July 18, 1971.

2381   "Dom Hélder Câmara sprach in Zürich und in Freiburg: 'Schwei-
        zervolk, handle nach deinem guten Ruf.'" Schweiz, July 19,
        1971.

2382   "Dom Hélder concede entrevista por ocasião da assembleia geral
        da CNBB." Centro Informativo Católico 968 (March 13, 1971).

2383   Dom Hélder contra violência." O Estado de São Paulo, April
        5, 1972.

2384   "Dom Hélder critica desnacionalização." O Estado de São
        Paulo, June 1, 1971.

2385   "Dom Hélder e a ação integralista." O Estado de São Paulo,
        May 24, 1968.

2386   "Dom Hélder é criticado." O Estado São Paulo, December 28,
        1967.

2387   "Dom Hélder e o comunismo." O Estado de São Paulo, October
        15, 1970.

2388   "Dom Hélder e o nordeste." O Estado de São Paulo, November
        11, 1967.

Brazil

Câmara, Hélder

2389 "Dom Hélder elogiado no Vaticano." O Estado São Paulo,
       February 27, 1971.

2390 "Dom Hélder: evangelização sem proselitismo." Centro Infor-
       mativo Católico 886 (June 14, 1969).

2391 "Dom Hélder fala de suas viagens." O Estado de São Paulo,
       October 3, 1970.

2392 "Dom Hélder fala sôbre a miséria." Centro Informativo Cató-
       lico 929 (May 2, 1970).

2393 "Dom Hélder irá à Conferência Ecumênica." Centro Informativo
       Católico 913 (December 20, 1969).

2394 "Dom Hélder irá ao Japão." Centro Informativo Católico 949
       (September 26, 1970).

2395 "Dom Hélder, la pasión." Primera Plana 198 (October 11-17,
       1966): 35-41.

2396 "Dom Hélder, nós e a historia." O Estado de São Paulo, Feb-
       ruary 23, 1968.

2397 "Dom Hélder: o astraso é nocivo como a guerra." O Estado de
       São Paulo, September 15, 1971.

2398 "Dom Hélder: o integralismo foi meu pecado la juventude."
       Manchete, September 28, 1968, pp. 74-77.

2399 "Dom Hélder: o padre estrangeiro é a presença viva da Igreja."
       Centro Informativo Católico 915 (January 3, 1969).

2400 "Dom Hélder prega reforma." O Estado de São Paulo, March 13,
       1968.

2401 "Dom Hélder, Prêmio Nobel da Paz." Centro Informativo Cató-
       lico 907 (November 9, 1969).

2402 "Dom Hélder promete fazer o impossível pelo povo." Centro
       Informativo Católico 918 (January 24, 1970).

2403 "Dom Hélder recebe o Prêmio Martin Luther King." Centro
       Informativo Católico 951 (August 22, 1970).

2404 "Dom Hélder responde as acusações." Centro Informativo Cató-
       lico 951 (October 3, 1970).

Câmara, Hélder

2405 "Dom Hélder se explica." Informaciones Católicas Interna-cionales 315 (July 1, 1968): 4.

2406 "Dom Hélder tem discordâncias." O Estado de São Paulo, June 18, 1968.

2407 "Dom Hélder tocuo na ferida do Brasil." Centro Informativo Católico 953 (November 9, 1970).

2408 "Dom Hélder vai ao encontro luterano." Centro Informativo Católico 970 (April 4, 1970).

2409 "Dom Rossi defende Dom Hélder." SEDOC 3 (1970): 643-644.

2410 "Dos facetas de la actual realidad brasileña." NADOC 144 (May 13, 1970).

2411 "En Brasil: frente a la miseria y la justicia Dom Hélder no está solo." Informaciones Católicas Internacionales 300 (November 2, 1967): 19.

2412 ENGEL, OTTO. "Vaticano censura a Monseñor Hélder Câmara y controla reunión de la CNBB." Noticias Aliadas 57 (July 19, 1969): 2.

2413 "Entrevista con Dom Hélder Câmara en Recife." Excelsior, September 22, 1972.

2414 "O estranho rito de natal de Dom Hélder." O Estado de São Paulo, December 28, 1971.

2415 "L'Express va plus loin avec Dom Hélder Câmara." L'Express 988 (June 15-21, 1970): 138-140, 145-166.

2416 GONZÁLES BALADO, J. L. Me llaman el Obispo Rojo. Madrid: Ediciones Paulinas, 1974. 224 pp.

2417 "Grave adoestação dos bispos do Brasil contra as violências e os abusos de poder." L'Osservatore Romano, October 25, 1970, p. 2.

2418 GUSKE, HUBERTUS. Hélder Câmara. Berlin: Union-Verlag, 1973. 85 pp., bibl.

2419 "Heads of Lettuce." America 110 (May 16, 1964): 663.

2420 "Hélder aponta erros do cristianismo." O Estado de São Paulo, October 24, 1970.

Brazil

Câmara, Hélder

2421 "Hélder Câmara." National Catholic Reporter 4 (May 8, 1968): 2.

2422 "Hélder: 'o tempo dirá.'" O Estado de São Paulo, October 25, 1970.

2423 "Hélder prega a Igreja politica." O Estado de São Paulo, June 26, 1972.

2424 "Hélder tem motivo." O Estado de São Paulo, August 14, 1970.

2425 "Hélder volta a criticar a Igreja." O Estado de São Paulo, June 27, 1972.

2426 HERNÁNDEZ, D. "La opción evangélica de un pacífico: Monseñor Hélder Câmara." Christus 38 (October, 1973): 5-8.

2427 IMBODEN, ROBERTO. "Encounter with the Third World: Dom Hélder and Brazil." Canadian Forum 54 (February, 1975): 11-15.

2428 "Interview with Dom Hélder Câmara." IDOC-International 54 (Summer, 1973): 15-19.

2429 JORGE, SALOMÃO. O diablo celebra a missa. São Paulo: L. Oren, 1969.

2430 "Jornal Carioca defende Dom Hélder." Centro Informativo Católico 934 (June 13, 1970).

2431 LARRAÍN, HERNÁN. "Dom Hélder Câmara." Mensaje 178 (May, 1969): 139-140.

2432 "Lettre du Cardinal Roy a Dom Hélder Câmara." La Documentation Catholique 1,611 (June 18, 1972): 596.

2433 MC CABE, H. "The Church and Social Problems." New Blackfriars 54 (January, 1973): 2-3.

2434 "Meditación pastoral de los obispos de Brasil: 25 de octubre, 1976." Christus 42 (September, 1977): 55-61.

2435 "Monseñor Câmara senala que amenazas de muerte no le atemorizan." Noticias Aliadas 87 (October 30, 1968).

2436 "Monseñor Hélder Câmara habla en EEUU sobre la seguridad nacional." ICIA 167 (March 15, 1978): 4.

Câmara, Hélder

2437 "Monseñor Hélder Câmara pide programa de habitación popular antes que templo lujoso." Criterio 1,529 (August 10, 1967).

2438 "Monseñor Hélder Pessoa Câmara: la libertad del hombre en el mundo de hoy." L'Osservatore Romano, August 1, 1971, p. 10.

2439 MORGAN, T. "Three Days with Archbishop Hélder." Catholic Digest 21 (August, 1967): 72-78.

2440 "Le Nonce Apostolique au Brésil a fait parvenir une chaleureuse lettre d'eloges à Dom Hélder Câmara, Archvêque de Recife, pour l'action pastorale qu'il projette de mener dans le nord-est du Brésil en 1972." La Documentation Catholique 1,603 (February 20, 1972): 191-192.

2441 "Nouvelles protestations d'évêques contre les tortures." La Documentation Catholique 1,612 (July 2, 1972): 642.

2442 "Novas Doenças na Igreja." Veja 2 (September 18, 1968): 52.

2443 "Padres católicos e padres comunistas." O Cruzeiro, August 24, 1968.

2444 PAGE, J. A. "The Church and Colonialism: The Betrayal of the Third World." Commonweal 91 (January 23, 1970): 462-463.

2445 PAPA, M. "Dom Hélder Enchants Educators with Justice: Upper Midwest Catholic Education Congress, Minneapolis, October, 1975." National Catholic Reporter 12 (October 31, 1975): 1.

2446 "Para Dom Hélder a paz vem do desenvolvimento." Jornal do Comércio, September 25, 1966.

2447 "Para Hélder Câmara piden Nobel de la Paz trabajadores de América Latina." Noticias Aliadas 97 (December 10, 1969).

2448 "Pastor of the Poor." Time, June 24, 1974, p. 61.

2449 "Paulo VI condena a violência." L'Osservatore Romano, October 25, 1970, p. 1.

2450 "Paulo VI no Brazil." Veja 66 (December 10, 1969): 34.

2451 "Pope's Man in Recife." Time, March 27, 1964, p. 60.

Câmara, Hélder

2452   "Por que Dom Hélder não recebeu o Prêmio Nobel." O Estado de
        São Paulo, October 22, 1970.

2453   PORRO, ALESSANDRO. "O Padre Hélder." Realidade 4 (July,
        1966): 117-120.

2454   "Pressão moral." Veja 5 (October 9, 1969): 22.

2455   "Refutação a Dom Hélder." O Estado de São Paulo, December 1,
        1967.

2456   "Roma desmiente que Dom Hélder sea 'censurado' pero el Arzo-
        bispo de Recife ha tenido que cancelar sus compromisos en
        el extranjero." Informaciones Católicas Internacionales
        341-343 (August, 1969): 15.

2457   ROSB, BETAP DE. Hélder Câmara, signo de contradicción.
        Salamanca: Ediciones Sígueme, 1974. 262 pp.

2458   ROSSI, JUAN JOSÉ. Iglesia y desarrollo: reportaje realizado
        a Dom Hélder Câmara sobre la problemática actual de América
        Latina y la Iglesia en el proceso de cambio. Buenos Aires:
        Ediciones Búsqueda, 1966. 63 pp.

2459   "Sad Days in Recife." Commonweal 99 (December 7, 1973): 256-
        257.

2460   "A Santa Sé e Dom Hélder." SEDOC 2 (1969): 321.

2461   SCHILLING, PAULO R. Hélder Câmara. Montevideo: Biblioteca
        de Marcha, 1969. 108 pp.

2462   SCHULTZ, ROGER. Violence des Pacifiques. Taizé: Les Presses
        de Taizé, 1968. 239 pp.

2463   SELSER, GREGORIO. "Brasil y Hélder Câmara: una Iglesia que
        retorna al evangelio." Cuadernos de Marcha 9 (January,
        1968): 55-57.

2464   "Sodré, Governador de São Paulo, sustenta suas acusações a
        Dom Hélder." O Estado de São Paulo, October 24, 1970.

2465   "Suaves mestres da moderação." Veja 128 (February 17, 1971):
        17.

2466   TAPIA DE REEDO, B. "Dom Hélder, el obispo comunista." Gaceta
        Illustrada, December 8, 1968.

Câmara, Hélder

2467   TAYLOR, JAMES A. "Giants of Our Faith." U.S. Catholic 39
        (December, 1974): 18-23.

2468   "El testimonio de Hélder." Informaciones Católicas Inter-
        nacionales 254 (December, 1965): 17.

2469   TYSON, BRADY. "Dom Hélder Câmara as a Symbolic Man." IDOC-
        International 22 (March 22, 1971): 20-42.

2470   Une journée avec Dom Hélder Câmara. Brussels: Desclée de
        Brouwer, 1970.

2471   VALDA PALMA, ROBERTO. Obispos Rojos, I--Dom Hélder Pessoa
        Câmara. Madrid: Propaganda Popular Católica, 1971.

2472   "Viagens de Dom Hélder Câmara em 1971." O Estado de São Paulo,
        June 12, 1971.

2473   "Violenta campaña contra Dom Hélder Câmara." Informaciones
        Católicas Internacionales 241 (June 7, 1965): 20.

2474   WARTENWEILER, FRITZ. Morgengrauen in Brasilien. Dom Hélder
        Câmara im Kampf. Zürich: Frau F. Hafner, 1972. 64 pp.

2475   "'... Wenn man mir die Nagel ausreisst.'" Der Spiegel 39
        (1970): 188-193.

CATHOLIC CHURCH AND SOCIAL CHANGE

2476   ALMEIDA, CANDIDO ANTÔNIO MENDES DE. Momento dos vivos: a
        esquerda católica no Brasil. Rio de Janeiro: Tempo Bra-
        sileiro, 1966. 256 pp.

2477   ALMEIDA, LUIS CASTANHO DE. "Clero secular diocesano brasileiro
        setecentista." Anais do Congresso Commemorativo do Bicen-
        tenario de Transferência da Sede do Governo do Brasil da
        Cidade do Salvador para o Rio de Janeiro 3 (1967): 41-103.

2478   ALVES, RUBEM. "Injusticia y rebelión." Cristianismo y Socie-
        dad 6 (1964): 40-53.

2479   ASSMANN, HUGO. "A dimensão social do pecado." In Pastoral
        da Penitência. Petrópolis: Editôra Vozes, 1970.

2480   BARBOSA, ROBERTO. "Catholic Church Renewal in Brazil: De-
        fending the Oppressed." Christian Century 90 (September
        5, 1973): 862-864.

Brazil

Catholic Church and Social Change

2481 _____. "Innovation in Brazil: Ecumenical Structure for Social
Problems." Christian Century 90 (May 2, 1973): 516-517.

2482 "Basic Reforms Sought by Brazil Priests." National Catholic
Reporter 4 (November 8, 1967): 5.

2483 BASTOS, SISTER IRANY. "Sisters in the Climate of Vatican II."
In The Religious Dimension in the New Latin America, edited
by John J. Considine, pp. 140-147. Notre Dame, Indiana:
Fides Publishers, 1966.

2484 BATISTA FRAGOSO, ANTONIO. "Evangelio y justicia social."
Cuadernos de Marcha 17 (September, 1968): 13-20.

2485 "Brazil, Dearth of Priests, Social Action." America 108
(February, 1963): 211-240.

2486 "Brazilian Bishop Lays Ills of Poor to the Rich." National
Catholic Reporter 5 (January 22, 1969): 5.

2487 BRUNEAU, THOMAS C. "Brazil's People of God: Prophets or
Martyrs?" America 124 (January 30, 1971): 91-94.

2488 _____. "Obstacles to Change in the Church: Lessons From Four
Brazilian Dioceses." Journal of Interamerican Studies and
World Affairs 15 (Novmeber, 1973): 395-414.

2489 _____. "Power and Influence: Analysis of the Church in Latin
America and the Case of Brazil." Latin American Research
Review 8 (Summer, 1973): 25-52.

2490 CÂMARA, HÉLDER. "Challenge to Latin America." America 110
(May 2, 1964): 590.

2491 _____. Church and Colonialism. London: Sheed and Ward,
1969. 181 pp.

2492 _____. Le dèsert est fertile. Paris: Desclée de Brouwer,
1971. 128 pp.

2493 _____. La Iglesia debe revisar su posición ante los problemas
sociales. Paraiba: [n.p.], 1966. 7 pp.

2494 _____. La Iglesia en el desarrollo de América Latina.
Algorta, Spain: Vizcaya Zero, 1970. 44 pp.

2495 _____. Iglesia y desarrollo. Buenos Aires: Búsqueda, 1968.

Catholic Church and Social Change

2496 _____. Pobreza, abundancia y solidaridad. Algorta, Spain:
Vizcaya Zero, 1970. 56 pp.

2497 _____. Pour arriver à temps. Paris: Desclée de Brouwer,
1970. 183 pp.

2498 _____. "Presencia de la Iglesia en el desarrollo de America
Latina: mensaje documentos." Mensaje 16 (January 2,
1967): 59-64.

2499 _____. Race Against Time. London: Sheed and Ward, 1971.
136 pp.

2500 _____. "Las religiones y los cambios necesarios de estructura
en el mundo de hoy." SEDOC 31 (1970): 765.

2501 _____. Revolução dentro da paz. Rio de Janeiro: Editora
Sabía, 1968. 203 pp.

2502 _____. Le tiers monde trahi. Paris: Desclée de Brouwer,
1968. 232 pp.

2503 _____. "La universidad y el desarrollo de América Latina:
conferencia pronunciada en ocasión de la apertura del año
académico de la Universidad Católica de Chile, abril 19 de
1969." Mensaje 18 (May, 1969): 189-192.

2504 CÂMPOS, RENATO CARNEIRO. Igreja, política e religião. Recife:
Instituto Joaquín Nabuco de Pesquisas Sociais, 1967. 61
pp., bibl.

2505 CÂRAMURU DE BARROS, RAIMUNDO. "Balanço da situação actual da
Igreja no Brasil." Revista Eclesiástica Brasileira 27
(1967): 350-366.

2506 CASTRO, L. DE. "Actualidade religiosa--a Igreja pobre ao
seguro de todos." Brotéria 78 (1964): 456-465.

2507 CAVALCANTI, JOSÉ KOSINSKI DE. Brasil: Igreja em transição.
Cuernavaca, México: Centro Intercultural de Documentación,
1970. 93 pp.

2508 "The Church in Brazil's Hunger Bowl." U.S. Catholic 29
(January, 1964): 53.

2509 CLOIN, TIAGO G. "Bishops on the March in Brazil." In The
Religious Dimension in the New Latin America, edited by
John J. Considine, pp. 105-116. Notre Dame: Fides Pub-
lishers, 1966.

Catholic Church and Social Change

2510   COMBLIN, JOSEPH. "Problems of the Church in Brazil." Clergy
        Review 57 (January, 1972): 3-15.

2511   "Communities of Moral Authority." America 134 (May 29, 1976):
        466.

2512   "Community Life in Brazil." Tablet 231 (January 8, 1977):
        45.

2513   "Conclusões da Mar del Plata sobre a presença ativa da Igreja
        no desenvolvimento e na integração da América Latina."
        Revista Eclesiástica Brasileira 27 (1967): 453-466.

2514   COTTER, JAMES P. "Brazil: Social Action." America 108
        (February 16, 1963): 222-223.

2515   DEELAN, GODOFREDO J. Diócese de Ponto Grossa, Paraná. Cuer-
        navaca, México: Centro Intercultural de Documentación,
        1968.

2516   _____. A sociologia a serviço da pastoral. Petrópolis:
        Editôra Vozes, 1966. 117 pp.

2517   DE KADT, EMMANUEL. "Religion, the Church and Social Change
        in Brazil." In The Politics of Conformity in Latin America,
        edited by Claudio Veliz, pp. 192-220. London: Oxford
        University Press, 1967.

2518   "Dom Hélder fala sobre a pobreza." Centro Informativo Cató-
        lico 954 (October 31, 1970).

2519   "Dom Hélder preve reformas com ou contra Igreja." Centro
        Informativo Católico 828 (May 4, 1968).

2520   DUNNE, GEORGE H. "To Hell and Gone." America 125 (October 2,
        1971): 224-227.

2521   FASSINI, ATICO. Igreja em tensão. Petrópolis: Editôra
        Vozes, 1971. 86 pp.

2522   FLANNERY, HARRY. "Brazil's Miserable Northeast." Catholic
        World 205 (August, 1967): 276-281.

2523   FLORIDI, ULISSE ALESSIO. Radicalismo cattolico brasiliano.
        Rome: Instituto Editoriale del Mediterraneo, 1968. 362 pp.

2524   FOYACA DE LA CONCHA, MANUEL. As encíclicas sociais. Rio de
        Janeiro: AGIR, 1967.

Catholic Church and Social Change

2525   FREEHAFER, VIRGINIA S. "Lighting a Candle in Northeastern
        Brazil." Worldmission 21 (Fall, 1970): 46-49.

2526   GALLET, PAUL. Freedom to Starve. Dublin: Gill and Macmillan,
        1970. 215 pp.

2527   _____. El padre. Paris: Editions Ouvrières, 1967. 270 pp.

2528   GREGORY, AFONSO FELIPPE, comp. Comunidades eclesiásticas de
        base: utopis ou realidade. Rio de Janeiro: Editôra
        Vozes, 1973. 189 pp., bibl.

2529   El grito del Tercer Mundo en un pueblo marginado: milagro
        brasileño? Testimonios. Buenos Aires: Merayo, 1974.
        137 pp.

2530   HARRIOT, JOHN. "Brazil's Tensions." Month 3 (May, 1971):
        131-135.

2531   HEIDEMANN, M. "A Igreja no Brasil e a previdência social."
        Revista Eclesiástica Brasileira 35 (September, 1975):
        606-623.

2532   "I Have Heard the Cry of My People: Statement of Bishops and
        Religious Superiors Northeast Brazil." IDOC Documentation
        Participation Project (May 6, 1973): 3-17.

2533   "Igreja do Brasil marcha do plano de pastoral de conjunto
        (PPC)." Catequesis Latinoamericana 2 (July, 1970): 382-
        386.

2534   IRELAND, ROWAN. "The Catholic Church and Social Change in
        Brazil: An Evaluation." In Brazil in the Sixties, edited
        by Riordan Roett, pp. 345-374. Nashville: Vanderbilt
        University Press, 1972.

2535   NO ENTRY

2536   LEPARGNEUR, FRANCOIS H. "The Christian Conscience of Brazil."
        Concilium 29 (October, 1967): 63-70.

2537   LERCARO, GIACOMO. "A pobreza na Igreja." Revista Eclesiástica
        Brasileira 23 (1963): 492-494.

2538   LIMA, DANILO GERALDO. Les documents de l'Episcopat brésilien
        sur le développement. Cuernavaca, Mexico: Centro Inter-
        cultural de Documentación, 1970.

Brazil

Catholic Church and Social Change

2539   MARANHÃO, LUIZ. "Marxistas e católicos: da mão estendida ao
       único caminho." Paz e Terra 6 (1968): 57-71.

2540   MARGERIE, BERTRAND DE. "Brazil: Dearth of Priests." America
       108 (February 16, 1963): 220-222.

2541   MEDINA, CARLOS ALBERTO DE. Participação e Igreja: estúdio
       dos movimentos e associações de leigos. Cuernavaca,
       México: Centro Intercultural de Documentación, 1971. 212
       pp.

2542   MOOY, SUITBERTO. Atualização da Igreja: comentário sobre a
       constitui ao gaudium et spes; curso para grupos e equipes
       paroquiais. Belo Horizonte, Brazil: Promação-da Família
       Editôra, 1970. 160 pp., bibl.

2543   MOREIRA ALVEZ, MARCIO. "Brazil: A Country Where Christians
       Are Outlaws." Catholic World 212 (November, 1970): 65-68.

2544   _____. O Cristo do povo. Rio de Janeiro: Ed. Sabía, 1968.
       295 pp.

2545   MUÑOZ, RONALDO. "O serviço da Igreja al homem: problemas e
       critérios teológico-pastorias." Revista Eclesiástica
       Brasileira 35 (December, 1975): 824-835.

2546   NEGROMONTE, A. "The Principal Remedy for Dechristianization
       in Brazil." Christ to the World 4 (1959): 353-358.

2547   "New Type of Parish in Brazil." L'Osservatore Romano, March
       19, 1970, pp. 11-12.

2548   OLIVEIRA, CARLOS JOSAPHAT PINTO DE. Evangelho e revolução
       social. São Paulo: Livraria Duas Cidades, 1962. 100 pp.

2549   _____. Evangelho e revolução social. São Paulo: Livraria
       Duas Cidades, 1963. 106 pp.

2550   POPE PAUL VI. "Palavras sobre a Igreja, nas audiéncias pub-
       licas." Revista Eclesiástica Brasileira 26 (1966): 955-
       971.

2551   _____. "Presença ativa da Igreja no desenvolvimento da América
       Latina. Carta de Paulo VI a X Reunião do CELAM." Revista
       Eclesiástica Brasileira 26 (1966): 931-935.

2552   "Les problèmes de l'Eglise au Brésil." Amérique Latine 8
       (February 23, 1965): 12-23.

Catholic Church and Social Change

2553   PROST, JUDE. "When the Church is Impoverished." Worldmission
       17 (Spring, 1966): 20-25.

2554   "Protest in Brazil." Herder Correspondence 5 (March, 1968):
       85-86.

2555   RANGEL, PASCHOAL. "O documento da comissão representativa da
       CNBB sobre pastoral social." Atualização 6 (1975): 468-
       477.

2556   RASHKE, R. "Brazil and the Church." National Catholic Re-
       porter 10 (March 29, 1974): 20.

2557   READ, WILLIAM R. New Patterns of Church Growth in Brazil.
       Grand Rapids, Michigan: W. B. Eerdman's Publishing Co.,
       1965. 240 pp., bibl.

2558   ROSSI, JUAN JOSÉ. Iglesia y desarrollo. Buenos Aires:
       [n.p.], 1968. 74 pp.

2559   RYAN, LEO V. "A Frontier Archbishop: Educational Endeavors
       in Brazil." Catholic School Journal 65 (November, 1965):
       37.

2560   SCHOOYANS, MICHEL. Chrétienté en contestation, l'Amérique
       Latine, essai de prospective pastorale. Paris: Editions
       du Cerf, 1969. 327 pp.

2561   _____. O desafio da seculaização. Subsídios para uma pros-
       pectiva pastoral. São Paulo: Editor Herder, 1968. 319 pp.

2562   SOUZA, LUIZ ALBERTO GÓMEZ DE, comp. Brasil: o confronto de
       duas gerações de cristãos, 1960. Cuernavaca, México:
       Centro Intercultural de Documentación, 1966. 7 pp.

2563   _____. O Cristão e o mundo. Petrópolis: Editôra Vozes, 1965.

2564   TAVORA, A. "Denies Reports Government Molesting Church in
       Brazil." Catholic Messenger 82 (June 25, 1964): 6.

2565   ZILLES, URBANO. Uma Igreja em discussão. Petrópolis: Editôra
       Vozes, 1969. 112 pp.

CATHOLIC CHURCH AND STATE

2566   Acción Católica Obrera. "De las iglesias particulares: en
       Brasil, tensión entre la Iglesia y el regimen." Informa-
       ciones Católicas Internacionales 271 (September 7, 1966):
       7-8.

2567 ANTOINE, CHARLES. Church and Power in Brazil. New York:
      Orbis Books, 1973. 275 pp.

2568 _____. "L'Episcopat brésilien face au pouvoir (1962-1969)."
      Etudes 333 (July, 1970): 84-103.

2569 ARAUJO, FRANCISCO DE. "¿Cuál es el papel de la Iglesia en el
      Brasil?" Mensaje 17 (July, 1968): 303-308.

2570 ARNS, PAULO EVARISTO. "Protest of Archbishop Arns of São
      Paulo in Brazil." L'Osservatore Romano, March 1971, p. 11.

2571 ASSMANN, HUGO. "La función legitimadora de la religión para
      la dictadura brasileña." Perspectivas de Diálogo 48
      (August, 1970): 171-181.

2572 _____. "Religion in Aid of Dictatorship." IDOC-International
      19 (February 13, 1971): 49-65.

2573 BARBOSA, ROBERTO. "Bishop of São Felix." Christian Century
      94 (May 4, 1977): 422-423.

2574 BONO, AGOSTINO. "Church Role as Critic in Brazil May End."
      National Catholic Reporter 10 (May 24, 1974): 15.

2575 _____. "Cross vs. Sword: Catholic Aid to Poor in Brazil Is
      Worsening Conflict with Military; Latin American Rules
      Fight Emerging Church Critics." Wall Street Journal 189
      (June 6, 1977): 1.

2576 Brazil. Washington: Division for Latin America, United
      States Catholic Conference, [n.d.]. 61 pp.

2577 "Brazil: Church-State Relations." Lutheran World 18 (1971):
      283-288.

2578 "Brazil Is Taking on the Church." Christian Century 90
      (October 10, 1973): 998.

2579 "Brazil: Order vs. Disorder." America 123 (December 19,
      1970): 536-537.

2580 "Brazil Regime Clamps Down on Progressive Churchmen." National
      Catholic Reporter 5 (January 1, 1969): 1+.

2581 "Brazil: The Bishops Attack." Christianity Today 21 (Decem-
      ber 17, 1976): 407.

Catholic Church and State

2582   "The Brazilian Priests' Plea to Their Bishop." Herder Corres-
       pondence 6 (October, 1969): 308-311.

2583   "Brazil's Bishops Speak Out." America 135 (December 11, 1976):
       407.

2584   BRUCE, JAMES. "Brazil: Muzzling the Outspoken Church."
       Christian Century 92 (October 22, 1975): 940-942.

2585   CÂMARA, HÉLDER. "Dom Hélder admite crise." Paz e Terra
       (April, 1968): 279.

2586   _____. "En 'respuesta a la crisis,' ¿que debéis hacer?"
       Vozes 5 (May, 1969): 425.

2587   "Challenge from the Church in Brazil." Tablet 227 (June 30,
       1973): 619-623.

2588   "Church and State in Brazil." Tablet 220 (September 17, 1966):
       1058.

2589   "The Church and the New Regime in Brazil." Tablet 218 (June
       13, 1964): 676.

2590   "Church-State Co-operation in Brazil: Bahia State." Tablet
       218 (August 8, 1964): 900.

2591   "Conscience and Power." America 130 (March 2, 1974): 143-144.

2592   DEEDY, JOHN G. "Bishops, Latin Style." Commonweal 95 (January
       21, 1972): 362.

2593   _____. "Embattled Brazil." Commonweal 93 (November 13, 1970):
       162.

2594   DELLA CAVA, RALPH. "Igreja e Estado do Brasil do século XX.
       Sete monografias recentes sobre o catolicismo brasileiro,
       1916-1964." Estudios CEBRAP 12 (April/June, 1975): 5-52.

2595   "Evolución de las relaciones entre la Iglesia y el Estado en
       el Brasil." Cuadernos de Marcha 9 (January, 1968): 29-53.

2596   "Four of His Priests Held, Superior Raps Brazil Regime."
       National Catholic Reporter 5 (January 15, 1969): 6.

2597   FRANCA, LEONEL. A Igreja, a reforma e a civilização. Rio de
       Janeiro: Livraria Artes Gráficas Indústrias Reunidas,
       1958. 476 pp., bibl.

2598   GRIFFIN, G. "Church and 'golpe' in Brazil." Ramparts 3
        (October, 1964): 41-44.

2599   "Holy War in Brazil." Tablet 220 (August 27, 1966): 978.

2600   "Iglesia-Estado, en el Brasil: la Iglesia paga el pato en la
        lucha contra la 'subverión'; 52 sacerdotes en prisión."
        Informaciones Católicas Internacionales 302 (December 2,
        1967): 9.

2601   KIRCHNER, DONNELL L. "Brazil Eight Years After." America
        126 (June 3, 1972): 589-591.

2602   KROHLING, A. "Brazilians Want Justice: Who Will Provide It?"
        Catholic Messenger 82 (February 6, 1964): 7.

2603   LIMA, ALCEU AMOROSO. Indicações políticas: da revolução a
        constituição. Rio de Janeiro: Civilização Brasileira,
        1936. 249 pp.

2604   LODWICK, ROBERT E. The Significance of the Church-State
        Relationship to an Evangelical Program in Brazil. Cuerna-
        vaca, México: Centro Intercultural de Documentación, 1969.
        220 pp.

2605   MAC EOIN, GARY. "A Pastor Bucks Brasília." Commonweal 98
        (September 7, 1973): 468-469.

2606   MATA MACHADO, EDGAR G. DA. "A Igreja voltada para o futuro,
        o governo, apegado ao que passou." Paz e Terra 2 (April,
        1968): 301-315.

2607   MEYER, JEAN A. "L'Eglise catholique au Brésil: histoire et
        structures; l'Eglise et l'Etat de 1960-1969; genèse du
        conflit entre l'Eglise et l'Etat; 1970--le rebondissement
        de la crise et l'apaisement." Note et Etude Documentaires
        18 (December 30, 1970): 47-56.

2608   MOREIRA ALVES, MARCIO. O cristo do povo. Rio de Janeiro:
        Sabía, 1968. 295 pp.

2609   NOVINSKY, ANITA. Cristãos novos na Bahia: história. São
        Paulo: Editôra Perspectiva, 1972. 238 pp.

2610   NO ENTRY

2611   OLIVEIRA, PLINIO CORREA DE. A Igreja ante a escalada da ameaça
        comunista. São Paulo: Editôra Vera Cruz, 1976. 223 pp.

Catholic Church and State

2612   "Pastoral Message to the People of God: National Conference
       of Brazilian Bishops." Catholic Mind 75 (April, 1977):
       55-64.

2613   "Les problèmes de l'Eglise au Brésil." Amérique Latine 8
       (February 23, 1965): 12, 23.

2614   QUIGLEY, THOMAS. "Brazil: New Generals vs. Renewal Bishops."
       Christianity and Crisis 34 (April 1, 1974): 61-64.

2615   ROSB, BETAP DE. "Brasil urgente: obispos frente a militares."
       Indice 233-234 (July/August, 1968): 28-40.

2616   SANDERS, THOMAS G. "Catholicism and Development: The Catholic
       Left in Brazil." In Churches and State: The Religious
       Institution and Modernization, edited by Kalman H. Silbert,
       pp. 81-99. New York: American Universities Field Staff,
       1967.

2617   "The Seething Pot Still Bubbles." America 115 (October 1,
       1966): 368.

2618   Seminar on Latin American History, University of South Carolina,
       1967. Conflicto e continuidade na sociedade brasileira. Rio
       de Janeiro: Civilização Brasileira, 1970. 351 pp.

2619   TRIGGS, WILLIAM. "Brazil: Bishops and Patriotism." IDOC-
       International 18 (January 30, 1971): 21-41.

2620   "Troubled Times in Brazil." Tablet 220 (August 13, 1966):
       929.

2621   TYSON, BRADY. "Not Yet Reduced to Silence." Christian Century
       90 (October 17, 1973): 1033-1034.

2622   VILLACA, ANTONIO CARLOS. História da questão religiosa. Rio
       de Janeiro: Livraria F. Alves Editôra, 1974. 177 pp.,
       bibl.

2623   WILLIAMS, MARGARET TODARO. "Integralism and the Brazilian
       Catholic Church." Hispanic American Historical Review 54
       (August, 1974): 431-452.

CATHOLIC CLERGY

2624   "Acción y no palabras: mensaje cristiano para el mundo de
       hoy." Mensaje 159 (June, 1967): 204-208.

Catholic Clergy

2625   ALENCAR, TITO DE. "The Gospel and Brazil." New Blackfriars
        54 (January, 1973): 4-12.

2626   BARBOSA, ROBERT. "ISER: Fellowship for Theological Reflection
        in Brazil." Christian Century 90 (June 27, 1973): 704-
        705.

2627   BATISTA FRAGOSO, ANTONIO. "Evangelio y justicia social."
        Cuadernos de Marcha 17 (September, 1968): 13-20.

2628   "Brazil's Angry Clergy." Newsweek, February 17, 1969, p. 68.

2629   CÂMARA, HÉLDER. La Iglesia en el desarrollo de América Latina.
        Algorta, Spain: Vizcaya Zero, 1969. 44 pp.

2630   "El Cardenal de Porto Alegre, Brasil, rebate acusaciones de
        comunismo a sacerdotes y obispos." ICIA 375-376 (January
        15, 1971): 4.

2631   "Ceris Report on Brazilian Bishops." Herder Correspondence 4
        (June, 1967): 179-180.

2632   CLOIN, TIAGO G. "Bishops on the March in Brazil." In The
        Religious Dimension in the New Latin America, edited by
        John J. Considine, pp. 105-116. Notre Dame, Indiana: Fides
        Publishers, 1966.

2633   "Declaração dos cardeais, arcebispos e bispos do Brasil."
        Revista Eclesiástica Brasileira 22 (1962): 485-490.

2634   "Grandes planos da Igreja no Brasil." Revista Eclesiástica
        Brasileira 26 (1966): 377-379.

2635   "Igreja do Brasil marcha do Plano de Pastoral de Conjunto
        (PPC)." Catequesis Latinoamericana 2 (July, 1970): 382-
        386.

2636   LODWICK, ROBERT W. The Significance of the Church-State Rela-
        tionship to an Evangelical Program in Brazil. Cuernavaca,
        México: Centro Intercultural de Documentación, 1969. 221
        pp.

2637   MARGERIE, BERTRAND DE. "Brazil: Dearth of Priests." America
        108 (February 16, 1963): 220-222.

2638   MARINS, JOSÉ. "Pesquisa sobre o clero do Brasil." Revista
        Eclesiástica Brasileira 29 (March 31, 1969): 121-138.

Catholic Clergy

2639   MEIRELLES, N. "O movimento catequético no Brasil." Catequesis
       Latinoamericana 1 (July/September, 1969): 95-98.

2640   NOVINSKY, ANITA. Cristãos novos na Bahia: história. São
       Paulo: Editôra Perspectiva, 1972. 238 pp.

2641   "Las nuevas palabras de los nuevos obispos." Cuadernos de
       Marcha 9 (January, 1968): 5-12.

2642   O'GRADY, D. "The Pope of Latin America: Brazil's New Cardinal
       Efficient Tiger for Work." National Catholic Reporter 12
       (July 16, 1976): 2.

2643   OZANAM DE ANDRADE, RAYMUNDO. "'Populorum Progresio': neo-
       capitalismo ou revolução." Paz e Terra 4 (August, 1967):
       209-221.

2644   PÉREZ RAMÍREZ, GUSTAVO. O problema sacerdotal no Brasil.
       Brussels: Bureau Internacional de Investigaçãos Sociais
       de FERES, 1965. 205 pp.

2645   ROMERO, ABELARDO. Heróis de Batina: pequena história do
       clero católico no Brasil. Rio de Janeiro: Conquista,
       1973. 237 pp.

2646   SCHOOYANS, MICHEL. "Le manque de vacations sacerdotales au
       Brésil." Nouvelle Revue Theologique 83 (November, 1964):
       1078-1098.

2647   SILVEIRA, GILSON JOSÉ. "Os seminaristas e a Igreja no Brasil."
       Revista Eclesiástica Brasileira 24 (1964): 375-380.

2648   VILLACA, ANTONIO CARLOS. História da questão religiosa. Rio
       de Janeiro: Livraria F. Alves Editôra, 1974. 177 pp.,
       bibl.

2649   "Visão positiva das inquierações doutrinários na Igreja pós-
       conciliar." Revista Eclesiástica Brasileira 27 (1967):
       367-373.

CHRISTIAN DEMOCRACY

2650   DEMANGE, EMÍLIO. A social democracia crista: como melhor
       regime do governo. São Paulo: Gráfica Urupês, 1967. 200
       pp.

Brazil

2651 FREI, MONTALVO EDUARDO. "Christian Democracy in Latin America."
Tablet 218 (September 5, 1964): 993-994; (September 12,
1964): 1021-1022; (September 19, 1964): 1050-1051.

2652 HUBNER GALLO, JORGE IVÁN. Los católicos en la política.
Santiago, Chile: Zig-Zag, 1959. 107 pp.

COMMUNISM

2653 CALLADO, ANTONIO. Tempo de arrães, padres e comunistas na
revolução sem violência. Rio de Janeiro: José Alvaro,
ed., 1964. 156 pp.

2654 CÂMARA, HÉLDER. "Conscience and Anti-Communism." Commonweal
81 (December 18, 1964): 407-408.

2655 CHILCOTE, RONALD H. The Brazilian Communist Party: Conflict
and Integration, 1922-1972. New York: Oxford University
Press, 1974. 361 pp., bibl.

2656 "Communists Infiltrate Church, Brazil Changes." National
Catholic Reporter 10 (February 22, 1974): 19.

2657 O cristão e o comunismo. Confronta. Rio de Janeiro: Centro
Cristiano de Literature, 1963. 87 pp.

2658 "Cuestiones sociales en el Brasil: los obispos rechazan 'la
falsa dicotomía capitalismo-comunismo.'" Informaciones
Católicas Internacionales 289 (June 7, 1967): 17.

2659 OLIVEIRA, PLÍNIO CORREA DE. A Igreja ante a escalada da amcaça
comunista: apelo aos bispos silenciosos. São Paulo: Editôra Vera Cruz, 1976. 223 pp.

DOCUMENTS

2660 "Action on Brazil: March 16, 1971." IDOC-International 27
(June 12, 1971): 52-58.

2661 Bishops of Brazil. "Brotherhood: The Responsibility of
Bishops Today." New Blackfriars 49 (April, 1968): 341-342.

2662 "Brazilian Bishops' Proposals for Realization of the Universal
Declaration of Human Rights." Catholic Mind 71 (October,
1973): 2-9.

Documents

2663   "A Call for an End to the Torture of Prisoners." IDOC-International 48 (November, 1972): 59-60.

2664   Conferencia Episcopal del Brazil. "Brasil: declaración colectiva del episcopado acerca de la nueva situación nacional." Informaciones Católicos Internacionales 218 (July 22, 1966): 8-9.

2665   Conferência Nacional dos Bispos do Brasil, Assembléia Geral Extraordinária, VII, Roma, 1966. Plano de Pastoral de Conjunto: 1966-1970. Rio de Janeiro: Livraria Dom Bosco, 1966. 159 pp.

2666   Conferência Nacional dos Bispos do Brasil. Plano de emergência para a Igreja do Brasil. Rio de Janeiro: Livraria Dom Bosco, 1963. 72 pp.

2667   "Cuestiones sociales en el Brasil: los obispos rechazan 'la falsa dicotomia capitalismo-comunismo.'" Informaciones Católicas Internacionales 289 (June 7, 1967): 17.

2668   "Do Not Oppress Your Brother: A Message of the Bishops of the State of São Paulo, Brazil." Catholic Mind 74 (September, 1975): 9-11.

2669   "Document pastoral de la conférence nationale des évêques du Brésil: May 16-17, 1970." La Documentation Catholique 67 (July 19, 1970): 685-691.

2670   "Dos cartas del clero brasileño a la asamblea de la CNBB." NADOC 79 (August 6, 1969): 1-9.

2671   "Exigences chrétiennes pour un ordre politique: déclaration de la conférence épiscopale du Brésil." La Documentation Catholique 74 (April 3, 1977): 315-319.

2672   FONSECA, GONDIN DA. Os gorilas, o povo, e a reforma agrária: manifestos dos bispos do Brasil. São Paulo: Editôra Fulgor, 1963. 77 pp.

2673   "Human Rights in Brazil." Clergy Review 59 (September, 1974): 627.

2674   LIMA, DANILO GERALDO. Les documents de l'episcopat brésilien sur le développement. Cuernavaca, México: Centro Intercultural de Documentación, 1970.

Brazil

2675   "Manifesto mineiro--Repercussões coincidências com a carta do
        Papa." Paz e Terra 2 (April, 1968): 198-215.

2676   "Manifesto of Bishops of the Northeastern Region of Brazil to
        Priests and Faithful in South America." New Blackfriars
        49 (December, 1967): 140-148.

2677   MASCARENHAS ROXO, R. "Sacramentos nas igrejas brasileiras;
        pastoral letter." Revista Eclesiástica Brasileira 33
        (March, 1973): 92-103.

2678   "Message des évêques de la région du nordeste brésilien; jan-
        vier, 1968." Lettre 117 (May, 1968): 4-6.

2679   MOREIRA ALVES, MARCIO. "El silencio de los pastores." Mensaje
        18 (October, 1969): 503-504.

2680   Obispos del Nordeste del Brasil. "Manifesto." CIAS 155
        (August, 1966): 29-30.

2681   POPE PAUL VI. "Radio Message to the Christians of the New
        Capital City of Brazil." Acta Apostolicae Sedis 60 (May
        31, 1968): 279-280.

2682   "A presença da Igreja no Brasil de hoje: documentário." Paz
        e Terra 2 (April, 1968): 149-179.

2683   "Report on Allegations of Torture in Brazil." IDOC-Interna-
        tional 48 (November, 1972): 7-33.

2684   Sacerdotes Brasileños. "300 padres contra opressão; padres
        denuncian: injustiças assassinam brasileiros e sustentam
        regime de miséria." Ultima Hora 17 (October 24, 1967):
        1-2.

2685   SCHOOYANS, MICHEL. Chrétienté en contestation: l'Amérique
        Latine. Paris: Cerf, 1969. 327 pp.

2686   TRIGGS, WILLIAM. "Brazil: Bishops and Patriotism." IDOC-
        International 18 (January 30, 1971): 21-41.

2687   VILLACA, ANTONIO CARLOS. O pensamento católico no Brasil.
        Rio de Janeiro: Zahar Editôres, 1975. 205 pp.

2688   "La violence et l'insecurité au Brésil: message e pastoral
        des évêques au peuple de Dieu." La Documentation Catholique
        73 (December 19, 1976): 1075-1081.

Economic Development

ECONOMIC DEVELOPMENT

2689   "Ação católico a política econômica." Paz e Terra 2 (April,
        1968): 247-250.

2690   ALVES, RUBEM. "Injusticia y rebelión." Cristianismo y Socie-
        dad 2 (1964): 40-53.

2691   ANDRADE, MANUEL CORREIRA DE OLIVEIRA. A terra o e homen no
        nordeste. São Paulo: Editorial Brasileira, 1964. 267 pp.,
        bibl.

2692   ARMSTRONG, JAMES. "People Are Doing...Badly in Brazil."
        Christian Century 88 (January 6, 1971): 14-16.

2693   ARRAES, MIGUEL. Brazil: The People and the Power. Harmonds-
        worth, England: Pelican Books, 1972. 232 pp.

2694   _____. "Yes, Brazil is Dominated." IDOC-International 34
        (October 31, 1971): 56-61.

2695   "Brazil: Two Images." IDOC-International 34 (October 30,
        1971): 49-55.

2696   CÂMARA, HÉLDER. "Diecisiete obispos del Tercer Mundo alientan
        a los pueblos pobres a defenderse contra la guerra sub-
        versiva del dinero." Informaciones Católicas Internacionales
        296 (September 2, 1967): 7-8.

2697   _____. "Presencia de la Iglesia en el desarrollo de América
        Latina." Mensaje 156 (January/February, 1967): 59-64.

2698   _____. "Un programa de acción para el subdesarrollo."
        Selecciones de Teología 8 (July/September, 1969): 249-252.

2699   CAMARGO, CÂNDIDO PROCIPIO FERREIRA DE. Igreja e desenvolvi-
        mento. São Paulo: Editôra Brasileira de Ciências and
        Centro Brasileiro de Análise e Planejamento (CEBRAP), 1971.
        218 pp., bibl.

2700   COMBLIN, JOSEPH. Teologia do desenvolvimento. Belo Horizonte,
        Brasil: Movimiento Familiar Cristiano, 1968. 32 pp.

2701   FERNANDES, FLORESTAN. Sociedade de classes e subdesenvolvi-
        mento. Rio de Janeiro: Zahar Editôra, 1968. 256 pp.

Labor and Laboring Classes

2702   FLANNERY, H. "Brazil's Miserable Northeast." Catholic World
        205 (August, 1967): 276-281.

2703   FRANK, ANDRE GÜNDER. Capitalism and Underdevelopment in Latin
        America. New York: Monthly Review, 1967. 298 pp., bibl.

2704   MARGOLIS, MAXINE L. The Moving Frontier: Social and Economic
        Change in Southern Brazilian Community. Gainesville: Uni-
        versity of Florida Press, 1973. 275 pp., bibl.

2705   VAZ DA COSTA, RUBENS. O primeiro passo: um testemunho sobre
        o nordeste brasileiro. Rio de Janeiro: Apec Editôra,
        1973. 405 pp.

2706   NO ENTRY

HUMANISM

2707   CÂMARA, HÉLDER. "Evangelização e humanização num mundo em
        desenvolvimento." Revista Eclesiástica Brasileira 25 (1965):
        296.

2708   QUAGLIANI, ANTÔNIO. "L'umanesimo rivoluzionario della Chiesa
        brasiliana." Mulino 18 (July/August, 1969): 800-806.

2709   SOUZA, LUIS ALBERTO GÓMEZ DE, comp. Brazil: o confronto de
        duas gerações de cristãos. Cuernavaca, México: Centro
        Intercultural de Documentación, 1966. 160 pp.

LABOR AND LABORING CLASSES

2710   CÂMARA, JAIME DE BARROS. A Igreja e os operários, carta pas-
        toral. Rio de Janeiro: Editorial S. Pio X, 1962.

2711   CASTRO, JOSUÉ DE. Sete palmos de terra e um caixão ensaio
        sobre o noreste, área explosiva. São Paulo: Editôra Bra-
        siliense, 1965. 222 pp., bibl.

2712   CERTEAU, MICHEL DE. "Desarrollo y justicia social; el mani-
        fiesto de la Acción Católica Obrera brasileña." Mensaje
        16 (July, 1967): 299-303.

2713   GALJART, BENNO. "Class and 'Following' in Rural Brazil."
        América Latina 7 (July/September, 1964): 3-24.

2714   "JOC quer reforma." Brasil, Urgente 1 (July 14-20, 1963): 12.

Labor and Laboring Classes

2715   OLIVEIRA, CARLOS. Evangelho e revolução social. São Paulo:
       Livraria Duas Cidades, 1962. 100 pp.

2716   PRICE, ROBERT E. Rural Unionization in Brazil. Madison:
       Wisconsin University Land Tenure Center, 1964. 83 pp.

2717   RIBEIRO, FÁBIO ALVES. "O trabalhismo brasileiro e os cató-
       licos." A Ordem 55 (May/June, 1956): 31-41.

2718   SPRINGER, JOSEPH FRANK. A Brazilian Factory Study, 1966.
       Cuernavaca, México: Centro Intercultural de Documentación,
       1969.

2719   TORRES, MAURILIO. "Operários da Sima, sem pão e sem teto, não
       contam com a justa a trabalhista." Ação Popular 1 (January,
       1962): 11.

2720   WIARDA, HOWARD J. The Brazilian Catholic Labor Movement: The
       Dilemnas of National Development. Amherst: Labor Relations
       and Research Center, University of Massachusetts, 1969.
       95 pp.

LIBERATION

2721   CÂMARA, HÉLDER. "Human Rights and the Liberation of Man in
       the Americas. Reflections and Responses." In Human Rights
       and the Liberation of Man in the Americas, edited by Louis
       M. Colonese, pp. 259-268. Notre Dame: University of Notre
       Dame Press, 1970.

MARXISM

2722   AMORIN DA COSTA, A. "Cristianismo o marxismo." Colaboração
       ou oposição?" Brotéria 10 (October, 1974): 289-304.

2723   MARANHÃO, LUIZ. "Marxistas e católicos: da mão estendida so
       único caminho." Paz e Terra 2 (April, 1968): 57-71.

2724   MOREIRA ALVES, MARCIO. "Christians, Marxists and Dictatorship
       in Brazil." Christian Century 87 (June 10, 1970): 723-
       727.

2725   NO ENTRY

Brazil

NATIONALISM

2726   MARTINS, HERMINIO. "Ideology and Development: Developmental
       Nationalism in Brazil." In Latin American Sociological
       Studies, edited by Paul Halmos, pp. 153-172. Keele, Stand-
       fordshire: Keele University, 1967.

PEASANTRY

2727   BASTIDE, ROGER. "Le messianisme raté." Archives de Sociologie
       des Religions 3 (January/June, 1958): 31-37.

2728   FLANNERY, H. "Brazil's Miserable Northeast." Catholic World
       205 (August, 1967): 276-281.

2729   LEEDS, ANTHONY. "Brazil and the Myth of Francisco Juliao."
       In Politics of Change in Latin America, edited by Joseph
       Ben Mayer and Richard Weatherhead, pp. 190-204. New York:
       Praeger, 1964.

2730   METRAUX, ALFRED. "Les messies de l'Amérique de Sud." Archives
       de Sociologie des Religions 2 (July/December, 1957): 108-
       112.

2731   PAULA, FRANCISCO JULÃO ARRUDA DE. Cambão. Cuernavaca, México:
       Centro Intercultural de Documentación, 1970. 16 pp.

2732   _____. Cambao: The Yoke. The Hidden Face of Brazil. Har-
       mondsworth: Penguin, 1972. 191 pp.

2733   _____. Ligas camponesas, outubro 1962-abril 1964. Cuernavaca,
       México: Centro Intercultural de Documentación, 1969. 555
       pp.

POLITICS

2734   "Ação católica contra a política econômica." Paz e Terra 2
       (April, 1968): 247-250.

2735   ANTOINE, CHARLES. Church and Power in Brazil. New York:
       Orbis Books, 1973. 275 pp.

2736   ARAÚJO, FRANCISCO DE. "Guerra y paz en Brasil: mucho ruído
       en relación a un 'silencio' para la paz." Informaciones
       Católicas Internacionales 292 (July 22, 1967): 8.

Politics

2737   ARMSTRONG, JAMES. "People Are Doing...Badly in Brazil."
       Christian Century 88 (January 6, 1971): 14–16.

2738   ARRAES, MIGUEL. Brazil: The People and the Power. Harmonds-
       worth: Penguin Books, 1972. 232 pp.

2739   BARROS, ADIRSON DE. Ascensão e queda de Miguel Arraes. Rio
       de Janeiro: Editôra Equador, 1965. 174 pp.

2740   BERRYMAN, PHILIP E. "The Miracle and Distansão." America
       132 (May 24, 1975): 396–399.

2741   "Bishops Reply." Time, September 2, 1966, p. 31.

2742   "Brazil: Two Images." IDOC–International 34 (October 30,
       1971): 49–55.

2743   "Brazil's Angry Clergy." Newsweek, February 17, 1969, p. 68.

2744   BRUNEAU, THOMAS C. The Political Transformation of the Bra-
       zilian Catholic Church. London: Cambridge University
       Press, 1974. 270 pp., bibl.

2745   _____. "Power and Influence: Analysis of the Church in Latin
       America and the Case of Brazil." Latin American Research
       Review 8 (Summer, 1973): 45–51.

2746   CAMPOS, RENATO CARNEIRO. Igreja, política e religião. Recife:
       Instituto Joaquim Nabuco de Pesquisas Sociais, 1967. 61
       pp., bibl.

2747   CASTRO PINTO, JOSÉ ALBERTO. "Cúria condena a violência pol-
       icial." Paz e Terra 2 (April, 1968): 287–292.

2748   CERTEAU, MICHEL DE. "Les chrétiens et la dictature militaire
       au Brésil." Politique Aujourd'hui 11 (November, 1969):
       39–53.

2749   COMBLIN, JOSEPH. "Problems of the Church in Brazil." Clergy
       Review 57 (January, 1972): 3–15.

2750   Conférence Nationale des Evêques du Brésil. "Les exigences
       chrétiennes d'un ordre politique." Dial 362 (March 10,
       1977): 9.

2751   Conferencia Episcopal del Brasil. "Brasil: declaración colec-
       tiva del episcopado acerca de la nueva situación nacional."
       Informaciones Católicas Internacionales 218 (July 22, 1966):
       8–9.

2752   Conferencia Nacional de Obispos del Brasil. "Brasil: exigen-
       cias cristianas de un orden político." SIC 394 (April,
       1977): 148-151.

2753   DELLA CAVA, RALPH. "Torture in Brazil." Commonweal 92 (April
       24, 1970): 129.

2754   "Direita comanda o jogo das esquerdas." Ação Popular 1 (Jan-
       uary, 1962): 10.

2755   ENGEL, OTTO. "Brazilian Cardinal Helps Launch Right-Wing Lay
       Catholic Movement." National Catholic Reporter 4 (October
       16, 1968): 2.

2756   "Exigences chrétiennes pour un ordre politique: déclaration
       de la Conférence Episcopale du Brésil." La Documentation
       Catholique 74 (April 3, 1977): 315-319.

2757   "Exigências cristas de uma ordem política." Revista Eclesiás-
       tica Brasileira 37 (March, 1977): 188-196.

2758   "Falência dos partidos marca a hora das forças populares."
       Ação Popular 1 (January, 1962): 12.

2759   GONÇALVES DA COSTA, JOSÉ D. "Igreja e política." Paz e Terra
       2 (April, 1968): 268-271.

2760   HARRIOT, JOHN. "Brazil's Tensions." Month 3 (May, 1971):
       131-135.

2761   IANNI, OCTAVIO. Crisis in Brazil. New York: Columbia Uni-
       versity Press, 1970. 244 pp., bibl.

2762   LEEDS, ANTHONY. "Brazil and the Myth of Francisco Juliao."
       In Politics of Change in Latin America, edited by Joseph
       Ben Mayer and Richard Weatherhead, pp. 190-204. New York:
       Praeger, 1964.

2763   LODWICK, ROBERT E. The Significance of the Church-State Rela-
       tionship to an Evangelical Program in Brazil. Cuernavaca,
       México: Centro Intercultural de Documentación, 1969. 220
       pp.

2764   "El MEB, la política y la Iglesia en el Brasil." CIDOC Informa
       1 (April, 1964): 7-9.

2765   MOREIRA ALVES, MARCIO. L'Eglise et la politique au Brésil.
       Paris: Editions du Cerf, 1974. 226 pp.

Politics

2766 _____. Os cristãos, a justiça e o governo. Brasília: Câmara dos Deputados Departamento de Imprensa Nacional, 1968. 13 pp.

2767 NERY, ADALGISA. "Nós, os católicos, e a esquerda." Ação Popular 1 (January, 1962): 13.

2768 "Noticias sobre el derrocamiento de Joao Goulart y consecuencias en la Iglesia del Brasil." CIDOC Informa 1 (April, 1964): 4-6.

2769 PINTO, M. "Believe Brazilian Church Caught Between Capitalists, Communists." Catholic Messenger 82 (April 9, 1964): 1.

2770 "Prelate Accepts Brazil Chief on Probation, Awaits Action." National Catholic Reporter 3 (April 19, 1967): 5.

2771 QUIGLEY, THOMAS. "Repression in Brazil: Protest vs. Protocol." Commonweal 93 (January 15, 1971): 366.

2772 REISKY DE DUBNIC, VLADIMIR. Political Trends in Brazil. Washington, D.C.: Public Affairs Press, 1968. 148 pp.

2773 SANTOS, PAULO DE TARSO. "Greve e revolução crista." Ação Popular 1 (February, 1962): 12.

2774 _____. Os cristãos e a revolução social. Rio de Janeiro: Zahar Editores, 1963. 135 pp., bibl.

2775 Seminar on Latin American History, University of South Carolina, 1967. Conflito e continuidade na sociedade brasileira. Rio de Janeiro: Civilização Brasileira, 1970. 351 pp.

2776 SKIDMORE, T. E. Politics in Brazil, 1930-1964. New York: Oxford University Press, 1967. 446 pp., bibl.

2777 VILELA, M. "Suppléance politique et couches populaires: l'Eglise au Brésil." Lumière 22 (November/December, 1973): 68-72.

REFERENCE

2778 Centro de Estadística Religiosa e Investigações Sociais. Anuário católico do Brasil, 1965. Rio de Janeiro: Editôra Vozes, 1,912 pp.

2779 _____. Anuário católico do Brasil, 1965. Suplemento no. 1.
Rio de Janeiro: Editôra Vozes, 1965. 335 pp.

2780 _____. Anuário católico do Brasil, 1965. Suplemento no. 2.
Rio de Janeiro: Editôra Vozes, 1965. 144 pp.

REVOLUTION

2781 ALENCAR, TITO DE. "The Gospel and Brazil." New Blackfriars
54 (January, 1971): 4-12.

2782 ANTOINE, CHARLES. Church and Power in Brazil. New York:
Orbis Books, 1973. 275 pp.

2783 ARAÚJO, FRANCISCO DE. "¿Cuál es el papel de la Iglesia en el
Brasil?" Mensaje 17 (July, 1968): 303-308.

2784 BARRETO, LEDO. Julião, nordeste, revolução. Rio de Janeiro:
Editôra Civilização Brasiliera, 1963. 145 pp.

2785 BELFRAGE, CEDRIC. "The Story Behind the 'Gorilla' Coup in
Brazil." National Guardian 16 (July 18, 1964): 5.

2786 "Brazil: Repression and Resistance." Christian Century 86
(November 5, 1969): 1,413.

2787 CALLADO, ANTÔNIO. Tempo de Arraes: padres e comunistas no
revolução sem violência. Rio de Janeiro: J. Alvaro, 1964.
158 pp.

2788 CÂMARA, HÉLDER. "Una alternativa a la revolución: la acción
no violenta organizada de Hélder Câmara." Eca 246 (March,
1969): 87-94.

2789 _____. O despertar da revolução brasileira. Lisbon: Empresa
de Publicidade Seara Nova, 1974.

2790 _____. "Ist Gewalt der einzige Weg?" In Diskussion zu 'Theologie der Revolution, edited by Ernst Feil, pp. 260-269.
Munich: C. Kaiser, 1969.

2791 _____. Revolução dentro da paz. Rio de Janeiro: Sabía, 1968.
203 pp.

2792 _____. Revolutie in Vredesnaami. Utrecht: Bruna Boeken,
1969.

Revolution

2793 _____. Révolution dans la paix. Paris: Editions du Seuil, 1970. 147 pp.

2794 _____. Revolution für Frieden. Brussels: Herder, 1970.

2795 _____. Spiral of Violence. Denville: Dimension Books, [n.d.]. 83 pp.

2796 CAMARGO, CANDIDO PROCOPIO. O movimento do Natal. Brussels: Centre de Documentation sur l'Action des Eglises dans le Monde, 1968.

2797 CASTRO, JOSÚE DE. Death in the Northeast. New York: Random House, 1966. 207 pp.

2798 CLARK, JAMES A. "Religion and Revolution South of the Rio Grande." American Ecclesiastical Review 159 (October, 1968): 256-260.

2799 Confederação Evangélica do Brasil, Setor de Responsabilidade Social da Igreja. Cristo e o processo revolucionário brasileiro. Rio de Janeiro: Loqui, 1962.

2800 "¿Conservador o revolucionario? El catolicismo en Brasil." Informaciones Católicos Internacionales 214 (April 22, 1964): 29-31.

2801 FERRARI, ALCEU. Igreja e desenvolvimento, o movimento de Natal. Natal: Fundação José Augusto, 1968. 354 pp.

2802 FREITAS, ALIPIO DE. "Carta del Padre ... al Cardenal Jaime Barros Câmara," Cristianismo y Revolución 1 (September, 1966): 5-6.

2803 "Grupo de leigos católicos fixa posição." Paz e Terra 2 (April, 1968): 166-175.

2804 HOROWITZ, IRVING LOUIS. Revolution in Brazil. New York: Dutton, 1964. 430 pp., bibl.

2805 MARGERIE, BERTRAND DE. "Pode o católico de 1963 dizerse neo-capitalista, revolucionário ou socialista?" Revista Eclesiástica Brasileira 23 (1963): 687-700.

2806 MARIGHELLA, CARLOS. For the Liberation of Brazil. Harmondsworth: Penguin Books, 1971. 191 pp.

2807   MOREIRA ALVES, MARCIO. A Grain of Mustard Seed: The Awakening
of the Brazilian Revolution. New York: Anchor, 1973. 194
pp.

2808   OZANAM DE ANDRADE, RAYMUNDO. "'Populorum Progressio': neo-
capitalismo ou revolução." Paz e Terra 4 (August, 1967):
209-221.

2809   PAULA, FRANCISCO ARRUDADE. Brasil: antes y después. México:
Editorial Nuestro Tiempo, 1968. 125 pp.

2810   PESSOA, FRANCISCO LAGGE. "Brasil: la Iglesia y el movimiento
revolucionario." In La Iglesia, el subdesarrollo y la
revolución, edited by Bernardo Castro Villagrana, pp. 160-
164. México: Editorial Nuestro Tiempo, 1968.

2811   ROCHA, MATEUS FREI. "A Igreja e a revolução de abril." Paz
e Terra 2 (April, 1968): 276-279.

2812   SANTOS, PAULO DE TARSO. "Aliança e incapaz de vivir sua revolução." Brasil, Urgente 1 (August 25-21, 1963): 10-11.

SOCIALISM

2813   AVILA, FERNANDO BASTOS DE. Neo-capitalismo, socialismo, soli-
darismo. Rio de Janeiro: Artes Gráficas Indústrias Re-
unidas, 1963. 176 pp.

2814   CÂMARA, HÉLDER. Cristianismo, socialismo, capitalismo.
Salamanca: Sígueme, 1975. 114 pp.

2815   CRAIG, ALEXANDER. "Socialism the Only Road in Brazil."
Guardian (June 9, 1968): 9.

2816   LYRA, ROBERTO. O socialismo para o Brasil: cristianismo,
nacionalismo, democracia. Rio de Janeiro: Editôra Civilização Brasileira, 1962. 107 pp.

2817   MARANHÃO, LUIZ. "Marxistas e católicos: da mão estendida ao
único caminho." Paz e Terra 6 (1968): 57-71.

2818   MARGERIE, BERTRAND DE. "Pode o católico de 1963 dizerse neo-
capitalista, revolucionário our socialista?" Revista Eclesiástica Brasileira 23 (1963): 687-700.

2819   MARGOLIS, MAXINE L. The Moving Frontier: Social and Economic
Change in a Southern Brazilian Community. Gainesville:
University of Florida Press, 1973. 275 pp., bibl.

Socialism

2820   MENEZES, JOSÉ RAFAEL DE. Cristianismo e socialização. Recife:
        Edição da Revista 'Horizontes', 1963. 123 pp.

VIOLENCE

2821   "Action in Brazil: March 16, 1971." IDOC-International 27
        (June 12, 1971): 52-58.

2822   ALARCÓN, RODRIGO. Brasil: represión y tortura. Santiago,
        Chile: Editorial Orbe, 1971. 180 pp.

2823   Amnesty International. Report on Allegations of Torture in
        Brazil. London: Amnesty International, 1974. 97 pp.

2824   "Another Crime of Passion." America 122 (March 14, 1970):
        260.

2825   "Ante el asesinato del P. Henrique." Víspera 3 (July, 1969):
        21-24.

2826   ARAÚJO, FRANCISCO DE. "O cristão e a violência." Paz e Terra
        2 (March, 1968): 99-111.

2827   BOLTON, ROBERT H. "Brazilian Torture: Specifically New,
        Specifically Terrible." Christian Century 87 (April 1,
        1970): 387-388.

2828   "Brazil Bishops Attack Problem of Violence." Justice and
        Peace 1 (February/March, 1977): 1.

2829   "Brazil Bishops Back Torture Charge." National Catholic
        Reporter 7 (February 26, 1971): 20.

2830   "Brazil Expels Belgian Priest: He Says He Was Tortured in
        Jail." National Catholic Reporter 5 (September 3, 1969):
        3.

2831   "Brazil Police Use Torture, Rebels Charge." National Catholic
        Reporter 6 (January 14, 1970): 3.

2832   "The Brazilian Priest's Plea to Their Bishops." Herder Cor-
        respondence 6 (October, 1969): 308-311.

2833   "Brazil's Angry Clergy." Newsweek, February 17, 1969, p. 68.

2834   BRUNE, JOHANNES MARIA, ed. Die papageienschaukel Diktatur und
        Folter in Brasilien, eine Dokumentation. Düsseldorf: Patmos,
        1971. 160 pp.

Brazil

2835 "A Call for an End to the Torture of Prisoners." IDOC-International 48 (November, 1972): 59-60.

2836 CÂMARA, HÉLDER. "Acción no violencia en América Latina." Mensaje 17 (November, 1968): 579-583.

2837 _____. Espiral de violencia. Salamanca: Sígueme, 1972.

2838 _____. "Is Violence the Only Solution?" U.S. Catholic 34 (March, 1969): 14-18.

2839 _____. Spirale de violence. Paris: Desclée de Brouwer, 1970. 87 pp.

2840 _____. "Tuve un sueño." Croissance de Jeunes Nations 104 (1970): 9-11.

2841 _____. "La violence, seule option?" Informaciones Católicas Internacionales 312 (May 2, 1968):

2842 _____. "La violencia: opción única?" Informaciones Católicas Internacionales 312 (May 2, 1968): 4-7.

2843 CASTRO PINTO, JOSÉ ALBERTO. "Cúria condena a violência policial." Paz e Terra 2 (April, 1968): 287-292.

2844 CRAIG, ALEXANDER. "Violence and Tension Threaten Brazil." Guardian (March 25, 1970): 3.

2845 DELLA CAVA, RALPH. "Torture in Brazil." Commonweal 92 (April 24, 1970): 129.

2846 DESROCHERS, I. "Le Brésil: terre de martyrs: une église qui garde de moins en moins le silence." Relations 36 (November, 1976): 291-292.

2847 "Dom Hélder aceita o desafio da violência." Fatos e Fotos 379 (May 9, 1968).

2848 EVANS, ROBERT DERVEL. Brazil: The Road Back from Terrorism. London: Institute for the Study of Conflict, 1974. 20 pp.

2849 FLORIDI, ULISSE ALESSIO. Radicalismo cattolico brasiliano. Rome: Instituto Editoriale del Mediterraneo, 1968. 362 pp.

2850 GAGNON, L. "La violence institutionnalisée au Brésil." Relations 353 (October, 1970): 262-263.

Violence

2851   HAMILTON-PATERSON, JAMES. "Brazil Under the Colonels: Behind
       the Christian Cant, Misery, Repression and Torture." New
       Statesman (June 26, 1970): 908-911.

2852   "Human Rights in Brazil." Clergy Review 59 (September, 1974):
       627.

2853   "Missionary Tells How Murder Was Added to Brazil Terror."
       National Catholic Reporter 5 (June 11, 1969): 2.

2854   MOREIRA ALVES, MARCIO. "Brazil: A Country Where Christians
       Are Outlaws." Catholic World 212 (November, 1970): 65-68.

2855   _____. "Heart Failure and Sealed Coffins: Military Terrorism
       in Brazil." Ave Maria 110 (October 25, 1969): 19-23.

2856   "Murder in Brazil." Herder 6 (August, 1969): 244.

2857   O'SHAUGHNESSY, HUGH. "Brazil Slides into a Nightmare of Vio-
       lence." Observer (September 7, 1969): 4.

2858   "Paulo VI condena a violência." L'Osservatore Romano, October
       25, 1970, p. 1.

2859   "Priest Tells of Torture." Christianity Today 15 (October 9,
       1970): 50.

2860   QUIGLEY, THOMAS. "Cold Blood in Brazil." Commonweal 90 (July
       17, 1969): 452-453.

2861   "Report on Allegations of Torture in Brazil." IDOC-Interna-
       tional 48 (November, 1972): 7-33.

2862   ROGERS, CORNISH. "Pride, Repression and Genocide in Brazil."
       Christian Century 91 (May 15, 1974): 524-525.

2863   "Sad Days in Recife: Abductions of Operation Hope Workers."
       Commonweal 99 (December 7, 1973): 256-257.

2864   SATTAMINI DE ARRUDA, MARCOS PENNA. "Living Freely in Brazil."
       IDOC-International 31 (September 11, 1971): 6-18.

2865   "La violence et l'insecurité au Brésil: message pastoral des
       êveques au peuple de Dieu." La Documentation Catholique
       73 (December 19, 1976): 1075-1081.

V Caribbean

GENERAL

2866   ALONSO, ISIDORO Y GARRIDO, GINES. La Iglesia en América Central y el Caribe. Friburg: Oficina Internacional de Investigaciones Sociales de FERES, 1962. 282 pp.

2867   BECKMAN, JOSEPH F. "Ecumenism to a Calipso Beat." America 129 (December 29, 1973): 504-505.

2868   DAY, MARK. "Ousted Puerto Rican Bishop Carries on Liberation Effort." Christian Century 90 (June 6, 1973): 655-656.

2869   GONZÁLEZ, JUSTO L. The Development of Christianity in Latin Caribbean. Grand Rapids, Michigan: William B. Eerdmans, 1969. 136 pp., bibl.

2870   "Die Kirche in der Dominikanischen Republik." Herder Korrespondence 15 (May, 1961): 353-355.

2871   MOSKIN, J. ROBERT. "Muñoz, the Practical Revolutionist." Look, January 17, 1961, pp. 30-33.

2872   SHARPE, KENNETH E. "La lucha campesina en la República Dominicana: poder, comunidad, Iglesia." Estudios Sociales 8 (October/December, 1975): 191-238.

2873   WIPFLER, WILLIAM LOUIS. The Churches of the Dominican Republic in the Light of History: A Study of the Root Causes of Current Problems. Cuernavaca, México: Centro Intercultural de Documentación, 1966. 300 pp.

2874   ZANCHOTTIN, CLAUDIO. "The Church in Haiti." New Blackfriars 52 (August, 1971): 363-367.

AGRARIAN REFORM

2875   BERAS ROJAS, OCTAVIO A., et al. "Reflexiones y sugerencias pastorales sobre las leyes agrarias." Estudios Sociales 21 (January/February/March, 1973): 54-64.

Agrarian Reform

2876   _____, and POLANCO, HUGO. "Situación campesina en la República
        Dominicana: declaración conjunta del Episcopado Dominicano
        sobre la situación campesina." Estudios Sociales 30 (Jan-
        uary/February/March, 1968): 60-64.

2877   "Dominican Farm Workers: Churchmen on Economic Matters."
        America 120 (March 15, 1969): 293.

2878   "Dominicano sobre la situación campesina." Estudios Sociales
        30 (January/February/March, 1968): 60-64.

2879   SHARPE, KENNETH E. "La lucha campesina en la República Domi-
        nicana: poder, comunidad, Iglesia." Estudios Sociales 32
        (1975): 191-238.

CATHOLIC CHURCH AND SOCIAL CHANGE

2880   ANDERSON, JAMES R. "Experiment in Love." Worldmission 15
        (Winter, 1965): 62-67.

2881   DOHEN, DOROTHY. Two Studies of Puerto Rico. Cuernavaca,
        México: Centro Intercultural de Documentación, 1966. 155
        pp.

2882   "Fidel Castro: reunión con los representantes de las iglesias
        de Jamaica." SIC 402 (February, 1978): 52-55, 89-92.

2883   PARRILLA BONILLA, ANTULIO. "Poder y desarrollo de la Iglesia
        en Puerto Rico." Desarrollo Indoamericano 6 (June, 1973):
        49-52.

2884   _____. Puerto Rico: Iglesia y sociedad, 1967-1969: confer-
        encias, discursos, entrevistas. Cuernavaca, México: Centro
        Intercultural de Documentación, 1970. 9 pp.

2885   _____. Puerto Rico: supervivencia y liberación. San Juan:
        Librería Internacional, 1971. 358 pp.

2886   ROBSON, JOHN. "West Indians and Pastoral Service." Clergy
        Review 61 (October, 1976): 379-382.

2887   SOUFFRANT, CLAUDE. "Un Catholicisme de résignation en Haiti:
        sociologie d'un recueil de cantiques religieux." Social
        Compass 17 (1970): 425-438.

2888   TRIEST, HUGO. "Reflections from Haiti." Worldmission 16
        (Summer, 1965): 72-77.

CATHOLIC CHURCH AND STATE

2889   ADAMS, BENJAMIN. "Reply to Puerto Rican Pastoral."
       Commonweal 73 (March 3, 1961): 588-589.

2890   CARGAS, H. "The Dominican Republic: Irony and Hope." Ave
       Maria 107 (March 23, 1968): 21-23.

2891   "Church Continues Muñoz Attack." Christian Century 78 (June
       21, 1961): 764.

2892   "The Church in Haiti." America 114 (May 21, 1966): 717-718.

2893   "Church in Politics." Newsweek, June 5, 1961, p. 56.

2894   "Church vs. Statism." Time, January 20, 1961, p. 36.

2895   DEEDY, JOHN G. "Puerto Rico Pastoral." Commonweal 73
       (December 2, 1960): 257.

2896   "The Ejected Churchman." Newsweek, December 5, 1960, p. 94.

2897   "Expulsion of Two Bishops." Commonweal 73 (January 27, 1961):
       448.

2898   "Haiti: lucha abierta entre el gobierno y la Iglesia."
       Mensaje 10 (March 4, 1961): 118-121.

2899   PARRILLA BONILLA, ANTULIO. "Poder y desarrollo de la Iglesia
       en Puerto Rico." Desarrollo Indoamericano 6 (June, 1973):
       49-52.

2900   "Peace in Puerto Rico." America 107 (October, 1962): 830.

2901   "Puerto Rico: The Pulpit Enters Politics." Life, November 7,
       1960, pp. 34-35.

2902   SISTER JANE MARY. "Spotlight Turned on Catholic Haiti."
       America 102 (December 5, 1959): 322-325.

2903   "Trujillo and the Church: Making and Breaking a Concordat."
       Tablet 215 (June 10, 1961): 569-570.

CATHOLIC CLERGY

2904   BERAS ROJAS, OCTAVIO A. and PLANCO, HUGO. "Situacion campesina
       en la Republica Dominicana: declaración conjunta del Epis-
       copado Dominicano sobre la situación campesina." Estudios
       Sociales 30 (January/February/March, 1968): 60-64.

Catholic Clergy

2905   CORRO, ALEJANDRO DEL, comp. Puerto Rico: obispos nativos,
        1962-1965: documentos y reacciones de prensa. Cuernavaca,
        México: Centro Intercultural de Documentación, 1967. 18
        pp.

2906   O'GRADY, D. "Caribbean Cooperation." National Catholic Re-
        porter 13 (April 1, 1977): 2.

2907   PARRILLA BONILLA, ANTULIO. Puerto Rico: supervivencia y
        liberación. San Juan: Librería Internacional, 1971.
        358 pp.

2908   ZAPELACK, EMILIAN. "El caso del padre Héctor Gallegos en
        Panamá." Noticias Aliadas (July 3, 1971): 10-15.

COMMUNISM

2909   "Fidel Castro: reunión con los representantes de las Iglesias
        de Jamaica." SIC 402 (February, 1978): 52-55, 89-92.

DOCUMENTS

2910   "Bishops. Puerto Rico. (Text of 2nd. Pastoral Letter)."
        Catholic Messenger 79 (November 24, 1960): 6.

2911   "Caribbean Catholics Participate Fully in Conference of
        Churches." National Catholic Reporter 12 (January 16,
        1976): 16.

2912   "The Catholic Church in Haiti." IDOC-International 6 (June
        27, 1970): 6-43.

2913   PARRILLA BONILLA, ANTULIO. Puerto Rico: Iglesia y sociedad,
        1967-1969: conferencias, discursos, entrevistas. Cuerna-
        vaca, México: Centro Intercultural de Documentación, 1970.

ECONOMIC DEVELOPMENT

2914   "Puerto Rico: Copper Mining." IDOC-International 21 (March
        13, 1971): 30-36.

LIBERATION

2915   DAY, MARK. "Ousted Puerto Rican Bishop Carries on Liberation
        Effort." Christian Century 90 (June 6, 1973): 655-656.

2916   PARRILLA BONILLA, ANTULIO.   Puerto Rico: supervivencia y
       liberación.   San Juan: Librería Internacional, 1971.   358
       pp.

MARXISM

2917   "Marxist Movements Concern Bishops of Puerto Rico."   Our Sunday
       Visitor 64 (May 2, 1976):   3.

POLITICS

2918   COUSINS, N.   "Sin and Political Freedom."   Saturday Review 43
       (December 3, 1960):   34.

2919   "Dominican Bishops Hit Injustices: Statement on Political
       Situation."   Catholic Messenger 81 (August 15, 1963):   1.

2920   "Here's Where Church Tried to Swing an Election."   U.S. News
       and World Report, November 7, 1960, pp. 59-61.

2921   LIGGETT, THOMAS.   "Catholic Political Party for Puerto Rico."
       Christian Century 77 (July 27, 1960):   870-871.

2922   _____.   "End of a Clerical Venture: Christian Action Party."
       Christian Century 78 (August 9, 1961):   952-954.

2923   NICHOLLS, DAVID.   "Politics and Religion in Haiti."   Canadian
       Journal of Political Science 3 (September, 1970):   400-414.

2924   OCAMPO, TARSICIO, comp.   Puerto Rico, Partido Acción Cristiana,
       1960-1962:   documentos y reacciones de prensa.   Cuernavaca,
       México: Centro Intercultural de Documentación, 1967.

2925   "Puerto Rican Bishops Crack Down on Christian Socialists."
       Our Sunday Visitor 65 (June 13, 1976):   3.

2926   "Roman Catholic Church Enters Politics."   Christian Century
       77 (July 20, 1960):   844.

2927   "Santo Domingo: causas y factores que determinarán la elec-
       ción del doctor Balaguer."   Carta de ISAL 3 (April, 1970):
       10-11.

Reference

REFERENCE

2928　ALONSO, ISIDORO and GARRIDO, GINES. La Iglesia en América Central y el Caribe: estructuras eclesiásticas. Bogotá: Oficina Internacional de Investigaciones Sociales de FERES, 1962. 282 pp.

2929　DOHEN, DOROTHY. Two Studies of Puerto Rico: Religion Data: The Background of Consensual Union. Cuernavaca, México: Centro Intercultural de Documentación, 1966. 155 pp., bibl.

SOCIALISM

2930　"Dos sacerdotes se separan de los cristianos para el socialismo." ICIA 125-126 (July 15/August 1, 1976): 3.

2931　"Puerto Rico: no a 'Cristianos por el Socialismo.'" El Catolicismo 2,234 (January 30, 1977): 15

VI Central America

GENERAL

2932   AGUIRRE, GERARDO G. La cruz de Nimajuyú: historia de la
       Parroquia de San Pedro La Laguna. Guatemala: [n.p.],
       1972. 474 pp.

2933   ALONSO, ISIDORO Y GARRIDO, GINES. La Iglesia en América Cen-
       tral y el Caribe. Friburg: Oficina Internacional de In-
       vestigaciones Sociales de FERES, 1962. 282 pp.

2934   APARICIO, PEDRO ARNOLDO. "Carta a las autoridades de El
       Salvador." Servicio de Información y Documentación 2
       (1975): 15-16.

2935   BENDAÑA, RICARDO. "Iglesia e ideologia en Guatemala."
       Diálogo 26 (1975): 4-7.

2936   BRAVO, FRANCISCO. The Parish of San Miguelito in Panama:
       History and Pastoral-Theological Evaluation. Cuernavaca,
       México: Centro Intercultural de Documentación, 1966. 348
       pp.

2937   "The Church in Central America." Pro Mundi Vita 46 (1973):
       22-36.

2938   "Dominica: Economic and Social Problems, Situation of the
       Church." Christian Order 3 (July, 1962): 401-410.

2939   FITZPATRICK, JOSEPH. "Parish of the Future." America 113
       (November 6, 1965): 521-523.

2940   MC GRATH, MARK G. "Algunas consideraciones sobre la relación
       entre evangelización y su proyección a la justicia en el
       istmo centroamericano." Búsqueda 3 (1975): 6-10.

2941   _____. "Ariel or Caliban?" Foreign Affairs 52 (October,
       1973): 75-95.

General

2942 _____. "La universidad católica: discurso pronunciado ...
el día de la inauguración de la universidad católica de
Panamá." CIDOC Informa 2 (September, 1965): 287-290.

2943 MAGNER, JAMES A. "Central American and the Church." Shield
38 (May, 1959): 4-5.

2944 NAVARRO O., ALFONSO, et al. "Dos manifestos del clero salvadoreño en torno al cardenalato de Monseñor Mario Casariego."
NADOC 58 (June 4, 1969): 1-4.

2945 PIKE, FREDERICK B. "The Catholic Church in Central America."
Review of Politics 21 (January, 1959): 83-113.

2946 VALENCIA, L. E. "Contra la Iglesia de avanzada: hechos en
Honduras y documento en Bolivia." Christus 41 (January,
1976): 4-6.

2947 VEGA, JUAN RAMÓN. "Algunos modelos de pastoral en América
Central." Pastoral Popular 26 (1975): 21-36.

2948 _____. "The Pastoral Work of Evangelizing in Central America."
Lumen Vitae 29 (December, 1974): 521-532.

2949 WAGLEY, CHARLES. "The Social and Religious Life of a Guate-
malan Village." In Latin American Social Organization and
Institutions, edited by Olen E. Leonard, and Charles P.
Loomis, pp. 67-83. East Lansing: Michigan State College
Press, 1953.

2950 WIPFLER, WILLIAM LOUIS. The Churches of the Dominican Republic
in the Light of History. Cuernavaca, México: Centro Intercultural de Documentación, 1966. 210 pp., bibl.

AGRARIAN REFORM

2951 "El Salvador: Agrarian Reform Manifesto." IDOC-International
11 (October 17, 1970): 38-42.

CATHOLIC CHURCH AND SOCIAL CHANGE

2952 BACIGALUPO, LEONARD. "The Church in Central America." Worldmission 11 (Spring, 1960): 57-65.

2953 CALDER, BRUCE JOHNSON. Crecimiento y cambio de la Iglesia
católica guatemalteca, 1944-1966. Guatemala: Seminario de
Integración Social Guatemalteca, 1970. 193 pp.

2954   EMERGY, GENNET MAXON. Protestantism in Guatemala: Its In-
       fluence on the Bicultural Situacion, With Reference to the
       Roman Catholic Background. Cuernavaca, México: Centro
       Intercultural de Documentación, 1970.

2955   FONSECA, JAIME. "Bishops' Appeal for Drastic Social Reforms
       in Central America Produces Limited Results." Catholic
       Messenger 81 (April 11, 1963): 9.

2956   "Guatemalan Bishops Stress Social Responsibility of All."
       Catholic Messenger 80 (October 25, 1962): 1.

2957   MORAN, E. "El Salvador, Wealth, Repression... Confront Church,
       Jesuits." National Catholic Reporter 13 (August 26, 1977):
       32-33.

2958   "No Class Distinction in Panama: Religious Ceremonies Reso-
       lutions of Ninth Annual Meeting." Tablet 218 (August 8,
       1964): 900.

2959   "Panamanians Protest Resignation of Bishop: McGrath Succeeds
       Him." National Catholic Reporter 5 (February 19, 1969):
       7.

2960   PARRILLI, R. E. "Church and Social Change in Guatemala."
       Revista de Derecho Puertorriqueño 11 (January/March, 1972):
       311-344.

2961   "Social Injustice in Nicaragua: Bishop Calderon's Pastoral."
       Tablet 216 (July 28, 1962): 725-726.

2962   TORTOLANI, PAUL. "Political Participation of Native and
       Foreign Catholic Clergy in Guatemala." Journal of Church
       and State 15 (Autumn, 1973): 407-418.

CATHOLIC CHURCH AND STATE

2963   BIMBI, LINDA. "The Death and Life of Hector Gallego." IDOC-
       International 51 (March, 1973): 7-9.

2964   BOSCH, JUAN. "El papel de la Iglesia en el golpe en la Re-
       pública Dominicana." Panoramas 14 [n.d.]: 120-129.

2965   "Church and Government in El Salvador." IDOC-International
       45 (April 15, 1972): 2-23.

2966   CLARK, JAMES A. "Church and the Dominican Crisis." Thought
       41 (Spring, 1966): 117-131.

Catholic Church and State

2967   DELANEY, ROBERT. "Analysis of the Political Function of a
Christian Community in Panama." Concilium 4 (1973): 24-
30.

2968   ESTRADA MONROY, AGUSTÍN. Datos para la historia de la Iglesia
en Guatemala. Guatemala: Tipografía Nacional, 1974. 804
pp.

2969   "The Explusion of Bishop Frey from Guatemala." IDOC-International 51 (March, 1973): 6-7.

2970   "Kirche und Staat in Guatemala." Herder-Korrespondenz 10
(July, 1956): 455-457.

2971   MAC EOIN, GARY. "Church-State Rift Grows in Panama." National
Catholic Reporter 8 (January 7, 1972): 1.

2972   OCAMPO V., TARSICIO, comp. Puerto Rico: Partido Acción
Cristiana, 1960-1962: documentos y reacciones de prensa.
Cuernavaca, México: Centro Intercultural de Documentación,
1967.

2973   SHEERIN, JOHN B. "The Bishops Confront Trujillo." Catholic
World 190 (March, 1960): 335-336.

2974   "Trujillo and the Bishops." America 102 (February 20, 1960):
603-604.

CATHOLIC CLERGY

2975   "Ahora en Honduras." Contacto 12 (December, 1975): 69-79.

2976   "Obispos guatemaltecos piden distribución de bienes mas justas."
Noticias Aliadas 36 (September 16, 1976): 1-3.

2977   "Situación anual de la catequesis." Catequesis Latinoamericana
3 (July/September, 1971): 402-410.

2978   TORTOLANI, PAUL. "Political Participation of Native and Foreign Catholic Clergy in Guatemala." Journal of Church and
State 15 (Autumn, 1973): 407-418.

2979   TURCIOS, CARLOS RAFAEL. "¿Y el evangelio ...? Problemas con
algunos jerarcas de la Iglesia católica en América Latina."
Contacto 13 (June, 1976): 44-48.

2980 WATTS, DAVID. "Why Priests Have Become Targets in El Salva-
       dor." Time, July 18, 1977, p. 12.

CHRISTIAN DEMOCRACY

2981 PAZ, MARCO ANTONIO DE. "El papel de la Iglesia en la formación
       de la nueva sociedad centroamericana." NADOC 53 (May 14,
       1969): 1-10.

2982 WALKER, THOMAS W. The Christian Democratic Movement in Nica-
       ragua. Tucson: University of Arizona Press, 1970. 71 pp.

COMMUNISM

2983 LIETZ, PAUL S. "Crossroads in Guatemala." America 96 (Decem-
       ber 29, 1956): 371-373.

DOCUMENTS

2984 BIMBI, LINDA. "The Death and Life of Hector Gallegos." IDOC-
       International 51 (March, 1973): 7-9.

2985 "Carta de la Iglesia católica de Honduras al jefe de estado y
       consejo superior de la defensa. Comunicado de la confer-
       encia episcopal de Honduras." CELAM 8 (1975).

2986 "Concenso mínimo: The Costa Rica Statement." IDOC-Interna-
       tional 43 (March 11, 1972): 3-10.

2987 "El Salvador: Agrarian Reform Manifesto." IDOC-International
       11 (October 17, 1970): 38-42.

2988 "El Salvador: mensaje de la Conferencia Episcopal sobre el
       momento actual que vive el país." L'Osservatore Romano,
       April, 1977. p. 6.

2989 Encuentro Pastoral, 1st Managua, 1969. De cara al futuro de
       la Iglesia en Nicaragua. [n.p.]: Ediciones Fichero Pas-
       toral, 1969, 263 pp.

2990 "The Explusion of Bishop William Frey from Guatemala." IDOC-
       International 51 (March, 1973): 6-7.

2991 "La Iglesia católica está presente en la vida del pueblo
       guatemalteco." Catequesis Latinoamericana 2 (October/
       December, 1970): 531-533.

Documents

2992 "In Honduras Episcopal Conference Issues Document at Close of
      Symposium." L'Osservatore Romano, June 3, 1971, p. 166.

2993 "Los Jesuitas ante el pueblo salvadoreño: dos documentos."
      Christus 42 (October, 1977): 45–50.

2994 "Principles Guiding the Church's Political Activity." Catholic
      Mind 71 (March, 1973): 43–49.

2995 RODRÍGUEZ Y QUIROZ. "Costa Rica: programa social." Mensaje
      10 (October, 1961): 508.

2996 "Episcopado de El Salvador frente a masacre de campesinos."
      Actualidad Pastoral 8 (1975): 54–55.

2997 "An Interview with Hector Gallego." IDOC-International 51
      (March, 1973): 9–13.

POLITICS

2998 "Apuntes para un análisis de la participación de la Iglesia
      en la situación actual de El Salvador." Christus 42
      (August, 1977): 9–18.

2999 CASEY, R. "Guatemala Missioners Claim Fraud in Elections."
      National Catholic Reporter 10 (May 24, 1974): 2.

3000 CLARK, JAMES A. "The Church and the Dominican Crisis."
      Thought 41 (Spring, 1966): 117–131.

3001 DELANEY, ROBERT. "Analysis of the Political Function of
      Christian Community in Panama." Concilium 4 (1973): 24–
      30.

3002 TURCIOS, CARLOS RAFAEL. "¿Y el evangelio ...? Problemas con
      algunos jerarcas de la Iglesia católica en América Latina."
      Contacto 13 (June, 1976): 44–48.

REFERENCE

3003 ALONSO, ISIDORO. La Iglesia en América Central y el Caribe:
      estructuras eclesiásticas. Bogotá: Centro de Información
      y Sociología de la Obra de Cooperación Sacerdotal Hispano-
      americana, 1962. 282 pp.

3004 STAHLKE, LEONARDO E. Estadísticas de la obra religioso-
cristiana en Guatemala. Guatemala: Iglesia Luterana,
1966. 235 pp.

REVOLUTION

3005 CLARK, JAMES A. "Religion and Revolution in the Dominican
Republic." American Ecclesiastical Review 156 (January,
1967): 35-38.

3006 GANNON, FRANCIS X. "Catholicism, Revolution and Violence in
Latin America: Lessons of the 1968 Guatemala Maryknoll
Episode." Orbis 11 (Winter, 1969): 1204-1225.

3007 MARTIN BARO, IGNACIO. "Una religiosa a la guerrilla." SIC,
Revista Venezolana de Orientación 31 (May, 1968): 212-214.

3008 MAURER, HARRY. "Radical Agitators: The Priests of Honduras."
Nation 222 (March 6, 1976): 266-269.

3009 MELVILLE, THOMAS. "Guatemala: Revolução, a unica saída."
Paz e Terra 2 (June, 1968): 217-225.

SOCIALISM

3010 "Concenso mínimo: The Costa Rica Statement." IDOC-International 43 (March 11, 1972): 3-10.

VIOLENCE

3011 AGUILERA PERALTA, GABRIEL EDGARDO. La violencia en Guatemala
como fenómeno político. Cuernavaca, México: Centro Intercultural de Documentación, 1971.

3012 BROCKMAN, JAMES R. "Persecution in El Salvador: Priests and
People Face Death, Beating and Exile." America 137 (July
2-9, 1977): 10-11.

3013 DEL CORRO, ALJANDRO, comp. Guatemala: La violencia, I-III;
posiciones ante el uso de la violencia en el cambio social:
prensa nacional, impresos clandestinos de tirajes reducidos,
prensa suprimida y marginal: 1960-1967. Cuernavaca,
México: Centro Intercultural de Documentación, 1968. 344
pp.

Violence

3014 Episcopado de El Salvador. "Exhortación pastoral--acerca de
la situación de violencia en el país." Búsqueda 3 (1975):
40-41.

3015 GALL, NORMAN. "Guatemala Guerrillas Slaughtered, Church
Objects to Bloodbath." National Catholic Reporter 3 (June
7, 1967): 1.

3016 HERNÁNDEZ PICO, JUAN. "Hacia una teología de la violencia:
reflexiones sobre la postura cristiana ante la violencia
revolucionaria." ECA 239 (July, 1968): 202-209.

3017 "Matter of Conscience." Newsweek, October 25, 1971, p. 127.

3018 SURVIL, B. "Letters Carry Hope to El Salvador." National
Catholic Reporter 13 (August 26, 1977): 27.

VII Chile

GENERAL

3019   ALONSO, ISIDORO. La Iglesia en Chile: estructuras eclesiás-
       ticas. Friburg: Oficina Internacional de Investigaciones
       Sociales de FERES, 1962. 223 pp.

3020   ARENEDA BRAVO, F. "Breve historia de la Iglesia en Chile."
       IDOC-International 1 (April 4, 1970): 51-52.

3021   CASASSAS CANTO, JOSÉ MARÍA. Noticias sobre la Iglesia cató-
       lica en la provincia de Antofagasta. Santiago, Chile:
       Editorial Orbe, 1968. 115 pp.

3022   "Les chrétiens chileiens contestent le visage actual de
       L'Eglise et la realité socio-economique de leur Pays."
       Lettre 124 (December, 1968): 32-39.

3023   Communaute Pacem in Terris. "L'Eglise catholique du Chili et
       les perspectivas démocratiques." Foi et Développement 41
       (November, 1976): 1-6.

3024   "En Chile, encuesta en Santiago: 'La Iglesia no se interesa
       en el hombre'." Informaciones Católicas Internacionales
       296 (September 2, 1967): 19-20.

3025   GALILEA, CARMEN and PUGA, JOSEFINA. Religiosidad y seculari-
       zación en Chile. Santiago, Chile: CISOC, 1974. 98 pp.

3026   GONZÁLEZ VIVES, JOSÉ. "La Iglesia en Chile." Educación
       Boletín 2 (1975): 35-38.

3027   HORNUNG, WARREN GEORGE. "Paulo Freire's Contribution to the
       Theological Education of the Protestant Laity in Chile."
       Claremont: School of Theology at Claremont, 1974. 347 pp.,
       bibl.

3028   "La Iglesia en tiempos difíciles: apuntes de un equipo cris-
       tiano chileno." Mensaje Iberoamericano 115 (1975): 16-19,
       22-23.

General

3029   LARRAÍN ERRÁZURIZ, MANUEL. Escritos sociales. Santiago,
       Chile: Ediciones del Pacífico, 1963. 279 pp.

3030   MC GRATH, MARK G. "Church in Chile: Inquietud." Apostolic
       Perspectives 4 (May, 1959): 32-35.

3031   _____. "Problems in Chile." Apostolic Perspectives 4 (March,
       1959): 12-16.

3032   MAC HALE, TOMAS P., ed. Chile: A Critical Survey. Santiago,
       Chile: Institute of General Studies, 1972. 324 pp.

3033   NOONAN, DANIEL P. "Latin America, Awakening Giant." World-
       mission 14 (Fall, 1963): 13-16.

3034   Los obispos de Chile hablan: el cristiano en el mundo actual
       y los de difusión. Santiago, Chile: Secretariado General
       del Episcopado de Chile, 1962. 99 pp.

3035   PIKE, FREDERICK B. "The Catholic Church and Modernization in
       Peru and Chile." Journal of International Affairs 20 (1966):
       272-288.

3036   ZOTTELE, PEDRO. "Clergy-Vatican Tension." Christian Century
       86 (August 27, 1969): 1120-1122.

AGRARIAN REFORM

3037   "Actions Which Speak Louder." Commonweal 75 (January 12, 1962):
       401.

3038   CHARLESWORTH, M. "Land Reform in Chile." Tablet 218 (May 23,
       1964): 575-576.

3039   CHONCHOL, JACQUES. "Agrarian Reform: One of the Issues."
       IDOC-International 53 (May, 1973): 52-54.

3040   DOMÍNGUEZ C., OSCAR. El campesino chileno y la acción cató-
       lica rural. Santiago, Chile: Centro de Investigación y
       Acción Social, 1961. 88 pp.

3041   Episcopado Chileno. "La Iglesia y el problema del campesino
       chileno: pastoral colectival del...." Mensaje 11 (May,
       1962): 185-194.

3042   "La Iglesia chilena inicia la reforma agraria." Mensaje 11
       (August, 1962): 362-364.

Catholic Church and Social Change

3043 "La Iglesia y el problema del campesino chileno." La Revista
     Católica 62 (January 4, 1962): 3325-3336.

3044 Sacerdotes Chilenos. "La tierra para los campesinos." Mensaje
     10 (August, 1961): 361-362.

3045 SILVA SOLAR, JULIO. Reforma Agraria. Santiago, Chile: Edi-
     ciones Sol, 1966. 162 pp.

3046 THIESENHUSEN, WILLIAM C. Chile's Experiments in Agrarian
     Reform. Madison: University of Wisconsin Press, 1966.
     230 pp.

CATHOLIC CHURCH AND SOCIAL CHANGE

3047 ALVÁREZ ANDREWS, OSCAR. Chile, monografía sociológica.
     México: Instituto de Investigaciones Sociales, Universidad
     Nacional, 1965. 231 pp.

3048 BAGÁ, JUAN. "Pursuit into the City." Worldmission 13 (Summer,
     1962): 44-47.

3049 Bishops of Chile. "Lead Social Reforms, Bishops Urge Chileans:
     Excerpts from Joint Pastoral Letter." Catholic Messenger
     80 (October 4, 1962): 1.

3050 Conferencia Episcopal de Chile. Comité Permanente. La Iglesia
     1976. Orientaciones pastorales para Chile. Santiago,
     Chile: CENCOSEP, 1976. 24 pp.

3051 ECHEGOYEN, MARUJA. "Priests and Socialism in Chile." New
     Blackfriars 52 (October, 1971): 459-466.

3052 Epsicopado Chileno. "El evangelio exige comprometerse en pro-
     fundas y urgentes renovaciones sociales." Mensaje 198
     (May, 1971): 190.

3053 FICHTER, JOSEPH H. Cambio social en Chile: un estudio de
     actitudes. Santiago, Chile: Editora Universidad Católica,
     1962. 225 pp.

3054 HENRÍQUEZ SILVA, RAUL. "Primacía del hombre en la vida de la
     Iglesia." Iglesia de Santiago (December, 1977): 16.

3055 JAVIER, FRANCISCO. El humanismo de Jorge Fernández Pradel.
     Santiago, Chile: Instituto Chileno de Estudios Humanísticos,
     1976. 68 pp.

Catholic Church and Social Change

3056   JIMÉNEZ, JULIO. "Sobre Iglesia y política en la historia
       chilena." Teología y Vida 3-4 (1971): 218-254.

3057   LARRAÍN ERRÁZURIZ, MANUEL. Escritos sociales. Santiago,
       Chile: Editorial del Pacífico, 1963. 279 pp.

3058   _____. El humanismo de Manuel Larraín. Santiago, Chile:
       Instituto Chileno de Estudios Humanísticos, 1975. 104 pp.

3059   _____. La voz profética de don Manuel Larraín E. Santiago,
       Chile: Ediciones Mundo, 1976. 88 pp.

3060   MAGSAM, CHARLES M. "We Reach Them Through Their Hearts."
       Worldmission 16 (Summer, 1965): 78-85.

3061   MALABRE, ALFRED L. "South America's Changing Church: Roman
       Catholicism is a Force for Some Surprising Liberalism in
       Latin Lands." Wall Street Journal, April 26, 1967, p. 16.

3062   Los obispos de Chile hablan: el deber social y el político en
       la hora presente. Santiago, Chile: Secretariado General
       del Epsicopado de Chile, 1964. 39 pp.

3063   Pastoral Colectiva del Episcopado de Chile. La Iglesia y el
       problema del campesinado chileno. Santiago, Chile: Edi-
       torial Universidad Católica, 1962. 37 pp.

3064   PIKE, FREDERICK B. "The Catholic Church and Modernization in
       Peru and Chile." Journal of International Affairs 20
       (1966): 272-288.

3065   POBLETE, RENATO. "The Church and Social Change in Chile."
       Month 6 (October, 1973): 329-333.

3066   SILVA HENRÍQUEZ, R. "Christian Solution to Chile's Social
       Problems." Catholic Messenger 82 (May 7, 1964): 7.

3067   SILVA SOLAR, JULIO. "Pluralidad de fuerzas e ideologías en la
       construcción del socialismo en Chile. Colaboración de
       marxistas y cristianos." In Chile: búsqueda de un nuevo
       socialismo, edited by Alejandro Foxley et al., pp. 206-231.
       Santiago, Chile: Nueva Universidad, 1971.

3068   SISTER, G. "A Pastoral Experiment in Chile." Tablet 219
       (February 13, 1965): 176-177.

3069   ZOTTELE, PEDRO. "Chilean Catholics Debate Allende's Socialism."
       Christian Century 88 (June 23, 1971): 778.

CATHOLIC CHURCH AND STATE

3070   AFFONSO, ALMINO, et al. Movimiento Campesino Chileno. San-
       tiago, Chile: ICIRA, 1970. 2 v., bibl.

3071   BONO, AGOSTINO. "The Cardinal and the Generals." IDOC-Inter-
       national 58 (December, 1973): 54-55.

3072   _____. "Chilean Church Moves to Retain Influence." National
       Catholic Reporter 10 (December 28, 1973): 14.

3073   _____. "Church Main Critic of Junta in Chile." National
       Catholic Reporter 10 (August 2, 1974): 20.

3074   _____. "Protest in Chile." Commonweal 103 (June 18, 1976):
       390-391.

3075   BROWN, JOHN PAIRMAN. "Chile Update: Peace Committee Replaced."
       Christian Century 93 (April 7, 1976): 334-338.

3076   "Chile and the Church." America 129 (October 13, 1973): 258.

3077   "Chile Drops Subversion Charges, Frees Priests." Our Sunday
       Visitor 64 (January 11, 1976): 3.

3078   "Chile: The Heat Is On." Christianity Today 18 (January 18,
       1974): 46-47.

3079   "Chilean Bishops Condemn Junta." National Catholic Reporter
       10 (May 3, 1974): 1.

3080   "Chilean Marxist Retracts Attack on Church in Senate." Catho-
       lic Messenger 82 (July 16, 1964): 6.

3081   "Chile's New President Declares Attitude on Religion." Chris-
       tianity Today 15 (January 1, 1971): 44.

3082   "Church and State in Chile: Where Activist Clergymen Stand."
       U.S. News and World Report, January 13, 1975, p. 58.

3083   "Church vs. State." Newsweek, May 6, 1974, pp. 43-44.

3084   Conferencia Episcopal de Chile. Comité Permanente. Chile,
       voluntad der ser. Santiago, Chile: Ediciones Paulinas,
       1968. 51 pp.

3085   DAUBECHIES, HUBERT. "Obispos Chilenos: el difícil camino de
       la colegialidad." Mensaje 245 (December, 1975): 584-586.

Catholic Church and State

3086   FERRANDO, MIGUEL ANGEL. "The Church in Chile Under Allende."
        Tablet 225 (April 10, 1971): 364-366.

3087   La Iglesia y la junta militar de Chile: documentos. Buenos
        Aires: Tierra Nueva, 1975. 168 pp.

3088   "La Iglesia y los derechos humanos. Entrevista al cardenal
        Raúl Silva Henríquez. (Chile)." Actualidad Pastoral 8
        (1975): 156-157.

3089   LANGTON, KENNETH P., and RAPOPORT, RONALD. "Religion and
        Leftist Mobilization in Chile." Comparative Political
        Studies 9 (October, 1976): 277-308.

3090   MAC EOIN, GARY. "Chile's Silent Church." Commonweal 103
        (July 18, 1975): 267-270.

3091   MAUROVICH, F. "Churchmen Still Resist Chile Regime." National
        Catholic Reporter 11 (June 20, 1975): 17.

3092   MOREAU, RON. "Church vs. State." Newsweek, November 15,
        1976, p. 45.

3093   OVIEDO CAVADA, CARLOS. "Carácter de la separación entre
        Iglesia y Estado en Chile." FINIS TERRAE 3 (Winter, 1968):
        99-113.

3094   PIKE, FREDERICK B. "Church and State and Political Develop-
        ment in Chile." A Journal of Church and State 10 (Winter,
        1968): 99-113.

3095   _____. "Church and State in Peru and Chile Since 1840: A
        Study in Contrasts." American Historical Review 73 (October,
        1967): 30-50.

3096   PRENAFETA JENKIN, S. "Los primeros cien días de gobierno en
        Chile." Christus 37 (March, 1972): 43-46.

3097   QUIGLEY, THOMAS. "Cardinal and the Junta." Commonweal 100
        (May 24, 1974): 278-279.

3098   SANDERS, THOMAS G., and SMITH, BRIAN. The Chilean Catholic
        Church During the Allende and Pinochet Regimes. [n.p.]:
        American University Field Staff, 1976. 25 pp.

3099   SANTOS ASCARZA, JOSÉ M. "Chile: Iglesia y Estado ayer y hoy."
        Mensaje Iberoamericano 115 (1975): 12-15.

Chile

3100 SILVA HENRÍQUEZ, R. "The Chilean People in Defense of the Church." L'Osservatore Romano, February 6, 1975, pp. 8-10.

3101 _____. "Positions of the Church in Chile." L'Osservatore Romano, November 22, 1973, p. 2.

3102 "Society and Church in Latin America." IDOC-International 1 (April 4, 1979): 37-69.

3103 ZOTTELE, PEDRO. "Clergy-Vatican Tension." Christian Century 86 (August 27, 1969): 1120-1122.

CATHOLIC CLERGY

3104 CID, FRANCISCO J. "Cristianos, sacerdotes y política." Mensaje 198 (May, 1971): 174-175, 177-179.

3105 Conferencia Episcopal de Chile. Comité Permanente. La Iglesia 1976: orientaciones pastorales para Chile. Santiago, Chile: CENCOSEP, 1976. 24 pp.

3106 "Declaración de los obispos de Chile." Política y Espíritu 321 (May, 1971): 67-68.

3107 ERRÁZURIZ, JOSÉ. "Training Catholic Leaders in Chile." Catholic World 191 (June, 1960): 147-152.

3108 "Les evénéments du Chili." La Documentation Catholique 70 (October 21, 1973): 881.

3109 FONTAINE, PABLO. "Algunos aspectos de la Iglesia chilena hoy." Mensaje 204 (June, 1975): 246-251.

3110 _____. "Situación actual de la Iglesia chilena." Mensaje 201 (August, 1971): 367-372.

3111 GONZÁLEZ, CARLOS C. Sacerdotes para un tiempo nuevo. Santiago, Chile: Paulinas, 1970. 96 pp.

3112 "La Iglesia hoy: orientaciones pastorales para Chile." Mensaje 240 (July, 1975): 325-330.

3113 "La pastoral de la reconciliación en Chile: pastoral letter, April 24, 1974." Christus 39 (August, 1974): 51-53.

3114 POBLETE BARTH, RENATO. Crisis Sacerdotal. Santiago, Chile: Editorial del Pacífico, 1965. 205 pp.

Catholic Clergy

3115   "La réconciliation au Chili: déclaration de l'Assemblée
        Pléniére de l'Episcopat chilien, Punta de Tralca, avril
        1974." La Documentation Catholique 71 (June 16, 1974):
        561-564.

3116   "Sacerdotes chilenos a su pueblo. Santiago de Chile, abril de
        1972." IDS-Iglesia de Santiago 66 (May/June, 1972): 28-
        30.

3117   SANDERS, THOMAS. "The Chilean Episcopate: An Institution in
        Transition." Fieldstaff Reports: West South American
        Series. 15 (August, 1968): 30.

3118   VILLOT, CARDENAL. "Mensaje del Santo Padre al Episcopado de
        Chile, Punta de Tralca (Chile), 7 de abril de 1972." IDS-
        Iglesia de Santiago 66 (May/June, 1972): 30.

CHRISTIAN DEMOCRACY

3119   AMMON, ALF, and FROEHLING, HEINZ. Die Christliche Demokratie
        Chiles: die Spaltung der Christdemokratischen Partei 1969.
        Bonn: Neue Gesellschaft, 1971. 159 pp.

3120   ANGELL, ALAN. "Chile: From Christian Democracy to Marxism?"
        World Today 26 (November, 1970): 488-496.

3121   _____. "Chile: The Christian Democrats at Mid-Term." World
        Today 23 (October, 1967): 434-443.

3122   _____. "Christian Democracy in Chile." Current History 58
        (February, 1979): 79-84.

3123   _____. Politics and the Labor Movement in Chile. London:
        Oxford University Press, 1972. 289 pp., bibl.

3124   BARAT, JOSEPH R. "Christianity and Marxism in Chile." Chris-
        tian Century 89 (June 7, 1972): 653-656.

3125   BARAT, THOMAS. "Chile: New Road to a Socialist Society?"
        Cross Currents 21 (Summer, 1971): 340-351.

3126   BECKET, JAMES. "Chile's Mini-Revolution." Commonweal 87
        (December 29, 1967): 406-408.

3127   BOIZARD B., RICARDO. La democracia cristiana en Chile: un
        mundo que nace entre dos guerras. Santiago, Chile: Edi-
        torial Orbe, 1963. 336 pp.

Chile

Christian Democracy

3128   BONO, AGOSTINO. "Protest in Chile." Commonweal 103 (June 18, 1976): 390–391.

3129   BRESLIN, PATRICK. "Chile's Coup Devours Its Godparents." America 130 (April 27, 1974): 327–329.

3130   CASTILLO, FERNANDO. "Christians for Socialism in Chile." In Christianity and Socialism, edited by Johann-Baptist Metz, pp. 106–112. New York: Seabury Press, 1977.

3131   CASTILLO VELASCO, JAIME. Las fuentes de la democracia cristiana. Santiago, Chile: Editorial del Pacífico, 1963. 103 pp., bibl.

3132   CASTRO, FIDEL. "En la democracia cristiana hay verdaderos revolucionarios." Punto Final. Documentos. 37 (September, 1967): 2–32.

3133   CESARETTI, CLAUDIO. "Para ser felices, los demócrata cristianos chilenos necesitan definirse verdaderos revolucionarios." Il Tempo (December 15, 1965).

3134   "Chile: The Expanding Left: From Christian Democrats to Anarchic Urban Terrorists." Time, October 19, 1970, pp. 23–24.

3135   "Chile's Christian Democratic Party: Power, Factions, and Ideology." Review of Politics 31 (April, 1969): 147–171.

3136   "Christian Democracy in Latin America." America 115 (November, 19, 1966): 645.

3137   CONDAMINES, CHARLES. "La tragique marginalisation des chrétiens socialistes au Chili." Esprit 1 (April/May, 1977): 93–105.

3138   DEEDY, JOHN G. "Change in Chile." Commonweal 93 (February 26, 1971): 506.

3139   DREKONJA, GERHARD. "Das Experiment des Eduardo Frei. Die ideologische Gärung in Lateinamerikas 'Democracia Cristiana.'" Wort und Wahrheit 22 (1967): 697–712.

3140   FANSTEAD, DONAL. "Breakthrough in Chile." Commonweal 82 (April 9, 1965): 82–83.

3141   FRANCIS, M. "The Perils of Power: Christian Democrats in Chile." Ave Maria 108 (October 26, 1968): 13–15.

Christian Democracy

3142   FREI MONTALVA, EDUARDO. "The Aims of Christian Democracy."
        Commonweal 81 (October 9, 1964): 63-66.

3143   FUENTEALBA, RENAE. En esta hora histórica, la Democracia
        Cristiana es quien mejor interpreta los anhelos populares.
        Santiago, Chile: Editorial del Pacífico, 1963. 31 pp.

3144   FUENTES CASTELLANOS, RICARDO. "El Partido Demócrata Cristiano
        y el comunismo en Chile." Estudios Centroamericanos 17
        (May, 1962): 136-139.

3145   GOLDENBERG, BORIS. "Wo steht die lateinamerikanische Revolu-
        tion?" Merkur 25 (1971): 222-223.

3146   GRAYSON, GEORGE W. "Chile's Christian Democratic Party:
        Power, Reactions, and Ideology." Review of Politics 31
        (April, 1969): 147-171.

3147   _____. El Partido Democrata Cristiano chileno. Santiago,
        Chile: Editorial Francisco de Aguirre, 1968. 517 pp.,
        bibl.

3148   GRIGULEVICH, I. "U vlasti levye katoliki." Nauka i Religiia
        5 (December, 1964): 82-83.

3149   GROSS, LEONARD. The Last, Best Hope: Eduardo Frei and
        Chilean Democracy. New York: Random House, 1967. 240 pp.

3150   GUILISASTI TAGLE, SERGIO. Partidos políticos chilenos. San-
        tiago, Chile: Editorial Nacimiento, 1964. 363 pp., bibl.

3151   HAMBURG, ROGER P. "Soviet Foreign Policy: The Church, the
        Christian Democrats, and Chile." Journal of Inter-American
        Studies and World Affairs 11 (October, 1969): 605-615.

3152   ITURIOZ, J. "Triunfo a la democracia cristiana en Chile."
        Razon y Fe 170 (September/October, 1964): 242-244.

3153   KLEIN REIDEL, FEDERICO. Las nacionalizaciones y la democracia
        cristiana. Santiago, Chile: Prensa Latinoamericana, 1964.
        88 pp.

3154   MAC CORMACK, ARTHUR. "Christian Democracy in Latin America."
        Month 33 (May, 1965): 302-310.

3155   MILLAS, ORLANDO. "Christian Democratic Reformism: The Chilean
        Experiment." World Marxist Review 8 (November, 1965): 65-
        69.

3156   MITCHELL, THOMAS. "Where Does Chile Go from Here. Christian
        Democratic Party." National Review 17 (April 6, 1965):
        275-277.

3157   Movimiento 'Camilo Torres.' "Carta abierta a los camaradas
        demócratas cristianos y al pueblo de Chile." Cristianismo
        y Revolución 5 (November, 1967): 37-38.

3158   NOHLEN, DIETER. Chile: Das Sozialistische Experiment. Ham-
        burg: Hoffmann und Campe, 1973. 432 pp., bibl.

3159   OGELSBY, J. C. M. "Christian Democracy in Chile." Canadian
        Forum 45 (December, 1965): 204-205.

3160   OLAVARRÍA BRAVO, ARTURO. Chile bajo la democracia cristiana.
        Santiago, Chile: Editorial Nacimiento, 1966.

3161   Partido Demócrata Cristiano. Programa del Partido Demócrata
        Cristiano. Documentos de la primera convención nacional.
        Santiago, Chile: Editorial del Pacífico, 1961.

3162   PERCEVAL (pseud.). ¡Ganó Allende! Santiago, Chile: Nueva
        Aurora, 1964. 133 pp.

3163   PETER, R. "Taps for Christian Democrats?" National Reporter
        21 (July 15, 1969): 700.

3163A   RANSTEAD, DONALD D. "Breakthrough in Chile." Commonweal 82
        (April 9, 1965): 82-83.

3164   "Rising Force: Christian Democrats.." Time, September 18,
        1964, pp. 48.

3165   SHAULL, RICHARD. The Church and Revolutionary Change: Con-
        trasting Perspectives. New York: Office of Student of
        World Relations, 1966. 13 pp.

3166   SIGMUND, PAUL E. "Chile's Christian Democrats." America 117
        (November 18, 1967): 602-604.

3167   _____. "Christian Democracy in Chile." Journal of Interna-
        tional Affairs 21 (1966): 332-342.

3168   SILVA, SERGIO. "El modelo ideológico de la democracia cristiana
        chilena (1962-1969) comparado con el de la doctrina social
        de la iglesia chilena (1962-1963) y latinoamericana (en Mar
        de la Plata, 1966)." Pasos 63 (August 3, 1973): 1-5.

Christian Democracy

3169   TARASOV, K. "La oligarquía financiera chilena." Punto Final
       23 (February 30, 1967): 1-9.

3170   TEITELBOIM, VOLODIA. "El verdadero carácter de la democracia
       cristiana." Documentos Políticos 8 (January/February,
       1964): 55-60.

3171   VISKOVIC, SERGIO. Diálogo con la democracia cristiana. Val-
       paraíso: Instituto Popular Valparaíso, [n.d.]. 38 pp.

3172   VITALE, LUIS. Esencia y apariencia de la democracia cristiana.
       Santiago, Chile: Arancibia Hermanos, 1964. 161 pp., bibl.

3173   VON LAZAR, ARPAD, and QUIROS VARELA, LUIS. "Christian Demo-
       cracy: Lessons in the Politics of Reform Management."
       Inter-American Economic Affairs 21 (Spring, 1968): 51-72.

3174   WANDELL, R. "Chile: Christianity or Communism." Today's
       Family 39 (May, 1964): 37-44.

3175   WYLAND-SMITH, GILES. The Christian Democratic Party in Chile.
       Cuernavaca, México: Centro Intercultural de Documentación,
       1969.

3176   ZEITLIN, MAURICE, and PETRAS, JAMES. "The Working Class Vote
       in Chile: Christian Democracy Versus Marxism." In Workers
       and Managers in Latin America, edited by Stanley M. Davis
       and Louis Wolf Goodman, pp. 308. Lexington, Massachusetts:
       D. C. Heath, 1972.

3177   ZWIEFELHOFER, H. "Christen für den Sozialismus." Stimmen
       der Zeit 190 (August 6, 1972): 133-136.

COMMUNISM

3178   ERRÁZURIZ, JOSÉ. "Training Catholic Leaders in Chile."
       Catholic World 191 (June, 1960): 147-152.

3179   HALPERIN, ERNEST. Nationalism and Communism in Chile. Cam-
       bridge, Massachusetts: M. I. T. Press, 1965. 267 pp.,
       bibl.

3180   "Los partidos comunistas y la Iglesia." Mensaje 11 (August,
       1962): 367-370.

3181   PERCEVAL, pseud. ¡Ganó Allende! Santiago, Chile: Nueva
       Aurora, 1964. 133 pp.

3182   SISTER MARY PATRICE. "How Sisters Warm Up in Chile." World-
        mission 15 (Summer, 1964): 87-94.

DOCUMENTS

3183   Bishops of Chile. "Lead Social Reforms, Bishops Urge Chileans:
        Excerpts from Joint Pastoral Letter." Catholic Messenger
        80 (October 4, 1962): 1.

3184   CAMUS, CARLOS. "We Cannot Remain Silent." IDOC-International
        64 (August, 1974): 124.

3185   "Canadian Missionaries Indignant/Manifesto." IDOC-Interna-
        tional 64 (August, 1974): 124.

3186   "Catholics and Socialism in Chile." Catholic Mind 70 (October,
        1972): 17-20.

3187   "Chilean Jesuits." IDOC-International 32 (September 25,
        1971): 27-30.

3188   "The Christian Loves and Acts: Chilean Bishop's Pastoral."
        Ave Maria 96 (October 20, 1962): 16.

3189   Conferencia Episcopal Chilena. "Evangelio y Paz." Ateismo e
        Diálogo 3 (September, 1976): 114-128.

3190   "Declaration of the Chilean Episcopate, 4th October, 1968."
        IDOC-International 1 (April 4, 1970): 56-58.

3191   "Ecumenical Aid for Victims Through the CCP.2" IDOC-Inter-
        national 64 (August, 1974): 125.

3192   "L'Eglise, la violence et la miséricorde: déclaration de
        l'archevêché, de Santiago de Chili." La Documentation
        Catholique 72 (December 21, 1975): 1074.

3193   Episcopado de Chile. Documentos del episcopado, 1970-1973.
        Santiago, Chile: Mundo, 1974. 240 pp.

3194   _____. "La Iglesia y el problema del campesino chileno:
        pastoral colectiva del...." Mensaje 11 (May, 1962):

3195   Evangelio, política y socialismos. Santiago, Chile: Confer-
        encia Episcopal de Chile, 1971. 91 pp.

Documents

3196   "Evangelio y paz: documento de trabajo del Comité Permanente
       del Episcopado de Chile."   Catequesis Latinoamericana 8
       (1976):   143-166.

3197   "Evangile et paix: document de travail du Comité Permanent
       de l'Episcopat du Chili."   La Documentation Catholique 72
       (November 2, 1975):   917-930.

3198   "Evangile, politique et socialismes: un document de travail
       de la conférence episcopale du Chili."   La Documentation
       Catholique 68 (September 19, 1971):   823-833.

3199   La Iglesia y la Junta Militar de Chile: Documentos.   Buenos
       Aires: Tierra Nueva, 1975.   168 pp.

3200   "An Interchurch Group, Reports on Torture."   IDOC-International
       64 (August, 1974):   126-129.

3201   "Manifiesto de los Camilos."   Cristianismo y Revolución 15
       (May, 1969):   12-13.

3202   "Manifiesto del 3 de marzo de 1972 publicado en Cuba por un
       grupo de sacerdotes y aspirantes al sacerdocio de Chile."
       Política y Espíritu 331 (April, 1972):   96.

3203   Militantes Católicos de Izquierda Cristiana de Chile.   "Mensaje
       al Sínodo Mundial de Obispos, 1974."   Cuadernos de Cris-
       tianismo y Sociedad 2 (1975):   16-20.

3204   Missioners' Committee on International Awareness.   "U.S. In-
       vestment in Chile: An Appraisal."   IDOC-International 49
       (December, 1972):   1-6.

3205   Obispos de Chile.   "Carta pública a un grupo de sacerdotes y
       aspirantes al sacerdocio, sobre 'sacerdocio y compromiso
       político,' Punta de Tralca, 11 de abril de 1972."   IDS-
       Iglesia de Santiago 66 (May/June, 1972):   6.

3206   PETRAS, JAMES.   "Chile."   The New Left Review   (March/April,
       1969):   54-59.

3207   PUÑERA CARVALLO, B., Bp.   "Ou em est l'Eglise du Chili en
       1977:   rapport."   La Documentation Catholique 74 (July 3,
       1977):   639-641.

3208   NO ENTRY

Chile

3209 "La réconciliation au Chili: déclaration de l'Assemblée
Pléniere de l'Episcopat chilien, Punta de Tralca, avril
1974." La Documentation Catholique 71 (June 16, 1974):
561-564.

3210 "Reconciliation in Chile." Catholic Mind 72 (September, 1974):
60-64.

3211 Sacerdotes Chilenos. "La tierra para los campesinos." Mensaje
10 (August, 1961): 361-362.

3211A SILVA HENRÍQUEZ, R. "Chilean Bishops Speak Out: The Easter
Statement." IDOC-International 64 (August, 1974): 123-
124.

3212 "Society and Church in Latin America." IDOC-International 1
(April 4, 1970): 37-69.

3213 TOMIC ROMERO, DRAGOMIR. Igualdad de oportunidades para todos
los niños chilenos. Santiago, Chile: Diario de Sesiones
del Senado, 1962. 16 pp.

3214 "U.S. Bishops Charge Junta." IDOC-International 64 (August,
1974): 124.

ECONOMIC DEVELOPMENT

3215 "Chile: Political and Socio-Economic Structures and the
Church in the Service of the Country." Pro Mundi Vita 49
(1974): 3-40.

3216 DORFMAN, ARIEL. "Chile: la resistencia cultural al imperialismo." Casa de las Américas 98 (September/October, 1976):
3-11.

3217 FRANK, ANDRE GUNDER. Capitalism and Underdevelopment in Latin
America. New York: Monthly Review, 1967. 289 pp., bibl.

3218 FREI MONTALVA, EDUARDO. Chile tiene un destino: pasado y
presente de una crisis. Santiago, Chile: Imprenta Raposo,
1962.

3219 HAREIDE, DAG, ed. Chile: Pa Vej Til Sosialismen. Oslo:
Pax, 1973. 207 pp.

3220 Missioners' Committee on International Awareness. "U.S. In-
vestment in Chile: An Appraisal." IDOC-International 49
December, 1972.

Education

EDUCATION

3221   BULNES A., JOSÉ, comp. Valparaíso: crisis de la Universidad
        Católica, junio-agosto 1967; documentos oficiales y re-
        acciones de prensa. Cuernavaca, México: Centro Intercul-
        tural de Documentación, 1968.

3222   "Carta abierta a todos los obispos de Chile, la Iglesia joven
        en marcha." Carta de ISAL 2 (July, 1969): 3.

HUMANISM

3223   BARRÍA SERÓN, JORGE I. El movimiento obrero en Chile: Sín-
        tesis histórica-social. Santiago, Chile: Universidad
        Técnica del Estado, 1971. 166 pp.

3224   Evangelio, política y socialismos. Santiago, Chile: Confer-
        encia Episcopal de Chile, 1971. 91 pp.

3225   LANDSBERGER, HENRY A. "Chile: A Vineyard Workers' Strike--A
        Case Study of the Relationship Between Church, Intellectuals,
        and Peasants." In Latin America Peasant Movements, edited
        by Henry Landsberger, pp. 210-273. New York: Cornell
        University Press, 1969.

3226   LARRAÍN ERRÁZURIZ, MANUEL. El humanismo de Manuel Larraín.
        Santiago, Chile: Instituto Chileno de Estudios Humanísticos,
        1975. 104 pp.

LABOR AND LABORING CLASSES

3227   ASSMAN, HUGO. El aporte cristiano al proceso de liberación
        de América Latina. Talca, Chile: Fundación Obispo Manuel
        Larraín, 1971. 12 pp.

3228   LARRAÑAGA DE ASPEITÍA, JESÚS. "Sacerdotes obreros en Chile."
        Mensaje 15 (June, 1966): 258-260.

3229   MALABRE, ALFRED L. "South America's Changing Church: Roman
        Catholicism is a Force for Some Surprising Liberalism in
        Latin Lands." Wall Street Journal 169 (April 26, 1967):
        16.

3230   "La semana política: solidaridad y liberación." Iglesia de
        Santiago (January/February, 1978): 29.

MARXISM

3231   BARNDT, JOSEPH R. "Christianity and Marxism in Chile."
       Christian Century 89 (June 7, 1972): 653-656.

3232   BERRYMAN, PHILLIP E. "Christian Delegates, Marxist Language."
       Commonweal 96 (June 16, 1972): 324-325.

3233   Chile: The Allende Years, the Coup, Under the Junta. New
       York: IDOC-North America, 1973. 78 pp.

3234   "Chilean Junta President Says Church Not Marxist." National
       Catholic Reporter 10 (July 5, 1974): 3.

3235   "Los cristianos en la vía socialista chilena." Víspera 23
       (April, 1971): 67-87.

3236   OSSA, MANUEL. "Cristianos y marxistas marchan juntos." Men-
       saje 16 (August, 1967): 368-370.

3237   PIÑERA, BERNARDINO. "La Iglesia chilena en medio de las
       corrientes ideológicas actuales: el marxismo." Pastoral
       Popular 67 (January/February, 1962): 5-19.

NATIONALISM

3238   HALPERIN, ERNEST. Nationalism and Communism in Chile. Cam-
       bridge, Massachusetts: M.I.T. Press, 1965. 267 pp., bibl.

3239   DOMÍNGUEZ C., OSCAR. El campesino chileno y la acción católica
       rural. Bogotá: Oficina Internacional de Investigaciones
       Sociales de FERES, 1961. 88 pp.

3240   EDWARDS PINTO, VICENTE. "A Pastor in Chile." Worldmission 14
       (Summer, 1963): 44-48.

3241   La Iglesia y el problema del campesinado. Santiago, Chile:
       Secretariado General del Epsicopado de Chile, 1962. 36 pp.

3242   LANDSBERGER, HENRY A., and CANITROT M., FERNANDO. Iglesia,
       intelectuales y campesinos: la huelga campesina de Molina.
       Santiago, Chile: Ediciones del Pacífico, 1967. 358 pp.

3243   Obispos de Los Angeles, Chillan y Talca. Carta a los cam-
       pesinos cristianos. Santiago, Chile: Mundo, 1975. 12 pp.

Nationalism

3244   Pastoral Colectiva del Episcopado de Chile. La Iglesia y el
        problema del campesinado chileno. Santiago, Chile: Edi-
        torial Universidad Católica, 1962. 37 pp.

POLITICS

3245   AMOR DE LA PATRIA, JOSÉ. Catecismo político cristiano.
        Buenos Aires: Francisco de Aguirre, 1969. 93 pp.

3246   ARIAS CALDERÓN, RICARDO. "Hacia una perspectiva cristiana de
        la política." Mensaje 159 (June, 1967): 217-227.

3247   BIRNS, LAWRENCE, comp. The End of Chilean Democracy. New
        York: Seabury Press, 1974. 219 pp.

3248   BONO, AGOSTINO. "Protest in Chile." Commonweal 103 (June 18,
        1976): 390-391.

3249   "Chile: Political and Socio-Economic Structures and the
        Church in the Service of the Country." Pro Mundi Vita 49
        (1974): 3-40.

3250   "Chile Prelate: Suppression Bound to Fall." National Catholic
        Reporter 10 (October 4, 1974): 18.

3251   Chile: The Allende Years, the Coup, Under the Junta. New
        York: IDOC-North America, 1973. 78 pp.

3252   "Chile: The Expanding Left: From Christian Democrats to
        Anarchic Urban Terrorists." Time, October 19, 1970, pp.
        23-24.

3253   Chile: Under Military Rule. New York: IDOC-North America,
        1974. 164 pp., bibl.

3254   CID, FRANCISCO J. "Cristianos, sacerdotes y política."
        Mensaje 148 (May, 1971): 174-175, 177-179.

3255   "Los cristianos en la vía socialista chilena." Víspera 23
        (April, 1971): 67-87.

3256   FONTAINE, PABLO. "Situación actual de la Iglesia chilena."
        Mensaje 201 (August, 1971): 367-372.

3257   GUILISASTI TAGLE, SERGIO. Partidos políticos chilenos.
        Santiago, Chile: Editorial Nacimiento, 1964. 363 pp.,
        bibl.

3258   HALPERIN, ERNEST. The Christian Democratic Alternative in
        Chile. Cambridge, Massachusetts: Massachusetts Institute
        of Technology, 1964. 27 pp.

3259   HARIEDE, DAG, ed. Chile: Pa Vei Til Sosilismen. Oslo:
        Pax, 1973. 207 pp.

3260   HENRY, JOHN F. "Chile's Agony." America 103 (July 2, 1960):
        408.

3261   JIMÉNEZ, JULIO. "Sobre Iglesia y política en la historia
        chilena." Teología y Vida 304 (1971): 218-254.

3262   MILLAS, ORLANDO. Los comunistas, los católicos y la libertad.
        Santiago, Chile: Editorial Austral, 1964.

3263   Obispos de Chile; "Carta pública a un grupo de sacerdotes y
        aspirantes al sacerdocio sobre 'sacerdocio y compromiso
        político,' Punta de Tralca, 11 de abril de 1972." Iglesia
        de Santiago 66 (May/June, 1972): 6.

3264   Los obispos de Chile hablan: el deber social y el político
        en la hora presente. Santiago, Chile: Secretariado General
        del Epsicopado de Chile, 1964. 39 pp.

3265   O'SHAUGHNESSY, H. "Chile's Political Future." Tablet 218
        (June 27, 1964): 714-715.

3266   "Padre Arrupe: en torno a la misión política y a los jesuitas."
        Iglesia de Santiago 66 (May/June, 1972): 24-28.

3267   Partido Demócrata Cristiano. "La revolución, democracia y
        el movimiento popular." Boletín Informativo Demócrata
        Cristiano (March, 1963): 6.

3268   PAYRO, ANA LÍA. Chile: cambio de gobierno o toma del poder?
        México: Editorial Extemporáneos, 1971. 203 pp., bibl.

3269   PETRAS, JAMES. Politics and Social Forces in Chilean Develop-
        ment. Berkeley: University of California Press, 1969.
        377 pp., bibl.

3270   Por qué triunfará Frei. Santiago, Chile: Imprenta Fantasía,
        1964. 47 pp.

3271   RANSTEAD, DONALD D. "Chile Turns Left." Commonweal 80 (Sep-
        tember 4, 1964): 594-596.

Politics

3272   RENTERÍA URALDE, JULIÁN, ed. La Iglesia y la política. San-
       tiago, Chile: Ediciones Paulinas, 1963. 172 pp.

3273   SEGURA, MANUEL. "La política chilena y la provincia."
       Noticias Jesuitas-Chile (March/April 1, 1972): 10-11.

3274   SILVA HENRÍQUEZ, R. "L'attitude de l'Eglise du Chili devant
       la situation politique." La Documentation Catholique 70
       (December 2, 1973): 1021-1022.

3275   URZUA VALENZUELA, GERMAN. Los partidos políticos chilenos,
       las fuerzas políticas. Santiago, Chile: Editorial Jurídica
       de Chile, 1968. 222 pp.

3276   VALENZUELO, ARTURO, and VALENZUELO, J. SAMUEL. Chile: Poli-
       tics and Society. New Brunswick, New Jersey: Transaction
       Books, 1976. 399 pp., bibl.

REFERENCE

3277   Centro de Investigaciones Sociológico-Religiosas. Anuario de
       la Iglesia en Chile: 1962-1963. Santiago, Chile: Oficina
       de Sociología Religiosa del Episcopado, 1962. 316 pp.

REVOLUTION

3278   BARNDT, JOSEPH R. "Revolutionary Christians Confer in Santi-
       ago." Christian Century 89 (June 14-21, 1971): 691-695.

3279   "Los Camilos de Chile." Cristianismo y Revolución 15 (May,
       1969): 27-33.

3280   "Chile: declaración de Navidad del Movimiento Camilo Torres."
       Cristianismo y Revolución 6-7 (April, 1968): 36.

3281   "Manifiesto de los Camilos." Cristianismo y Revolución 15
       (May, 1969): 12-13.

3282   "Revolution in Four Steps." America 114 (February 12, 1966):
       214-215.

SOCIALISM

3283   "Arzobispado no autoriza reunión de 'Cristianos por el Social-
       ismo." 18 de abril de 1972." Iglesia de Santiago 66 (May/
       June, 1972): 9.

3284   BARAT, THOMAS. "Chile: New Road to a Socialist Society?"
       Cross Currents 21 (Summer, 1971): 340-351.

3285   Centro de Estudios para el Desarrollo e Integración de América
       Latina. "Iglesia chilena y 'Cristianos por el Socialismo.'
       Crónica IV." Tierra Nueva 4 (1975): 38-58.

3286   "Christians for Socialism: What the Bishops of Chile Think."
       Christ to the World 20 (1975): 124-131, 212-213.

3287   Conferencia Episcopal de Chile. Evangelio, política y social-
       ismo: documento de trabajo. Santiago, Chile: Secretariado
       del CECH, 1971. 91 pp.

3288   COSTE, RENÉ. "Les chrétiens et le socialisme. A propos de la
       reunión des 'Chrétiens pour le Socialisme' á Santiago du
       Chili." Pasos 12 (July 31, 1972): 2.

3289   DONOSO LOERO, TERESA. Historia de los Cristianos por Social-
       ismo en Chile. Santiago, Chile: Vaitea, 1976. 209 pp.

3290   FRANÇOU, FRANÇOIS. Le Chili, le socialisme et l'Eglise.
       Paris: France-Empire, 1976. 268 pp., bibl.

3291   FREI MONTALVA, EDUARDO. El social cristianismo: una fórmula
       eficaz y constructiva de gobierno. Santiago, Chile: Radio
       Cooperativa Vitalicia, 1951.

3292   GIRARDI, GIULIO. "Après la conférence de Santiago du Chili.
       Des chrétiens qui se veulent socialistes." Informations
       Catholiques Internationales 409 (June, 1972): 15-18.

3293   "Jerarquías chilena y mexicana, ante el primer encuentro
       latinoamericano de Cristianos por el Socialismo." Christus
       37 (September, 1972): 41-50.

3294   "Mensaje del Presidente de la República de Chile, Dr. Salvador
       Allende, a los delegados al Primer Encuentro Latinoamericano
       de 'Cristianos por el Socialismo,' Santiago, 28 de abril
       de 1972." IDS-Iglesia de Santiago 66 (May/June, 1972):
       9-10.

3295   MORRIS, DAVID J. We Must Make Haste--Slowly: The Process of
       Revolution in Chile. New York: Random House, 1973. 308
       pp., bibl.

3296   "Reunión del Cardenal Silva con delegados al Encuentro 'Cris-
       tianos por el Socialismo'." IDS-Iglesia de Santiago 66
       (May/June, 1972): 11-12.

Socialism

3297 SILVA SOLAR, JULIO. "Pluralidad de fuerzas e ideologías en
     la construcción del socialismo en Chile. Coloboración de
     marxistas y cristianos." In Chile: búsqueda de un nuevo
     socialismo, edited by Alejandro Fozley et al., pp. 206-231.
     Santiago, Chile: Nueva Universidad, 1971.

3298 TORRES RESTREPO, CAMILO. "Chile: declaración de Navidad del
     Movimiento Camilo Torres." Cristianismo y Revolución 6-7
     (April, 1968): 36.

3299 YRARRÁZAVAL, DIEGO. "¿Qué hacer? Cristianos en el proceso
     socialista." Pasos 37 (December 2, 1973): 1-23.

3300 ZOTTELE, PEDRO. "Christian Socialists Meet in Chile."
     Christian Century 90 (February 21, 1973): 242.

3301 ZWIEFELHOFER, H. "Christen für den Sozialismus." Stimmen
     der Zeit 190 (August 6, 1972): 133-136.

VIOLENCE

3302 "Amor cristiano, violencia y asesinato." Mensaje 200 (July,
     1971): 261-263.

3303 "Catholics Arrested, Raided During Chile Coup." National
     Catholic Reporter 9 (October 5, 1973): 1.

3304 "Chile Cardinal Reports Threats Against His Life." National
     Catholic Reporter 10 (April 26, 1974): 2.

3305 DOWDEN, R. "Chile: Tale of Prayer, Torture Told." National
     Catholic Reporter 12 (January 16, 1976): 1-2.

3306 "L'Eglise, la violence et la miséricorde: déclaration de
     l'archevêché, de Santiago du Chili." La Documentation
     Catholique 72 (December 21, 1975): 1074.

3307 Episcopado de Chile. Comité Permanente. "Evangelio y paz."
     Mensaje 24 (October, 1975): 462-473.

VIII Colombia

GENERAL

3308 ALZATE R., MANUEL. Libertad religiosa en Colombia. Cali:
Pacífico, 1969. 122 pp.

3309 _____. Plataforma conciliar. Cali: Pacífico, 1968. 80 pp.

3310 BECKER, G. "Kolumbien." Stimmen der Zeit 195 (March, 1977):
169-178.

3311 BECKMAN, JOSEPH F. "If Your Parish Were in South America."
Catholic Digest 39 (September, 1975): 27-33.

3312 BORRAT, HÉCTOR. "El gran impulso." Víspera 2 (October, 1968):
3-5.

3313 "Colombian Bishops Have Criticism of Radicals." Our Sunday
Visitor 65 (January 2, 1977): 2.

3314 "Colombian Priests Protest: Against Closing Down of Catholic
Newspapers." Tablet 220 (October 29, 1966): 1229.

3315 "Colombie: réactions a la déclaration des Evêques. Des
groupes chrétiens de Bogotá s'adressant a l'opinion pub-
lique, Bogotá le 10 Decembre 1976." DIAL 351 (January 20,
1977): 3.

3316 Eveques Colobiens. "Synthèse du document des evêques colombiens
sur identité chrétienne dans l'action pour la justice."
DIAL 354 (February 3, 1977): 6.

3317 FALS BORDA, ORLANDO. Subversion and Social Change in Colombia.
New York: Columbia University Press, 1969. 238 pp., bibl.

3318 GILLY, ADOLOFO. "Bogotá: el programa del cura Camilo."
Marcha 27 (July 2, 1965): 23.

General

3319   HADDOX, BENJAMIN EDWARD. Sociedad y religión en Colombia:
        estudio de las instituciones religiosas colombianas.
        Bogotá: Ediciones Tercer Mundo y Facultad de Sociología,
        Universidad Nacional, 1965. 180 pp.

3320   HAVENS, A. EUGENE. Támesis: estructura y cambio: estudio
        de una comunidad antioqueña. Bogotá: Ediciones Tercer
        Mundo y Facultad de Sociología, Universidad Nacional, 1966.
        384 pp., bibl.

3321   "Kidnapping by Canon Law." Christian Century 77 (June 29,
        1969): 767.

3322   LOETSCHER, HUGO. "Die Kirche spricht verschieden Katholich.
        Kolumbien--noch ein 'El Dorado,'" Weltwoche 35 (1967):
        15-17.

3323   MEJIA, JORGE. "El pequeño concilio de Medellín." Criterio
        41 (September 15, 1968): 651-653; 686-689.

3324   PARRA SANDOVAL, RODRIGO. Las actitudes de los seminaristas.
        Bogotá: Facultad de Sociología, Universidad Nacional, 1964.
        60 pp., bibl.

3325   SCHOULULTZ, LARS. "Reform and Reaction in the Colombian
        Catholic Church." The Americas 30 (October, 1973): 229-
        250.

3326   TORRES RESTREPO, CAMILO. Camilo Torres (1956-1966). Cuerna-
        vaca, México: Centro Intercultural de Documentación, 1966.
        377 pp., bibl.

3327   _____. "Carta latinoamericana." Cristianismo Social 74 (Sep-
        tember/October): 549-551.

3328   _____. Escrits et paroles. Paris: Editions di Seuil, 1968.
        319 pp.

3329   _____. "Encruzilhadas da Igreja na América Latina (duas con-
        ferencias do padre)." Paz e Terra 2 (April, 1968): 117-
        137.

3330   _____. La proletarización de Bogotá, ensayo de metodología
        estadística. Bogotá: Universidad Nacional de Colombia,
        1961. 42 pp.

3331   _____. "Mensaje a los desocupados." Cristianismo y Revolución
        4 (March, 1967): 33.

Catholic Church and Social Change

3332 _____. "Mensaje a los estudiantes." Cristianismo y Revolución
2-3 (October/November, 1966): 19.

3333 _____. "O caso de padre...." Paz e Terra 1 (July, 1968):
254-263.

3334 VARGAS CELIS, JAIME. "Paulo VI en Bogotá: mensaje signos del
tiempo." Mensaje 17 (October, 1968): 493-495.

3335 VERSTRAELEN, F. J. "Church and Society in Conflict. Manipu-
lation and Movement in Colombia." Exchange 15 (December,
1976): 1-27.

3336 ZEA, VIRGILIO. "¿Es posible institucionalizar a Colombia?"
Revista Javeriana 428 (September, 1976): 23-30.

AGRARIAN REFORM

3337 BETANCUR, BELISARIO. El rostro anhelante: imágen del cambio
social en Colombia. Bogotá: Editorial Colombiana, 1966.
84 pp.

3338 DUFF, ERNEST A. "Agrarian Reform in Colombian Problems of
Social Reform." Journal of Inter-American Studies and
World Affairs 8 (January, 1966): 75-88.

3339 PEREZ RAMIREZ, GUSTAVO. El campesinado colombiano, un problema
de estructura. Bogotá: Editorial Iqueima, 1959. 230 pp.,
bibl.

3340 "La plataforma del Frente Unido." Frente Unido 1 (August 26,
1965): 4-6.

CATHOLIC CHURCH AND SOCIAL CHANGE

3341 "The Bishops of Colombia for the Defense of Life." L'Osservatore Romano, April 8, 1976, p. 8.

3342 "Carta de Colombia." Cristianismo y Revolución 8 (July, 1968):
24-25.

3343 Centro de Investigación y Acción Social. Socialismo y cristianismo. Bogotá: Centro de Investigación y Acción Social
and Instituto de Doctrina y Estudios Sociales, 1971. 48 pp.

Catholic Church and Social Change

3344   Centro de Investigación y Educación Popular. ¿Iglesia en
        conflicto? Bogotá: Centro de Investigación y Educación
        Popular, 1976. 133 pp.

3345   CHIAPPE, C., and URIBE, J. Iglesia y aspiraciones del pueblo
        colombiano. Bogotá: Centro de Investigación y Acción
        Social and Instituto de Doctrina y Estudios Sociales, 1971.
        37 pp.

3346   "Colombian Bishops Make Plea for Intensified Social Action."
        Catholic Messenger 81 (March 7, 1963): 3.

3347   CONCHA, LUIS. El derecho de propiedad. Bogotá: Editorial
        Lume Christi, 1965. 2 pp.

3348   FALS BORDA, ORLANDO. Subversion and Social Change in Colombia.
        New York: Columbia University Press, 1969. 238 pp., bibl.

3349   FUNK, RICHARD HARRIES. Camilo Torres Restrepo and the Chris-
        tian Left in the Tradition of Colombian Church-State Rela-
        tions. [n.p.], 1972. 471 pp.

3350   GALILEA, SEGUNDO. A los pobres ¿se les anuncia el evangelio?
        Bogotá: Consejo Episcopal Latinoamericano, [n.d.]. 38 pp.

3351   GUTIÉRREZ, GUSTAVO MERINO. "De la Iglesia colonial a Medellín."
        Víspera 16 (April, 1970): 3-8.

3352   HADDOX, BENJAMIN EDWARD. Sociedad y religión en Colombia:
        estudios de las instituciones religiosas colombianas.
        Bogotá: Ediciones Tercer Mundo y Facultad de Sociología,
        Universidad Nacional, 1965. 180 pp.

3353   JIMÉNEZ CADENA, GUSTAVO. The Role of the Rural Parish Priest
        as an Agent of Social Change in Central Colombia. Madison:
        University of Wisconsin, 1965. 235 pp.

3354   _____. Sacerdote y cambio social. Bogotá: Ediciones Tercer
        Mundo, 1967. 296 pp.

3355   MALDONADO PIEDRAHITA, RAFAEL. Conversaciones con un sacerdote
        colombiano: puntos de choque con la Iglesia. Bogotá:
        Antares, 1957. 102 pp.

3356   PARRA SANDOVAL, RODRIGO. Las actitudes de los seminaristas.
        Bogotá: Facultad de Sociología, Universidad Nacional de
        Colombia, 1964. 60 pp.

Colombia

3357   PÉREZ RAMIREZ, GUSTAVO, and WUST, ISSAC. La Iglesia en
       Colombia, estructuras eclesiásticas. Bogotá: Oficina
       Internacional de Investigaciones Sociales de FERES, 1961.
       195 pp.

3358   "Pills from the Bishops." Newsweek, July 30, 1973, pp. 40-41.

3359   PLOWMAN, EDWARD E. "Spiritual Boom in Bogota." Christianity
       Today 20 (April 9, 1976): 41-43.

3360   RESTREPO, GUILLERMO BOTERO. Cartas de un vicario. Cali:
       Editora Feriva, 1968. 342 pp.

3361   SCHWAN, HUBERT, and UGALDE, ANTONIO. "Orientations of the
       Bishops of Colombia Toward Social Development, 1930-1970."
       Church and State 16 (Autumn, 1974): 473-492.

3362   TORRES RESTREPO, CAMILO. Camilo, el cura revolucionario: sus
       obras. Buenos Aires: Ediciones Cristianismo y Revolución,
       1968. 313 pp.

3363   _____. Camilo Torres: biografía, plataforma, mensajes.
       Medellín: Ediciones Carpel-Antorcha, 1966. 104 pp.

3364   _____. Camilo Torres: His Life and His Message. The Text
       of His Original Platform and All His Messages to the Colom-
       bian People. Springfield, Illinois: Templegate Publishers,
       1968. 128 pp.

3365   _____. Con las armas en la mano. México: Editorial Diógenes,
       1971. 183 pp.

3366   _____. Cristianismo y revolución. México: Ediciones Era,
       1970. 611 pp.

CATHOLIC CHURCH AND STATE

3367   "Banned Colombian Catholic Journal Folds." Christian Century
       87 (April 29, 1970): 527.

3368   BLISS, SHEPHERD, and HOLSTEYN, ENRIQUE. "Colombia's Church-
       State Rite Denounced by Catholic Churchmen." Christian
       Century 88 (October 6, 1971): 1178-1179.

3369   CASTILLO CARDENAS, GONZALO. The Colombian Concordat in the
       Light of Recent Trends in Catholic Thought Concerning
       Church-State Relations and Religious Liberty. Cuernavaca,
       México: Centro Intercultural de Documentación, 1968.

Catholic Church and State

3370   Centro de Investigación y Educación Popular. Iglesia en
           conflicto. Bogotá: Centro de Investigación y Educación
           Popular, 1976. 133 pp.

3371   "Conflict in Colombia." America 134 (June 19, 1976): 528.

3372   DAILEY, SUZANNE. "Religious Aspects of Colombia's 'La Vio-
           lencia': Explanations and Implications." Journal of
           Church and State 15 (Autumn, 1973): 381-405.

3373   DEEDY, JOHN G. "Angelic Rhetoric: Reactions to Pastrana's
           Statement." Commonweal 95 (November 5, 1971): 122.

3374   DOERR, EDD. "Church, State, and Freedom in Colombia." Church
           and State 20 (December, 1967): 30-32.

3375   LEVINE, DANIEL H., and WILDE, ALEXANDER W. "The Catholic
           Church, 'Politics,' and Violence. The Colombian Case."
           The Review of Politics 2 (April, 1977): 220-249.

3376   LÓPEZ, FRANCISCO. Proceso al poder religioso en Colombia.
           Bogotá: Ediciones Hispana, 1968. 245 pp., bibl.

3377   "Religious Freedom in Colombia." America 115 (July 9, 1966):
           22.

CATHOLIC CLERGY

3378   GRENIER, JOSÉ ENRIQUE. "Los curas, la política y Cristo."
           In Los universitarios colombianos frente a Cristo, edited
           by José Enrique Grenier, pp. 170-176. Bogotá: Centro de
           Investigación y Acción Social, 1972.

3379   _____. "La imagen de Cristo." In Los universitarios colom-
           bianos frente a Cristo, edited by José Enrique Grenier,
           pp. 32-43. Bogotá: Centro de Investigación y Acción
           Social, 1972.

3380   _____. "Teología comprometida: un método para esta teología;
           hacia una teología colombiana; nuestro Cristo colombiano."
           In Los universitarios colombianos frente e Cristo, edited
           by José Enrique Grenier, pp. 294. Bogotá: Centro de In-
           vestigación y Acción Social, 1972.

3381   MEJÍA ESCOBAR, JESÚS. Obispos antiqueños. Medellín: Edi-
           torial Granamerica, 1971. 176 pp.

3382   PÉREZ RAMÍREZ, GUSTAVO. El problema sacerdotal en Colombia.
       Bogotá: Oficina Internacional de Investigaciones Sociales
       de FERES, 1962. 176 pp.

3383   Social-Activist Priests: Colombia, Argentina. Washington,
       D.C.: Division for Latin America--United Stated Catholic
       Conference, [n.d.]. 70 pp.

3384   TORRES, J. "Colombian Quandary: Irremovable Pastor, Irre-
       sistible Bishop Take Insoluble Case to Infallible Rome."
       National Catholic Reporter 3 (February 15, 1967): 2.

CHRISTIAN DEMOCRACY

3385   CASTILLO VELASCO, JAIME. Las fuentes de la democracia cris-
       tiana. Santiago, Chile: Editorial del Pacífico, 1966.
       46 pp.

3386   JARAMILLO, FRANCISCO DE PAULA. La democracia cristiana. Una
       nueva perspectiva para Colombia. Bogotá: Ediciones del
       Caribe, 1962. 121 pp.

3387   PLÁ RODRIGUEZ, AMÉRICO. Los principios de la democracia
       cristiana. Bogotá: Ediciones del Caribe, 1962. 99 pp.,
       bibl.

COMMUNISM

3388   CONCHA, LUIS. Carta pastoral de su excelencia reverendisima...
       sobre el comunismo. Bogotá: Editora Lumen Christi, [n.d.].
       7 pp.

3389   ORDUZ, JULIO CESAR. ¿El comunismo es verídico y por tanto
       inevitable? Bogotá: Ediciones Paulinas, 1962. 33 pp.

3390   VEGA, GUILLERMO, and BETANCOURT, OCTAVIO. Brillante camino.
       Medellín: Editorial Impresos Jiménez, 1970. 208 pp.

DOCUMENTS

3391   Conferencia Episcopal Colombiana. Identidad cristiana en la
       acción por la justicia. Bogotá: Secretariado Permanente
       del Episcopado Colombiano, 1976. 73 pp.

3392   _____. La Iglesia ante el cambio. Bogotá: Secretariado
       Permanente del Episcopado Colombiano, 1969. 160 pp.

Documents

3393   _____. La justicia en el mundo. Textos sinodales: aportes
        de la Igelsia colombiana. Bogotá: Secretariado Permanente
        del Episcopado Colombiana, 1972. 157 pp.

3394   _____. (XXVII Asamblea Plenaria). Informe sobre el esquema
        sinodal: 'la justicia en el mundo.' Bogotá: Comisión
        Teológica, 1971. 12 pp.

3395   Conferencia General del Episcopado Colombiano. "Colombia:
        carta colectiva del episcopado sobre la situación social."
        Informaciones Católicas Internacionales 245-256 (August,
        1965): 8-9.

3396   Episcopado Colombiano. "De las iglesias particulares: en
        Colombia, el episcopado impulsa a la Iglesia en un gran
        esfuerzo de evangelización." Información Católica Inter-
        nacional 269-270 (August, 1966): 9.

3397   _____. "Reforma agraria: declaración del...." Mensaje 9
        (December, 1960): 554-557.

3398   GALILEA, SEGUNDO. "La conferencia de Medellín. Una lectura
        de sus lineas de fuerza pastorales." Sal Terrae 8-9
        (August/September, 1976): 573-582.

3399   "The Golconda Declaration." Catholic Mind 68 (March, 1970):
        48-53.

3400   MALDONADO PÉREZ, OSCAR, comp. Colombia, la jerarquía catolica
        y los problemas de control de la natalidad, enero-marzo
        1967: algunos documentos clave. Cuernavaca, México:
        Centro Intercultural de Documentación, 1968. 305 pp.

3401   Partido Social Demócrata Cristiano. Declaración de principios.
        Bogotá: Editorial Kelly, 1966. 40 pp.

3402   Sacerdotes Colombianos. "Lutter sans relache pur la trans-
        formation sociale: document d'un groupe de pretres de
        Colombia." Lettre 126 (February, 1969): 39-43.

ECONOMIC DEVELOPMENT

3403   HAGEN, EVERETT EINAR. El cambio social en Colombia. El factor
        humano en el desarrollo económico. Bogotá: Ediciones
        Tercer Mundo, 1963. 108 pp.

Colombia

3404   TORRES RESTREPO, CAMILO. Consecuencias de la programación
económica para el apostolado en los países subdesarrollados.
Bogotá: Segundo Congreso Internacional de Pro Mundi Vita,
1964. 49 pp.

3405   _____. La proletarización de Bogotá. Bogotá: Facultad de
Sociología, Universidad Nacional de Colombia, 1961. 42 pp.

LABOR AND LABORING CLASSES

3406   MEDHURST, KENNETH. "The Church and Labor in Colombia." Clergy
Review 57 (February, 1972): 96-107.

3407   TORRES RESTREPO, CAMILO. La proletarización de Bogotá: ensayo
de metodología estadística. Bogotá: Universidad Nacional,
Facultad de Sociología. 1961. 42 pp.

LIBERATION

3408   GUTIÉRREZ, GUSTAVO. "De la Iglesia colonial a Medellín."
Víspera 16 (April, 1970): 3-8.

3409   PERESSÓN, MARIO. "Lineas de orientación de una experiencia de
evangelización liberadora de los jovenes colombianos."
Catequesis al Día 42 (May/June, 1970): 6-19.

PEASANTRY

3410   FARR, T., and BLISS, S. "Colombia: Death of a Campesino."
IDOC-International 32 (September 25, 1971): 31-34.

POLITICS

3411   "Colombian Bishops Ask Elections Be Postponed." Our Sunday
Visitor 64 (March 28, 1976): 3.

3412   "Colombians Vote on Easter, Are Warned." Our Sunday Visitor
64 (April 18, 1976): 1.

3413   Concientizar y organizar a las masas. Bogotá: Editorial
América Latina, 1974. 395 pp., bibl.

3414   CORR, EDWIN G. The Political Process in Colombia. Denver,
Colorado: University of Denver, Graduate School of International Studies and the Social Science Foundation, 1972.
149 pp., bibl.

Politics

3415   DE HAINAUT, RAYMOND K. "New Alliance of Christians of Libera-
       tion in Colombia Comes into the Open." Christian Century
       91 (July 17, 1974): 729-731.

3416   "Heritage of Lleras Camargo." Time, August 10, 1962, p. 25.

3417   "Iglesia y poder político en Colombia (I): ligada con la
       historia." Nueva Frontera 108 (November/December, 1976):
       16-17.

3418   "Iglesia y poder político en Colombia (II): patronato de
       reyes y presidentes." Nueva Frontera 110 (December, 1976):
       16-17.

3419   "Iglesia y poder político en Colombia (III): entre radicales
       y conservadores." Nueva Frontera 111 (December, 1976):
       16-17.

3420   LEVINE, DANIEL H., and WILDE, ALEXANDER W. "The Catholic
       Church, Politics, and Violence: The Colombian Case."
       Review of Politics 39 (April, 1977): 220-249.

3421   LÓPEZ, FRANCISCO. Proceso al poder religioso en Colombia.
       Bogotá: Editorial Hispana, 1968. 245 pp.

3422   MAULLIN, RICHARD L. Soldiers, Guerrillas and Politics in
       Colombia. London: D.C. Heath Books, 1973. 168 pp., bibl.

3423   PAYNE, JAMES L. Patterns of Conflict in Colombia. New Haven:
       Yale University Press, 1968. 358 pp., bibl.

3424   PRADA CÁCERES, JOSÉ MARÍA. Mancha de sangre: la verdad
       jurídica y la realidad social colombiana. Quito: Editorial
       Santo Domingo, 1962. 119 pp.

3425   RESTREPO JARAMILLO, GONZALO. "El absurdo político colombiano."
       Universidad Pontificia Boliviana 90 (1962): 195-212.

3426   RUÍS NOVOA, ALBERTO. El gran desafío. Bogotá: Ediciones
       Tercer Mundo, 1965. 146 pp.

3427   SMITH, DONALD EUGENE, ed. Religion, Politics and Social
       Change in the Third World. New York: The Free Press,
       1971. 286 pp., bibl.

3428   TORRES RESTREPO, CAMILO. Camilo Torres: biografía, plata-
       forma, mensajes. Medellín: Ediciones Carpel-Antorcha,
       1966. 104 pp.

3429   _____. Cristianismo y revolución. México: Era, 1970. 611
        pp.

3430   _____. Ecrits et paroles. Paris: Editions du Seuil, 1968.
        320 pp.

3431   _____. Revolutionary Priest: The Complete Writings and
        Messages of Camilo Torres. New York: Random House, 1971.
        460 pp.

3432   URAN ROJAS, CARLOS H. Participación política de la Iglesia
        en el proceso histórico de Colombia. Lima: MIEC-JECI,
        Secretariado Latinoamericano, 1974. 92 pp., bibl.

REFERENCE

3433   PÉREZ RAMÍREZ, GUSTAVO, and WUST, ISSAC. La Iglesia en Colom-
        bia: estructuras eclesiásticas. Bogotá: Centro de In-
        vestigaciones Sociales, Departamento Socio-Económico, 1961.
        195 pp.

3434   WATSON, GAYLE HUDGENS. Colombia, Ecuador, and Venezuela: An
        Annotated Guide to Reference Materials in the Humanities
        and Social Sciences. Metuchen, New Jersey: Scarecrow
        Press, 1971. 279 pp., bibl.

REVOLUTION

3435   ALVAREZ GARCÍA, JOHN, and RESTREPO CALLE, CHRISTIAN. Camilo
        Torres: His Life and His Message. Springfield, Illinois:
        Templegate Publishers, 1968. 128 pp.

3436   ANDRADE, VICENTE. "The Death of Camilo Torres." America 114
        (March 12, 1966): 355.

3437   BERMUDEZ, LUIS A. Colombia hacia la revolución. Caracas:
        Editorial Domingo Fuentes, 1971. 128 pp.

3438   BERNARDI, BERNARDO. "In the Fringeland of Colombia." World-
        mission 14 (Spring, 1963): 36-44.

3439   BOTERO RESTREPO, GUILLERMO. Cartas de un vicario. Un aporte
        pacífico a la revolución de Colombia. Cali: Editora
        Feriva, 1968. 339 pp.

Revolution

3440 "Camilo Torres, vida, acción y revolución: testimonio de un
       comandante del ELN de Colombia." Cristianismo y Revolución
       5 (November, 1967): 21-23.

3441 CHAIGNE, HERVE. "Bogotá et la révolution nécessaire." Frères
       du Monde 57 (1969): 31-62.

3442 "The Church Embattled." Economist 228 (August 24, 1968): 23.

3443 GERASSI, JOHN, ed. Revolutionary Priest. The Complete
       Writings and Messages of Camilo Torres. New York: Random
       House, 1971. 460 pp.

3444 MADURO, OTTO. Revelación y revolución. Mérida, Venezuela:
       Ediciones del Recotrado, Universidad de los Andes, Departa-
       mento de Publicaciones, 1970. 133 pp.

3445 OLAYA, NOEL, and ZAVALA, GERMÁN. "En la ruta de Golconda."
       Víspera 8 (November, 1969): 36-39.

3446 RESTREPO, FRANCISCO JAVIER DARIO. "Priest-Guerrillas." IDOC-
       International 8 (August 15, 1970): 58-65.

3447 "Revolution in Colombia: The Church and the Recent Changes."
       Tablet 209 (May 25, 1957): 486-487.

3448 TORRES RESTREPO, CAMILO. Camilo, el cura revolucionario:
       sus obras. Buenos Aires: Ediciones Cristianismo y Revo-
       lución, 1968. 313 pp.

3449 _____. Camilo Torres, el cura que murió en las guerrillas.
       Barcelona: Editorial Nova Terra, 1968. 297 pp.

3450 _____. Cristianismo y revolución. México: Ediciones Era,
       1970. 611 pp., bibl.

3451 _____. La revolución: imperativo cristiano. Bogotá: Edi-
       ciones del Caribe, 1965. 58 pp., bibl.

3452 _____. "Latin America: Some Problems of Revolutionary
       Strategy." In Latin America Radicalism, pp. 499-531. New
       York: [n.p.], 1969.

3453 _____. Liberación o muerte. Havana: Instituto del Libro,
       1967. 206 pp.

3454 _____. "Mensaje a los cristianos." Frente Unido 1 (August 26,
       1965): 3.

Colombia

3455   . "Mensaje del padre...." Cristianismo y Revolución 2 (September, 1966): 21.

3456   . Obras escogidas. Montevideo: Provincias Unidas, 1968. 254 pp.

3457   . "Por qué no voy a las elecciones." Frente Unido 1 (August 26, 1965): 1, 8.

3458   . Revolutionary Writings. New York: Herder and Herder, 1969. 371 pp.

SOCIALISM

3459 ANDRADE, VICENTE. "Doctrina social. Voz de alerta del episcopado colombiano." El Catolicismo 2,234 (January 30, 1977): 6.

3460 ROUX LOPEZ, RODOLFO DE, et al. Socialismo y cristianismo. Bogotá: Centro de Investigación Social e Instituto de Doctrina y Estudios Sociales, 1971. 48 pp.

TORRES, CAMILO

3461 ALLAZ, TOMÁS G. ¿Hambre o revolución? La Iglesia contra la pared. México: Editorial Nuestro Tiempo, 1971. 244 pp.

3462 ANDRADE, VICENTE. "Rebel Priest in Colombia." America 113 (September 18, 1965): 287.

3463   . "The Death of Camilo Torres." America 114 (March 12, 1966): 355.

3464 ARENAS, JAIME. La guerrilla por dentro: análisis del ELN colombiano. Bogotá: Ediciones Tercer Mundo, 1971. 204 pp.

3465 BENOIT, ANDRÉ. "L'histoire tragique de Camilo Torres." Lettre 97-98 (September 10, 1966): 29-38.

3466 BERRYMAN, PHILLIP E. "Camilo Torres: Revolutionary Theologian." Commonweal 96 (April 21, 1971): 164-166.

3467 BIGO, PIERRE. "Enseñanza de la Iglesia sobre la violencia." Mensaje 174 (November, 1968): 574-578.

Torres, Camilo

3468   BOJORGE, HORACIO, et al. El ciervo. Retrato de Camilo Torres.
       México: Editorial Grijalbo, 1969. 158 pp.

3469   _____, et al. Retrato de Camilo Torres. México: Editorial
       Grijalbo, 1969. 158 pp.

3470   BRODERICK, WALTER J. Camilo Torres: A Biography of the
       Priest-Guerrilero. New York: Doubleday, 1975. 370 pp.,
       bibl.

3471   "Camilo o el Papa." Cristianismo y Revolución 9 (September,
       1968): 1.

3472   "Camilo Torres: presentación del sondeos no. 5, titualdo:
       Camilo Torres por el P. Torres Restrepo, Camilo." CIDOC
       Informa 4 (June 1, 1967): 187-188.

3473   "Camilo Torres, prêtre et guerrillero." Lettre 117 (May,
       1968): 7-16.

3474   "Camilo Torres, vida, acción y revolución: testimonio de un
       comandante del ELN de Colombia." Cristianismo y Revolución
       5 (November, 1967): 21-23.

3475   "Camilo Torres y los universitarios." Mensaje 17 (March 5,
       1968): 113-115.

3476   "O caso do padre Camilo Torres." Paz e Terra 1 (July, 1966):
       254-263.

3477   CASTILLO CARDENAS, GONZÁLO. "A morte do sacerdote Camilo
       Torres." Paz e Terra 1 (July, 1966): 264-266.

3478   _____. "From Protest to Revolutionary Commitment." Inter-
       national Review of Mission 60 (April, 1971): 212-222.

3479   _____. Violencia contra sacerdotes en Colombia: la persecu-
       ción oficial se intensifica contra los curas comprometidos
       con la causa popular. Bogotá: [n.p.] 1969. 7 pp.

3480   CASTRO, FIDEL. "Cuba: la madre de Camilo Torres con Fidel
       Castro." Cristianismo y Revolución 12 (March, 1969): 12.

3481   CAYCEDO, OLGA DE. El padre Camilo Torres: o, la crisis de
       madurez de América. Barcelona: Ediciones Aura, 1972.
       402 pp.

Colombia

3482 Confederación Latinoamericana de Sindicatos Cristianos, ed.
Padre Camilo Torres: su pensamiento, su actitud, su
ejemplo.... Antioquia [n.p.], 1967. 6 pp.

3483 CORRO, ALEJANDRO DEL, comp. Colombia: Camilo Torres; un
símbolo controvertido, 1962-67. Cuernavaca, México:
Centro Intercultural de Documentación, 1967.

3484 "Cuatro documentos de Camilo Torres." Cuadernos de Marcha 9
(January, 1968): 121-123.

3485 DAUBECHIES, HUBERT. "Camilo Torres ¿la revolución desesperada?"
Mensaje 15 (March/April, 1966): 120-124.

3486 GALLY, HECTOR, ed. Camilo Torres: con las armas en la mano.
México: Editorial Diógenes, 1971. 183 pp.

3487 GARCÍA ELORRIO, JUAN. "Bajo el signa de Camilo." Cristianismo
y Revolución 4 (March, 1967): 2-3.

3488 GILLY, ADOLFO. "El programa del cura Camilo Torres." Marcha
(June 4, 1965).

3489 GÓMEZ DE SOUZA, LUIS ALBERTO. "O testemunho de Padre Camilo
Torres." Paz e Terra 1 (July, 1966): 267-272.

3490 GONZÁLEZ RUÍZ, JOSÉ MARÍA. "Camilo Torres o el buen samari-
tano." Perspectivas de Diálogo 25 (July, 1968): 139-141.

3491 Grupo Sacerdotal Golconda. "Los herederos de Camilo: documentos revolucionarios de Buenaventura." Cristianismo y
Revolución 12 (March, 1969): 21-25.

3492 GUZMÁN CAMPOS, GERMÁN. Camilo, el cura guerrillero. Bogotá:
Servicios Especiales de Prensa, 1967. 257 pp.

3493 _____. Camilo, presencia y destino. Bogotá: Servicios
Especiales de Prensa, 1967. 257 pp.

3494 _____. Camilo Torres. New York: Sheed and Ward, 1969. 310
pp.

3495 _____. "Colombia: Camilo, o padre guerrilheiro." Paz e
Terra 2 (June, 1968): 259-265.

3496 _____. El padre Camilo Torres. México: Siglo Veintiuno,
1968. 321 pp.

Torres, Camilo

3497   HABEGGER, NORBERTO. Camilo Torres: el cura guerrillero.
       Buenos Aires: A. Peña Lillo, 1967. 312 pp.

3498   _____. Camilo Torres prete e gerrigliero. Florence, Italy:
       Cultura Editrice, 1968. 71 pp.

3499   HOCHMAN, ELENA, and SONNTAG, HEINZ RUDOLF. Christentum und
       Politsche Praxis: Camilo Torres. Frankfurt: Suhrkamp,
       1969. 136 pp., bibl.

3500   HORNMAN, WIM. De Rebel: Roman Over Camilo Torres. Haarlem,
       The Netherlands: J.H. Gottmer, 1968. 320 pp.

3501   _____. The Rebel Priest. London: Collins, 1971. 319 pp.

3502   _____. The Stones Cry Out: (A novel of Camilo Torres).
       Philadelphia: Lippincott, 1971. 323 pp.

3503   HOURDIN, GEORGE. "A justa violencia dos oprimidos." Paz e
       Terra 2 (April, 1968): 73-88.

3504   HOUTART, FRANCOIS. "Camilo sacerdote..." Cristianismo y
       Revolución 4 (March, 1967): 13-15.

3505   JARAMILLO, FRANCISCO DE PAULA. Camilo: 8 ensayos apasionados.
       Bogotá: Editorial Revista Colombiana, 1970. 139 pp.

3506   JIMENES GRULLON, JUAN ISIDRO. El camilismo y la revolución
       dominicana. [n.p.]: 1973. 169 pp., bibl.

3507   LARA-BRAND, JORGE. Revolution in the Western Hemisphere.
       New York: Office of Student World Relations, 1966. 6 pp.

3508   LEVINE, DANIEL H., and WILDE, ALEXANDER W. "The Catholic
       Church, Politics, and Violence: The Colombian Case."
       Review of Politics 39 (April, 1977): 220-249.

3509   LÓPEZ OLIVA, ENRIQUE. El camilismo en la América Latina.
       Havana: Casa de las Américas, 1970. 97 pp.

3510   LÜNING, HILDEGARD. Camilo Torres, Priester Guerrillero.
       Darstellung, Analyse, Dokumentation. Hamburg: Furche-
       Verlag, 1969. 168 pp.

3511   MALDONADO PÉREZ, OSCAR. "A propósito de Camilo Torres."
       CIDOC Informa 3 (March 16, 1966): 90-101.

Colombia

3512 _____. "Camilo Torres, Priester und Rebell." Junge Kirche
7 (July 10, 1967): 368-376.

3513 MAZA, ENRIQUE. "Los sacerdotes revolucionarios." Excélsior,
July 7, 1965.

3514 OSPINA R., WILLIAM. ¿Qué es el Frente Unido del Pueblo?
Bogotá: Ediciones Siete de Enero, 1968. 90 pp.

3515 OSSA, MANUEL. Camilo Torres. Buenos Aires: Centro Editor
de América Latina, 1972. 280 pp., bibl.

3516 PANTOJA, CARLOS. "Camilo Torres, un camino en la liberación
de Colombia." La Gaceta 3 (September/December, 1966):
2-16.

3517 PAREJA, CARLOS. El padre Camilo Torres: el cura guerrillero.
México: Nuestra América, 1968. 262 pp.

3518 PÉREZ MALDONADO, OSCAR. "A propósito de Camilo Torres."
Reconstrucción 24 (April, 1966): 3-9.

3519 PÉREZ RAMÍREZ, GUSTAVO. "Camilo Torres." IDOC-International
32 (September 25, 1971): 21-26.

3520 PRADES, ALBERTO. "Camilo Sociólogo." Cristianismo y Revolución 4 (March, 1967): 10-12.

3521 _____. "Camilo Torres en tant que sociologue." In Camilo
Torres en tant que prêtre sociologue et Colombines, edited
by François Houtart, Alberto Prades, and Fabil Gutiérrez
Correa. Louvan: Cercle des Etudiants Colombines, 1966.

3522 "¿Quién es el padre Camilo Torres?" La Nueva Prensa 117
(June 16, 1964): 32.

3523 RESTREPO, ISABEL. "Qué entreguen el cuerpo de mi hijo."
Cristianismo y Revolución 9 (September, 1968): 49.

3524 RESTREPO, JAVIER DARÍO. "Priest-Guerrillas." IDOC-International 8 (August 15, 1970): 58-65.

3525 ROSIER, IRENEO. "Camilo Torres, señal de contradicción."
Mundo Nuevo 28 (October, 1968): 4-12.

3526 "El sacerdote y la revolución: hace tres meses murió, el
sacerdote Camilo Torres." Informaciones Católics Internacionales 265 (June 7, 1966).

Torres, Camilo

3527   NO ENTRY

3528   SALAZAR, MARÍA CRISTINA, et al. Inquietudes: láicos a la
       hora del concilio: el "caso" del padre Camilo Torres.
       Bogotá: Ediciones Tercer Mundo, 1965. 79 pp.

3529   SANGER, CLYDE. "Priest Leads Guerrillas in Colombia."
       Guardian (January 10, 1966): 9.

3530   SEGUNDO, JUAN LUIS. "Camilo Torres, sacerdocio y violencia."
       Víspera 1 (May, 1967): 71-75.

3531   SOTO APARICIO, FERNANDO. La siembra de Camilo: novela.
       Bogotá: Talleres de la Editorial Colombia Nueva, 1971.
       236 pp.

3532   "Study on Death: la violencia en Colombia." Time, February
       1, 1963, p. 19.

3533   SUÁREZ, LUIS. "Sacerdote y guerrillero, Camilo dejó a Colom-
       bia un legado de angustia y de dignidad." Siempre 71
       (March 29, 1967): 32-33.

3534   THEISEN, GERALD. "The Case of Camilo Torres Restrepo."
       Journal of Church and State 16 (Spring, 1974): 301-315.

3535   TORRES CALLE, CRISTIAN, ed. Camilo Torres, bibliografía,
       plataforma, mensajes. Medellín: Carpel-Antorcha, 1966.

3536   TORRES RESTREPO, CAMILO. Compendium of His Writings. (1956-
       1966). Cuernavaca, México: Centro Intercultural de Docu-
       mentación, 1966.

3537   _____. El cura que murió en las guerrillas. Barcelona: Edi-
       torial Nova Terra, 1968. 297 pp.

3538   _____. La violencia y los cambios socio-culturales en las
       áreas rurales colombianas. Bogotá: Memoria del Primer
       Congreso Nacional de Sociología, 1963.

3539   _____. Revolução na América Latina: vida e obra do padre
       guerriheiro. Salvador, Brasil: Editora Mensajeiro da Fé
       1968. 220 pp.

3540   _____. Revolutionary Priest: The Complete Writings and
       Message of Camilo Torres. New York: Random House, 1971.
       460 pp.

Colombia

3541   VALENCIA TOVAR, ALVARO. El final de Camilo. Bogotá: Ediciones Tercer Mundo, 1976. 257 pp.

3542   WEISS, ANITA, and BELALCAZAR, OCTAVIO, eds. Golconda: el libro rojo de los curas rebeldes. Bogotá: Editorial Cosmos, 1969. 200 pp.

3543   "Why Men Join Guerrillas." Tablet 221 (August 26, 1967): 915.

3544   WOMACK, JOHN. "Priest of Revolution." New York Review of Books 13 (October 23, 1969): 13-16.

3545   ZAMBRANO, H., et al. "Informe: presencia y memoria de Camilo Torres." Víspera 1 (May, 1967): 54-72.

VIOLENCE

3546   "Frente Unido del Pueblo." Frente Unido 1 (August 26, 1965): 4-5.

3547   GAITÁN MAHECHA, BERNARDO. Misión histórica del frente nacional. Bogotá: Editorial Revista Colombiana, 1966. 88pp.

3548   LEVINE, DANIEL H., and WILDE, ALEXANDER W. "The Catholic Church, Politics, and Violence: The Colombian Case." The Review of Politics 2 (April, 1977): 220-249.

3549   LIPMAN, AARON, and HAVENS, A. EUGENE. "The Colombian Violencia: An Ex Post Facto Experiment." Social Forces 44 (December, 1965): 238-45.

3550   ¿Revolución violenta? Bogotá: Editorial Andes, 1965. 157 pp.

3551   SMITH, ROBERT F. "Till We Have Built Jerusalem." Nation 208 (June 30, 1969): 829-830.

IX Cuba

GENERAL

3552 ARDATOVSKII, V. "Sviatye Ottsy na Kube." Nauka i Religiia
      3 (November, 1961): 47-49.

3553 BLANQUART, PAUL. "Au Congres Cultural de la Havane: Cuba,
      premier territoire libre d'Amérique, foyer de la lutte
      anti-impérialiste." Lettre 115 (March, 1968): 24.

3554 CARDENAL, ERNESTO. En Cuba. Buenos Aires: Ediciones Carlos
      Lohle, 1972. 370 pp.

3555 "The Church in Cuba: Vindicated or Not?" Tablet 219 (May 22,
      1965): 588.

3556 COLONNESE, LOUIS M. "Religion in Cuba Today." Christian Cen-
      tury 88 (August 11, 1971): 953.

3557 "Confessions of the Cuban Church." Tablet 219 (May 29, 1965):
      616-617.

3558 CRAHAN, MARGARET E. "Religion, Cuba." IDOC-International 69
      (January, 1975): 17-21.

3559 DETIEGE, HENRI. "Cuba et les chrétiens." Eglise Vivante 15
      (1962): 379-380.

3560 DEWART, LESLIE. Cuba, Church and Crisis. New York: Sheed
      and Ward, 1964. 320 pp.

3561 _____. "The Current Mood of the Cuban Church." Blackfriars
      45 (February, 1964): 50-60.

3562 "Dyversanty v Sutanakh." Voiovnychyi ateist 1 (January, 1961):
      62.

3563 FERNÁNDEZ, MANUEL. "La Iglesia en Cuba ante nuevas expecta-
      tivas." Amérique Latine 24 (June, 1975): 7-10.

General

3564　GARCÍA FRANCO, RAIMUNDO, and BATISTA GUERRA, ISRAEL. "Christians in Cuba." IDOC-International 45 (April 15, 1972): 68-81.

3565　GRIGULEVICH, I. "Ten'kresta nad Kuboi i Kongo." Kommunist (Vilnius) 10 (1960): 67-70.

3566　GUZMÁN CAMPOS, GERMÁN. "Reportaje a Monseñor ... a su regreso a Colombia." Cristianismo y Revolución 8 (July, 1968): 26-29.

3567　"How Catholic Faith Survives in Cuba." U.S. Catholic 29 (February, 1964): 55.

3568　La Iglesia en Cuba: informe especial. Buenos Aires: Editorial Auca, 1972. 52 pp.

3569　MC GOWAN, FELIX. "The Catholic Church and Cuba: An Inside View." The Militant 30 (February 21, 1966): 4-5.

3570　"A New Note From Havana." America 118 (March 16, 1968): 338-339.

CATHOLIC CHURCH AND SOCIAL CHANGE

3571　CEPEDA, RAFAEL. "La conducta cristiana en una sociedad revolucionaria." Cristianismo y Sociedad 3 (1965): 91-95.

3572　DEWART, LESLIE. "The Church in Cuba: A Universal Dilemna." Commonweal 79 (October 11, 1963): 67-69.

3573　FERNÁNDEZ, MANUEL. "Eleven Years Later: The Church in Cuba." IDOC-International 8 (August 15, 1970): 43-53.

3574　HIGGINS, JAMES. "New Church in New Cuba." Commonweal 96 (July 28, 1972): 399-402.

3575　"Una Iglesia vitalmente incorporada en el actual contexto social: exhortación del episcopal cubano a los sacerdotes, religiosos, religiosas y fieles." Mensaje Iberoamericano 115 (1975): 9.

3576　MAC EOIN, GARY. "Cuba's Catholic Ground Swell." Sign 38 (November, 1958): 34-36.

3577　MESLAY, JOHN. "Algo mas sobre Cuba." Mensaje 11 (January, 1962): 47-49.

3578   MIANO, V. "Two Documents on the Relationship Between Communism
        and Religion: Cuba and Spain." L'Osservatore Romano,
        April 28, 1977, pp. 10-11.

3579   ORDOÑEZ, JACINTO. "Cuba: las iglesias a la búsqueda de un
        ecumenismo social." Circular del Centro Ecuménico 3 (1975):
        21-27.

3580   RENES, CARLOS GERMÁN. "La Iglesia cubana, ¿tragedia o esper-
        anza?" Mensaje Iberoamericano 44 (June, 1969): 4-9.

CATHOLIC CHURCH AND STATE

3581   "L'agonie de l'Eglise de Cuba: editorial." Relations 240
        (December, 1960): 311.

3582   AGUIRRE, M. "The Persecutions in Cuba." Catholic World 193
        (April, 1961): 35-38.

3583   BOZA MASVIDAL, EDUARDO. "Cuba: The Explusion of Priests."
        New Blackfriars 45 (July/August, 1964): 307-311.

3584   _____. "¿Es la Iglesia católica en Cuba una iglesia per-
        seguida?" Mensaje 118 (May, 1963): 184-187.

3585   "Captive in Church." Time, April 22, 1966, pp. 34-35.

3586   CARR, AIDAN M. "Castro vs. Catholic Priest." Homiletice and
        Pastoral Review 62 (December, 1961): 249.

3587   "Castro and the Church: Report from French Writer Just Back
        From Cuba." Ave Maria 93 (March 4, 1961): 5-12.

3588   "Castro vs. the Church." Time, October 2, 1960, pp. 84-85.

3589   "Castro vs. the Witnesses." Newsweek, March 25, 1963, p. 72.

3590   "The Church and Castro." Herder Correspondence 5 (August,
        1968): 243-247.

3591   "The Church in Cuba." America 111 (December 12, 1964): 769.

3592   "Church vs. State." Newsweek, August 22, 1960, pp. 49-50.

3593   "Cuba: La Iglesia católica y Fidel Castro." Mensaje 10
        (June, 1966): 235-239.

Catholic Church and State

3594   "Cuban Catholic Leader Says There's No Freedom in Cuba." Our
       Sunday Visitor 64 (August 3, 1975): 3.

3595   "Cuban Expulsions." Commonweal 75 (October 6, 1961): 30-31.

3596   "Declaración de la CLASC sobre la revolución y el gobierno de
       Fidel Castro." Pensamiento Político 1 (November, 1966):
       31-32.

3597   DEWART, LESLIE. A Catholic Speaks on Cuba. Toronto: Fair
       Play for Cuba Committee, 1961. 6 pp.

3598   DONOVAN, JOHN. "Cuban Church Not Persecuted." Catholic
       Messenger 82 (April 16, 1964): 1.

3599   _____. "Donovan Denies He Said Church Not Tied in Cuba."
       Catholic Messenger 82 (April 30, 1964): 1.

3600   FERNÁNDEZ, MANUEL. "Eleven Years Later: The Church in Cuba."
       IDOC-International 8 (August 15, 1970): 43-53.

3601   _____. "La Iglesia en Cuba a los diez años de la revolución."
       Mensaje Iberoamericano 42 (April, 1969): 1073.

3602   GENDLER, E. E. "Cuba and Religion: Challenge and Response."
       Christian Century 86 (July 30, 1969): 1013-1016.

3603   GILLY, ADOLFO. "La OEA, la Iglesia y Cuba." Marcha 20
       (July 10, 1964): 14-21.

3604   GLICK, E. B. "Castro and the Church." Commonweal 75 (October
       13, 1961): 67-69.

3605   GRIGULEVICH, I. "Revoliutsionnaia Kuba i Tserkov." Nauka i
       Religiia 2 (October, 1960): 75-76.

3606   GUTIÉRREZ, CARLOS MARÍA. "Fidel, el cristiano: reportaje al
       Nuncio del Papa en Cuba." Cristianismo y Revolución 6-7
       (April, 1969): 18-20.

3607   HIGGINS, JAMES. "New Church in New Cuba." Commonweal 96
       (July 28, 1972): 399-402.

3608   HORGAN, J. "Kyrka Och Stat Pa Kuba." Svensk Missionstidskrift
       59 (1971): 80-87.

3609   "La Iglesia en Cuba: reportaje a un nuevo obispo." Cris-
       tianismo y Revolución 18 (July, 1969): 36-38.

3610   JULIEN, C. "Church and State in Cuba: Development of a Con-
       flict." Cross Currents 11 (Spring, 1961): 186-192.

3611   NO ENTRY

3612   MAURER, R. "Distrust of Church in Cuba Fades." National
       Catholic Reporter 8 (November 19, 1971): 3-4.

3613   MENÉNDEZ RODRÍGUEZ, MARIO. "La Iglesia y la revolucion cubana."
       SUCESOS, September 17, 1966.

3613A NOVOA, EDUARDO. "La situación religiosa en Cuba." Mensaje
       167 (March/April, 1968): 104-107.

3614   O'GRADY, D. "The Church in Cuba: Text of an Exchange Between
       Exiled Bp. Boza Masvidal and the Cuban Ambassador to the
       Vatican." Ave Maria 97 (April 13, 1963): 5-8.

3615   POWER, ANNE. "The Church in Cuba." Commonweal 89 (March 7,
       1969): 704-705.

3616   "Religious Liberty in Cuba." Tablet 221 (July 22, 1967): 814.

3617   "Sees Church-State Peace in Cuba." National Catholic Reporter
       4 (March 6, 1968): 7.

3618   SUHOR, M. "Church and State in Fidel's Cuba." National
       Catholic Reporter 8 (December 24, 1971): 18.

3619   SWAREN, BEVERLY. "The Church in Today's Cuba." America 119
       (September 21, 1968): 211-213.

3620   ZACCHI, CÉSAR. "La Iglesia católica y la revolución cubana:
       reportaje al Nuncio Papal en la Habana." Cristianismo y
       Revolución 5 (November, 1967): 19-20.

CATHOLIC CLERGY

3621   "Belgian Priests for Cuba." Tablet 218 (February 1, 1964):
       140.

3622   "Kogo Proslavliat 'Pailot'?" Nauka i Religiia 4 (May, 1963):
       42.

3623   "National Service for Cuban Priests and Seminarians." Tablet
       220 (August 27, 1966): 978.

Catholic Clergy

3624   PÉREZ SERVANTES, E.   "The Situation in Cuba: Pastoral Letter
        of May 17, 1960."   Catholic Mind 59 (February, 1961):   89-
        95.

3625   ROCA, BLAS.   "La lucha ideológica contra las sectas religiosas."
        Cuba Socialista 3 (June, 1963):   28-41.

3626   "Two Consecrated Bishops in Havana."   Catholic Messenger 82
        (June 4, 1964):   8.

COMMUNISM

3627   CASTRO, FIDEL.   "Govorit Fidel' Kastro."   Nauki i Religiia 4
        (June, 1963):   34-35.

3628   "The Embattled Catholics."   Newsweek, May 30, 1960, p. 56.

3629   HAGEMAN, ALICE L., and WHEATON, PHILIP, eds.   Religion in
        Cuba Today: A New Church in a New Society.   New York:
        Association Press, 1971.   317 pp.

3630   LISTOV, V.   "Bitaia Karta Imperializma."   Nauka i Religiia 4
        (June, 1963):   36-38.

3631   MONTERO RODRÍGUEZ, CELSO.   Cristianos en la revolución cubana:
        diario de un periodista.   Estella: Verbo Divino, 1975.
        325 pp.

3632   TORRES RESTREPO, CAMILO.   Cuba, paraíso perdido.   Bogotá:
        Aedita Eitores, 1962.   160 pp.

DOCUMENTS

3633   "Communist Influence in Cuba: Pastoral Letter of August 7,
        1960."   Catholic Mind 59 (June, 1961):   273-276.

3634   Confederación Latinoamericana de Sindicatos Cristianos.   "La
        CLASC y la revolución cubana: declaración de la CLASC
        sobre la revolución cubana y el gobierno de Fidel Castro."
        Mensaje 9 (December, 1960):   541-542.

3635   Cuba Resource Center.   "Papers Toward Trading with Cuba."
        IDOC-International 49 (December, 1972):   9-12.

3636   PÉREZ SERVANTES, E.   "The Situation in Cuba: Pastoral Letter
        of May 17, 1960."   Catholic Mind 59 (February, 1969):   89-95.

ECONOMIC DEVELOPMENT

3637   "El concilio mundial de iglesias y las relaciones con Cuba."
       Carta de ISAL 2 (November, 1969): 3.

3638   Cuba Resource Center. "Papers Toward Trading with Cuba."
       IDOC-International 49 (December, 1972): 9-12.

MARXISM

3639   ROCA, BLAS. "La lucha ideológica contra las sectas religiosas."
       Cuba Socialista 3 (June, 1966): 28-41.

3640   TISEYRA, OSCAR. Cuba marxista vista por un católico. Buenos
       Aires: Jorge Alvarez, 1964. 197 pp.

POLITICS

3641   DEWART, LESLIE. Cuba, Church and Crisis: Christianity and
       Politics in the Cuban Revolution. London: Sheed and Ward,
       1964. 320 pp.

3642   Pasión de Cristo en Cuba. Santiago, Cuba: Departamento de
       Publicaciones del Secretariado de Difusión, 1962. 76 pp.

3643   "Rapports entre politique et religion: résolution du congres
       du parti communiste cubain." La Documentation Catholique
       73 (December 19, 1976): 1084-1085.

3644   RASCO, JOSÉ IGNACIO. Cuba 1959: artículos de combate.
       Buenos Aires: Ediciones Diagrama, 1962. 125 pp.

3645   TORRES RESTREPO, CAMILO. Cuba, paraíso perdido. Bogotá:
       Aedita Editores, 1962. 160 pp.

3646   TSCHUY, THEO. "The Cuban Miracle and the Church's Prison."
       Cross Currents 21 (Summer, 1971): 335-339.

REVOLUTION

3647   ASSMAN, HUGO, ed. Habla Fidel Castro sobre los cristianos
       revolucionarios. Montevideo: Tierra Nueva, 1972.

3648   CEPEDA, RAFAEL. "La conducta cristiana en una sociedad revo-
       lucionaria." Cristianismo y Sociedad 3 (1965).

Revolution

3649 Confederación Latinoamericana de Sindicatos Cristianos. "La CLASC y la Revolución Cubana: declaración de la CLASC sobre la revolución cubana y el gobierno de Fidel Castro." <u>Mensaje</u> 9 (December, 1960): 541-542.

3650 Congreso Cultural de la Habana. "Ponencia de los sacerdotes catolicos." <u>Cristianismo y Revolución</u> 6-7 (April, 1968): 75.

3651 DAUBECHIES, HUBERT. "Fidel Castro habla a los 'Ochenta'." <u>Mensaje</u> 206 (January/February, 1972): 57-63.

3652 DEWART, LESLIE. <u>Christianity and Revolution: The Lesson of Cuba</u>. New York: Herder and Herder, 1963. 320 pp.

3653 FERNÁNDEZ, MANUEL. "La Iglesia en Cuba a los diez años de la revolución." <u>Mensaje Iberoamericano</u> 42 (April, 1969): 1073.

3654 HOUTART, FRANÇOIS, and ROUSSEAU, ANDRE. <u>The Church and Revolution: From the French Revolution of 1789 to the Paris Riots of 1968: From Cuba to Southern Africa: From Vietnam to Latin America</u>. Maryknoll: ORBIS, 1971. 371 pp.

3655 "Die Kirche und die soziale Revolution in Kuba." <u>Herder Korrespondence</u> 15 (December, 1960): 124-128.

3656 Priestly Secretariat of Christians for Socialism. "The 80 Priests Meet with Fidel Castro." <u>LADOC</u> 26 (March, 1972): 2.

X Ecuador

GENERAL

3657   BECKMAN, JOSEPH F. "A Census in Milagro." America 130 (May
        25, 1974): 418-419.

3658   GRIGULEVICH, I. "Ten' nad Ekvadorom." Nauka i Religiia 4
        (September, 1963): 36-39.

3659   GRISERI, AGUSTIN. "Labor de los religiosos en El Salvador."
        ECA 18 (December, 1963): 386-391.

3660   "Otro paso adelante: ISPLA: resumen da varios artículos del
        P. Segundo Galilea y definición de ISPLA." CIDOC-Informa
        1 (July, 1964): 1-6.

3661   PIKE, FREDERICK B. The United States and the Andean Republics:
        Peru, Bolivia and Ecuador. Cambridge: Harvard University
        Press, 1977.

CATHOLIC CHURCH AND SOCIAL CHANGE

3662   BRAVO, ELAINE HUBARD DE. Roman et société en Equateur: 1930-
        1949. Cuernavaca, México: Centro Intercultural de Docu-
        mentación, 1970.

3663   "The Church in Ecuador Undertakes Agrarian Land Reform."
        Reportaje DESAL 1 (July/December, 1968): 3.

3664   "Ecuador: formas organizativas que han asumido los cristianos."
        Educación Popular en América Latina 1 (1975): 5-8.

3665   Episcopado Ecuatoriano. "No haga más ricos y miserables a
        los pobres." Noticias Aliadas 23 (June, 1976): 6-8.

3666   MAC EOIN, GARY. "Church Renewal on Trial in Ecuador."
        America 129 (August 4, 1973): 61-63.

Catholic Church and State

CATHOLIC CHURCH AND STATE

3667   "Ecuador Arrests 57 in Move Seen Aimed at Latin Church."
       National Catholic Reporter 12 (August 27, 1976): 5.

3668   PROAÑO, LEONIDAS. "Church and Politics in Ecuador." Con-
       cilium 71 (1972): 99-105.

CATHOLIC CLERGY

3669   BELTRÁN, EDGARD. "Ecuador: abuso de fuerza o algo mas
       grande." Noticias Aliadas 37 (October, 1976): 3-5.

3670   "The Bishops of Ecuador: Joint Statement, Excerpt." Tablet
       215 (August 5, 1961): 762.

3671   FONTAINE, PABLO. "La Iglesia católica chilena y los últimos
       '20 años." Mensaje 202-203 (September/October, 1971):
       422-432.

3672   "Seventeen Prelates Expelled During Pastoral Meeting: Docu-
       mentation Concerning the Case of Arresting in Ecuador."
       L'Osservatore Romano, November 11, 1976, p. 5.

COMMUNISM

3673   CHÁVEZ Y GONZÁLEZ, LUIS. Vigésima novena carta pastoral del
       Excmo. y Revmo. Arzobispo de San Salvador ... sobre los
       peligros del comunismo y la eficaz solución de la "Cuestión
       Social". San Salvador: Imprenta Criterio, 1961. 16 pp.

3674   Conferencia Episcopal Ecuatoriana. "La integridad del mensaje
       cristiano. Catequesis Latinoamericana 33 (1976): 75-89.

3675   Episcopado Ecuatoriano. "Reforma agraria en Ecuador: carta
       pastoral colectiva del...." Mensaje 10 (May, 1961):
       187-188.

DOCUMENTS

3676   "La integridad del mensaje cristiano: Conferencia Episcopal
       Ecuatoriana." Catequesis Latinoamericana 8 (1976): 75-84.

Ecuador

POLITICS

3677   BIALEK, ROBERT W. Catholic Politics: A History Based on
       Ecuador. New York: Vantage Press, 1963. 144 pp., bibl.

REFERENCE

3678   WATSON, GAYLE HUDGENS. Colombia, Ecuador, and Venezuela: An
       Annotated Guide to Reference Materials in the Humanities and
       Social Sciences. Metuchen: Scarecrow Press, 1971. 279
       pp., bibl.

XI Mexico

GENERAL

3679   "The Ban on CIDOC." Herder Correspondence 6 (April, 1969):
        117-119.

3680   BASTIDE, ROGER. "Contributions a une sociologie des religions
        en Amérique Latine: les publications du CIDOC, Mexique
        (1968-1971)." Archives de Sciences Sociales des Religions
        18 (1973): 139-150.

3681   CAMPION, D. R. "Out of Many Things: Center for Intercultural
        Documentation at Cuernavaca, Out of Bounds to Priests and
        Religious." America 120 (February 1, 1969): 120.

3682   CASTILLO, ALFONSO. "Tragedia en la Iglesia mexicana." Christus
        37 (March, 1972): 8-9.

3683   Catholic Church. Conferencia del Episcopado Católico de
        México. Carta pastoral de episcopado mexicano sobre el
        desarrollo e integración del pais. México: [n.p.], 1968.
        63 pp.

3684   "Catholic Revival in Mexico." Tablet 216 (February 3, 1962):
        117-118.

3685   CERTEAU, MICHEL DE. "Cuernavaca: el Centro Cultural y mon-
        señor Illich." Mensaje 18 (October, 1969): 493-495.

3686   COWAN, WAYNE H. "Interview with Ivan Illich." Christianity
        and Crisis 29 (August 4, 1969): 213-219.

3687   "Cuernavaca: centro de formación intercultural." Mensaje 11
        (June, 1962): 246-248.

3688   "Cuernavaca Decision Sadly Received." Tablet 221 (June 24,
        1967): 707.

3689   "The Cuernavaca Dossier." Herder Correspondence 6 (April,
        1969): 110-111.

General

3690 "Cuernavaca's Illich Quits Priesthood." National Catholic
Reporter 5 (April 2, 1969): 1+.

3691 CUEVAS, MARIANO. Historia de la Iglesia en México. El Paso:
Editorial Revista Católica, 1928. 502 pp., bibl.

3692 DEELEN, GODOFREDO J. Diócese de Caraveles. Cuernavaca,
México: Centro Intercultural de Documentación, 1969. 498
pp.

3693 "Development at Cuernavaca." Tablet 221 (June 17, 1967): 681.

3694 DU PLESSI GRAY, FRANCINE. Divine Disobedience: Profiles in
Catholic Radicalism. New York: Knopf, 1970. 322 pp.

3695 GANNON, FRANCIS X. "Shortcoming." Christianity and Crisis
29 (December 8, 1969): 319-320.

3696 "Get Going and Don't Come Back: Vatican Investigations of
Center for Intercultural Documentation in Cuernavaca,
México." Time 93 (February 14, 1969): 48-53.

3697 GUTIÉRREZ CASILLAS, JOSÉ. Historia de la Iglesia en México.
México: Editorial Porrúa, 1974. 509 pp., bibl.

3698 "Illich Bares 85-Point Bill of Complaints Used in Holy Office
Grilling." National Catholic Reporter 5 (February 13, 1969):
1+.

3699 "Illich Says Criticism Costs Center $64,800." National Cath-
olic Reporter 3 (March 8, 1967): 3.

3700 "Illich Tells Seper Why He Won't Answer." National Catholic
Reporter 5 (February 12, 1969): 7.

3701 Institute Supérieur de Pastorale Catéchétique. Cuernavaca:
mentalidad religiosa popular. Cuernavaca, México: Centro
Intercultural de Documentación, 1969. 367 pp.

3702 LEMERCIER, G., and ARCEO, S. "Monks of Cuernavaca Using
Psychoanalysis." Catholic Mind 65 (September, 1967): 5-8.

3703 LEÑERO, VICENTE. "Catolicismo a la mexicana." Siempre 799
(May 29, 1968): 8.

3704 MANDOUZE, ANDRÉ. "Quelques questions au nouveau Saint-Office."
Lettre 129 (May, 1969): 8-9.

Catholic Church and Social Change

3705   MEDIAVILLA, MANUEL. "Cuernavaca: libertad al son de los
        mariachis." Pueblos del Tercer Mundo 52 (1975): 40-47.

3706   MÉNDEZ ARCEO, SERGIO. "Homilía de Mons ... Obispo de Cuerna-
        vaca." NADOC 78 (July 30, 1969): 1-3.

3707   MOHS, MAYO. "Catholic Cuernavaca ... Christianity Unconfined."
        Critic 30 (May/June, 1972): 44-59.

3708   MORFIN, L. "¿Es la Iglesia en México un buen patron?"
        Christus 37 (January, 1972): 5-6.

3709   ORSY, LADISLAS M. "Questions About a Questionnaire: Contro-
        versy Over the Cuernavaca Center, with Text of Letter from
        I. Illich." America 120 (February 15, 1969): 185-189.

3710   "Rome Puts CIDOC Off Blacklist ... If, Illich Says Thanks,
        but No Thanks." National Catholic Reporter 5 (June 25,
        1969): 3+.

3711   SCHRAG, P. "Ivan Illich: The Christian as Rebel." Saturday
        Review 52 (July 19, 1969): 14-19.

3712   SPIELBERGER, W. "Ivan Illich: Cuernavaca Era Ends, CIDOC
        Gone." National Catholic Reporter 12 (February 27, 1976):
        1-2.

3713   SUÁREZ, LUIS. "Sacerdote de los nuevos tiempos ... el padre
        Felipe Pardiñas." Siempre 741 (1967): 33-34, 70.

CATHOLIC CHURCH AND SOCIAL CHANGE

3714   CABEZA M., MACELINO. Misión y pastoral nueva. México: Mayela,
        1969. 107 pp.

3715   "El compromiso cristiano ante las opciones sociales y la polí-
        tica; mensaje del episcopado mexicano al pueblo de México."
        Christus 39 (February, 1974): 48-62.

3716   FITZPATRICK, JOSEPH P. "Training Center at Cuernavaca."
        America 106 (February 24, 1962): 678-680.

3717   GARCÍA, SAMUEL RUÍZ. "A Mexican Plan for Rural Areas." In
        The Religious Dimension in the New Latin America, edited
        by John J. Considine, pp. 117-126. Notre Dame: Fides
        Publishers, 1966.

Catholic Church and Social Change

3718   Institut Supérieur de Pastorale Catéchétique. Cuernavaca:
       mentalidad religiosa popular. Cuernavaca, México: Centro
       Intercultural de Documentación, 1969.

3719   LÓPEZ, BALTÁZAR, comp. Cuernavaca: fuentes para el estudio
       de una diócesis: documentos y reacciones de prensa, 1959-
       1968. Cuernavaca, México: Centro Intercultural de Docu-
       mentación, 1968. 2 v.

3720   MACCOBY, MICHAEL. Social Change and Social Character in Mexico
       and the United States. Cuernavaca, México: Centro Inter-
       cultural de Documentación, 1970.

3721   MAZA, ENRIQUE. "La situatión social de México y de la Iglesia
       ante Jesucristo y ante los pobres." Christus 36 (April,
       1971): 4-5.

3722   OCAMPO V., TARSICIO, comp. México: "entredicho" del Vaticano
       a CIDOC, 1966-1969: documentos y reacciones de prensa.
       Cuernavaca, México: Centro Intercultural de Documentación,
       1969. 5 pp.

3723   PARDINAS, FELIPE. "Tasks for the Future." Month 33 (February,
       1965): 104-111.

3724   RAMOS, RUTILIO. La Iglesia en México. Friburg: Oficina
       Internacional de Investigaciones Sociales de FERE, 1963.
       119 pp., bibl.

3725   SÁENZ Y ARRIAGA, JOAQUÍN. Cuernavaca y el progresismo reli-
       gioso en México. México: n.p., 1967. 240 pp.

3726   ZENTENO, ARNALDO. Liberación social y Cristo: apuntes para
       una teología de la liberación. México: Secretariado Social
       Mexicano, 1971. 87 pp., bibl.

CATHOLIC CHURCH AND STATE

3727   ALEIXO, JOSÉ CARLOS. The Catholic Church and Elections.
       Cuernavaca, México: Centro Intercultural de Documentación,
       1969.

3728   ECKSTEIN, SUSAN. "Politics and Priests: The Iron Law of
       Oligarchy and Interorganizational Relations." Comparative
       Politics 9 (July, 1977): 463-481.

3729 GARCÍA TREVIÑO, RODRIGO. El católico-munismo. México: Editora Sociopolíticas, 1970. 118 pp.

3730 MABRY, DONALD J. Mexico's Acción Nacional: A Catholic Alternative to Revolution. Syracuse: Syracuse University Press, 1973. 269 pp., bibl.

3731 "The Middle Way." Christian Century 78 (November 1, 1961): 1312-1314.

3732 OLIVERA DE BONFIL, ALICIA. "La Iglesia en México, 1926-1970." In Contemporary Mexico: Papers of the IV International Congress of Mexican History, edited by James W. Wilkie, pp. 295-316. Los Angeles: University of California Press, 1976.

3733 OLIVERA SEDANO, ALICIA. Aspectos del conflicto religioso de 1926 a 1929, sus antecedente y consecuencias. México: Instituto Nacional de Antropología e Historia, 1966. 292 pp., bibl.

3734 RICE, ELIZABETH ANN. The Diplomatic Relations Between the United States and Mexico, as Affected by the Struggle for Religious Liberty in Mexico, 1925-1929. Washington, D.C.: Catholic University of America Press, 1959. 224 pp., bibl.

3735 SCHUSTER, E. "The Church and Social Revolution in Mexico." Social Justice Review 63 (August, 1970): 112-121.

3736 TORO, ALFONSO. La Iglesia y el Estado en México. Jalapa: Talleres Linotipográficos del Gobierno del Estado, 1932. 613 pp., bibl.

3737 TURNER, FREDERICK C. "The Compatibility of Church and State in Mexico." Journal of Inter-American Studies 9 (October, 1967): 591-602.

CATHOLIC CLERGY

3738 BULNES ALDUNATE, JUAN. Sacerdocios y dominación. Cuernavaca, México: Centro Intercultural de Documentación, 1971. 190 pp.

3739 "Carta pastoral del episcopado mexicano." Mensaje 170 (July, 1968): 322-325.

Catholic Clergy

3740   "La justicia en México: síntesis del estudio nacional para el
        sínodo mundial de obispos, 1971." Servir 34 (August, 1971):
        447-492.

3741   MOLINA, P. MANUEL. El progresismo religioso: orígenes,
        desarrollo y crítica. México: Tradición, 1975. 244 pp.

3742   "Monsignor Illich's Hot Blast at U.S. Bishop's Latin Program
        Gets a Cool Response from the Prelates." U.S. Catholic 32
        (April, 1967): 56-67.

CHRISTIAN DEMOCRACY

3743   FUENTES DÍAZ, VICENTE. La democracia cristiana en México.
        México: Editorial Altiplano, 1972. 125 pp.

3744   ROBERT, SCOTT E. "Social Justice Without Christian Democracy
        in Mexico." In The Conflict Between Church and State in
        Latin America, edited by Frederick B. Pike, pp. 225-232.
        Notre Dame: University of Notre Dame, 1964.

3745   Youth Organization of the Party of National Actions. "Social
        Justice and Christian Democracy in Mexico." In The Conflict
        Between Church and State in Latin America, edited by
        Frederick B. Pike, pp. 218-224. Notre Dame: University of
        Notre Dame, 1964.

COMMUNISM

3746   KUEHNELT-LEDDIHN, ERIK MARIA RITTER VON. "Socialism sí, com-
        munism no." National Review 10 (January 28, 1961): 46.

3747   SCHMITT, KARL MICHAEL. Communism in Mexico: A Study in Poli-
        tical Frustration. Austin: University of Texas Press,
        1965. 290 pp., bibl.

DOCUMENTS

3748   Acción Católica Mexicana. "México: en declaración solemne,
        la Acción Católica reconoció los aspectos positivos de la
        revolución mexicana." Informaciones Católicas Interna-
        cionales 218 (June 22, 1964): 12.

3749   Congress for Bishops. "Moreliensis-Zamorensis in Mexico:
        Decreturm de Finium Mutatione." Acta Apostolica Sedis 66
        (October 31, 1974): 581-582.

3750   "Declaración del episcopado mexicano." Christus 36 (February,
        1971): 29.

3751   "El episcopado mexicano pide sugerencias para perfeccionar el
        enfoque en algunas áreas educativas." Christus 40 (May,
        1975): 50-52.

3752   ILLICH, IVAN D. "Mgr. Illich's Letter to Cardinal Seper."
        Herder Correspondence 6 (April, 1969): 115-117.

3753   LOPEZ, BALTÁZAR, comp. Cuernavaca: fuentes para el estudio
        de una diócesis: documentos y reacciones de prensa, 1959-
        1968. Cuernavaca, México: Centro Intercultural de Docu-
        mentación, 1968. 2 v.

3754   "El respeto a la vida humana: declaración del episcopado
        mexicano." Catequesis Latinoamericana 8 (1976): 105-112.

ECONOMIC DEVELOPMENT

3755   "Como se explota a los braceros latinoamericanos en los EE.UU."
        Carta de ISAL 3 (April, 1970): 12-13.

3756   VERDUZCO, PARDO A. "Situación económica actual del clero en
        México." Christus 38 (October, 1973): 57-59.

EDUCATION

3757   CORRO, ALEJANDRO DEL, comp. México: movimiento universitario
        de renovadora orientación, 1961-1966: reacciones de prensa.
        Cuernavaca, México: Centro Intercultural de Documentación,
        1967.

3758   HARO BARRIOS, MARÍA DEL CARMEN. Intereses religiosos y éticos
        en los alumnos de psicología de las universidades Nacional
        Autónoma de México e Iberoamericana. Cuernavaca, México:
        Centro Intercultural de Documentación, 1968. 88 pp.

3759   OCAMPO V., TARSICIO, comp. México: conflicto estudiantil,
        1968: documentos y reacciones de prensa. Cuernavaca,
        México: Centro Intercultural de Documentación, 1969. 2 v.

3760   _____. México: huelga de la UNAM, marzo-mayo, 1966: docu-
        mentos y reacciones de prensa. Cuernavaca, México: Centro
        Intercultural de Documentación, 1967.

Humanism

HUMANISM

3761   Institut Supérieur de Pastorale Catéchétique. Cuernavaca:
       mentalidad religiosa popular. Cuernavaca, México: Centro
       Intercultural de Documentación, 1969.   319 pp., bibl.

LABOR AND LABORING CLASSES

3762   "Como se explota a los braceros latinoamericanos en los EE.UU."
       Carta de ISAL 3 (April, 1970):   12-13.

MARXISM

3763   CAREAGA, GABRIEL.   Los intelectuales y la política en México.
       México: Editorial Extemporáneos, 1971.   140 pp., bibl.

3764   MC CLAVE, JORDÁN.   Cristianismo radical y marxismo.   México:
       Editora Nuestro Tiempo, 1970.   107 pp.

PEASANTRY

3765   MAC LEAN Y ESTENÓS, ROBERTO.   Status socio-cultural de los
       indios de México.   México: Instituto de Investigaciones
       Sociales, Universidad Nacional Autónoma de México, 1960.
       192 pp.

3766   MEDIAVILLA, MANUEL   "Héctor Gallego ... mártir de la lucha
       campesina."   Pueblos del Tercer Mundo 55 (1975):   2-29.

POLITICS

3767   Acción Católica Mexicana.   "México: La Acción Católica se
       preocupa de las responsabilidades políticas de los cris-
       tianos."   Informaciones Católicas Internacionales 234
       (February 22, 1969):   11.

3768   "La actitud de la Iglesia de México frente a las elecciones."
       CIDOC-Informa 1 (June, 1964):   12-15.

3769   ALEIXO, JOSÉ CARLOS.   The Catholic Church and Elections.
       Cuernavaca, México: Centro Intercultural de Documentación,
       1969.

3770   GONZÁLEZ LUNA MORFÍN, EFRAÍN. Cuestiones políticas y sociales.
       México: Ediciones de Acción Nacional, 1965. 81 pp.

3771   _____. El puño y la mano tendida. México: Ediciones de
       Acción Nacional, 1965. 91 pp.

3772   _____. Justicia y reforma social. México: PAN, 1976. 63 pp.

3773   "México: lucha popular." IDOC-International 33 (October 16,
       1971): 39-44.

REFERENCE

3774   Centro Intercultural de Documentación. Catálogo de adquisi-
       ciones de los archivos CIDOC. Cuernavaca, Méxcio: Centro
       Intercultural de Documentación, 1967.

3775   _____. Indice a CIDOC dossier nos. 1-37, 1966-1971. Cuerna-
       vaca, México: Centro Intercultural de Documentación, 1971.

3776   GONZÁLEZ RAMÍREZ, MANUEL R. La Iglesia mexicana en cifras.
       México: Centro de Investigación y Acción Social, 1969.
       200 pp., bibl.

3777   RAMOS, RUTILIO. La Iglesia en México: estructuras eclesiás-
       ticas. Bogotá: Centro de Información y Sociología de la
       Obra de Cooperación Sacerdotal Hispanoamericana, 1963.
       119 pp.

REVOLUTION

3778   GONZÁLEZ NAVARRO, MOISÉS. "México: la revolución disequili-
       brada." In Obstáculos de la transformación en América
       Latina, edited by Claudio Veliz, pp. 196-214. México:
       Fondo de Cultura Económica [n.d.].

3779   GRIMES, LARRY M. The Revolutionary Cycle in the Literary
       Production of Martín Luis Guzmán. Cuernavaca, México:
       Centro Intercultural de Documentación, 1969. 102 pp.

3780   GUISA Y AZAVEDO, JESUS. Acción Nacional es un equívoco.
       México: Editorial Polis, 1966. 236 pp.

3781   MAGNET, ALEJANDRO. "Biografía de 3 revoluciones: México,
       Bolivia y Cuba." Mensaje 123 (October, 1963): 652-666.

Revolution

3782   TARIK, ALI. <u>Los nuevos revolucionarios: la oposición de</u>
        <u>izquierda</u>. México: Editora Grijalbo, 1971. 463 pp.

SOCIALISM

3783   CASTILLO, ALFONSO. "Un hecho: cristianos por el socialismo.
        ¿Como interpreta la prensa mexicana?" <u>Christus</u> 37 (July,
        1972): 15-19.

3784   "Jerarquías chilena y mexicana, ante el primer encuentro
        latinoamericano de cristianos por el socialismo." <u>Christus</u>
        37 (September, 1972): 41-50.

3785   KUEHNELT-LEDDIHN, ERIK MARIA RITTER VON. "Socialism sí, com-
        munism no." <u>National Review</u> 10 (January 28, 1961): 46.

XII Paraguay

GENERAL

3787   "Collision in Latin America." Time, February 9, 1970, p. 44.

3787   MENA PORTA, ABIBAL. "Después de un silencio cómplice de años, los obispos paraguayos presionados por las bases, optan por denunciar esta injusticia." Cristianismo y Revolución 13 (April, 1969): 28.

3788   WESTHUES, KENNETH. "American Catholicism in a Latin Setting." Missiology 3 (July, 1975): 265-285.

CATHOLIC CHURCH AND SOCIAL CHANGE

3789   CARRÓN, JUAN MARÍA. "El cambio social y el clero en el Paraguay." Revista Paraguaya de Sociología 4 (January/August, 1967): 129-132.

3790   La chiesa del Paraguay al servizio dell'uomo. Rome: Azzociazione per gli studi e la documentazione dei problemi socio-riligiosi dell'America Latina, 1974. 253 pp., bibl.

3791   Conferencia Episcopal Paraguaya. Las exigencias de la doctrina social cristiana ante el insuficiente desarrollo del país. Asunción: Secretariado Permanente de la Conferencia Episcopal Paraguaya, 1963. 31 pp.

CATHOLIC CHURCH AND STATE

3792   "Bishops and the Dictator." America 122 (June 6, 1970): 604-605.

3793   CARRÓN, JUAN MARÍA. "El cambio social y el clero en el Paraguay." Revista Paraguaya de Sociología 4 (January/August, 1967): 129-132.

Catholic Church and State

3794   "Christ in Paraguay?" Christian Century 87 (January 21, 1970):
       68.

3795   DEEDY, JOHN G. "CRS in Paraguay." Commonweal 93 (October 9,
       1970): 34.

3796   _____. "Paranoid Paraguay." Commonweal 94 (May 7, 1971):
       204.

3797   _____. "Peril in Paraguay." Commonweal 94 (April 9, 1971):
       98.

3798   "Distaff Thugs in Paraguay." America 124 (April 17, 1971):
       396.

3799   GIMÉNEZ, GILBERTO. "Church and Politics in Paraguay." IDOC-
       International 41 (February 11, 1972): 47-64.

3800   GREENE, G. "Paraguay: Where the Living is Easy, So..."
       Holiday, April, 1969, pp. 68-71.

3801   HICKS, FREDERIC. "Politics, Power and the Role of the Village
       Priest in Paraguay." Journal of Inter-American Studies and
       World Affairs 9 (April, 1967): 273-282.

3802   "Indigestion in Paraguay." America 120 (March 29, 1969): 347-
       348.

3803   MONZON, P. UBERFILS. "Repression in Paraguay: the Monzon
       Case." IDOC-International 41 (February 11, 1972): 42-46.

3804   "Paraguay Church Told to Stop All Charities." National Catho-
       lic Reporter 6 (January 21, 1971): 1.

3805   "Paraguay Ends Church Relief." America 122 (January 24, 1970):
       61.

3806   "Paraguay: universidad, Iglesia y Estado." Mensaje 18 (July,
       1069): 300-303.

CATHOLIC CLERGY

3807   HICKS, FREDERIC. "Politics, Power and the Role of the Village
       Priest in Paraguay." Journal of Inter-American Studies and
       World Affairs 9 (April, 1967): 273-282.

3808   NÚÑEZ, M. SECUNDINO. "Nueva imagen del sacerdote rural."
        Revista Paraguaya de Sociología 5 (April, 1968): 93-96.

DOCUMENTS

3809   "Entre las persecuciones del mundo y los consuelos de Dios:
        Hablan los obispos de Paraguay, Asunción, el 12 de junio
        de 1976." Christus 42 (March, 1977): 40-44.

3810   Obispos de Paraguay. "Paraguay: los obispos denuncian una
        ley represiva inicua e inhumana." Cristianismo y Revolución
        20 (September, 1969): 29-31.

3811   "Paraguay: organizaciones católicas exigen definiciones a la
        Iglesia ante la dramática situación de los presos políticos:
        carta dirigida a la Conferencia Episcopal Paraguaya."
        Cristianismo y Revolución 13 (April, 1969): 25-27.

LIBERATION

3812   HORNUNG, WARREN GEORGE. Paulo Freire's Contribution to the
        Theological Education of the Protestant Laity in Chile.
        Claremont: School of Theology at Claremont, 1974. 347 pp.,
        bibl.

PEASANTRY

3813   "Paraguay: violenta represión de campesinos." Amérique
        Latine 21-22 (1975): 3-8.

POLITICS

3814   "Overview: Paraguay in the 70's." IDOC-International 41
        (February 11, 1972): 2-41.

3815   Partido Liberal Radical. "A pesar de las reclamaciones
        oficiales de la Iglesia se sigue torturando y asesinando
        a los presos políticos: José Farias." Cristianismo y
        Revolución 13 (April, 1969): 29.

3816   SÁNCHEZ, CONCEPCIÓN. "Paraguay: una Iglesia profética contra
        un régimen dictatorial." Pueblos del Tercer Mundo 54
        (1975): 42-44.

Reference

REFERENCE

3817   Conferencia Episcopal Paraguaya. "Anuario eclesiástico del
          Paraguay." Revista Eclesiástica 22 (September, 1963):
          1-128.

SOCIALISM

3818   Episcopado Paraguayo. Las exigencias de la doctrina social
          cristiana ante el insuficiente desarrollo del país. Asun-
          ción: Conferencia Episcopal Paraguaya, 1963. 32 pp.

3819   Obispos de Paraguay. "Paraguay: los obispos denuncian una
          ley represiva, inicua, e inhumana." Cristianismo y Revo-
          lución 20 (September, 1969): 29-31.

VIOLENCE

3820   Arzobispo de Asunción-Paraguay. "Sobre la violenta represión
          a sacerdotes y fieles en Asunción." Criterio 42 (November
          13, 1969): 778.

3821   "Paraguay Bishops Denounce Torture and Oppression." Our Sunday
          Visitor 65 (July 18, 1976): 1.

3822   "Paraguay: violenta represión contra una comunidad cristiana."
          Mensaje 239 (June, 1975): 252-256.

3823   "Paraguay: violenta represión de campesinos." Amérique
          Latine 12-22 (1975): 3-8.

3824   Partido Liberal Radical. "A pesar de las reclamaciones
          oficiales de la Iglesia se sigue torturando y asesinando
          a los presos políticos: José Farias." Cristianismo y
          Revolución 13 (April, 1969): 29.

3825   "Techniques of Repression." America 134 (May 29, 1976):
          466-467.

XIII Peru

GENERAL

3826　ALONSO, ISIDORO, and TRUMIR, JULIO. La Iglesia en Perú y
　　　Bolivia, estructuras eclesiásticas. Friburg: Oficina
　　　Internacional de Investigaciones Sociales de FERES, 1962.
　　　201 pp., bibl.

3827　BARTRA, ENRIQUE. "Problematic Pastoral in Peru." Lumen Vitae
　　　17 (December, 1962): 747-749.

3828　DAMMERT BELLIDO, JOSE A. "Orientaciones para la acción social
　　　de la Iglesia: de una conferencia dada por Mons ... obispo
　　　auxiliar de Lima en la primera semana social del Peru tenida
　　　en Lima del 1 al 9 de agosto de 1959." Mensaje 9 (November,
　　　1960): 502-504.

3829　ILLICH, IVAN D., and CUSHING, R. "Se reinicia controversia
　　　entre Monseñor Illich and el Cardenal Cushing." Noticias
　　　Aliadas 18 (March 4, 1967): 1.

3830　METSINGER, LUCIEN M. "A Once Great Nation." Worldmission 17
　　　(Summer, 1966): 86-93.

3831　NEIRA SAMANEZ, HUGO. Cuzco: tierra y muerte. [n.p.], Ed
　　　Populibros, 1964. 125 pp.

3832　O'KANE, OWEN. "No Simple Solution: Here Is an Honest Apprai-
　　　sal of the Problems of the Church in South America." The
　　　Far East (March, 1962): 1-3.

3833　PIKE, FREDERICK B. "The Catholic Church and Modernization in
　　　Peru and Chile." Journal of International Affairs 20
　　　(1966): 272-288.

3834　_____. "The Modernized Church in Peru: Two Aspects." Review
　　　of Politics 26 (July, 1964): 307-318.

3835　_____. The United States and the Andean Republics: Peru,
　　　Bolivia, and Ecuador. Cambridge: Harvard University Press,
　　　1977. 493 pp.

General

3836   WESTHUES, KENNETH. "American Catholicism in a Latin Setting."
       Missiology 3 (July, 1975): 265-285.

AGRARIAN REFORM

3837   Episcopado Peruano. "Declaración del ... sobre reforma
       agraria." NADOC 77 (July 2, 1969): 1-2.

3838   "Perú: dentro de la lucha de la reforma agraria, el diario
       'La Prensa' retira públicamente sus acusaciones contra un
       sacerdote." Informaciones Católicas Internacionales 210
       (February 22, 1964): 12-13.

3839   "Sacerdotes peruanos apoyan la reforma agraria." Cristianismo
       y Revolución 20 (September/October, 1969): 37-39.

CATHOLIC CHURCH AND SOCIAL CHANGE

3840   ANTOCICH, RICARDO. "Lima: cristianos en un mundo de injus-
       ticia." Mensaje 200 (July, 1971): 307-308.

3841   "Bishops in Peru Say Church Will Teach Social Justice." Our
       Sunday Visitor 65 (November 21, 1976): 3.

3842   Comisión Episcopal Peruana de Acción Social. "Participación
       popular: una visión cristiana." Mensaje 250 (July, 1976):
       312-315.

3843   CROWLEY, MICHAEL. "Peru: Whose Mea Culpa?" Worldmission 15
       (Spring, 1964): 59-63.

3844   "Declaración en apoyo del Comité Organizador de Trabajadores
       Granjeros Unidos." Carta de ISAL 3 (April, 1970): 13-14.

3845   HEGY, PIERRE M. Introducción a la sociología religiosa del
       Perú. Peru: Ediciones Librería Studium, 1971. 161 pp.

3846   "Informe de la Comisión Episcopal de Acción Social del Perú,
       al departamento de acción del CELAM." Christus 38 (May,
       1973): 55-60.

3847   MALLON, VINCENT T. "The Church in Peru Today." Homiletic
       and Pastoral Review 62 (March, 1962); 495-503.

3848   MICHENFELDER, JOSEPH. Gringo Volunteers. Maryknoll, New
       York: Maryknoll Publications, 1969. 96 pp., bibl.

3849 NEGRE RIGOL, PEDRO. Sicuani, 1968: estudio socio religioso.
Cuernavaca, México: Centro Intercultural de Documentación,
1970. 383 pp.

3850 "Obispos de la región andina denuncian la represión del
gobierno contra las protestas populares." ICIA 153
(September 1, 1977): 2.

3851 "Peru: Justice in the World." IDOC-International 37 (December 11, 1971): 2-18.

3852 PIKE, FREDERICK B. "The Modernized Church in Peru: Two
Aspects." Review of Politics 26 (July, 1964): 307-318.

3853 "Situación del pueblo y responsabilidad cristiana: declaración
del Movimiento Sacerdotal ONIS (Organización Nacional de
Iglesia Solidaria) del Perú, enero de 1977." Christus 42
(March, 1977): 37-39.

3854 TULLIS, F. LA MOND. Lord and Peasant in Peru: A Paradigm of
Political and Social Change. Cambridge: Harvard University
Press, 1970. 295 pp.

3855 VERHOEVEN, THOMAS W. "New Army of Catechists in the Andes."
In The Religious Dimension in the New Latin America, edited
by John J. Considine, pp. 127-139. Notre Dame, Indiana:
Fides Publishers, 1966.

CATHOLIC CHURCH AND STATE

3856 "Difficulties for the Church in Peru." Tablet 215 (August 12,
1961): 777.

3857 GUTIÉRREZ, GUSTAVO MERINO. "La separación de la Iglesia y el
Estado en el Peru." NADOC 18 (January 8, 1969): 1-5.

3858 PIKE, FREDERICK B. "Church and State in Peru and Chile Since
1840. A Study in Contrasts." American Historical Review
73 (October, 1976): 30-50.

CATHOLIC CLERGY

3859 CORREA, BELARMINO, et al. "Pastoral Misionera." In Antropoligía y teología en la acción misionera, edited by
Vicariato Apostólico de Iquitos, Perú, pp. 117-133. Bogotá:
Indo-American Press Service, 1972.

Catholic Clergy

3860   Evêques du Perou. "Message de L'Episcopat peruvien: 'reflex-
        ions chrétiennes sur le moment present." DIAL 336 (October
        28, 1976): 10.

3861   GUTIÉRREZ, GUSTAVO. "De la teología de la misión al teología
        del encuentro." In Antropología y teología en la acción
        misionera, edited by Vicariato Apostólico de Iquitos, Perú
        pp. 79-86. Bogotá: Indo-American Press Service, 1972.

3862   "La justicia en el mundo." Mensaje 204 (November, 1971):
        569-574.

3863   "Obispos de la región andina denuncian la represión del
        gobierno contra las protestas populares." ICIA 153
        (September 1, 1977): 2.

3864   Obispos del Peru. "Obispos del Peru--carta pastoral." SPES
        30 (October, 1976): 25-30.

3865   "Primer encuentro de pastoral de misiones en el Alto Amazonas."
        In Antropología y teología en la acción misionera, edited
        by Vicariato Apostólico de Iquitos, Perú, pp. 151-167.
        Bogotá: Indo-American Press Service, 1972.

3866   "Recogiendo el clamor, reflexiones de algunos obispos de Perú,
        julio 10, 1977." Christus 42 (October, 1977): 53-54.

3867   Vicariato Apostólico de Iquitos, Perú. Antropología y teología
        en la acción misionera. Bogotá: Indo-American Press
        Service, 1972. 167 pp.

CHRISTIAN DEMOCRACY

3868   ACURIO, GASTÓN, et al. "Balance y vaticinios en el Perú:
        cuatro líderes opinan de sus partidos y de sus adversios."
        Oiga 155 (December, 1965): 1-9.

3869   CORNEJO CHÁVEZ, HÉCTOR. Democracia cristiana y revolución.
        Lima: [n.p.], 1968. 37 pp.

3870   _____. ¿Que les propone la democracia cristiana? Lima:
        Ediciones del Sol, 1962. 144 pp.

3871   Partido Demócrata Cristiano. Democracia cristiana: nuevos
        principios para un nuevo Perú. Lima: Imprenta El Escritor,
        1960. 20 pp.

3872   _____. Una tercera posición. (Discursos demócrata-cristianos
         en los ultimos cuatro años). Lima: Editorial Universitaria,
         1960. 171 pp.

3873   Partido Demócrata Cristiano, Perú. Declaración de principios
         y el A.B.C. de la democracia cristiana. Santiago, Chile:
         Partido Cristiano, 1960. 20 pp.

DOCUMENTS

3874   Epsicopado Peruano. "Declaración del ... sobre reforma
         agraria." NADOC 77 (July 2, 1969): 1-2.

3875   _____. La justicia en el mundo. Documento del episcopado
         peruano para el sínodo. Lima: Editorial Universitaria,
         1969. 32 pp.

3876   "Lineas pastorales de evangelización: documento de la XLII
         asamblea episcopal peruana." Catequesis Latinoamericana
         8 (1976): 84-104.

3877   Obispos del Perú. "Mensaje del episcopado peruano al pueblo
         de Dios." L'Osservatore Romano, November 14, 1976, pp. 7-8.

3878   "Peru: Justice in the World." IDOC-International 37 (Decem-
         ber 11, 1971): 2-18.

3879   "Post-Earthquake Peru." IDOC-International 16 (December 26,
         1970): 83-96.

3880   Sacerdotes Peruanos. "Perú, nación proletaria: declaración
         de un grupo de sacerdotes peruanos." Mensaje 17 (May,
         1968): 170-173.

3881   "Sacerdotes peruanos apoyan la reforma agraria." Cristianismo
         y Revolución 20 (September/October, 1969): 37-39.

3882   "Situación del pueblo y responsabilidad cristiana: declaración
         del movimiento sacerdotal ONIS (Organización nacional de
         Iglesia solidaria) del Perú, enero 1977." Christus 42
         (March, 1977): 37-39.

ECONOMIC DEVELOPMENT

3883   "In a Lima Slum: Mother Suzanna Buckley." Catholic Digest
         30 (January, 1965): 94-95.

Labor and Laboring Classes

LABOR AND LABORING CLASSES

3844   "Declaración en apoyo del comité organizador de trabajadores
        granjeros unidos." Carta de ISAL 3 (April, 1970): 13-14.

3845   "La justicia en el mundo." Mensaje 204 (November, 1971):
        569-574.

PEASANTRY

3886   Aspectos sociológicos del desarrollo en el Perú: cambios en
        sociedad (rural). Cuernavaca, México: Centro Intercultural
        de Documentación, 1968.

3887   HABERBUSH, DAVID. "A Pastor in Peru." Worldmission 14
        (Summer, 1963): 49-54.

3888   HANDELMAN, HOWARD. Struggle in the Andes: Peasant Political
        Mobilization in Peru. Austin: University of Texas Pub-
        lishers, 1975. 303 pp.

3889   MARZAL, MANUEL M. Estudios sobre religión campesina. Lima:
        Rustica, 1977. 306 pp.

3890   ZUTTER, PIERRE DE. Campesinado y revolución. Lima: Instituto
        Nacional de Cultura, 1975. 312 pp.

POLITICS

3891   ACURIO, GASTÓN, et al. "Balance y vaticinios en el Perú:
        cuatro líderes opinan de sus partidos y de sus adversarios."
        Oiga 155 (December 23, 1965): 1-9.

3892   ANTONCICH, RICARDO. "La presencia de la Iglesia." Víspera 3
        (November/December): 107-110.

3893   ASTIZ, CARLOS ALBERTO. La Iglesia católica en la política:
        el caso peruano. Asunción: Centro Paraguayo de Estudios
        Sociológicos, 1971. 16 pp.

3894   HANDELMAN, HOWARD. Struggle in the Andes: Peasant Political
        Mobilization in Peru. Austin: University of Texas Pub-
        lishers, 1975. 303 pp.

3895   KANTOR, HARRY. El movimiento aprista peruano. Buenos Aires:
        Pleamar, 1964. 254 pp.

3896   Obispos del Perú. "Tenemos fe en el Perú." Actualidad Pas-
        toral 105 (March, 1977):   30-34.

3897   "Strong Language by Peruvian Bishops: Responsibility of
        Catholic Voters." Tablet 216 (May 19, 1962):   486.

REFERENCE

3898   ALONSO, ISIDORO. La Iglesia en Perú y Bolivia: estructuras
        eclesiásticas. Bogotá: Centro de Información y Sociología
        de la Obra de Cooperación Sacerdotal Hispanoamericana,
        1961.   271 pp.

REVOLUTION

3899   BRADY, P. "Peru: Revolution, Church, Salvation." Furrow 23
        (March, 1972):   140-153.

3900   MONTAGNE, E. "La Iglesia ante el actual progreso revolucionario
        en el Perú." Christus 37 (February, 1972):   27-33.

3901   "Revolution in Peru?" IDOC-International 33 (October 16,
        1971):   45-51.

SOCIALISM

3902   Comisión Episcopal Francesa del Mundo Obrero. Obispos, mili-
        tantes y socialismo. Lima: Centro de Estudios y Publica-
        ciones, 1972.   26 pp.

3903   "Peru's Bishops Speak Up." America 120 (March 15, 1969):   293.

VIOLENCE

3904   "The Clerical Toll." IDOC-International 58 (December, 1973):
        55.

XIV Uruguay

GENERAL

3905   Centro de Estudios Cristianos. Aspectos religiosos de la
       sociedad uruguaya. Montevideo: Centro de Estudios Cris-
       tianos, 1965. 143 pp.

3906   DIBAR, MIGUEL. La Iglesia uruguaya postconcilio. Montevideo:
       Sandino, 1969. 40 pp.

3907   Episcopado Uruguayo. "Carta pastoral sobre la misión de la
       Iglesia." Criterio 48 (1975): 745-749.

3908   FUIDIO, WALTER. Un Uruguay nueva. Montevideo: [n.p.], 1973.
       126 pp., bibl.

3909   SEGUNDO, JUAN LUIS. Funciones de la Iglesia en la realidad
       rioplatense. Montevideo: Barreiro y Ramos, 1962. 81 pp.

3910   SOBRADO, ENRIQUE E. "Influencia social en la Iglesia católica
       en el Uruguay." Aportes 10 (October, 1968): 106-135.

3911   "Uruguay: católicos militantes en una manifestación contra
       el nuncio." Informaciones Católicas Internacionales 245-
       246 (August, 1965): 10-11.

3912   "Uruguay: una 'especie de Concilio' se prepara en Montevideo."
       Informaciones Católicas Internacionales 266 (June 22, 1966):
       12.

3913   VETRANO, VICENTE O. "La Iglesia en Uruguay." Criterio 39
       (May 26, 1966): 366-368.

CATHOLIC CHURCH AND SOCIAL CHANGE

3914   Administración Apostólica de Montevideo. "Misión de la Iglesia
       en la actual situación del Uruguay." Criterio 41 (February
       15, 1968): 65-69.

Catholic Church and Social Change

3915   CASTRO, EMILIO. "Conversion and Social Transformation." In
       The Church Amid Revolution, edited by Harvey Cox, p. 256.
       New York: Association Press, 1967.

3916   SANTA ANA, JULIO DE. "From the Mobilization of Human Resources
       to the Creation of a Human Society." IDOC-International 13
       (November 14, 1970): 19-49.

3917   SOBRADO, ENRIQUE. "Influencia social de la Iglesia católica
       en el Uruguay." Aportes 10 (1968): 106-135.

3918   _____. La Iglesia uruguaya: entre pueblo y oligarquía.
       Montevideo: Editorial Alfa, 1969. 123 pp.

3919   ZENTENO, ARNALDO. "Contribución de las iglesias al proceso de
       liberación: documentos de una consulta en Montevideo."
       Cristianismo y Sociedad 24-25 (1970): 83-90.

CATHOLIC CHURCH AND STATE

3920   CULHANE, EUGENE K. "Strange Alliance in Uruguay." America
       132 (May 17, 1975): 382-383.

CATHOLIC CLERGY

3921, PLÁ RODRÍGUEZ, AMÉRICO. Los principios de la democracia
       cristiana. Montevideo: Imprenta Don Orione, 1959. 99 pp.

CHRISTIAN DEMOCRACY

3922   CORSO, EDUARDO J. El cristiano y el frente amplio. Montevideo:
       Talleres Gráficos Barreiro y Ramos, 1971. 70 pp.

3923   Partido Demócrata Cristiano. "Desarrollo y resoluciones de
       la convención." El Ciudadano 8 (July 2, 1964): 4-6.

3924   PETER, ROBERT. "Taps for Christian Democrats." National
       Review 21 (July 15, 1969): 700.

COMMUNISM

3925   PETER, ROBERT. "Cassocks and Communism." National Review 23
       (December 31, 1971): 1468-1469.

DOCUMENTS

3926   Administración Apostólica de Montevideo. "Misión de la Iglesia en la actual situación del Uruguay." Criterio 41 (February 15, 1968): 65-69.

3927   Confederación Latinoamericana de Sindicatos Cristianos. "Seminario de CLASC en el Uruguay." Cristianismo y Revolución 6-7 (April, 1968): 35.

3928   SOBRADO, ENRIQUE. La Iglesia uruguaya: entre pueblo y oligarquía. Montevideo: Editorial Alfa, 1969. 123 pp.

LABOR AND LABORING CLASSES

3929   Confederación Latinoamericana de Sindicatos Cristianos. "Seminario de CLASC en el Uruguay." Cristianismo y Revolución 6-7 (April, 1968): 35.

LIBERATION

3930   ZENTENO, ARNALDO. "Contribución de las Iglesias al proceso de liberación: documentos de una consulta en Montevideo." Cristianismo y Sociedad 24-25 (1970): 83-90.

NATIONALISM

3931   WHITAKER, ARTHUR P. "Nationalism and Religion in Argentina and Uruguay." In Religion, Revolution and Reform. New Forces for Change in Latin America, edited by William V. D'Antonio, pp. 75-90. New York: Praeger, 1964.

POLITICS

3932   "Les troubles politiques en Uruguay." Doctrine Catholique 69 (December 17, 1972): 1122-1123.

3933   NO ENTRY

REVOLUTION

3934   GILIO, MAVIA ESTER. The Tupamaro Guerrillas: The Structure and Strategy of the Urban Guerrilla Movement. New York: Saturday Review Press, 1970. 204 pp.

Revolution

3935   The Tupamaros: Urban Guerrillas in Uruguay. New York:
            Penguin, 1973. 168 pp.

TORRES, CAMILO

3936   ZAFFARONI, JUAN CARLOS. "La juventud uruguaya frente al
            ideario político de Camilo Torres." Cristianismo y Revo-
            lución 6-7 (April, 1968): 32-35.

3937   _____. "Uruguay: los cristianos y la violencia." Cristianismo
            y Revolución 9 (September, 1968): 31-32.

XV Venezuela

GENERAL

3938   ALONSO, ISIDORO, et al. La Iglesia en Venezuela y Ecuador.
        Estructuras eclesiásticas. Friburg: Oficina Internacional
        de Investigaciones Sociales de FERES, 1962. 201 pp., bibl.

3939   "Calling the Kettle Black." America 100 (January 3, 1959):
        389.

3940   KUZNETSOV, I. "Na Strazhe Diktatorov Venesuely." Nauki i
        Religiia 4 (August, 1963): 37-40.

AGRARIAN REFORM

3941   POWELL, JOHN DUNCAN. Political Mobilization of the Venezuelan
        Peasant. Cambridge: Harvard University Press, 1971. 259
        pp.

CATHOLIC CHURCH AND SOCIAL CHANGE

3942   CUNNINGHAM, PHILLIP J. "Vocationless Venezuela: Shortage of
        Native Born Priests." Catholic World 201 (June, 1965):
        189-193.

3943   ISAZA RESTREPO, RUBIÉN. Carta pastoral de saludo a la Arqui-
        diócesis de Cartagena. Cartagena: Editora Alfa y Orso,
        1976.

3944   UGALDE, LUIS. "¿Qué hemos hecho en Venezuela con 'el progreso
        de los pueblos'?" SIC 393 (March, 1977): 125-127.

CATHOLIC CHURCH AND STATE

3945   BONO, AGOSTINO. "The Venezuelan Hierarchy and Presidential
        Politics." America 129 (December 1, 1973): 421-422.

Catholic Church and State

3946   DEEDY, JOHN G. "Calder's Calderon." Commonweal 93 (November
        13, 1970): 162.

CHRISTIAN DEMOCRACY

3947   CALDERA RODRÍGUEZ, RAFAEL. Democracia cristiana y desarrollo.
        Caracas: Ediciones IFEDEC, 1964. 99 pp.

3948   _____. El bloque latinoamericano. Santiago, Chile: Editorial
        del Pacífico, 1961. 128 pp.

3949   _____. La actitud del social-cristianismo en defensa de la
        democracia. Caracas: Gráfica Americana, 1960. 39 pp.

3950   _____. "The Christian Democrat Idea." America 107 (April,
        1962): 12-15.

3951   Juventudes Demócratas Cristianas, ed. La espada y el escudo
        de los pobres: primer congreso mundial. Caracas: [n.p.],
        1962. 4 pp.

3952   OCAMPO V., TARSICIO, comp. Venezuela: "Astronautas" de
        COPEI, 1965-1967: documentos y reacciones de prensa.
        Cuernavaca, México: Centro Intercultural de Documentación,
        1968. 100 pp.

3953   _____, comp. Venezuela: ley orgánica de educación, 1966:
        reacciones de prensa. Cuernavaca, México: Centro Inter-
        cultural de Documentación, 1968. 12 pp.

ECONOMIC DEVELOPMENT

3954   BLASLOV, E. Ayuda en sacerdotes y ayuda económica para las
        diócesis latinoamericanas. Caracas: [n.p.], 7 pp.

3955   GONZÁLEZ GONZÁLEZ, GODOFREDO. Contra los des-equilibrios
        económicos. Caracas: Fracción Parlamentario de COPEI,
        1964. 705 pp.

LABOR AND LABORING CLASSES

3956   CALDERA RODRÍGUEZ, RAFAEL. Derecho del trabajo. Buenos
        Aires: El Ateneo, 1960.

POLITICS

3957 CALDERA RODRÍGUEZ, RAFAEL. La actitud del social-cristianismo en defensa de la democracia. Caracas: Gráfica Americana, 1960. 39 pp.

3958 LEVINE, DANIEL H. "Democracy and the Church in Venezuela." Journal of Interamerican Studies and World Affairs 18 (February, 1976): 3-23.

3959 Partido Social-Cristiano. COPEI frente al estatuto electoral y la actual situación política. Caracas: Fracción Parlamenta, Publicaciones Caracas, 1951. 16 pp.

3960 RIVERA OVIEDO, JOSÉ ELÍAS. Los social cristianos en Venezuela. Caracas: Impresos Hermar, 1969.

REFERENCE

3961 Centro de Investigaciones Sociales y Socio-religiosas, CISOR. Anuario de la Iglesia católica en Venezuela. Caracas: Ediciones Paulinas, 1969. 387 pp.

3962 MALDONADO, FRANCISCO. Anuario católico de la arquidiócesis de Caracas, 1964-1965. Colombia, Venezuela: Ediciones Paulinas, 1965. 267 pp.

3963 WATSON, GAYLE HUDGENS. Colombia, Ecuador and Venezuela: Annotated Guide to Reference Materials in the Humanities and Social Sciences. Metuchen, New Jersey: Scarecrow Press, 1971. 279 pp., bibl.

REVOLUTION

3964 LINDENBERG, KLAUS. "Zur Krise der revolutionären Linken in Latein-Amerika: das Beispiel Venezuela." In Der Ostblock und die Entwicklungsländer, pp. 281-308. Hanover: Forschungsinstitut der Friedrich-Ebert-Stiftung, 1968.

SOCIALISM

3965 Partido Social-Cristiano. Carta fundamental del magisterio socialcristiano de Venezuela. Caracas: Ediciones Cantaclaro, 1960. 245 pp.

Violence

VIOLENCE

3966   CORRO, ALEJANDRO DEL, comp. <u>Venezuela: la violencia</u>.
         Cuernavaca, México: Centro Intercultural de Documentación,
         1968. 5 v.

Author Index

Author Index

Bermejo, J.   0025
Bermudez, Luis A.   1484, 3437
Bernardi, Bernardo   3438
Bernardin, Joseph L.   0377
Berrigan, Daniel   1654
Berryman, Phillip E.   0378,
   0755, 1198, 1199, 1362, 2124,
   2740, 3232, 3466
Berton, Norberto   0325
Bessière, Gérard   1655
Betancourt, Alfonso   2104
Betancur, Belisario   1065, 3337
Bentacur Mejía, Gabriel   1134B
Bialek, Robert W.   3677
Bianchi, E.   1485
Bigo, Pierre   0026, 0380, 0752,
   1363, 1656, 1925, 3467
Bilheimer, Robert   0027, 0381
Bimbi, Linda   2963, 2984
Bingaman, Joseph W.   1606
Birns, Lawrence   3427
Bishop M., Jordan   0382, 1141,
   1200, 1364, 1486, 1657, 1658,
   1659, 2117, 2168
Bishops' Commission for Social
   Action, Lima   0989
Bishops of Brazil   2661
Bishops of Chile   3049, 3183
Bishops of Latin America   1134C
Blakemore, H.   2079
Blanquart, Paul   1834, 3553
Blaslov, E.   3954
Blásquez, Carmona Feiciano
   2340
Bliss, Shepherd   0028, 3368
Bocket, Richard J.   0326
Boeninger, Eduardo   0029
Boersner, Demetrio   0880
Boff, Leonardo   0030, 1201
Boizard,B., Ricardo   3127
Bojorge, Horacio   0383, 1202,
   3468, 3469
Bolo Hidalgo, Salomón   0031
Bolton, Robert H.   2827
Bonilla, Adolfo   1172
Bonino-Miguez, José   0032, 0384,
   0385, 1203
Bono, Agostino   0033, 0034,
   0386, 2574, 2575, 3071, 3072,
   3074, 3128, 3248, 3945
Borah, Woodrow   1486A

Borello, G. M.   0035
Borisov, S.   0036, 0037
Bornewasser, Hans   0387
Borrat, Héctor   0038, 0039, 0040,
   0041, 0388, 0389, 0390, 0391,
   0757, 0758, 1204, 1205, 1206,
   1365, 1487, 1660, 3312
Bosc, Robert   1926
Bosch, Juan   2964
Botero Restrepo, Guillermo   3439
Bouchard, Paul   0809, 1366, 1488
Boza Masvidal, Eduardo   0042,
   0393, 3583, 3584
Brady, P.   3899
Brando, Avelar   0327
Bravo, Carlos   0394
Bravo, Eliane Hubard de   3662
Bravo, Francisco   2936
Breslin, Patrick   3129
Brilla, Rudolf   1661
Brockman, James R.   0759, 1968,
   3012
Broderick, Walter J.   3470
Bröker, W.   1367, 1662
Broucker, José de   0342, 2342
Brown, John Pairman   3075
Bruck, James   2584
Brugarola, M.   0043
Brune, Johannes Maria   2834
Bruneau, Thomas C.   0395, 0760,
   2200, 2201, 2487, 2488, 2489,
   2744, 2745,
Brunn, Stanley,D.   1607
Bulnes A., José M.   3221
Bulnes Aldunate, Juan   0810,
   3738
Büntig, Aldo J.   0396, 0397,
   0811, 1207, 1969
Buntig, P.   1987, 2032, 2119,
   2133
Burgeon, Roger   2343
Burks, David D.   0940
Burns, E. B.   0044
Busacca, Salvador   2038
Buston, Ismael   1663
Bustos, Ismael   1835

Cabal, Latorre   0398
Cabero, Juan A.   1664
Cabeza M., Marcelino   3714
Cabral Duarte, L.   0046

Author Index

Author Index

Title Index

Title Index

Amérique Latine aujoud'hui et
demain; politique, développement, révolution, socialisme
0908

L'Amérique Latine entre la
réthorique et la violence
1954

Amérique Latine et conscience
chretienne   0008

L'Amérique Latine: jeunesse et
politiques   1516

Amérique Latine 1967   1629

El amor cristiano al próximo en
la era tecnológica   0321

Amor cristiano, violencia y
asesinato   3302

Análisis del proceso de secularización en América Latina
0093

Análisis filosófico del conflicto
social   1442

El ánalisis marxista en el documento del primer encuentro
latinoamericano de cristianos
por el socialismo   1408,
1976

Análisis político del conflicto
social en América Latina y
compromiso cristiano   1556

Análisis psico-social de la
situación pre-revolucionaria
de América Latina   1817

Angelic Rhetoric: Reactions to
Pastrana's Statement   3373

Un año después del concilio
0230

Another Crime of Passion   2824

Ante el asesinato del P. Henrique
2825

Antecedentes para el estudio de
la teología de la liberación.
Comentario bibliográfico
segunda parte   1342, 1343

Anti-Communism in Latin America
0936

Antikommunismo en América Latina.
Radiografía del proceso hacia
una nueva colonización
0937

Antropología y evangelización: Un
problema de la Iglesia en
América Latina   0077

Antropología y teología en la
acción misionera   3867

Anuario católico de la Arquidiócesis de Caracas, 1964-1965
3962

Anuário católico do Brasil, 1965
2778

Anuário católico do Brasil, 1965.
Suplemento no. 1   2770

Anuário católico do Brasil, 1965.
Suplemento no. 2   2780

Anuario de la Iglesia católico en
Venezuela   3961

Anuario de la Iglesia en Chile:
1962-1963   3277

Anuario eclesiástico del Paraguay
3817

Apertura eclesial y oclusión
política en América Latina
1487

El aporte cristiano al proceso de
liberación de América Latina
1187, 3227

Aportes para la liberación   1335

Un apóstol social en América
Latina   0317

Après la conférence de Santiago
du Chili. Des chrétiens qui
se veulent socialistes   3292

Apuntes de ...   1957

Apuntes para un análisis de la
participación de la Iglesia
en la situación de El Salvador
2998

Apuntes para un programa de reconstrucción en la teología
1059

Apuntes para una interpretación
de la Iglesia Argentina   1977

Apuntes para una teología de la
liberación   1259

Apuntes para una teología para la
liberación   1260

Apuntes sobre Iglesia y liberación
1276

Archbishop Criticised for Demanding
Reform   2329

L'Archevêque des favelles   2343

Title Index

347

Title Index

Title Index

Title Index

Title Index

Title Index

Title Index

Title Index

Title Index

Title Index

Title Index

Title Index

Title Index

Title Index

Title Index

Title Index

409